PSYCHOSOCIAL ASPECTS OF DEPRESSION

Edited by
JOSEPH BECKER
University of Washington
ARTHUR KLEINMAN
Harvard Medical School

LAWRENCE ERLBAUM ASSOCIATES, PUBLISHERS
1991   Hillsdale, New Jersey   Hove and London

RC
537
.P768
1991

Copyright © 1991 by Lawrence Erlbaum Associates, Inc.
All rights reserved. No part of this book may be reproduced in an form, by photostat, microform, retrieval system, or any other means, without the prior written permission of the publisher.

Lawrence Erlbaum Associates, Inc., Publishers
365 Broadway
Hillsdale, New Jersey 07642

Library of Congress Cataloging-in-Publication Data
Psychosocial aspects of depression / edited by Joseph Becker, Arthur Kleinman.
  p. cm.
  Includes bibliographical references and indexes.
  ISBN 0-8058-0079-4 (cloth)
  1. Depression, Mental. 2. Depression, Mental—Social aspects.
I. Kleinman, Arthur.
RC537.P768 1990
616.85'27—dc20   90-44663
                                                             CIP

Printed in the United States of America
10 9 8 7 6 5 4 3 2 1

Contents

Preface vii

1. **Epidemiological Studies of Depression: Definition and Case Finding**   1
   George W. Brown

   Current Instruments   2
   Measuring Symptoms   4
   Diagnostic Algorithms   7
   Definition of a Case   9
   Hierarchy and Exclusion Rules   15
   Heterogeneity in Aetiological Research   17
   Time Order   18
   Subtypes of Depression   22
   Choice of a Diagnostic Instrument   28
   References   31

2. **Theoretical and Empirical Issues in Differentiating Depression from Anxiety**   39
   Lee Anna Clark and David Watson

   Introduction   39
   Relations Between Current Measures of Depression and Anxiety   41
   Common and Distinctive Aspects of Anxiety and Depression   48
   The Structure of Mood and Personality   56
   Toward a New Model for Understanding Anxiety and Depression and Their Relation   58
   Conclusion   60
   References   61

3. Cross-Cultural Studies of Depression   67
Janis H. Jenkins, Arthur Kleinman, and Byron J. Good

Cross-Cultural Aspects of Depression: Introduction   67
The Cultural Construction of Emotion   68
The Ethnopsychology of Emotion   69
Culture and Depressive Affect   71
Somatization and Depression   73
Gender and Depression   75
Socioeconomic Status and Depression   79
Depression Among Refugees and Immigrants   81
Depression and Family Factors   83
Depression and Social Change   86
Methodological Problems in Cross-Cultural Research on Depression   87
Directions for Future Research   90
References   92

4. Life Stress and Depression   101
Scott M. Monroe and Richard A. Depue

Historical Background   102
Conceptual and Measurement Issues in Life-Stress Research   106
Life Stress and the Onset of Depression: Integrative Models and Subtype Distinctions   111
Concurrent Life Stress: Exacerbation, Remission, Relapse, and Recurrence   118
Concluding Remarks   124
References   125

5. Interpersonal Aspects of Depression from Psychodynamic and Attachment Perspectives   131
Joseph Becker and Karen Schmaling

Interpersonal Aspects of Psychodynamic Theory   132
Attachment and Depression   145
Social Support and Depression   158
Some Methodological Cautions   161
An Integrative Speculation   162
Summary   164
References   164

6. Empirical Studies of the Interpersonal Relations of Adult Depressives   169
Karen Schmaling and Joseph Becker

Interaction Between Depressed Persons and Strangers   *170*
Significance of Marital Factors and Characteristics
  of Marital Interaction   *172*
Characteristics of the Spouses of Depressed Patients   *176*
Marital Interaction Factors Related to Relapse   *177*
Interactions Between Depressed Mothers
  and Their Children   *178*
Methodological Critique of the Studies   *179*
Design and Analysis/Statistical Issues   *181*
Treatment Implications and Theoretical Implications   *182*
References   *182*

7. Life Stressors, Social Resources, and the Treatment of Depression   187
Rudolf H. Moos

Integrating Theory and Program Evaluation   *187*
Comparing Depressed Patients and Community
  Controls   *191*
Treatment Selection and Allocation   *195*
Pretreatment Life Contexts, Treatment,
  and Treatment Outcome   *196*
Posttreatment Life Contexts and Treatment Outcome   *201*
Remitted Patients' Functioning and Life Contexts   *204*
The Spouses of Depressed Patients   *205*
Future Directions   *207*
Implications for Clinicians and Program Evaluators   *210*
References   *211*

8. An Integrative Perspective on Recurrent Mood Disorders: The Mediating Role of Personality   215
Hagop S. Akiskal

Conceptual and Methodologic Considerations   *216*
Heredofamilial Factors and Affective Temperaments   *217*
Early Development and Character Pathology   *220*

Gender, Temperament, and Affective Episodes   224
An Interactional Model   225
Precipitating Circumstances   226
Future Perspectives   226
References   230

Author Index   237
Subject Index   251

Preface[1]

PART I: OVERVIEWS

General

Most authorities on depression seem to agree that psychosocial factors play a significant role in the predisposition, onset, lifetime course, and systems impact of depressive disorders. However, psychosocial variables such as life events and social support which had initially appeared to significantly influence these aspects of depressive disorders have not proven to be as consistently replicable or predictive as expected. Many investigators attribute much of the mixed findings obtained to the heterogeneity of depressive diagnoses, therefore our first three papers address various facets of the heterogeneity issue.

We were desirous of identifying factors relatively unique to depression, and especially, unique to subtypes of depression. Regrettably, our hopes in this regard remain largely unrequited. While there is widespread recognition of the desirability of such specificity, promising developments are only now getting well underway. It remains to be seen whether the paucity of factors identified as relatively unique to depressions is inherent or more a function of conceptual and methodological shortcomings in contemporary research in psychopathology.

---

[1] In part I of the Preface, Kleinman wrote the comments on the papers by Brown, Clark, and Watson, and on Akiskal. In addition, he contributed Part II "What is Depression?" Since the latter deals with important aspects of the paper by Jenkins, Kleinman, and Good, only a brief overview of that paper is provided in Part I. Becker prepared the remainder of the Preface.

Regrettably, the range of depression related psychosocial topics included within this volume is by no means exhaustive. Space limitations precluded focal concern with a number of relevant interpersonal domains such as social cognition, impression management, circumplex models or the impacts of immigration, unemployment, political upheaval and the drug culture on depressive phenomena.

Because the editors believe that well-validated, empirically significant, and theoretically relevant findings on the psychosocial aspects of depression are still relatively fragmentary we did not seek a tightly integrated set of papers. Such a goal seemed premature to us. By the same token, we did not urge our contributors to restrict themselves to the discussion of methodologically rigorous studies. As the late J. Mc V. Hunt was wont to say "too much rigor leads to rigor mortis." Given the difficulties with replicability of studies to date there seems to us to be substantial need for broadened perspectives, fresh concepts, innovative methodologies, and longitudinal studies. Likewise there is need for much greater attention to developing more meaningful operational criteria for subject selection as a means for reducing sample heterogeneity. Only as this is accomplished are we likely to determine relationships relatively unique to the variants of depressive disorders.

We provided contributors with rather extensive guidelines but indicated our awareness of the impracticality of obsessive compliance with them given space limitations. Therefore we explicitly encouraged our contributors to write about those aspects of their topic that concerned them most. Our conviction that they would thereby be maximally informative has been well vindicated.

Some differences in perspective between the editors will become evident in the remainder of Part I of the Preface. Kleinman was primarily responsible for the remarks about the papers by Brown, Clark and Watson, Jenkins et al. and Akiskal, and Becker for the remainder.

Individual Papers

George Brown's chapter reminds us that advances in the epidemiological data base and the methodologies and taxonomies that sow the seeds for that rich harvest, psychosocial research, is bedeviled by exceedingly complex problems that result from the human nature of depressed patient and researcher as much as from technical issues.

Brown is for the use of multiple diagnostic approaches that take account of a wider scope of symptoms. He is for the elicitation of illness narratives in order to provide a rich text from which time order can be more accurately worked out. He is for openness about how decisions on symptoms are reached in the research setting. He is against unneeded and potentially constricting rigidity, in the use of diagnostic algorithms, for example. He believes that we must be honest about or final dependence in measuring symptoms on experts and their agreement. All of which strikes the editors like the good common sense of a journeyman researcher who believes that in addition to the problems of the verification of observations (reliability) and the verification of suppositions (validity), there are also the crucial conceptual problems embedded in the methods themselves.

Those methods that see depressive disorder as a dyscrasia or diathesis in the person, a thing, an it, separate from experience and its human sources, seek to measure courses that unfold as natural outcomes of preset disease programs. Whatever the techniques used to cover and control measurement problems, those very measures are tied to a view of reality that has not in fact been established. In a sense there is no *natural course* of depression or any other disorder—e.g., cancer of the lungs, heart disease, diabetes—inasmuch as disorders are experienced by individuals whose resources, supports, and responses alter, potentially at least, almost every aspect of the condition from perception of symptoms, experience of distress, expression of complaints, help seeking, compliance, second opinions, treatment change, and even decisions about whether to participate in research. Does a major depressive disorder in a Taiwanese peasant farmer with no access to outpatient psychiatric care who focuses on somatic symptoms over existential ones and seeks care from a primary care practitioner, and major depressive disorder in a Manhattan investment banker who enters psychoanalysis and whose expectation, unlike his Chinese counterpart, is that the treatment will be long term, psychologically oriented and will absorb his full attention—do these conditions share a *natural course* that can be mapped to subtype depression?

The time-limited format of epidemiological research is likely to strike the ethnographer or the historian, or for that matter the psychotherapist, as possibly biased toward superficial assessments that leave out the full range of symptoms—especially those that usually get lumped together as somatic complaints and those that are most intimate and difficult to reveal—and that create a narrow template that is more methodologically driven than empirically emergent. Thus, primary care physicians complain that the cases they see are neither full blown examples of *DSMIII-R or ICD-9* categories nor merely *borderline cases.* They are perhaps different subtypes of depression. Indeed, since most cases of depression are seen in primary care settings, these subtypes may indeed claim greater priority in the psychiatric taxonomy and the research methodologies. Pain, fatigue, sleeplessness, and other common bodily experiences among patients with clinical depression are a vast uncharted territory at the very center of the psychiatric epidemiology of depression.

Because it can be a symptom, or normal feeling as well as a disease, depression is the quintessential instance of *"what is a case"?* The points Brown reviews about borderline *"caseness,"* comorbidity, the fuzzy edges of definitions and the production of different findings by different technologies—i.e., *PSE, SADS, DIS*—are the nub of another vexing conceptual difficulty: namely, how to evaluate the experience of suffering within which depression is embedded. Brown's tactic is to gather in as much information as is relevant, give the researcher the opportunity to sift and weigh all of it, compare his assessment to computer program determinations, in a flexible iterative *process* that feeds back to refine definition and instrument while making visible the inner workings of the determination. This process of epidemiological research scholarship seems well suited to the uncertainties and complexity of mood disorders. Brown's contention that structured interviews that fail to adequately probe patient's experiences and that treat the question of interpretation as one that can be solved via narrowly technical "fixes" are inadequate should lead us to rethink the purposes and scope of epidemiological research in depression. The *provisional* appellation he wishes to affix to the measures should be the label for the field itself. In the absence of pathognomonic biological markers, epidemiological assessment is best regarded as a scholarly process of provisional interpretations whose epistemological limits are as important to recognize as its statistical ones.

Nonetheless, for all that, it is impressive to review how much we have in fact learned about depression. The chapter by Clark and Watson offers a rich illustration. Tackling the perennially vexing controversy over whether depressive and anxiety disorders are distinctive or inseparable conditions, Clark and Wilson disclose how psychometric instruments structure the controversy by the tendency of self-report forms to fail to discriminate these conditions. Rather than settling for the qualified confusion of the vastly complex technical issues, Clark and Watson, following Eysenck, Gotlib, Tellegen, and others, interpret the disparate findings as evidence of a common construct of negative affectivity (NA) that is shared by both depressive and anxiety disorders. Reviewing a wide variety of clinical rating scales, Clark and Watson demonstrate key consequences of the findings from clinical rating scales and self-report measures to the effect that patients' perceptions of depression and anxiety against the backup of negative affect is a type of figure and ground phenomenon. Thus, when specific treatments are at stake, depression and anxiety are more highly differentiated by clinical assessments.

The analytic grid created by independent constructs of negative affect and positive affect in either trait or state configuration and each ranging across a continuum from high to low that emerges from Clark and Watson's analysis of existing measures of depression and anxiety enables these authors to reason that the depression factor picked up by these measurements is a more general *distress* dimension of negative affectivity that crosses diagnostic categories while the anxiety factor relates more specifically to the category of panic anxiety. Generalized anxiety splits across the two. And this conceptual solution receives support from their empirical findings as well. The conceptual and analytic advance provided by this model of the experiential structure of mood and its disorders is that it offers both a larger, more complex framework and a subtler combination of components to handle the varieties of distress from worry to guilt and fear and of a more constitutional fatigue, while mapping their opposites from ebullience and competence through relaxation. The parameters support a more discriminating description of types of depressive conditions and anxiety disorders, and their relationship.

But if a two dimensional state/trait model is so availing, one might well wonder if other structural axes might not even further advance our understanding of mood. For example, a somatic perception axis that encompasses both amplification and damping of symptoms, a social axis that ranges from isolation and withdrawal to support and mastery, again both constitutionally and situationally configured, or a cultural axis that relates the components of mood to a particular family and ethnic values applied to major life cycle transitions or to the subject's explanatory model of his condition would offer an even more richly human mapping. What is refreshingly thought provoking in this chapter is the deconstruction of mood into structures and also processes of their interaction (about which the authors are only suggestive) that are both empirically measurable and conceptually resonant with the diverse patterns and textures of normal and abnormal experience. Perhaps beyond the significance of the specific details of their analysis, the approach to rethink the forms and content of mood suggests that the academic and clinical discourses have gotten stuck into a cul de sac of routine and increasingly less useful ways of configuring (and measuring) mood from which we might with profit turn back to more fundamental questions before engaging the always messier clinical realities.

Jenkins, Kleinman, and Good's paper provides an anthropological perspective on controversies in psychosocial research on depression. The authors argue that the cross-cultural validity of contemporary concepts and models of depression is a precondition for the development of a comprehensive scientific theory of depression. Theories of depression must be based on an understanding of culturally specific ethnopsychologies of dysphoric emotion; cross-cultural data provide an understanding of how indigenous views of emotion affect the range of dysphoric affects and illness states. A critical examination of the major research findings of the past three decades is presented. A proposal is advanced for an integrated framework of depression that incorporates an understanding of how culture mediates the psychobiological experience and expression of depressive illness. Additional aspects of this paper are elaborated in Part II of this Preface.

The relationship of aversive life events to depression has probably generated more controversy, speculation, and research than any other aspect of depression. As Monroe and Depue's paper indicates, perhaps the principal gains from these efforts have been illumination of the sheer complexity of the issues involved and the development of promising concepts and methods for eventually elucidating these issues. An excellent example of the complexity of the problem is provided by the seeming paradox that a relatively small proportion of persons who experience severely aversive life events become clinically depressed yet a very substantial proportion of persons with clinical depressions have experienced significantly more severe life events than nondepressed controls within a few months before the onset of their depressive episodes.

Thus a major issue addressed in this paper is why some people may be more vulnerable than others to depression as a result of severe life events. These issues encompass biogenetics, psychogenetics, and their resultant interactions vis-a-vis personality dispositions, psychopathology, and biological viability. These factors in turn affect current life circumstances in such manner as to affect the likelihood of occurrence of severe life events and the availability of moderating resources for coping with such adversity.

It is increasingly clear that severe life events account for a rather limited proportion of variance in the onset of depressive disorders overall. But there are promising indications that we may yet be able to specify what kind of severe life events are more likely to result in what type, severity, and course (including relapse and recurrence) of depression.

As the work of G. Brown and his associates perhaps most notably suggests, it is the context within which life events occur rather than their objective characteristics per se that determines their import for depressive reactions.

A lack of consistent findings has bedeviled theoretical and empirical progress on relations between stress and depression. The old psychometric truism that reliability limits validity is probably in part responsible for these inconsistencies. While it is critically important not to stifle innovation in such an inadequately explored domain as stress and depression, a greater degree of standardization of concepts, instruments, and research designs might enable the field to sort the wheat from the chaff more readily.

Consensus already appears to be emerging in some theory and research aspects on the relationship of stress to depression. For example, it seems increasingly clear that aversive psychosocial events are probably more related to the onset of initial episodes of depressive disorders than to later ones, or a relatively circumscribed life event such as disruption of a significant interpersonal relationship is a relatively specific preceding life event for many depressions and such disruptions are related to a more favorable prognosis. Many such interesting trends are cited along with a variety of frustrating conundrums.

Becker and Schmaling first provide an historical perspective on interpersonal aspects of depression from psychodynamic perspectives and their elaboration in attachment theory and research. They contend that much of contemporary psychosocial theory and many hypotheses under investigation have been repeatedly adumbrated in this earlier literature. The troubled interpersonal relations of many depression-prone persons from early childhood on, their tendencies toward excessive dependency and/or perfectionism, problems with assertiveness, social skills, and hostility have long been noted in the psychodynamic literature. It is also their contention that this literature which is largely based on intensive prolonged observation of depressives uninfluenced by biological treatments may still prove to be a source of fruitful psychosocial hypotheses.

Becker and Schmaling also cite intriguing though speculative attempts at an integrative biopsychosocial etiological theory of depressive disorders, in particular work dealing with the disruption of synchronized circadian rhythms by psychosocial events or so called "zeitgebers." Contemporary research on various aspects of depression is much more rigorously and systematically investigating the validity and significance of these and other observations. However, only very recently are these studies being done with the longitudinal studies and appropriate control groups that may eventually clarify what is relatively unique in the etiology, onset, course, and impact of the depressive disorders. As the review of the empirical literature on the social interaction of depressives by Schmaling and Becker indicates, probably the best validated findings so far are that many of the depression-prone start life in emotionally and socially troubled environments that negatively affect self-esteem and that are conducive to subsequent unfortunate life experiences which frequently eventuate in ungratifying matings. Genetics and assortative mating are probably significant contributors especially in more severe, recurrent depressive disorders. Depressed persons have an as yet poorly understood tendency to not only diminish the nurturance and support which is often initially forthcoming from significant others, but to eventually antagonize and alienate these persons. These consequences reinforce depressives' sense of helplessness, distrust, and self-denigration.

Moos sets forth an empirically buttressed systems model that encompasses the major psychosocial constructs thus far identified as influential factors in the onset and course of depressive reactions. As he notes, the roles of stress and social support on the onset of depression have been fairly extensively investigated, but their effects on the kind and amount of treatment received and on concurrent and subsequent treatment response have been relatively neglected. As he convincingly shows, this neglect has probably contributed to serious inadequacies in designing interventions and in assessing their impact.

Moos reviews the literature related to the several aspects of his model and then integrates these with the findings of his research group. Particularly stimulating are his comparisons of remitting, partially remitting, and nonremitting depressives and their spouses with a well-matched nonpsychiatric control group drawn from the community. This is surely the largest scale study to date with such a well-conceived and operationalized conceptual framework. His data on the dismayingly high relapse rate of persons treated for depressive disorders makes this contribution an especially timely one.

Implementing the broad-gauged treatment approach Moos envisages and largely justifies would have difficult barriers to overcome. Most mental health practitioners are not taught the range of skills that are probably needed for durable interventions nor do third-party insurance carriers readily reimburse for the simultaneous, multifaceted interventions that would ideally be needed to initiate and sustain long-term improvements. But before appreciable changes in our training and treatment occurs, the need has to be well established and Moos' paper provides a forceful impetus to such endeavors.

In several now classical papers in the mid 70s Hagop Akiskal and William McKinney summarized the research findings that supported a multifactorial conceptualization of depression. Later work by Akiskal convinced him that predisposition to, at least, recurrent mood disorder was established in childhood. Latterly, Akiskal has come to view personality processes as the mediator of the causal nexus between heredity and early life experience *and* depression. To make this argument, at least for heredity, Akiskal has to model depression as bipolar disorder, with unipolar depression as a *less penetrant* form of that disorder. To some this may seem a bit casuistic inasmuch as the evidence for a hereditary contribution to the highly prevalent unipolar condition is less impressive than that for the less common and phenomenologically quite distinctive bipolar condition. In the absence of convincing data on either genotype or latent trait for either dyscrasia, Akiskal's attribution of the two to a shared *underlying* heredity, though certainly courageous, is a model somewhat in advance of the data. Notwithstanding the uncertainty of the proof, the theorem is a major one, widely shared by researchers, deserving to be seriously considered. Evidence for the early developmental source of adult depressions would seem somewhat more secure, if for no other reason than its hoary pedigree among the major psychopathology thinkers of the past century. Curiously, Akiskal gives this familial influence a modifying rather than a pathogenetic role, thus reaffirming the deeply embedded psychiatric framework of pathogenetic and pathopsychiatric influences which represents something akin to a creed among researchers.

Akiskal's sensibility to shared clinical psychiatric conventions is also visible in his view of temperament—the *innercore* of personality—as the mediator between gene and vulnerability to depression. But he seeks to go beyond the temperamental traits—cyclothymia and dysthymia—to elaborate more characteristic mechanics. Akiskal's speculation of how personality mediates this causative process draws on the clinician's retrospection that depressed adults, at least those who seek out mental health services, are introverted and lack social adroitness—characteristics which psychological research has long associated with a propensity toward psychosocial distress. Akiskal adds to this list an ecumenical perspective which combines psychodynamic, cognitive, and behavioral explanatory features. This integrated theory easily accommodates precipitating factors and sparks off interesting testable hypotheses.

Whether or not the reader is convinced by the particular details of Akiskal's persuasive argument, the real value of the framework that he has adapted and reworked over the past two decades is the effort to establish a unifying grounds where biological, psychological and social antecedents and consequences of clinical depression can be viewed as contributing to and resulting from a shared causal pathway, even a mechanism. Integrating risk factors and precipitating factors through some obdurate grain of personhood even for the most narrowly focused empirically oriented researchers must be attractive because it creates both a complete picture and resonates with the clinical intuition that depression is grounded in what is most deeply at stake in our human condition. Surely, even if the picture is no longer avant garde and the weighty framework seems a bit tarnished, even out of date, there is an abiding security in a vision that unifies virtually all the dimensions around intimate yet researchable processes of the self. In this sense, Akiskal's work, regardless of changing emphasis—now on biology, earlier on psychology—represents a balance that seems both old fashioned and alluring in this age of the romance with biological reductionism. It leaves us with the hope that perhaps even in these greatly fragmented times, we can put it all together—if not in this traditional way then in ways emergent in current studies. This desire to *put it all together* via the human nature of the person may be the most abiding common grounds of psychosocial researchers that this master at *bricolage* intuits.

PART II: What is Depression?

Arthur Kleinman

Depression is obviously a cover term for several different kinds of things. It is important to be clear about each and to indicate what we mean by depression in this volume.

Depression is a feeling state. That feeling state seems to be found in many societies. Is it universal? To be universal suggests a "natural" phenomenon. While depression is widespread across continents and epochs, it is not "natural." As Jenkins, Good, and Kleinman show in this volume, ethnopsychological categories differ greatly for different cultures. They all do not conceive of depressed emotion in the same way as we do in North American society. The meanings differ. Those meanings shape the sentiment itself: its significance but also its expression and experience.

Thus, from the anthropological perspective the emotion depression may well involve the same physiological processes in Papua New Guinea highlanders and inner city Blacks in Detroit and upper middle class White Londoners. But as a psychological phenomenon it is a *lived experience*—"to feel depressed"—that is the result of physiological processes interacting with meaning systems and social relationships.

Depression is also a symptom in the course of other conditions—schizophrenia, bipolar disorder, cancer.

Depression is also a disorder. In this volume we are principally concerned with this definition of depressive phenomena, but necessarily the other definitions are implied at times as well. In the chapter by Jenkins, Good, and Kleinman we see that major depressive disorder appears to be found in every society for which we possess adequate clinical data. But as Jenkins et al. point out, it is essential to keep in mind a series of questions that affect how we measure depression in different settings. These questions are the questions of normative uncertainty, centricultural bias, indeterminacy of meaning, narrative context and category validity. We feel that readers should think through these questions and their implications for research, before deciding that investigating depressive disorder in different cultural or ethnic groups is the same as studying clinical depression among the mainstream Caucasian population in North America or Western Europe.

While these anthropologists who refuse to give major depressive disorder the status of a disease can be shown to have an inadequate understanding of the empirical findings, their opposites who regard major depressive disorder as a cut and dried *biological* entity independent of cultural category and culturally shaped experience are also off the mark.

Suffering is a cross-cultural universal. Certain forms of suffering are part of clinical depression. But what suffering means and how it is elaborated—even if all the vegetative complaints as well as despondent mood characteristic of depression are present—requires an exploration of local social worlds: worlds of significance and relations that can be radically distinctive even for the chap next door. The question of suffering is always a moral question because it calls into question the existential conditions of lived experience, the meaning of those conditions and the humanity of the sufferers.

The question is whether one can study clinical depression without examining the question of suffering. Jenkins, Good, and Kleinman—while acknowledging clinical depression as a disease—say you cannot. Once suffering is taken into account, depressive disease is seen to affect real human beings and not to be an impersonal psychobiological process separate from the person. The disease is lived by the person. By its construction of categories, psychopathology limits its object, for good or bad, to a congeries of affect, cognition, and behavior. But the problem of suffering argues for recognition of a human condition of being-in-the-world—an aspect of the human spirit—that is left out of psychological research with considerable gain in measurement, but with considerable impoverishment in the understanding of sick persons and their illness experiences.

The problem for psychosocial research is how to configure mood disorders so that the issue of suffering is not neglected, but also so that attention to this profoundly ethical aspect of depression does not undermine attempts at measurement. We have no answer to this dilemma, but we do feel that researchers of depressed persons should grapple with this vexing problem so that our research frameworks and methods are up to the humanity of depression as a human experience.

THE STUDY OF MOOD DISORDERS
IN INTERNATIONAL PERSPECTIVE

The world is going through a health transition that is as profound in our times as have been demographic changes. Mortality rates have declined in all societies, though the smallest decline is in the poorest nations. Communicable diseases as a source of mortality have declined and been joined by chronic disorders. This means that morbidity has become as important as mortality. The third phase of the health transition touches the theme of this book. For we are seeing a pandemic of disturbed behavioral conditions come to occupy center stage of the world's health. These behavioral conditions are shared by rich and poor societies. They include alcohol and drug abuse and related violence, nicotine addiction and associated health effects, urbanization with associated family breakdown and abandonment of, and violence to spouse, child and the elderly, suicide, delinquency, dementia associated with the aging of the world's population, and, most pertinent for our purposes, depressive and anxiety disorders. Whether or not the last two disorders have actually increased in prevalence or have merely been more accurately reported is still a controversy. But there is suggestive evidence from developing societies to indicate the rates are actually rising (see the Chapter by Jenkins et al.). In the event, depressive and anxiety disorders constitute between 10 and 20% of all patient visits to outpatient health care services in the developing world. In Africa and Asia and Latin America, these conditions together have a higher prevalence in primary care settings than do infectious disease. Sadness is as common a symptom as fever or physical pain (Sugar, Kleinman & Eisenberg, in preparation).

Yet for all its high prevalence and equally high cost, mood disorder is virtually ignored in international health. In most Third World primary care settings it is neither diagnosed nor treated. Hardly any monies are devoted to mood disorders—the most common primary health problem—by ministries of health in the developing world.

We present this stark scenario, because we wish to argue that this is a crucial issue for behavioral scientists studying mood disorders. By far most patients with mood disorders reside in the developing world, where they receive neither effective treatment nor significant research attention. Surely, it is the responsibility of researchers and clinicians in the richer societies to do something about this tragedy. It would be regarded by international health experts and biomedical researchers as scandalous if a serious medical condition accounted for an equally high prevalence of cases yet went undiagnosed and untreated, especially where there are reasonably effective treatments and the bases of knowledge to begin to develop preventative programs. We believe it is time that psychologists and psychiatrists took up the question of what is to be done about mood disorders in the Third World societies. We believe that the salience of these disorders, and their neglect by both national and international agencies, requires that they receive serious attention from researchers. We would argue that both international research and research with disadvantaged groups in the West must occupy a more substantial place in the research agenda. Furthermore, practical policy implications of psychosocial research are especially crucial in this context.

Acknowledgments

First and foremost we would like to express our appreciation to our contributors, the quality of whose papers lived up so well to our hopes and expectancies. Our publisher showed splendid forbearance in the face of some very frustrating and unforeseen impediments to the timely completion of this work. Dr. Becker would like to express particular appreciation to Nancy Monihan and Janet Campbell whose exemplary typing of this manuscript occurred despite heavy work loads and multiple distracting moves. Dr. Kleinman likewise wishes to express his appreciation to his administrative assistant, Joan Gillespie for her excellent contributions to this project.

We both feel immensely indebted to our respective families whose ongoing support has so invaluably facilitated our work. And finally we wish to dedicate this volume to those innumerable persons world-wide who have been afflicted with depressive disorders. Our sincerest hope is that the content of this volume may in some measure contribute to the prevention and alleviation of these disorders.

1 Epidemiological Studies of Depression: Definition and Case Finding

George W. Brown
University of London

During the last 20 years systematic psychiatric interviews such as the Present State Examination (PSE), and the Schedule for Affective Disorders and Schizophrenia (SADS) have had a major impact on psychiatric research. Each consists of a series of questions and possible probes, a parallel series of definitions of symptoms, and rating scales that allow each symptom to be rated by the interviewer in terms of severity. Their influence has derived from the improved reliability in the recognition and rating of symptoms and the improvement in psychiatric diagnosis that this has made possible (Spitzer & Fleiss, 1974). It is important to note that the basic advance has been in the categorizing of individual symptoms. This has made it worthwhile to take the further and quite distinct step of reaching agreement about diagnostic labels to be given to clusters of symptoms. The various innovations have been heavily influenced by psychiatric hospital experience, and led in 1980 to the influential third edition of the American Psychiatric Association's Diagnostic and Statistical Manual of Mental Disorders (DSM-III); and a revised edition (DSM-III-R) has recently been published (American Psychiatric Association, 1987). The introduction to this latest edition notes how "The impact of DSM-III has been remarkable. Soon after its publication, it became widely accepted in the United States as the common language of mental health clinicians and researchers, and in the seven years since its publication over two thousand articles that directly address some aspects of it have appeared in the scientific literature."

Some further developments have included clinical interview schedules to reflect DSM-III diagnostic categories (Spitzer & Williams, 1983); and this has been used with some success to differentiate anxiety and major depressive disorder (Riskind et al., 1987). The publication of DSM-III also coincided in 1980 with the ninth edition of the International Classification of Diseases (ICD-9), and a new edition is planned to coincide with DSM-IV in the 1990s. There have been many other related developments, but most epidemiological research has been based on either the PSE or the SADS, or, more recently, the highly standardized Diagnostic Interview Schedule (DIS) especially developed for use in large-scale inquiries (Robins, Helzer, Croughan, & Ratcliff, 1981) and specifically designed with DSM-III in mind. The DIS is the most controversial development and the apotheosis of the wave of enthusiasm and confidence ushering in this return to nosological concerns by psychiatry. In coming to terms with these acronyms (and unfortunately there are more to follow) it is helpful to keep in mind the point already made that the semistructured interview and systematic procedures for rating symptoms seen in the PSE and SADS need to be distinguished from the parallel schemes for establishing diagnosis—in these two instances these consist of a computerised scheme (CATEGO) for the PSE and Research Diagnostic Criteria (RDC) for the SADS. Schemes such as DSM-III are only concerned with the task of diagnosis, although, as already noted, a parallel interview has recently been developed.

CURRENT INSTRUMENTS

It is essential to establish the presence or not of particular symptoms before attempting to reach a decision about diagnosis or caseness. Instruments have been based on one or other of two radically different approaches to this basic task. In one, the job of measurement is largely handed over to the respondent who, in answer to standard questions, classifies him or herself by agreeing or disagreeing about the presence of particular symptoms. In this sense the approach is *respondent-based*. As part of this tradition there are a number of brief screening questionnaires which have a high correlation with measures of self-esteem, helplessness, dread, anxiety, sadness and confused thinking, all of which are facets of what Frank (1973) has called "demoralization" (Dohrendwend et al., 1980). They are in other words very imperfectly related to diagnosable mental illness. Measurement is carried out entirely by the respondent. On the basis of this experience a number of more sophisticated psychometric instruments have been developed. For example, the General Health Questionnaire (GHQ) for use in general practice (Goldberg, 1972), the Centre for Epidemiological Studies-Depression scale (CES-D) specifically for the study of depression (Boyd et al., 1982; Radloff, 1977; Weissman et al., 1977), and a set of screening scales from the Psychiatric Epidemiology Research Interview (PERI) (Shrout, Dohrenwend, & Levav, 1986). Most sophisticated of all is the Diagnostic Interview Schedule (DIS) where the respondent-based approach has been used to deal with diagnostic groupings. It is respondent-based as the interviewee still largely takes on the job of settling the presence of relevant symptoms in terms of his or her answers, but standard probes are used to clarify any answer considered ambiguous, and to use them the interviewer must understand the purpose of each question (Robins et al., 1981).

Some of these instruments can be used in the form of a written questionnaire. The alternative investigator-based approach used in instruments such as the PSE and SADS must be carried out by interview, and the interviewer takes on a far more central role than in the DIS. It is the interviewer alone who makes a decision about whether a symptom is present, using prior definitions and probes that may go well beyond the standard ones provided by the interview schedule. (The respondent-based DIS does not have the same kind of flexibility and its designers have had to do their best to frame its questions so that answers will parallel those of the alternative, less structured approach.) There are a number of variations in the application of investigator-based instruments. For example, the ratings made during the interview need not be final. Tape-recorded interviews have usually been used in population surveys in the UK and this enables the interviewer after the interview to amend provisional ratings made during the interview itself. It also allows a coworker to make ratings independently, either by reading a transcription or by listening to the tape-recorded interview.

After symptom material has been rated, both approaches usually rely on formal rules to reach a decision about diagnosis or caseness (in so far as these are considered); that is such decisions are usually carried out in an automatic manner—typically by computer-based algorithms. They allow broad diagnostic ratings such as depression or anxiety to be made as well as subtypes within such broad categories. Therefore the investigator plays no further part once symptoms have been collected—whatever his or her role has been in collecting the symptom material. (I will comment later on this curious demotion of the investigator's role.) As already noted, the PSE has an accompanying CATEGO Programme for reaching both case identification and diagnostic rating (Wing, Cooper, & Sartorius, 1974), and the SADS utilizes the well-known Research Diagnostic Criteria—RDC (Endicott & Spitzer, 1978). Therefore, although the interviewer has to be trained to recognize symptoms of clinical relevance in investigator-based instruments, it is strictly unnecessary for him or her to be trained to carry out diagnostic ratings.

The 9th edition of the PSE, the version used so far in population surveys, defines 140 symptoms ranging from worrying and tension pains to incoherence of speech and neologisms, although a shorter version has usually been used for epidemiological research (Wing et al., 1974). It was the first instrument to include fairly extensive definitions of individual symptoms and in this sense it is superior to alternative instruments such as the SADS that leave definitions more vague. As an example, for "Neglect due to brooding" we are given in the PSE Instruction Manual:

> The subject is so preoccupied with unpleasant worries, fears or experiences which are beyond his ability to stop, that he cannot cope with the affairs he should be dealing with. The effects are seen in quality and speed of work, whether domestic or vocational.

Moderate impairment includes a falling off in standard or speed of work. Severe impairment occurs when the subject has to take time off, or when a housewife is unable to complete some important part of her duties at all (such as shopping or cooking or cleaning or going to work) (Wing et al., 1974).

For instruments such as the PSE, interview schedules have had to be developed that are capable of collecting the basic symptom material, and in addition training programs arranged to enable both clinicians and lay persons to use instruments reliably. In the recent emphasis on the development of decision rules for diagnosis there has been a tendency to overlook that the success of such rules is bound to depend on the interviewer's ability to obtain satisfactory material about particular symptoms. And here definition is not enough: "Reliability is not determined solely through the use of criteria, but also through their application by interviewers who are sufficiently knowledgeable to elicit the relevant data in a clinically meaningful way across the range of psychopathology that will be encountered" (Rabkin & Klein, 1987, p. 30). For this task of eliciting relevant data all interviews other than the DIS have been semistructured in the sense that the interviewer is encouraged to go beyond set questions (or to omit questions if sufficient material has already emerged spontaneously). There has been a certain amount of controversy about the employment of lay interviewers for this (e.g., Bebbington, 1986). However, given suitable training and ongoing guidance from psychiatrists, it is clear that lay persons can achieve satisfactory levels of reliability. (For the PSE see Cooper et al., 1977; Wing, Nixon, Mann, & Leff, 1977a; Duncan-Jones, 1980; and Craig, Brown & Harris, 1987). I know of no study that would suggest otherwise.

There can be no doubt of the achievements that have followed these efforts at systematization. Epidemiological research has been transformed since the early large-scale pioneering studies in the 1950s, and there is a warranted sense that knowledge has begun to accumulate. However, I take these achievements largely for granted and deal with the inevitable shortcomings. The sad fact is that current achievement is a good deal less firmly based than might at first appear. I deal particularly with the necessity to avoid circularity of definition, and contamination of measures by factors that may play an actiological role; and the need for measures that reflect clinical experience, which deal with time order and employ flexible definitions. In all, I argue that investigator-based instruments are likely to prove superior and in the long run will almost certainly be a much better bet both scientifically and economically.

MEASURING SYMPTOMS

So far I have emphasized the need for accuracy in recording symptoms. But this does not mean there is no place for less accurate instruments. The General Health

Questionnaire (GHQ) developed by Goldberg (1972), for example, which makes no attempt to establish particular symptoms with any validity, has been successfully employed as a screening instrument. But experience suggests that such instruments cannot be used for diagnostic purposes—say to differentiate between depressive and anxiety disorders. With instruments, such as the PSE, designed for a diagnostic role it is essential to strive for as much accuracy as possible about particular symptoms. At present there is no conceivable way of judging such accuracy other than to rely on the consensus of experienced psychiatrists, and assessments concerning both reliability and accuracy are in essence, levels of agreement between, or with, such experts. In the end, of course, these will need to be shown to be useful in a practical and theoretical sense, and ultimately it can be hoped that some at least will be validated by criteria such as treatment response or biological marker.

Given this dependence on experts, it is interesting that many of the crucial observations and decisions of psychiatrists in everyday practice appear to be made very early on in an interview. For example, in one study where psychiatrists were shown films of diagnostic interviews lasting some 25 minutes, half the symptoms detected had been reported during the first 3 minutes (Sandifer et al., 1970). Moreover in three-quarters of instances the "preferred diagnosis" after 3 minutes is the same as the final diagnosis. Others have reported that diagnostic impressions are very often within the first 30 to 60 seconds (Gauron & Dickinson, 1966a, 1966b, 1969). Kendell (1973) found that in interviews lasting 5 minutes, diagnoses made by psychiatric judges agreed with those of the hospital in almost two-thirds of instances. Moreover accuracy did not differ with either length of experience or self-confidence of the rater.

Such practice may go some way to explain the puzzling fact that current interview schedules can involve what can appear an endless series of topics covered by literally hundreds of questions, and yet are usually completed in a reasonable period of time. This occurs in spite of specific instructions to encourage the respondent to talk at length and to obtain examples of the last instance of a symptom, its worst manifestation, and so on (Wing et al., 1974). In so far as ideas about diagnosis are formed early on, it seems likely that they will be used to lighten the burden of the question-answer-exploration sequence. In short, the amount of curiosity shown by the interviewer is likely to be influenced by an early assessment of what is wrong.

It does not follow that bias will inevitably follow such anticipation. This will depend on the validity of the underlying assumptions that have prompted whether or not further questions are asked. At the point, say, a respondent denies feelings of self-depreciation, the interviewer may persist (perhaps in response to a slight hesitation) because he or she has already made a decision about the likely presence of clinical depression and given this, that self-depreciation may well be present. Let us assume that self-depreciation often does turn out to be present in such instances. This will contribute to the overall validity of the approach as long as the interviewer's judgment about the presence of a depressive disorder and what symptoms tend to occur together in such a depressive disorder are correct. But while such short-cuts may in this sense be largely benign, the desirability of introducing some control here is obvious. The regular critical scrutiny of tape-recorded interviews by a second investigator would help in so far as it would reduce any tendency to rate the presence or absence of symptoms on too little evidence. The definitions of each symptom also need to be made as explicit as possible. And here it is surprising that neither the PSE nor the SADS-RDC include detailed examples in their training manuals—both of what and what not to include. This point is perhaps best made with an example: one taken from the notes made about an interview with a school teacher. The commentary contains a mixture of the woman's reply to the PSE questions about brooding and the interviewer's remarks about them.

"Oh yes, I was brooding all the time, even in relatively happy years." She went on, "I was still brooding in the background; things were no good; they were radically wrong; they never got sorted out—even when I was doing a job I liked." She went on to describe how she never read for the subject she was teaching, even though it interested her, and that she would get through by trading on her teaching skills. She said she was sure of this since "80% of me was elsewhere."

"Brooding" as a PSE symptom, however, was not rated. It was decided that there was not enough evidence to suggest the presence of negative effects in terms of "quality and speed of work" outlined in the definition (see earlier definition). However, "lack of interest" was rated and it would have been understandable if the interviewer had succumbed to a halo effect here—that is, had stopped short of the necessary probing to settle whether the "quality and speed" of the woman's work (necessary to rate brooding) had been significantly effected. I conclude there is an urgent need to develop such examples; and that in general, there is a need to generate more concern and discussion about the rules concerning individual symptoms.

But rather than providing such examples in terms of inclusion and exclusion, the PSE relies on a common tradition of psychiatric practice (European/Maudsley Hospital/Institute of Psychiatry), and the underlining of these previously inculated thresholds during training for the PSE itself. There are obvious dangers here. Such training is usually based on video-recordings of interviews with in-patients and many symptoms will therefore comfortably reach the threshold necessary for inclusion. But it does not follow that somewhat less severe manifestations found more commonly in out-patient clinics and the general population will be so accurately rated; and it is well known that bias in rating is most likely to arise in rating borderline or ambiguous material (Hyman 1954). Moreover, lay interviewers will not have prior psychiatric training to draw upon.

It should also be borne in mind that knowledge about a person's status as a psychiatric patient may subtly influence ratings. It is probably easier to make a decision to include as a symptom somewhat marginal phenomena if the person has already been considered to be disturbed enough to require psychiatric care. It is also possible that under such circumstances a person may more readily report certain symptoms. Those not contacting psychiatric services may well show less interference with everyday functioning even when severity of symptomatology is taken into account. In short, as a group, nonpatients may have greater coping skills and sources of support that enable them to function with less impairment even when symptoms are apparently equivalent.

But most of this is speculation: We know surprisingly little about how decisions about symptoms are reached in a research setting (Cicourel, 1986). Given this, there are two ways to proceed. First, in the tradition of instruments such as the PSE, to encourage the respondent to talk at some length and to seek out examples of anything that might prove relevant—that is, for the respondent to say how things are in the context of his or her life. As long as this is done it will not matter greatly whether or not a particular question is interpreted in the way intended by the interviewer. If there is sufficient talk it should become clear how a question has been interpreted, and given this, any response, even if based on a misunderstanding of the question, is likely to provide valuable material when using investigator-based instruments. The onus is on the interviewer to interpret replies appropriately, irrespective of whether the respondent has understood a particular question in the way it was intended. This principle must, however, not be taken too far. It is not unreasonable to attempt to formulate questions in a way that will maximize their chance of being understood. The point is that such understanding is not essential. The basic requirement is to get the respondent to talk, and one of the main dangers is that, because of time pressure, too much will be assumed and too little explored by the interviewer. This solution is, of course, in any case clearly of no help with a respondent-based approach.

Second, discussion of the interview material with a coworker not present at the interview will serve several functions: It will enable training to be extended, help to maintain rating standards, and provide an invaluable opportunity to elaborate on the basic definitions and examples provided by the training manual.

DIAGNOSTIC ALGORITHMS

If it is possible to sense a certain lack of zeal in attending to these intricacies concerning symptoms, this cannot be said about recent efforts to increase diagnostic precision. Paradoxically, and in direct contrast to the definition of symptoms, there is a danger with such diagnostic judgments of taking definitions too seriously and thereby bringing unwelcome rigidity to aetiological research. Staddon (1971) in a review of a book by Ghiselin on Darwinian methods contrasts

Darwin's approach to definition and measurement to that traditionally taught in psychology. Far from being careful about definitions, operational or otherwise, he "does not bother to define his terms any more than is necessary to allow his readers to make the distinction he has in mind" (Ghiselin, 1969, p. 201). The strength of this more relaxed approach is its recognition that a term cannot be well understood until it is part of an established theory. "It would have been senseless for Newton to have been exact in his use of the term "force" before he discovered the laws of motion; afterwards the proper definition was obvious" (Staddon, 1971, p. 690). Such flexibility makes it possible for diagnostic schemes to be amended in the light of new insights and thereby kept in line with developing theoretical ideas. And as long as the basic symptom material is fully documented at the time it is collected, it is possible to carry out this kind of reevaluation years after the original interview. With this kind of flexibility in mind Kaplan has emphasized the importance of processual definitions that are theoretical and provisional, and undergo modification as inquiry proceeds (Kaplan, 1946, p. 281). Of course, the many versions of the PSE and the various editions of DSM-III can be seen in part of such a "processual" procedure. Unfortunately, there is also much about these schemes that encourages rigidity.

Although in texts about research methods there is an understandable emphasis on the need for agreement, actual advances in science probably arise far more from disagreement—from clashes of perspective and the need to resolve them. One of the worries about current instruments is the degree to which the use of in-built diagnostic decisions (at least for a particular edition of the instrument) means that the to and fro of debate by experienced clinicians aimed to iron out differences about particular sets of symptoms is absent. Indeed, the use of diagnostic rules may even inhibit *any* diagnostic judgment on the investigator's part and thereby the possibility of tension between the formal diagnostic rules and a personal assessment. (In some schemes the rules are so complex that the study diagnosed is only likely to emerge a good deal later from the computer.) One obvious way to proceed is to do both: To have a study diagnosis based on formal criteria and also one in terms of a clinical-type judgment. Where the formal criteria are straight-forward (as for example in the DSM-III criteria for "major depression") the two can be immediately compared and the reason for any discrepancy discussed at once among the workers involved. In the longer term this kind of continuous evaluation and debate can only add to the ultimate validity of an instrument. It can provide a parallel set of diagnostic judgments for particular pieces of research, and also provide case material for the periodic revisions that have proved necessary for instruments such as the PSE.

It is now possible, having discussed diagnosis, to turn to the consideration of the controversy that has surrounded the problem of case definition—that is, what should count as of psychiatric relevance. It also provides a parallel perspective on these same issues.

DEFINITION OF A CASE

A recent statement by a distinguished commentator in the *Archives of General Psychiatry* expresses disquiet about the achievements of these recent diagnostic efforts. "We have learnt how to make reliable diagnoses but we still have no adequate criterion for their validity, and this achievement focuses attention on the failures. We draw the boundaries between one syndrome and another, and between illness and normality, in widely different places and using widely different criteria and we have no adequate means of deciding which is right, or even which is preferable for a given project" (Kendell, 1988, p. 374). A good place to begin in any consideration of such difficulties is with an important survey by the MRC Epidemiological Research Unit in Edinburgh using four diagnostic schemes (Dean, Surtees, & Sashidharan, 1983). I deal with three of them: the PSE, the SADS, and the Bedford College scheme based on the PSE. The survey used the shortened 40-item version of the PSE, which deals mainly with neurotic symptoms (Wing et al., 1977a). A computer program (CATEGO) incorporates the complex set of diagnostic rules (Wing & Sturt, 1978). The issue of caseness is dealt with by a distinct 8-point Index of Definition of psychiatric disorder (Wing et al., 1978): both severity and specificity are taken into account and an individual with ID 5 (or a higher rating of 6 to 8) is considered to have a diagnosable condition and counted as a case. As already noted, the Research Diagnostic Criteria (RDC) follow somewhat similar lines but the definitions are not as explicit. One difference is that for the PSE-CATEGO system depressed mood must be present for a diagnosis of depression to be made. However, for RDC the entry criteria for major depression is the presence of either depressed mood *or* loss of interest. Minor depression requires depressed mood (Spitzer, Endicott, & Robins, 1977). However, there are more important differences in the definition of symptoms between the two, and the Edinburgh investigators were faced with the problem of reconciling these definitions. A positive score on the SADS for poor concentration means that the individual is "definitely aware of limited attention span but it causes no difficulties" whereas the PSE threshold demands more—at least a "moderate" form of symptom present during the past month (e.g., can read a short article, can concentrate if tries hard), or intense less than 50% of the time, or for the more severe rating in intense form (e.g., cannot attempt to read or concentrate) more than 50% of the past month. Where possible, the tougher PSE equivalent symptom for RDC symptoms was used and this undoubtedly meant some tendency to underestimate RDC caseness. Despite this, using the respective diagnostic criteria, the rate of caseness of "depression" in a population of 576 women was still higher using RDC: 8.7% (7.0% major depression and 1.0% minor depression) compared with the ID system of the PSE of 5.9% (1.6% for ID 6 and 4.3% for ID 5). A direct comparison of the two systems for women allocated a diagnosis on either shows that only two-thirds (33/50) of those who were classified as depressive by RDC received a PSE diagnosis of depression—but only 1 diagnosed on the PSE did not receive an RDC diagnosis of depression.[1] Almost all the disagreement concerns women rated as minor depression by RDC. Therefore even when ignoring the somewhat idiosyncratic method of rating episodes in the RDC system (to be discussed later) there is a good deal of disagreement. (This is even greater for anxiety conditions.)

The third, Bedford College, scheme has been the basis of a good deal of the aetiological research on affective disorder in the UK. The initial threshold for defining a case was settled by two psychiatrists (John Copeland and John Cooper) who had previously worked on the PSE in the context of the UK–US Diagnostic Project (Brown & Harris, 1978). In setting the threshold they went by their experience of affective disorder in outpatient practice. Such an approach left unclear just what symptoms were being used to define caseness; but with the completion of a number of population surveys, it was possible to establish what PSE symptoms best predicted caseness of depression (Finlay-Jones et al., 1980). The resulting empirically derived criteria turned out to be not dissimilar to those reached independently on a priori grounds in the SADS-RDC and DSM-III.

For the diagnosis of a *case of depression* both A and B must be present for at least 2 weeks:

(A) Depressed mood.
(B) Four or more of the following symptoms: hopelessness, suicidal ideas or actions, weight loss, early waking, delayed sleep, poor concentration, neglect due to brooding, loss of interest, self-depreciation, and anergia.

In practice, many other symptoms covered by the PSE are also always to be found present.

The two criteria for the diagnosis of a *borderline case of depression* are:

(A) Depressed mood.
(B) Between one and three of the symptoms listed above.

---

[1]

RDC diagnosis		PSE diagnosis
Definite or possible:	Caseness depression	Caseness involving other diagnoses or not assigned
Major depression	22	2
Minor depression	11	15
Other diagnoses or not assigned	1	20

A similar system for anxiety disorders covered most of the women in the general population considered to be cases or borderline cases (Finlay-Jones et al., 1980; Brown, Craig, & Harris, 1985.) (A more complex weighting scheme gives much the same results as the simple one—Finlay-Jones et al., 1980). Borderline case conditions in the Bedford College scheme have significant symptoms and are often treated by general practitioners, but are not typically seen by psychiatrists.

However, reliance on these rules is not absolute. Clinical judgments are still encouraged and on occasions clinical-type decisions about caseness or diagnosis are allowed to override the formal rules. For example, depression at a caseness level may occasionally be rated in spite of lack of depressed mood if a person shows significant bodily signs, say, in terms of facial expression or because of profound loss of interest. In this respect the scheme is closer to DSM-III. It is also possible to define a person as a case overall when neither depressive nor anxiety components on their own reach caseness. While such instances are fairly rare, the procedure does ensure that every set of symptoms is considered (and discussed with colleagues) in broad diagnostic terms.

The Bedford College scheme when used in the Edinburgh survey gave a much lower rate of 3.2% for caseness of depression than the other two schemes: The rate for borderline caseness of depression was 6.1%. Bedford College cases were practically always rated "cases" by the PSE and RDC schemes.

These results might at first appear to confirm the earlier gloomy conclusion, but probably not too much should be made of the differences, as such, as there are obvious definitional reasons for them. The problem is much less a need to understand the differences than to come to terms with their significance for aetiological research, and here matters do not appear so gloomy. But it first must be admitted that there is some problem with symptom definition. The Edinburgh workers note that the differences would have been larger if PSE equivalent symptoms had not been employed for RDC. They also make the point that RDC tends to regard impairment of function as the criterion by which symptom or syndrome is regarded as pathological, whereas according to PSE criteria a symptom has to be out of proportion to the circumstances, unpleasant, and not easily turned off by the patient's own efforts or external distractions. They go on to note that by "using the recommended PSE cut-offs we found that many of the women, whose audiotapes we listened to, had symptoms which could not be rated . . . this meant that women with symptoms did not necessarily fulfill the criteria for a diagnosis, even though they frequently had impairment of function, and regarded themselves as unlike their usual self." They conclude that there may be an argument for devising new criteria, for use in the community which would enable such marginal cases to be classified. This is not an uncommon view. Shepherd and Wilkinson (1988), for example, argue that existing classificatory schemes are unsatisfactory for use in the general population because they have been developed for hospital patients suffering from "major" affective illness. They recommend the use of a multi-axial approach capable of taking into account physical and social problems. However, such vague nostrums are unlikely to lower current uncertainty. This particular issue is, in any case, unlikely to prove fundamental as additional "cases" will mainly fall into the "borderline case" categories of the present schemes; and some account of other dimensions should in any case play a part in any epidemiological inquiry. The fundamental question is the impact of the differences reviewed on the results of aetiological research. Most of our knowledge here rests with research based on the Bedford College scheme and before proceeding it may be useful to summarize some of its core findings.

Large social class differences in both incidence and prevalence of caseness depression have emerged in inner-city populations with an overall prevalence among women aged between 18 and 65 of some 15% in a 1-year period. Half the cases at any point in time will have lasted at least 1 year (Brown et al., 1985). While social class differences based on occupation are apparently lacking in rural populations, depression appears to be much greater among those least integrated into the traditional way of life (Brown & Prudo, 1981). The great majority of the onsets of caseness of depression are provoked by major losses and disappointments, and there is evidence that the chronic conditions are often perpetuated by ongoing major difficulties (Brown & Harris, 1978, 1986). There is also evidence that recovery from chronic depressive conditions is highly associated with a reduction in such difficulties or the occurrence of a "fresh start event" promising some hope of relief from an ongoing difficulty or a situation of deprivation (Brown, Adler, & Bifulco, 1988). These aetiological findings appear to be reasonably secure and much recent research has concentrated on the issue of vulnerability—why only some 1 in 5 women experiencing a major loss or disappointment go on to develop depression at a caseness level. Lack of social support and low self-esteem have been shown to be critical for such vulnerability and to be highly relevant phenomena (Brown et al., 1986). And this issue of vulnerability is a good point at which to return to the question of diagnosis and caseness. While onset of anxiety conditions is highly related to the presence of severely threatening events, they typically relate to the experience of danger: the onset of depression appears to require the experience of an actual loss or disappointment (Finlay-Jones & Brown, 1961). (Danger is a threatened rather than an actual loss or disappointment.) However, there also appears to be an important element of specificity in vulnerability. Lack of support appears to be critical in depression but not in anxiety (see Brown & Harris, 1986b for a review of studies dealing with depression, and Finlay-Jones, 1989, for its role in anxiety states.) Table 1.1 represents a typical result for onset of depression in relation to provoking agent (typically a severe loss or disappointment) and vulnerability in the form of lack of social support. The result is from a recent longitudinal study in Islington in North London, with women with depression at a caseness level at the time of first contact with them excluded, and tests for a vulnerability effect—that

TABLE 1.1
Vulnerability Factor, Presence of a Provoking Agent and Onset of
A. Caseness and B. Borderline Caseness of Depression
(303 Islington Women Excluding Chronic Cases of Depression)

A. *Onset of Caseness (N = 303)*

Provoking Agent	Vulnerability Factor	
	Yes	No
	Percentage Onset	
yes	29 (28/95)	2 (1/56)
no	4 (2/55)	1 (1/97)
	p < .001	NS

B. *Onset of Borderline Caseness, Excluding Cases (N = 271)*

Provoking Agent	Vulnerability Factor	
	Yes	No
yes	22 (15/67*)	2 (1/55)
no	17 (9/53)	3 (3/96)
	NS	NS

*Cases in this table are excluded from denominators of table A, e.g., in this instance 95 -28 = 67.

is, that certain background characteristics such as poor support do not increase risk of onset of depression unless a provoking agent has occurred. Table 1.1 makes clear the importance of vulnerability for depression at a caseness level, but *not* at a borderline case level. It suggests that the nonvulnerable do not escape risk of depression altogether, but are more likely to develop the milder form after a major loss. The important point about the results for the present argument is that it indicates that choice of threshold for defining caseness is of importance for aetiological research. But this same research program also indicates that it is highly unlikely that just *one* threshold will prove of importance. For example, serious accidents to children are considerably raised after their mothers develop case *or* borderline case depression (Brown & Davidson, 1981), and here it would be silly to suggest that only the higher threshold is used. Alcoholism provides a second example. A number of studies have shown that relatively few males develop depressive disorder prior to alcohol abuse (e.g., Robins et al., 1977; Schuckit, 1985). Nonetheless a recent intensive inquiry in Great Britain has suggested an important intervening role for depression. This difference appears to be the result of differing diagnostic criteria and thresholds (Gorman, 1987). The British study used for the measurement of alcohol dependence indicators of changed behavior such as drinking more than one's former companions and giving up previous interests. This means that onset will often have been dated a good many months, if not years, before that of the American studies that use criteria such as alcohol related problems and withdrawal phenomenon (of RDC) which typically take longer to develop. Moreover, in the British study, criteria of onset of depression at a borderline caseness level was used, the American studies focusing on a more severe form of depression. It is not a matter of one approach being correct—rather that the British study, by use of different criteria, was able to document a highly important link between severely threatening events, the onset of borderline depressive symptoms and the later onset of alcohol dependence. These insights do not necessarily conflict with the American research: Here depressive conditions at a borderline case level may only have reached caseness after the development of alcohol related problems and this worsening might well have been provoked by physiological and social changes associated with heavy and longlasting alcohol abuse.

The importance of these examples is that they illustrate that worry about differences of definition often become irrelevant once they can be shown to have different empirical consequences—it is clear that both cases and borderline cases in the Bedford College scheme at times will need to be considered, and that it would be wise, on present evidence, for schemes such as SADS–RDC to make a parallel division whatever other thresholds or diagnostic categories it entertains. The result also reminds us that definitions are not about delineating the world in any absolute sense but to enable us to gain understanding and control. This, it should be added at once, is not to fall into the notorious trap surrounding the notion of operational definition that suggests that phenomena are no more than their definition, but it does insist that definitions are judged by their practical and theoretical usefulness.

But at this point it may well be asked why the question of choice of threshold cannot be avoided altogether by taking a noncategorical approach to caseness and diagnosis. Psychiatric epidemiology, after all, has frequently been content to conceive of depression as a continuum, typically employing scores from questionnaire items for this purpose. While there has been a good deal of uncertainty about the status of such scales, present evidence indicates that they are accurate enough to serve as screening instruments (Boyd et al., 1982). Unfortunately, the use of continuous scores does not solve the problem of threshold and may well complicate matters by misleading the unwary. This can be illustrated by returning to the data in table 1.1. In this table, cases of depression at time 1 have been excluded and attention concentrated on caseness of depression developing by time 2. However, instead of using such a dichotomy it is possible to characterize the same women in terms of symptom scores at time 1 and time 2. (As just noted, by definition none of the women at time 1 will have reached caseness in a categorical sense.) We employed a general measure of depression formed by adding to the 11 core symptoms (see earlier), further PSE symptoms of depression, usually quite rare, together with symptoms largely dealing with tension and worry—widely used in scales such as the Hamilton Rating Scale (Hamilton,

1960). If multiple regression is then used with depression measured on both occasions in continuous terms, there is no inkling of the presence of an interactive effect involving provoking agent, vulnerability factor, and a high score at time 2. Moreover, the various main effects (in terms of beta weights) are difficult to interpret. In the regression analysis the depression score at time 1 is highly predictive of that at time 2, and in addition the time 1 measure is shown to be much more important than the social factors at time 1 in predicting time 2 score. However, a quite different result emerges when a *categorical* measure of depression at time 2 is used in the regression. In this instance the time 1 continuous depression is of no importance in predicting case or borderline caseness of depression. The failure of the multiple regression analysis to show an interactive effect appears to be a function of the generality of the continuous measure. When a measure using only the 11 core symptoms is employed evidence for such an effect does emerge (Brown, Harris, & Lemyre, in press). However, the weight given to the importance of time 1 symptoms appears to be a function of using a continuous measure. The most plausible explanation is that a continuous measure, unlike that of caseness, is essentially one of well-being rather than depression in a clinically relevant sense. Therefore the high beta weight for initial symptoms is largely reflecting the ability of the *absence* of symptoms at time 1 to predict the same at time 2 (op cit). It is easy to fall into the trap of believing that we see reflected in such regression results the relative importance of psychiatric and psychosocial factors in determining clinically relevant depression and this, indeed, appears to be the most usual interpretation in the literature of such a patterning of results (e.g., Warheit, 1979). Such an interpretation is likely to be profoundly misleading.

Nonetheless once such pitfalls are recognized (and avoided) there is reason for optimism. In the end, success in diagnostic terms must be judged by what findings prove to be useful and there are already many replicated results using categorical measures of depression. It is also possible to make certain recommendations. There appears to be a general agreement that at least one threshold of caseness should reflect the level of severity of depression typically met in outpatient practice. (This is probably broadly reflected by criteria such as DSM-III major depression, but this needs further elucidation.) But at the same time, both higher and lower thresholds will at times need to be considered depending on the problem tackled. Such decisions should not be bypassed by the use of continuous scores, although there is no reason to rule out the use of the latter as long as they are carried out alongside categorical analyses.

HIERARCHY AND EXCLUSION RULES

I have argued so far for the importance of a certain openness in the approach to diagnoses and caseness. But this should not be muddled with the quite separate question of how much a definition should encompass. There is unfortunately a real danger of including too much in our definitions—that is that they will display too little restriction. And equally unfortunately the needs of research and clinical practice at this point may diverge. For the research worker considerable advantages are to be gained by restricting the range of a definition. If phenomena playing distinct roles in the aetiological process are encompassed in a definition, it may well be impossible to sort out what is going on.

In clinical practice the reverse will tend to hold: here it can be more important to know a classification works—say in predicting response to treatment—than to know *why* it works. A scheme such as DSM-III, developed with both research and clinical needs in mind, is particularly subject to such problems, and this is seen clearly in its various exclusion and hierarchical rules. These are employed in most current diagnostic schemes in an attempt to deal with the wide range of symptoms typically displayed by psychiatric patients. Since it is often impossible to reduce symptoms to one diagnostic category, it is tempting to exclude certain diagnostic possibilities by fiat—for example, that "major depression" should not be diagnosed in the presence of heavy drinking; or, even when this kind of problem is absent, to give priority to just one diagnostic category—say, major depression rather than that of anxiety state. The DSM-III has many such rules, none of which have been subjected to systematic evaluation. In promulgating them, there is often an implication that one disorder has brought about another, but no guidelines are provided for determining this (Barlow et al., 1986). In a revealing exercise comparing discrepancies between a clinical-based interview and the DIS (which follows DSM-III rules) a fifth of the discrepancies in diagnosing major depression were found to involve alcohol abuse where the clinicians, because they lacked evidence that depressive symptoms had been present in the absence of alcohol-related organic states, did not rate major depression' (Anthony et al., 1985, p. 673). Apparently the possibility of rating both conditions was not considered, nor any attempt made to document the history of the conditions and in this way to settle the matter in empirical terms.

The CATEGO-ID system of the PSE is also hierarchial and when symptoms of both depression and anxiety are present it will often subsume anxiety under depression. The Bedford College system, by contrast, enables two diagnoses to be made. The scheme is flexible in the sense that it is possible to have, say, onset case depression:chronic borderline case anxiety. This in turn enables a number of aetiological questions to be tackled. For example, it has already been shown that different types of life event provoke depression (loss) and anxiety (danger), and further that women developing a joint case depression:case anxiety condition experience far more events involving both loss and danger (Finlay-Jones & Brown, 1981). The distinction makes it possible to consider whether the two conditions take a different course, and whether different types of social risk factors are involved (Brown & Prudo, 1981; Prudo, Brown, Harris, & Dowland, 1981). This kind of analysis would be impossible, say, within the CATEGO system of the PSE (Brown, 1981).

The advantage of a more flexible approach has been increasingly recognized (see Monroe, in press). The DIS, for example, allows hierarchical rules to be ignored (Robins et al., 1981). However, the temptation to introduce hierarchical rules is obviously strong and these at times can threaten the very intellectual basis of epidemiological research. The revised DSM-III has made important changes but still retains the assumption of the earlier version that depression following bereavement should not be classified as major depression (although it meets formal criteria for such a diagnosis) if it is "a normal reaction to the death of a loved one" and therefore uncomplicated bereavement. It is noted, however, that morbid preoccupation with worthlessness, suicidal ideation, marked functional impairment or psychomotor retardation of prolonged duration, would suggest the bereavement has been complicated by major depression (APA, 1987).

Whatever the importance of such a distinction in clinical terms (and I certainly do not wish to argue against its usefulness), it is illogical and confusing in the context of aetiological research. It needs to be established, for instance, whether patterning of symptoms and course are different. It also overlooks the fact that many of the conditions labeled major depression follow events such as divorce, disappointing love affairs, and the like (Brown, Harris, 1989, ch. 2). How do such events differ from bereavements? And how can it be justified to class conditions provoked by them as major depression and not those following bereavement?

HETEROGENEITY IN AETIOLOGICAL RESEARCH

Blumenthal (1971) in an important paper has discussed these problems of over-inclusion in diagnostic schemes in terms of a broader principle covering the heterogeneity associated with affective disorder. She argues that at least three kinds need to be recognized—symptoms, treatment response, and aetiology. Her key point is that such domains are not necessarily at all closely related. A series of reports, for example, have now failed to confirm the common assumption that "endogenous" depressive disorders show little or no link with prior life events—that is, it is now reasonably clear that patients showing a classic pattern of symptoms associated with the idea of endogenous depression such as retardation and early waking have frequently had the condition provoked by a major loss or disappointment (see Katschnig, Pakesch, & Egger-Zeidner, 1986, for an excellent review). This is not to say the idea of endogenous depression is worthless—some forms of depression are almost certainly endogenous in a literal sense. The point is that there appear to be many exceptions and that we will never learn about the extent of this as long as judgments about the presence or not of provoking events is built into the diagnostic category itself (see discussions by Derogatis, Klerman, & Lipmann, 1972; Ni Bhrolchain, 1979; Cooke, 1982).

The need to segregate domains (e.g., symptoms and aetiological factors) is so critical that some instruments probably should be avoided altogether because of such mixing. There has been a long and costly effort in psychiatry to relate subtypes of depression to biological measures such as the Dexamethasone Suppression Test (DST). Results have been conflicting and will be discussed later—but one of the most successful measures so far has been the Newcastle Scale (Carney & Sheffield, 1972). This is a straightforward 15-item measure relying on clinical judgments. Unfortunately it involves making decisions about the presence of precipitating factors and other nonsymptomatic aspects of the disorder, and such general assessments about the presence of precipitating factors are known to be unreliable. Moreover, Katschnig and his colleagues (1986) have shown that whether or not the item concerning precipitation is rated as positive on the Newcastle Scale has a considerable effect on the proportions of depressed patients assigned to endogenous or nonendogenous subgroups. Given this kind of shortcoming, the main function of such contaminated measures would appear to be to hold out some promise that there is something of scientific significance in the endogenous/nonendogenous distinction.

The issue of heterogeneity is not restricted to the three categories outlined by Blumenthal—it is possible to add personality, degree of handicap, the presence of coterminous disorders such as anxiety, and processes influencing who receives psychiatric care. As a general rule such domains should not form part of the basic diagnostic scheme. To do so would almost certainly involve assuming a good deal more than has been reasonably established, and their inclusion would leave no way of testing these same assumptions. New insights may well be inhibited and somewhat narrow views reinforced. However, since such assumptions are most unlikely to be eliminated from everyday clinical work, their complete exclusion from instruments such as DSM-III is likely to prove difficult. However, it is not unrealistic to work to reduce them and to allow (and encourage) research workers to opt out of them at will—a point to which I return. It should be added that the use of additional axes or dimensions in schemes such as DSM-III avoids the problem presented by heterogeneity, although it needs to be added that there has so far been a good deal of wish fulfillment in their promulgation. Basic developmental work in terms of measurement has been skimped and their usefulness is likely to be minimal until there has been considerable investment of resources. This may well explain why in practice they have been very little used. However, they have served the useful function of making it easier to ignore nonclinical material in basic diagnostic decisions.

TIME ORDER

The problem of time is perhaps the most neglected of all the major issues concerning diagnosis. Instruments such as the Present State Examination were almost literally about the present and for most of its life users have been urged to deal with only the 1-month period before interview (Wing et al., 1967, 1974).

However, it is of very limited use for aetiological research if employed so narrowly: It is obvious that much could have changed since the time of onset and that in any case it is essential to date the actual data of onset if we are to consider the role of factors of possible aetiological importance. However, by and large, the research community has not concentrated on reconstructing recent history— say the prior year. It has either stuck to dealing with the present or, surprisingly, gone to the other extreme of dealing with the far more difficult (and perhaps intangible) notion of life-time disorder. As will be seen there is now a good deal to suggest that much can be done to reconstruct reasonably accurately recent clinical history and material is certainly good enough to tackle key aetiological issues. Unfortunately, however, we know practically nothing about our ability to reconstruct the distant past in terms of particular signs and symptoms. Just because it is possible to be confident about establishing the date of onset of caseness depression based on core symptoms such as depressed mood, early waking, weight loss, and suicidal plans, it does not follow that we are as effective in picking up, say, anergia or in making even more subtle distinctions (say quality of depressed mood) on which some diagnostic distinctions may rely. Bearing this particular knowledge gap in mind, I return to current epidemiological research which often appears confused about the question of time.

It is necessary to distinguish time order that emerges as a matter of course from the study of the same people at different points in time from that established by intensive interviewing aimed to reconstruct the past from the perspective of just one point in time. It should also be realized that a longitudinal inquiry will typically not obviate altogether the need for the latter kind of reconstruction. Although an ongoing inquiry will establish clinical state at particular points of time, it will usually also be necessary to establish changes occurring *between* such points—and this can only be achieved by retrospective questioning. For example, in some longitudinal inquiries life events in the period immediately *before* time 1 have been related to any new disorder occurring between time 1 and time 2. But since studies typically contact people about every 6 months, and life events of aetiological importance usually occur in a matter of weeks before onset many relevant events will be bound to be missed since those falling in the period between time 1 and onset will not be recorded. It is surprising how common this fatal shortcoming can be found in published inquiries and how little appreciation there has been of the problem (Brown & Harris, 1989, ch. 2).

Such difficulties concerning time have a number of origins. There has been widespread scepticism (quite unnecessary in terms of published work concerning the recent past) about what can be achieved by retrospective questioning—e.g., Zimmerman, Coryell, Pfohl, & Stangl, 1986, p. 236. The PSE, as already noted, for most of its history was only concerned with the 1 month prior to interview. In order to make it possible to use it in life-event research, it was necessary to deal with the course of depression disorders over a 1-year period and this in turn involved the development of the notion of *change-points* to take account of changes in clinical state (either in terms of increasing or decreasing severity). The detailed questioning that makes this possible usually starts with the present and then goes on to deal with the past (Brown & Harris, 1978; Copeland, 1983). The interviewing of depressed patients and near relatives (Brown & Harris, 1978), and the reinterviewing of respondents after 1 year (Brown et al., 1985), suggest that such reconstructions are accurate enough for systematic aetiological inquiry, and that clinical changes can be juxtaposed in time with important changes in a person's life.

But scepticism on occasions has given way to surprising, and, on the face of it, naive optimism. The SADS has a life-time version and the DIS is centrally concerned with life-time prevalence (Robins et al., 1981); Von Korff and Anthony, 1982). Its nonprobing, highly standardized mode of questioning has already been noted and clearly the task faced in reconstructing the past is more daunting than with the more flexible SADS, although in practice the two may not differ all that much over this issue. The DIS first asks about the presence of particular depressive symptoms in terms of a whole life time (e.g., "Has there ever been a period of a week or longer when you lost your appetite?"). At this point in the interview, however, nothing has been established about possible episodes of disorder. And when this issue is raised it is not in terms of asking about such episodes. Instead, if a person in terms of the life-time measure has been rated on depressed mood and at least four other depressive symptoms (out of 16) he or she is asked, "You said you've had a period of feeling depressed or blue and also said you've had some problems like (SYMPTOMS MENTIONED). Has there been a time when the feelings of depression and some of these other problems occurred together, that is, within the same month?" In other words only symptoms already mentioned in response to the questioning about life-time experience are at this second stage asked about and no systematic attempt is made to ask the interviewee about any episode or possible episode in detail. One obvious shortcoming is that a very great deal depends on the effectiveness of coverage of the opening questions about life-time prevalence. In practice, it is highly likely that some symptoms about the past are missed in the initial questioning; this is likely if only because respondents are not questioned about *particular* episodes. Moreover, given at the second stage of questioning that the total range of symptoms involved in a particular episode are not discussed together as such, there is no opportunity to add to the symptoms already reported. The point is critical because presence of major depression is settled in terms of the presence of 5 or more core symptoms. Where fewer than 5 have been mentioned it is not be possible to increase them during the final questioning and thereby turn a possible episode into one of major depression. Kovess and Fournier 1988) have discussed such reasons and report evidence that symptoms are in fact missed in this way and this may go some way to explain the apparent underreporting of depression by the DIS discussed later in this review. The nonprobing questioning probably also helps to explain why the reliability of reporting past episodes has been dismal (e.g., Bromet et al., 1986).

Aneshensel and her colleagues (1987) have carried out a thorough review of such attempts to document past episodes. Pulver and Carpenter (1983), for example, found that in a third of instances the DIS failed to detect a history of psychotic illness leading to a hospital admission. The best hope of improving this disheartening performance is to turn to a less structured and more probing approach that emphasizes the importance of obtaining narrative accounts—if you like, stories. There is now a good deal of evidence for its efficacy. In one study, women in the general population were interviewed by two different interviewers 1 year apart and the level of agreement about symptoms at time 1 in terms of the categories of case, borderline case and noncase was .75 on kappa (Brown, Craig, & Harris, 1985). In addition there was no evidence of fall-off in reporting with increase in time between onset and interview. In another study disorder during adulthood was considered with encouraging evidence concerning validity when case records of general practitioners were checked (Harris, Brown, & Bifulco, 1986). Results for nonpsychiatric phenomena are also highly encouraging. But these are at best intimations of what might be achieved. The approach in any case, of course, requires skilled interviewing and a good deal of time during the interview itself (see, for example, Neilson, Brown, & Marmot, 1989, who cover a 10-year period for life events).

These problems of the DIS about past episodes are also reflected in its ability to establish a current episode. In order to decide whether an episode is present at the time of interview, a person is further asked: "Are you in one of those spells of feeling low or disinterested and having some of these problems now?" and "When did your period like that end?" But, as with questioning about the past, the respondent is simply asked about the presence or not of such a spell and not about particular symptoms. The questions therefore do not provide the information needed to discriminate between subjects who currently meet the full criteria for major depressive episode and those who formerly met the full criteria, but now only meet *some* criteria—Anthony et al., 1985, p. 673.

Other problems in current instruments concerning time are less blatant, but still have a considerable potential for confusion. The investigator-based SADS-RDC system used in the Edinburgh survey discussed earlier applies diagnostic rules to symptom information obtained for the whole episode, and this rule was applied in the aetiological aspect of the Scottish inquiry. The research was longitudinal and in the light of this rule a number of women not considered to be "cases" at the time of first interview were retrospectively redefined as cases on the basis of the follow-up interview because they had developed caseness in the intervening period (Ingham et al., 1987). Thus a woman who had had mild tension symptoms for a lengthy period at first interview would in retrospect be redefined as having major depression for the *whole* of this period if a case condition had developed during the intervening period. As it happened, the exclusion from the analysis of 11 women in this ambiguous category made a difference to the conclusions reached about the role of self-esteem in predicting onset of depression. It is again a matter of avoiding being caught up willy-nilly in the consequences of extraneous rules built into a diagnostic scheme. It is yet another example of the mixing of domains. In this instance, it would have been better to avoid the confusion of such a built-in rule by plotting as accurately as possible what actually occurred in terms of "change-points" and then dealt with the issue in empirical terms. (It is of interest that a comparable North American approach (LIFE) to such change-points has recently been described—Keller et al., 1987).

The need for the accurate dating of changes in disorder derives not only from a concern with aetiology. There is worrying evidence for lack of stability in sub-diagnostic groupings of depression—e.g., the RDC endogenous subtype (Young et al., 1987). Barrett (1986) also reminds us that the long-term course taken by disorders has been, in the past, a principal means of validating diagnostic groupings. But, as already noted, the heterogeneity issue also applies here. In Barrett's discussion the course of disorder is seen in some way as resulting from *within* the person, from the very nature of the disorder itself, and course used to characterize two subgroups of patients. This might turn out to be a useful classification—but the implicit assumption about subtypes may at the same time be quite false. A more open and in the long run probably a more profitable strategy would be to use a quite separate dimension to deal with course. This would rule out possible circularity and allow for the consideration of alternative mechanisms—for example, perhaps that a certain personality type results in incompetence in developing supportive relationships and that this lack of support in turn contributes to the chronicity of any depressive disorder that happens to develop.

SUBTYPES OF DEPRESSION

One of the main concerns of the recent increased interest in psychopathology has been to isolate diagnostic subtypes; for depression this has meant concern with the perennial endogenous-reactive distinction. Undoubtedly the most important approach has been an intuitive one. The influential syndromes in psychiatry were identified by clinical observers and not statistically armed research workers. But Paykel (1981) in an authoratative review, is not enthusiastic in terms of future knowledge about either an intuitive or statistical approach: "There may yet be more symptomatic syndromes awaiting discovery, where the retentive observer's eye is likely to be more illuminating than the blanket statistical technique, which can easily miss infrequent exceptional individuals. However, most of the opportunities for such insights are past" (p. 360). Paykel argues that the considerable overlap between the various subgroupings of depression (other than bipolar) is probably genuine and that, in all likelihood, we will need to live with this untidiness and capitalize on the modest help statistical techniques have to offer. Such pessimism is probably realistic, but it might be unwise to cut oneself off altogether from this intuitive tradition and the chance of feeding any insights back into the research process—a point I made earlier in discussing the potential rigidity of classificatory schemes. One statistical technique, discriminant analysis, relates directly to this since diagnostic subgroups must already have been decided intuitively before it can be used. Discriminant analysis will then produce a linear combination of weighted symptoms (or any item for that matter) which will produce the best separation between the original subgroups. Paykel (1981) notes how the statistical power of discriminant analysis can maximize chance findings and produce invalid differences between groups. Nonetheless, the technique is nicely placed to bridge the gap between clinical judgment and empirical findings. To illustrate: it has been used to separate *psychotic* and *neurotic* depressive patients in a study of life events and onset. Differences between the two diagnostic groups in terms of such events were minimal even when they were split into extreme and less extreme halves in terms of the discriminant function (Brown & Harris, 1978, ch. 14). But the matter was not left there. The 5% of the psychotic group with the least psychotic scores were reassigned to the neurotic group and the 5% of the neurotic group with the least neurotic scores were reassigned to the psychotic group, and in three further exercises 10%, 15% and 20% were reallocated in the same way. For the 20% reallocation, a statistically significant difference did emerge—52% of the psychotics and 73% of the neurotics had experienced a severe event before onset (Ni Bhrolchain, Brown, & Harris, 1979; table 1). While 20% is a substantial reallocation it is probably about as large as might be expected to be necessary from what is known about diagnostic reliability. The strength of the exercise was that it enabled a particularly severe test of the null hypothesis to be carried out. In spite of the substantial reallocation only a modest difference in the hypothesized direction was obtained. And the original conclusion therefore remained: that there is a large overlap in the experience of provoking agents in subtypes of depression aimed to reflect the classical endogenous/reactive distinction. Katschnig, Pakesch, and Egger-Deidner (1986) have carried out an exhaustive review of the field and arrived at the same general conclusion. It should be added that the problem of statistical power is, of course, bypassed if a finding is replicated.

Statistical inquiries into subgroup classifications of depression, however, have typically employed factor analysis or cluster analysis rather than discriminant analysis (Garside & Roth, 1978; Kendell, 1975; Paykel, 1981). Cluster analytic studies have been fewer, but a group of endogenous or psychotic depressives—usually severely ill—have consistently emerged. A second feature of such studies is that there has been a general failure of nonendogenous depression to emerge as a single group rather than in several groups. There is also clear overlap in some of the additional groups which have emerged in different studies (see Paykel, 1981, p. 359). There can be no doubt that there has been a convincing demonstration by factor analysis that endogenous and neurotic forms of depression can be contrasted, but there is still uncertainty about the best discriminants at a symptom level. Given that cluster analysis is typically producing more than two subgroups of depression perhaps more can be expected from this approach. However, Paykel concludes his review on a cautious note. Studies have failed convincingly to demonstrate any clear-cut distinction between *endogenous* and *neurotic* domains and it is clear that we must recognize large numbers of intermediate cases—the very reason for resorting to multivariate statistics in the first place. Our present need is to relate these tentative schemes to alternative domains—such as underlying pathology, biochemical measures, social correlates, and so on.

There remains the third approach, a development of the intuitive—that of devising formal criteria by fiat. Instruments such as PSE-CATEGO, SADS-RDC, and DIS have relied on the development of formal algorithms for isolating subtypes of depression and a good deal of research has been concerned with evaluating their effectiveness. A recent study by Zimmerman and his colleagues (1986a) provides a representative example of such research. Four diagnostic systems were compared, three of which have already been discussed—DSM-III, RDC, Newcastle, and a fourth by Feinberg and Carroll (FC) (1982) developed by the use of discriminant function. RDC have provided the most frequently used definition of endogenous-type depression. The DSM-III criteria for melancholia are the influential official criteria of the American Psychiatric Association. Both promulgated criteria by fiat: No empirical justification for RDC criteria has been given (Spitzer et al., 1977), and Williams and Spitzer (1982) suggest that DSM-III criteria for melancholia were intended to reduce the heterogeneity within the RDC endogenous depressive group. Zimmerman and his coworkers note that the major difference between the two sets of criteria is that DSM-III melancholics must exhibit pervasive or near pervasive anhedonia and be unreactive to pleasurable environmental stimuli, whereas there are no absolutely necessary criteria for RDC endogenous depression, the change reflecting Klein's conceptualization of the core symptoms of endogenomorphic depression (Klein, 1974). The Newcastle scale was empirically derived on the basis of a multiple regression analysis of 35 items collected for depressed patients receiving electro-convulsive therapy (ECT) and aimed to predict ECT response (Carney, Roth, & Garside, 1965). Several studies have shown the scale predicts treatment response (Carney & Sheffield, 1972; Abou-Saleh & Coppen, 1983, Rao & Coppen, 1979; Vlissides & Jenner, 1982) and also response to the dexamethasone suppression test (DST) (Coppen et al., 1983; Holden, 1983). The FC criteria were chosen because the research on DST has had a major influence on work on the biological classification of depression (Carroll et al., 1981).

To return to the study; Zimmerman and his colleagues established from a literature review various clinical, demographic, familial, and psychosocial criteria that should discriminate endogenous and nonendogenous depression, and then looked at a consecutive series of 152 unipolar depressive in-patients. The most notable result was the modest degree of association they showed with other characteristics of the person; and also between some of the definitions of depression. Endogenous depression was most frequently diagnosed by RDC and FC with almost two-thirds diagnosed as definite. In contrast, less than half were endogenous according to DSM-III and Newcastle. Kappa coefficients between the various instruments ranged from 0.18 to 0.69. All four schemes found that endogenous patients were more seriously disturbed in terms of various methods of assessment and that nonendogenous patients had more nonserious suicide attempts—e.g., by RDC criteria 47% versus 15%. The Newcastle scale was the only one finding a difference in the experience of separation-divorce—33% among the nonendogenous versus 18%. Life events were unrelated to diagnostic criteria, and, quite contrary to expectation, DSM-III and RDC endogenous were more likely to lack a confidant. Personality disorder was significantly less frequent in Newcastle endogenous depressives—27% versus 60%, but not in the other systems. A family history of alcoholism was more frequent in all systems for nonendogenous patients—but the proportion involved were modest—e.g., for the Newcastle measure 12% versus 7%.

The correlates of these measures to the dexamethasone suppression test was also considered. As expected endogenous patients had a significantly higher rate of nonsuppression than nonendogenous patients according to the DSM-III and Newcastle definitions, but not according to RDC or FC. The differences were modest—44% versus 28% for DSM-III and 48% versus 28% for Newcastle (Zimmerman et al., 1985, 1986b).

I have gone to some length to review these findings as they are probably typical of what can at present be expected (see, for example, Andreasen et al., 1986; and Copolov et al., 1986). Similar conclusions can almost certainly be made about other current methods of classifying depression—for example, primary and secondary disorders (Grove et al., 1987; Nelson & Charney, 1980). Many interesting findings have been reported in the literature, but inconsistent results are not uncommon and the degree of overlap between the diagnostic subgroups is often considerable. We appear to meet here a stubborn inability to produce clear-cut findings on the part of efforts to subclassify depression. Because of this there has been increasing uncertainty about objectives. In a stimulating discussion, Van Praag and his colleagues (1987) have reacted to the emerging failure of serotonin (5-hydroxytryptamine, 5-HT) dysfunction to be restricted to one psychiatric disorder, let alone to subtypes of depression. They point out the bewildering range of disorders involved in 5-HT dysfunction— depression, anxiety states, schizophrenia, and alcoholism. They argue that 5-HT disturbance is, nonetheless, only nonspecific in terms of a nosological/categorical approach to disorder. If a dimensional approach is taken, such disturbance can be seen in specific terms. It is, for example, correlated with characteristics such as hostility. The fact that they can be manifested in a range of disorders explains its nonspecificity in ordinary diagnostic terms.

Such a stance does not necessarily reject a categorical component in diagnosis—but it would underline the importance of considering additional dimensions, such as hostility, even within the "symptom" level—and it may provide one way forward in the somewhat unrewarding attempts to distinguish clear subtypes of depression.

The important question is what more can be done. There is a chance that symptom definition is still too vague. A study by Rush and his colleagues (Rush et al., 1989) is an important exception in finding marked differences in DST response in terms of endogenous and nonendogenous depressed patients according to RDC. (They also found an impressive link between the two groups and REM latency). They note that their findings are at some variance with other reports. They suggest that the differences could be accounted for by the conservative way they applied RDC criteria and the fact that their center approximates a primary rather than a tertiary care centre. Nonetheless, even with this strict usage, the endogenous and bipolar groupings formed as many as 71% (114/160) of the patient series. The results of this study are certainly highly encouraging, but the investigators would probably be the first to agree that the reason for the difference in result is as yet unclear and given the present uncertain situation, it would appear most appropriate at present to take a polydiagnostic approach in current research (Katschnig & Berner, 1983, p. 206). That is, to use several diagnostic formulations on the same population. But this needs to go with continued concern about the validity of ratings at a symptom level; it may also be desirable to take account of symptoms rarely included in present schemes, but often considered clinically important—such as distinct quality of depression (Ramas-Brieva et al., 1987.) It should here be borne in mind that some of the most useful symptoms for distinguishing endogenous depression may turn out to be derived primarily from observation (Nelson & Carney, 1980).[2]

In addition it is necessary to entertain the possibility that at times genuine endogenous conditions may be indistinguishable clinically from reactive conditions. In a recent inquiry considering depressive disorders arising in the few weeks after a birth were found to be the least likely to have a provoking stressor. However, it was not possible to distinguish in clinical terms this temporarily restricted postpartum group from other major depressive conditions occurring to prepartum and postpartum women, many more of whom had adverse life circumstances associated with onset (Martin et al., 1989).

Finally, it needs to be recognized that it is likely that selective factors influencing who is channelled into psychiatric care may be greatly complicating attempts to establish subtypes of depression (Brown & Harris, 1978; ch. 14), a point probably best conveyed by an example. Cases of depression in a population

---

[2]These same authors also make the interesting point on the basis of their literature review that changes in sleep, appetite, and weight loss long considered basic neurovegative symptoms very often occur in "nonendogenous" conditions.

survey in London who were referred to psychiatrists were not more severely disturbed in terms of PSE symptoms of depression than cases not referred. However, the women were more likely to have tried to harm themselves and more often to show evidence of alcohol abuse or drug addiction. In other words, they were of more potential trouble to their general practitioners or to themselves and those in their immediate milieu. Such referred women were much more likely to have lost a mother in childhood by separation but *not* by death (Brown, Craig, & Harris, 1985). Another study had earlier shown that hostile cognitive sets and self-harm to be more common among women with early loss of mother by separation but not among those losing a mother by death (Brown & Harris, 1978). Given this, it is important to consider the possibility that effects may arise via the influence of a factor on symptom-formation (and hence admission) rather than because of any genetic diathesis inherent in a diagnostic characteristic (Harris et al., 1986, 1987). In the work of Zimmerman reviewed earlier there are a number of possible examples—say of the correlation of family alcoholism or marital separation in parents and type of depression.

There have been a number of attempts to isolate specific symptoms for "reactive/neurotic depressives" (e.g., Matussek, Luks, & Nagel, 1982; Matussek, Soldner, & Nagel, 1982; Akiskal et al., 1978), but the results just reviewed raise the possibility that findings have been influenced by selective factors determining who receives psychiatric care. The work of Angst and his colleagues in Zurich is of particular interest here as it is based on a longitudinal study of a general population sample of 20- and 21-year-old men and women which therefore avoids bias arising from the use of a patient series. A depressive syndrome was first defined by the simple presence or absence of changes in mood and drive. The resulting conditions were then classified by duration of episode. The conclusions reached are radical in that once this had been done, no qualitative differences were found in terms of other symptom characteristics—only a trend for somatic symptoms to become more prominent with increasing duration of episode. Considerable emphasis was given to nonsymptom criteria such as subjective impairment, social impairment, and illness behavior and all favored a continuum of depression from normal to pathological (Angst & Dobler-Mikola, 1984). Of particular interest is the importance placed on the study of physical symptoms such as "syndromes" concerning stomach, intestine, respiration, and exhaustion; and in this way they isolated a group of short-lasting depressive states with a very high rate of somatic symptoms and "pronounced subjective suffering and a remarkable frequency of treatment." Unfortunately the method of data collection has many of the shortcomings already outlined. The research as a whole runs into serious problems when dealing with time because of its reliance on questionnaires, checklists, and highly general questioning (see Brown & Harris, 1982 and Schmid, Scharfetter, & Binder, 1981 for a discussion of the approach to life events). Nonetheless it is an excellent example of a refreshing open and descriptive approach that is capable of throwing up many stimulating ideas, and this innovative program clearly needs to be carried out with measures less subject to criticism.

CHOICE OF A DIAGNOSTIC INSTRUMENT

Epidemiological inquiries can now choose to study depression by a variety of instruments. (An excellent account can be found in a recent review by Rabkin and Klein, 1987.) Consideration of cost is likely to play a role in any choice, and here it is well to recall that investigator-based instruments, although more costly in terms of a single study, in the long-term will be bound to be cheaper in so far as they more often lead to cumulative findings. Two fundamental advantages of the approach are that it is in a much better position to improve the accuracy of the basic symptom ratings on which everything else is built, and can also deal with the question of time. It also has the advantage that the investigator is likely to be brought into more intimate contact with the phenomenology of depression. I have emphasized how a precious means of moving beyond the limited insights encapsulated in our measurement procedures would be lost if we did not allow some tension between the *rules* of the instrument and possible *insights* from grappling with the full clinical picture.

Undoubtedly the critical choice at present is whether to use the highly structured Diagnostic Interview Schedule (DIS) in population inquiries. The choice here has recently been enlarged by the introduction of the Composite International Diagnostic Interview (CIDI). This has been designed at the request of the World Health Organization and the US Alcohol, Drug Abuse, and Mental Health Administration, and is based on questions from the DIS, but includes additional questions to elicit Present State Examination (PSE) items (Robins et al., 1988). The claims made for it can be judged by the following brief extract arguing for its advantages:

> A highly structured interview is required to reduce the observer, information, and criterion variance that can result from using less standardized procedures for diagnostic assessment. Such a structured instrument not only assures investigators in different settings that their diagnostic results with respect to shared diagnoses will be comparable, but it also provides a basis for cross-cultural comparison of local diagnostic systems that include conditions thought to be culture specific. In addition, a high degree of structure makes it possible to use nonclinicians as interviewers. . . .
>
> To be usable by nonclinicians, the interview questions must be fully spelled out and 'closed ended' (i.e., answerable with a number or by choosing among predetermined alternatives) so that the nonclinicians can get reliable and valid answers when read as written, without requiring interpretation by interviewers who have no more medical or psychological information than that available to any well-educated

member of the local society. These questions must also rule out the common difficulties of everyday life and the symptoms of physical disease that resemble psychiatric symptoms, to avoid inflated estimates of psychopathology. For the interview to be useful throughout the population in societies with varying levels of education and literacy, its language needs to be simple; to facilitate use in many countries, it must avoid idiomatic phrases that do not translate cross-culturally.

In the light of the arguments of this essay, all this needs to be treated with the utmost caution. However, the CIDI does have the considerable advantage of not relying on a life-time approach and ultimately does focus on questions concerning severity in the last month. However, the documentation of validity (either of CIDI or DIS) as yet is far from convincing, and such claims, not least in the context of cross-cultural research, cannot but appear immoderate and cannot in any case be transferred to DIS. A recent paper has in fact compared the item-by-item agreement between the PSE and the CIDI. The former interview was carried out by research psychiatrists and the latter by a specially trained psychologist. Both interviews were given to 30 subjects representing a wide range of diagnoses, including hospital psychotic patients, subjects attending an Eating Disorder Unit, and out-patients with milder neurotic symptoms. The results confirmed what would be expected on the basis of this review—that agreement between the two instruments about individual symptoms was low. However, when broader issues such as syndrome classification, diagnostic class, and severity, were considered, agreement reached statistical significance (Farmer, Katz, & McGuffin, & Bebbington, 1987). Unfortunately a closer look at the material still leads to a pessimistic conclusion about the likely usefulness of the instrument for population surveys. Agreement was highest for the psychotic patients. When these were excluded sensitivity was 71% in terms of whether the patient reached threshold level for caseness (i.e., ID 5). This must be counted as a disappointing result given that all those involved were attending clinics regularly, and its usefulness for epidemiological research must at present be uncertain. Results were more favorable in another study comparing the use of the DIS by a lay interviewer and a psychiatrist, the latter empowered to add questions he thought necessary (Robins et al., 1981, 1982); but in a later report of a general population survey sensitivity was low (Helzer et al., 1985). For example, the sensitivity of the physicians' DIS compared with further coverage to establish the physicians' best clinical judgment was .63; and a comparison between a lay DIS and a physicians' best estimate .42. Interestingly, the basic failure of the DIS was in the underreporting of depression—a point touched on earlier when discussing the nature of the questions about symptoms and episodes. Of the 101 instances of major depression rated by clinicians in terms of their best estimate only 42 were rated when the DIS was used by lay interviewers, whereas of the 67 diagnoses of major depression made by the DIS most (42) were also made by the clinicians best estimate. Parker (1987) has recently published a very useful discussion of evidence for the validity of the prevalence estimates based on the DIS. His review is sceptical in tone and he is particularly critical of its use to measure lifetime prevalence. There have been various other negative reports (e.g., Anthony et al., 1985; Anthony and Dryman, 1987). It needs also to be borne in mind that the job of collecting material in the general population can be onerous and at times threatening and that the morale and training of lay interviewers has almost certainly got to be high. Probably a special effort has to be made to achieve this in inner-city areas. Bearing all this in mind I conclude that the DIS is likely to be most useful for establishing simple correlations with demographic-type variables. And even here valid results are only likely to emerge in so far as errors in diagnostic ratings tend to cancel out. (Robins [1985] has argued that this in fact occurred in the St Louis data of the Epidemiologic Catchment Area programme (ECA).) However, even if this should turn out to be correct, such an instrument (and also CIDI) is unsuitable for more complex analyses where there is concern with models dealing with the impact of a number of factors; for this it is essential to have accurate measurement at the individual level. Here the DIS is just not accurate enough and it follows its economic advantage with large population samples is no longer compelling. Nonetheless pressure (not least economic) to produce such all-purpose instruments is clearly considerable. This means that they are unlikely to be entirely dropped for some time from epidemiological inquiries. Given this, it would be highly desirable, both on scientific and economic grounds, to carry out in any study using the DIS a parallel more intensive one on a smaller sample from the same population, using an investigator-based approach. In the end, claims and counterclaims in this area are best assessed in terms of the degree of convergence in findings. However, here it needs to be borne in mind the neither the DIS nor CIDI are capable of dating onset (within, say, a period of 1 year) and their use in a good deal of aetiological research that requires close attention thereby is ruled out.

There are, as already noted, shortcomings, albeit less fundamental, in the alternative investigator-based instruments. The SADS life-time version is probably as suspect as the life-time DIS. Unlike the current SADS it does not set out to determine the clinical significance of each symptom but only its presence or absence. It appears possible to include symptoms on relatively little evidence and detailed definitions are rarely given. Earlier it was argued that insufficient attention, even if much less marked than this, is given to the definition of individual symptoms in instruments such as SADS (current) and PSE. Moreover present investigator-based instruments frequently need supplementing in terms of particular research objectives. The 9th edition of the PSE, for example, only covers 1 month, psychosomatic and sexual disturbances cannot be evaluated, and it does not assess social problems and social consequences of psychological disturbance (Angst & Dobler-Mikola, & Binder, 1984). While (in this instance) a 10th edition will meet some of these gaps, research workers will often need to develop new components for the instrument of their choice.

Because it is essential for scientific progress that we utilize as far as possible common instruments, it is fortunate that there seems no good reason why the kind of investigator-based ones that I have discussed should not be built upon, bearing in mind that some of their rules may need to be relaxed, particularly those concerning hierarchy and exclusion (Meehl, 1986). In more general terms, our biggest danger may well be to assume that achievements have been greater than they have been. The whole paraphernalia of the language of science and the need for large sums of money to carry out epidemiological research will tend to push us in the direction of overstatement. The recognition that definitions in science are processual may be helpful in the sense of making it easier to accept that our measures are bound to be provisional. At the same time, since comparison and replication are important virtues, instruments should ideally be created so that more than one diagnostic scheme can emerge. There are welcome signs that many are moving towards such flexibility, and if this is combined with continued interest in ratings at a symptom level, the future for epidemiological psychiatry must, on recent performance, be a hopeful one.

ACKNOWLEDGMENTS

This chapter could not have been written without the influence and generous help of the psychiatrists with whom I have worked over the last 16 years—John Copeland, John Cooper, Ray Prudo, Robert Finlay-Jones, Elaine Murphy, and Tom Craig. I have also benefitted greatly from the clinical experience of Tirril Harris, who also, with Tom Craig, made invaluable comments on this chapter.

REFERENCES

Abou-Saleh, M. T., & Coppen, A. (1983). Classification of depression and response to antidepressive therapies. *British Journal of Psychiatry, 143,* 601–603.

Akiskal, H. S., Bitar, A. H., Puzantian, V. R., Rosenthal, T. L., & Walker, P. W. (1978). The nosological status of neurotic depression. A prospective three- to four-year follow-up examination in light of the primary-secondary and unipolar-bipolar dichotomies. *Archives of General Psychiatry, 35,* 756–766.

American Psychiatric Association (1987). *Diagnostic and statistical manual of mental disorders* (Third edition–revised). DSM-III-R.

Andreasen, N. C., Scheftner, W., Reich, T., Hirschfeld, R. M. A., Endicott, J., & Keller, M. B. (1986). The validation of the concept of endogenous depression—A family study approach. *Archives of General Psychiatry, 43,* 246–251.

Aneshensel, C. S., Estrada, A. L., Hansell, M. J., & Clark, V. A. (1987). Social psychological aspects of reporting behaviour: Lifetime depressive episode reports. *Journal of Health & Social Behaviour, 28,* 232–246.

Angst, J., Dobler-Mikola, A., & Binder, J. (1984). The Zurich study—a prospective epidemiological study of depressive, neurotic and psychosomatic syndromes. I. Problem and methodology. *European Archives of Psychiatry & Neurological Sciences, 234,* 13–20.

Angst, J., & Dobler-Mikola (1984). The Zurich study. II. The continuum from normal to pathological depressive mood swings. *European Archives of Psychiatry & Neurological Sciences, 234,* 21–29.

Anthony, J. C., & Dryman, A. (1987, September). *Analysis of discrepancy in life-time diagnosis of mental disorder: Results from the NIMH catchment area program.* Presented at the meeting of the World Psychiatric Association Section on Epidemiology and Community Psychiatry, Reykjavik, Iceland.

Anthony, J. C., Folstein, M., Romanoski, A. J., von Korff, M. R., Nestadt, G. R., Chahal, R., Merchant, A., Brown, C. H., Shapiro, S., Kramer, M., & Gruenberg, E. M. (1985). Comparison of the Lay Diagnostic Interview Schedule & a standardized psychiatric diagnosis. Experience in Eastern Baltimore. *Archives of General Psychiatry, 42,* 667–675.

Barlow, D. H., DiNardo, P. A., Vermilyea, J., & Blanchard, E. B. (1986). Co-morbidity and depression among the anxiety disorders. Issues in diagnosis and classification. *The Journal of Nervous and Mental Disease, 174,* 63–73.

Barrett, J. (1986). Case identification for category validation: The challenge of disorder-specific assessment. *Comprehensive Psychiatry, 27,* 81–100.

Bebbington, P. (1986). Depression, distress or disease? *British Journal of Psychiatry, 148,* 479.

Blumenthal, M. D. (1971). Heterogeneity & research on depressive disorders. *Archives of General Psychiatry, 24,* 524–531.

Boyd, J. H., Weissman, M. M., Douglas Thompson, W., & Myers, J. K. (1982). Screening for depression in a community sample: Understanding the discrepancies between depression symptom and diagnostic scales. *Archives of General Psychiatry, 39,* 1195–1200.

Bromet, E. J., Dunn, L. O., Connell, M. M., Dew, M. A., & Schulberg, M. C. (1986). Long-term reliability of diagnosing lifetime major depression in a community sample. *Archives of General Psychiatry, 43,* 435–440.

Brown, G. W., (1981). Aetiological studies and the definition of a case. In J. K., Wing, P., Bebbington, & L. N. Robins (Eds.), *What is a case? The problem of definition in psychiatric community surveys.* London: Grant McIntyre.

Brown, G. W., Adler, Z., & Bifulco, A. (1988). Life events, difficulties and recovery from chronic depression. *British Journal of Psychiatry. 152,* 487–498.

Brown, G. W., Andrews, B., Harris, T. O., Adler, Z., & Bridge, L. (1986). Social support, self-esteem and depression. *Psychological Medicine, 16,* 813–831.

Brown, G. W., Birley, J. L. T., & Wing, J. K. (1972). Influence of family life on the course of schizophrenic disorders: a replication. *British Journal of Psychiatry, 121,* 241–258.

Brown, G. W., Craig, T. K. J., & Harris, T. O. (1985). Depression: Distress or disease? Some epidemiological considerations. *British Journal of Psychiatry, 147,* 612–622.

Brown, G. W., & Davidson, S. (1978). Social class, psychiatric disorder of mother, and accidents to children. *Lancet, 1:* 378–381.

Brown, G. W., & Harris, T. O. (1978). *Social origins of depression: A study of psychiatric disorder in women.* London: Tavistock.

Brown, G. W., & Harris, T. O. (1979). Psychotic and neurotic depression: Part 3. Aetiological and background factors. *Journal of Affective Disorders, 1,* 195–211.

Brown, G. W., & Harris, T. O. (1982). Fall-off in the reporting of life events. *Social Psychiatry, 17,* 23–28.

Brown, G. W., & Harris, T. O. (1986). Stressor, vulnerability & depression: A question of replication. *Psychological Medicine, 16,* 739–744.

Brown, G. W., & Harris, T. O. (1989a). Depression. In G. W. Brown and T. O. Harris (Eds.), *Life events and illness.* Guilford Press.

Brown, G. W., & Harris, T. O. (1989b). *Life events and illness.* New York: Guilford Press.

Brown, G. W., Harris, T. O., & Peto, J. (1973b). Life events and psychiatric disorders. Part 2: Nature of causal link. *Psychological Medicine, 3,* 159–176.

Brown, G. W., Harris, T. O., & Lemyre, L. (in press). Now you see it, now you don't—Some considerations of multiple regression. In D. Magnusson, L. R. Bergman, E. Rudinger, & B.

Törestad (Eds.), *Problems and methods in longitudinal research: Stability and change*. Cambridge, England: Cambridge University Press.

Brown, G. W., & Prudo, R. (1981). Psychiatric disorder in a rural and an urban population: 1. Aetiology of depression. *Psychological Medicine, 11*, 581–599.

Brown, G. W., Sklair, F., Harris, T. O., & Birley, J. L. T. (1973a) Life events & psychiatric disorders. Part 1: Some methodological issues. *Psychological Medicine, 33*, 74–87.

Carney, M. W. P., Roth, M., & Garside, R. F. (1965). The diagnosis of depressive syndrome and the prediction of ECT response. *British Journal of Psychiatry, III*, 659–674.

Carney, M. W. P., & Sheffield, B. F. (1972). Depression and the Newcastle Scales: Their relationship to Hamilton's Scale. *British Journal of Psychiatry, 121*, 35–40.

Carroll, B. J., Feinberg, M., Greden, J. F., Tarika, J., Albala, A. A., Haskett, R. F., James, N. M., Kronfol, Z., Lohr, N., Steiner, M., de Vigne, J. P., and Young, E. (1981). A specific laboratory test for the diagnosis of melancholia: Standardization, validation and clinical utility. *Archives of General Psychiatry, 38*, 15–22.

Cicourel, A. V. (1986). Social measurement as the creation of expert systems. In D. W. Fiske and R. A. Shweder (Eds.), *Metatheory in social science*. Chicago: University of Chicago Press.

Cooke, D. J. (1982). Life events and psychological distress: some problems in design and analysis. In C. J. Main (Ed.), *Clinical psychology and medicine: A behavioural perspective*. New York: Plenum.

Cooper, J. E., Copeland, J. R. N., Brown, G. W., Harris, T. O., & Gourlay, A. J. (1977). Further studies on interview training and inter-rater reliability of the Present State Examination (PSE). *Psychological Medicine, 7*, 517–523.

Copeland, J. R. M. (1983). Psychotic and neurotic depression: discriminant function analysis and five-year entrance. *Psychological Medicine, 13*, 373–383.

Copolov, D. L., Rubin, R. T., and Mander, A. J., Sashidharan, S. P., Whitehouse, A. M., Blackburn, I. M., Freeman, C. P., & Blackwood, D. H. R. (1986). DSM-III melancholia: Do the criteria accurately and reliably distinguish endogenous pattern depression? *Journal of Affective Disorders, 10*, 191–202.

Coppen, A., Abou-Saleh, M., Miln, P., Metcalfe, M., Harwood, J. & Bailey, J. (1983). Dexamethasone suppression test in depression and other psychiatric illnesses. *British Journal of Psychiatry, 142*, 498–504.

Craig-Nelson, J., & Charney, D. S. (1981). The symptoms of major depressive illness. *The American Journal of Psychiatry, 138*, 1–13.

Craig, T. K. J., Brown, G. W., & Harris, T. O. (1987). Depression in the general population: comparability of survey results. *British Journal of Psychiatry, 150*, 707–708.

Dean, C., Surtees, P. G., & Sashidharan, S. P. (1983). Comparison of research diagnostic systems in an Edinburgh community sample. *British Journal of Psychiatry, 142*, 247–256.

Derogatis, L. R., Klerman, G., & Lipman, R. S. (1972). Anxiety states and depressive neurosis: Issues in nosological discrimination. *Journal of Nervous and Mental Disease, 155*, 392–403.

Dohrenwend, B. P., Shrout, P. E., Egri, G., & Mendelsohn, F. S. (1980). Non-specific psychological distress and other dimensions of psychopathology: Measures for use in the general population. *Archives of General Psychiatry, 37*, 1229–1236.

Duncan-Jones, P., Henderson, S., & Byrne, D. G. (1980). The Present State Examination: Its use without formal training in a population survey. *Social Psychiatry, 15*, 91–93.

Endicott, J., & Spitzer, R. L. (1978). A diagnostic interview. The schedule for affective disorders and schizophrenia. *Archives of General Psychiatry, 35*, 837–844.

Farmer, A. E., Katz, R., McGuffin, P., & Bebbington, P. (1987). A comparison between the Present State Examination and the Composite International Diagnostic Interview. *Archives of General Psychiatry, 44*, 1064–1068.

Feinberg, M., Carroll, B. J. (1982). Separation of subtypes of depression using discriminant analysis. *British Journal of Psychiatry, 140*, 384–391.

Finlay-Jones, R. (1989). Anxiety. In G. W. Brown & T. O. Harris (Eds.), *Life events & illness*. New York: Guilford Press.
Finlay-Jones, R., & Brown, G. W. (1981). Types of stressful life event and the onset of anxiety and depressive disorders. *Psychological Medicine, 11*, 803–815.
Finlay-Jones, R., Brown, G. W., Duncan-Jones, P., Harris, T. O., Murphy, E., & Prudo, R. (1980). Depression and anxiety in the community: Replicating the diagnosis of a case. *Psychological Medicine, 10*, 445–454.
Frank, J. D. (1973). *Persuasion and healing*. Baltimore: The John Hopkins University Press.
Garside, R. F., & Roth, M. (1978). Multivariate statistical methods and problems of classification in psychiatry. *British Journal of Psychiatry, 133*, 53–67.
Gauron, E. F., & Dickinson, J. K. (1966a). Diagnostic decision making in psychiatry: Information usage. *Archives of General Psychiatry, 14*, 225–232.
Gauron, E. F., & Dickinson, J. K. (1966b). Diagnostic decision making in psychiatry: Diagnostic styles. *Archives of General Psychiatry, 14*, 233–237.
Gauron, E. F., & Dickinson, J. K. (1969). The influence of seeing the patient first on diagnostic decision making in psychiatry. *American Journal of Psychiatry, 126*, 199–205.
Ghiselin, M. T. (1969). *Triumph of the Darwinian method*. Berkeley: University of California Press.
Goldberg, D. P. (1972). *The detection of psychiatric illness by Questionnaire*. London: Oxford University Press.
Gorman, D. M. (1987). Measures of onset of 'caseness' in studies of stressful life events and alcohol abuse. *British Journal of Addiction, 82*, 1017–1020.
Gorman, D. M. (1988). *The role of life events and other social factors in the aetiology of alcohol dependence*. Doctoral thesis, University of Essex, Colchester, UK.
Grove, W. M., Andreasen, N. C., Clayton, P. J., Winokur, G., & Coryell, W. H. (1987). Primary and secondary affective disorders: Baseline characteristics of unipolar patients. *Journal of Affective Disorders, 13*, 249–257.
Hamilton, M. (1960). A rating scale for depression. *Journal of Neurology, Neurosurgery and Psychiatry, 23*, 56–62.
Harris, T. O., & Brown, G. W. (1985). Interpreting data in aetiological studies of affective disorder: Some pitfalls and ambiguities. *British Journal of Psychiatry, 147*, 5–15.
Harris, T. O., Brown, G., & Bifulco, A. T. (1986). Loss of parent in childhood and adult psychiatric disorder: The role of lack of adequate parental care. *Psychological Medicine, 16*, 641–659.
Helzer, J. E., Robins, L. N., McEvoy, L. T., Spiznagel, E. L., Stoltzman, R. K., Farmer, A., & Brockington, I. F. (1985). A comparison of clinical and diagnostic interview schedule diagnoses. *Archives of General Psychiatry, 42*, 657–666.
Holden, N. L. (1983). Depression and the Newcastle Scale: Their relationship to the Dexamethasone suppression Test. *British Journal of Psychiatry, 142*, 505–507.
Hyman, H. H. (1954). *Interview in social research*. Chicago: University of Chicago Press.
Ingham, J. G., Kreitman, N. B., Miller, P. McC., Sashidharan, S. P., & Surtees, P. G. (1987). Self-appraisal, anxiety and depression in women—A prospective enquiry. *British Journal of Psychiatry, 150*, 643–651.
Katschnig, H., & Berner, P. (1985). The polydiagnostic approach in psychiatric research. In ADAMHA/WHO: *Mental disorders, alcohol and drug related problems: International perspectives on their diagnosis and classification* (pp 113–20). Amsterdam: Elsevier Scientific Publications.
Katschnig, H., Pakesch, G., & Egger-Zeidner, E. (1986). Life stress and depressive subtypes: A review of present diagnostic criteria and recent research results. In *Life events and psychiatric disorders: Controversial issues*. Heinz Katschnig (Ed.), New York: Cambridge University Press.
Kaplan, A. (1946). Definition and specification of meaning. *The Journal of Philosophy, 43*, 281–288.
Keller, M. B., Lavori, P. W., Friedman, B., Nielsen, E., Endicott, J., McDonald-Scott, P., & Andreasen, N. C. (1987). The longitudinal internal follow-up evaluation. A comprehensive

method for assessing outcome in prospective longitudinal studies. *Archives of General Psychiatry, 44,* 540–548.
Kendell, R. E., Everitt, B., Cooper, J. E., Sartorius, N., & David, M. E. (1968). Reliability of the Present State Examination. *Social Psychiatry, 3,* 123–129.
Kendell, R. E. (1973). Psychiatric diagnoses: A study of how they are made. *British Journal of Psychiatry, 122,* 437–445.
Kendell, R. E. (1975). *The role of diagnosis in psychiatry.* Oxford: Blackwell Scientific Publications.
Kendell, R. E. (1988). What is a case? Food for thought for epidemiologists. *Archives of General Psychiatry, 45,* 374–376.
Klein, D. F. (1974). Endogenomorphic depression: A conceptual and terminological revision. *Archives of General Psychiatry, 31,* 447–454.
Kovess, V., & Fournier, L. (1988). *A short and effective measure of mental health disorders: The DISSA, a self-administered, abridged version of DIS.* (Final Report, Project 6605 216 46, NHRDP, Ottawa, Canada).
Maier, W., Philipp, M., Buller, R., & Benkert, O. (1986). Sources of disagreement between clinical (ICD-9) and operational (RDC, DSM-III) diagnosis of endogenous depression (melancholia). *Journal of Affective Disorders, 11,* 235–243.
Martin, C. J., Brown, G. W., Goldberg, D. P., & Brockington, I. F. (1989). Psychosocial stress and puerperal depression. *Journal of Affective Disorders, 16,* 283–93.
Matussek, P., Luks, O., & Nagel, D. (1982). Depression symptom patterns. *Psychological Medicine, 12,* 765–773.
Matussek, P., Soldner, M. L., & Nagel, D. (1982). Neurotic depression—results of cluster analyses. *Journal of Nervous and Mental Disease, 170,* 588–597.
McGuffin, P., Katz, R., & Aldrich, J. (1986). Past and Present State Examination: The assessment of 'Lifetime ever' psychopathology. *Psychological Medicine, 16,* 461–465.
Meehl, P. E. (1986). Diagnostic taxa as open concepts: Metatheoretical and statistical questions about reliability and construct validity in the grand strategy of nosological revision. In T. Millon & G. L. Klerman (Eds.), *Contemporary directions in Psychopathology: Towards the DSM-IV.* New York: Guilford Press.
Mendels, J., & Cochrane, C. (1968). The nosology of depression: The endogenous-reactive concept. *American Journal of Psychiatry, 124,* 1–11.
Monroe, S. M. (in press). Psychosocial factors in Anxiety and depression. In J. D. Master & C. R. Cloniger (Eds.), *Comorbility in anxiety mood disorders.* Washington, D.C.: American Psychiatric Press.
Neilson, E. M., Brown, G. W., & Marmot, M. (1989). Life events and myocardial infarction. *In*: G. W. Brown & T. O. Harris (Eds.), *Life events and illness.* New York: Guilford Press.
Nelson, J. C., & Charney, D. S. (1980). Primary affective disorder criteria and the endogenous-reactive distinction. *Archives of General Psychiatry, 37,* 787–793.
Ni Bhrolchain, M. (1979). Psychotic and neurotic depression: 1. Some points of method. *British Journal of Psychiatry, 134,* 87–93.
Ni Bhrolchain, M., Brown, G. W., & Harris, T. O. (1979). Psychotic and neurotic depression: 2. Clinical characteristics. *British Journal Psychiatry, 134,* 94–107.
Parker, G. (1987). Are lifetime prevalence estimates in the ECA study accurate? *Psychological Medicine, 17,* 275–282.
Paykel, E. S. (1981). Have multivariate statistics contributed to classification? *British Journal of Psychiatry, 139,* 357–362.
Prudo, R., Brown, G. W., Harris, T. O., & Dowland, J. (1981). Psychiatric disorder in a rural and an urban population: 2. Sensitivity to loss. *Psychological Medicine, 11,* 601–616.
Pulver, A. E., & Carpenter, W. T. (1983). Lifetime psychotic symptoms assessed with the DIS. *Schizophrenia Bulletin, 9,* 377–382.
Rabkin, J. G., Klein, D. F. (1987). The clinical measurement of depressive disorders. In A. J.

Marsela, R. M. A. Hirschfeld, & M. M. Katz (Eds.), *The measurement of depression*. New York: Guilford Press.

Radloff, L. S. (1977). The CES-D scale: A self-report depression scale for research in the general population. *Applied Psychological Measurement, 1,* 385–401.

Ramos-Brieva, J. A., Cordero-Villafafila, A., Ayuso-Mateos, J. L., Rios, B., Montejo, M. L., Rivera, A., Caballero, L., Ponce, C., & Canas, F. (1987). Distinct quality of depressed mood, an attempt to develop an objective measure. *Journal of Affective Disorders, 13,* 241–248.

Rao, V. A. R., & Coppen, A. (1979). Classification of depression and response to amitriptyline therapy. *Psychological Medicine, 9,* 321–325.

Riskind, J. H., Beck, A. T., Berchick, R. J., Brown, G., & Steer, R. A. (1987). Reliability of DSM-III diagnoses for major depression and generalized anxiety disorder using the structures clinical interview for DSM-III. *Archives of General Psychiatry, 44,* 817–820.

Robins, E., Gentry, K. A., Munoz, R. A., & Marten, S. (1977). Characteristics of patients with three or more common illnesses. *Archives of General Psychiatry, 34,* 269–281.

Robins, L. N. (1985). Epidemiology: reflections on testing the validity of psychiatric interviews. *Archives of General Psychiatry,* 918–924.

Robins, L. N., Helzer, J. E., Croughan, J., & Ratcliff, K. S. (1981). National Institute of Mental Health Diagnostic Interview Schedule. Its history, characteristics, and validity. *Archives of General Psychiatry, 38,* 381–389.

Robins, L. N., Helzer, J. E., Ratcliff, K. S., & Seyfried, W. (1982). Validity of the Diagnostic Interview Schedule, version II: DSM-III Diagnoses. *Psychological Medicine, 12,* 855–870.

Robins, L. N., Wing, J., Wittchen, H. U., Helzer, J. E., Babor, T. F., Burke, J., Farmer, A., Jablenski, A., Pickens, R., Regier, D., Sartorius, N., & Towle, L. H. 1988. The composite international diagnostic interview: An epidemiologic instrument suitable for use in conjunction with different diagnostic systems and in different cultures. *Archives General Psychiatry, 45,* 1069–107.

Rush, A. J., Schlesser, M. A., Giles, D. E., Weissenburger, J. E., Fulton, C. L., Orsulak, P. J., Fairchild, C. J., & Roffwarg, H. P. (1989). *Two neuroendocrine tests and REM latency validate the RDC endogenous/nonendogenous dichotomy.* (Manuscript).

Sandifer, M. G., Hordern, A., & Green, L. M. (1970). The psychiatric Interview: The impact of the first three minutes. *American Journal of Psychiatry, 126,* 968–973.

Sashidharan, S. P. (1985). Definitions of psychiatric syndromes—comparison in hospital patients and general population. *British Journal of Psychiatry, 147,* 547–551.

Schmid, I., Scharfetter, C., & Binder, J. (1981). Lebensereignisse in Abhangigkeit von Soziodemographischen Variablen. *Social Psychiatry, 16,* 63–68.

Schukit, M. A. (1985). The clinical implications of primary diagnostic groups among alcoholics. *Archives of General Psychiatry, 42,* 1043–1049.

Shepherd, M., & Wilkinson, G. (1988). Primary care as the middle ground for psychiatric epidemiology. *Psychological Medicine, 18,* 263–267.

Shrout, P. E., Dohrendwend, B. P., & Levav, T. (1986). A discriminant role for screening cases of diverse diagnostic types: Preliminary results. *Journal of Consulting and Clinical Psychology, 54,* 314–319.

Spitzer, R. L., & Fleiss, J. L. (1974). A reanalysis of the reliability of psychiatric diagnosis. *British Journal of Psychiatry, 125,* 341–347.

Spitzer, R. L., Endicott, J., & Robins, E. (1977). *Research Diagnostic Criteria for a selected group of functional disorders, edition 3.* New York, Biometrics Research Division, New York State Psychiatric Institute.

Spitzer, R. L., & Williams, J. B. (1983). *Instruction manual for the Structural Clinical Interview for DSM-III (SCID).* New York, Biometrics Research Department, New York State Psychiatric Institute.

Staddon, J. E. R. (1971). Darwin explained: An object lesson in theory construction. *Contemporary Psychology, 16,* 689–691.

Van Praag, H. M., Kahn, R. S., Asnis, G. M., Wetzler, S., Brown, S. L., Bleich, A., & Korn, M. L. (1987). Review: Denosologization in biological psychiatry or the specificity of 5-HT disturbances in psychiatric disorders. *Journal of Affective Disorders, 13,* 1–8.

Vlissides, D. N., & Jenner, F. A. (1982). The response of endogenously and reactively depressed patients to electroconvulsive therapy. *British Journal of Psychiatry, 141,* 239–242.

Von Korff, M. R., & Anthony, J. C. (1982). The NIMH Diagnostic Interview Schedule modified to record current mental status. *Journal of Affective Disorders, 4,* 365–371.

Warheit, G. J. (1979). Life events, coping, stress, and depressive symptomatology. *American Journal of Psychiatry, 136,* 502–507.

Weissman, M. M., Sholomskas, D., Pottenger, M., Prusoff, B. A., & Locke, B. Z. (1977). Assessing depressive symptoms in five psychiatric populations: A validation study. *American Journal of Epidemiology, 106,* 203–214.

Williams, J. B. N., & Spitzer, R. L. (1982). Research Diagnostic Criteria & DSM-III: An annotated comparison. *Archives of General Psychiatry, 39,* 1283–1289.

Wing, J. K., Birley, J. L. T., Cooper, J. E., Graham, P., & Isaacs, A. D. (1967). Reliability of a procedure for measuring and classifying 'Present Psychiatric State'. *British Journal of Psychiatry, 113,* 499–515.

Wing, J. K., Cooper, J. E., & Sartorious, N.(1974). *The measurement and classification of psychiatric symptoms: an instruction manual for the Present State Examination and CATEGO Programme.* Cambridge England: Cambridge University Press.

Wing, J. K., Nixon, J. M., Mann, S. A., & Leff, J. P. (1977a). Reliability of the PSE (Ninth Edition) used in a population study. *Psychological Medicine, 7,* 505–516.

Wing, J. K., Henderson, A. S., & Winckle, M. (1977b). The rating of symptoms by a psychiatrist and a non-psychiatrist: A study of patients referred from general practice. *Psychological Medicine, 7,* 713–715.

Wing, J. K., & Sturt, E. (1978). *The PSE-ID-CATEGO system.* Supplementary Manual. London: MRC Social Psychiatry Unit.

Wing, J. K., Mann, S. A., Leff, J. P., & Nixon, J. M. (1978). The concept of a 'case' in psychiatric population surveys. *Psychological Medicine, 8,* 203–217.

Wing, J. K. (1980). Methodological issues in psychiatric case-identification. *Psychological Medicine, 10,* 5–10.

Young, M. A., Keller, M. B., Lavori, P. W., Scheftner, W. A., Fawcett, J. A., Endicott, J., & Hirschfeld, R. (1987). Lack of stability of the REC endogenous subtype in consecutive episodes of major depression. *Journal of Affective Disorders, 12,* 139–143.

Zimmerman, M., Coryell, W., Pfohl, B., & Stangl, D. (1985). Four definitions of endogenous depression and the Dexamethasone Suppression Test. *Journal of Affective Disorders, 8,* 37–45.

Zimmerman, M., Coryell, W., Pfohl, B. (1986). The validity of dexamethsaone suppression test as a marker for endogenous depression. *Archives of General Psychiatry, 43,* 347–355.

Zimmerman, M., Coryell, W., Pfohl, B., & Stangl, D. (1986a). The validity of four definitions of endogenous depression. II. Clinical, demographic, familial, and psychosocial correlates. *Archives of General Psychiatry, 43,* 234–244.

2 Theoretical and Empirical Issues in Differentiating Depression from Anxiety

Lee Anna Clark
David Watson
Southern Methodist University

INTRODUCTION

The problem of differentiating between depression and anxiety has plagued both clinicians and researchers for many years. The view that anxiety and depression can both be subsumed within a more general class of disorders of mood originated over 50 years ago (e.g., Lewis, 1934; Mapother, 1926), and still has its proponents (e.g., Johnstone et al., 1980; Pollitt & Young, 1971). The data supporting this view are plentiful:

1. diverse measures of anxiety and depression—both self-report and clinical ratings—show poor discriminant validity (e.g. Mendels, Weinstein, & Cochrane, 1972; Zuckerman, Persky, Eckman, & Hopkins, 1967);

2. a substantial proportion of patients rated as having either a depressive or anxiety syndrome also show significant features of the other type (e.g., Foa & Foa, 1982; Johnstone et al., 1980);

3. approximately half of all patients diagnosed with an anxiety disorder (e.g., panic disorder, agoraphobia and other phobias, and generalized anxiety disorder) also meet criteria for a depressive disorder and vice versa (e.g., Breier, Charney, & Heninger, 1984);

4. family and pharmacological studies indicate that there is a particularly strong relation between panic disorder and major depression (e.g., Breier, Charney, & Heninger, 1985; Leckman, Weissman, Merikangas, Pauls, & Prusoff, 1983); and

5. a number of symptoms are shared by depressive and anxiety disorders

(e.g., insomnia, fatigue), and at the symptom level, few consistent prevalence differences are found between anxious and depressed patients (Clark, 1989).

Despite these findings, most researchers maintain that the basic distinction is valid. They contend that the two types of disorders are conceptually and empirically distinguishable on the basis of course, relative severity of each syndrome in a patient, associated symptoms, and physiological correlates, for example (e.g., Akiskal, 1985; Breier et al., 1985; Derogatis, Klerman, & Lipman, 1972; Klerman, 1977; Roth & Mountjoy, 1982). This point of view also has clear empirical support:

1. factor analytic studies of depressive and anxiety symptoms have frequently found separate depression and anxiety factors, or else a bipolar factor with melancholic depression versus panic as its poles (see Clark, 1989);

2. although many patients show a mixed anxious-depressed pattern, in most cases one or the other syndrome tends to be dominant (Clark, 1989);

3. a small core of symptoms have been found to distinguish reliably between patients with a panic syndrome from those with a major depressive syndrome (e.g., Roth, Gurney, Garside, & Kerr, 1972);

4. although clinical, family, and pharmacological studies have established a strong relation between major depression and panic, they have by no means shown them to be simply variants of each other. Further, no relation has been established between any of the other anxiety or depressive disorders (see Breier et al., 1985);

5. certain physiological correlates, such as the disturbance of REM sleep in depression, appear to be unique to one or the other syndrome (e.g., Akiskal, 1985).

Thus, on the basis of existing evidence, one must conclude that future research should not focus on the general issue of whether anxiety and depression are continuous or distinct, but rather on the precise degree, nature, and underlying causes of both the similarities and the differences that have been shown to exist: What biological, psychological, or social communalities and distinctions can be found? Are either anxious or depressive phenomena causally primary, or does their association stem from yet-unidentified variables underlying both types of disturbance?

In this chapter we first review psychometric and other data regarding the measurement of depression and anxiety both in self-reports and clinicians' ratings, and investigate various explanations for the findings. We also consider briefly the diagnostic, familial, and pharmacological data mentioned above. We then focus on two dominant dimensions of emotional experience—Positive and Negative Affect—that may be useful in understanding the relation between anxiety and depression. Each of these broad affective dimensions can be measured either as a state (i.e., transient fluctuations in mood) or as a trait (i.e., stable individual differences in general affective tone, in which case they have been termed Positive and Negative Affectivity; Tellegen, 1982). Finally, we explore hypotheses concerning how these variables may contribute to both the distinctive and overlapping features of anxiety and depression.

RELATIONS BETWEEN CURRENT MEASURES OF DEPRESSION AND ANXIETY

Self-report Measures

A large number of scales have been developed to assess depression and anxiety via self-report (see Gotlib & Cane, 1989, for a review). The focus and range of these scales is quite variable, with some measuring state or trait depressed or anxious mood, others assessing diverse sets of depressive or anxiety symptoms, and still others providing a measure of syndromic severity or diagnosis. These scales generally possess adequate reliability and appropriate levels of stability (Gotlib & Cane, 1989). The issue of validity is more complex, however, as it is important to consider both the convergent and discriminant validity of these measures. To establish convergent validity, the critical issue is the extent to which scales purportedly assessing the same construct actually correlate with each other; that is, are various measures that are all intended to assess depression (or anxiety) in fact significantly interrelated? In contrast, to establish discriminant validity, it is necessary to show that scales supposedly tapping different constructs are in fact unrelated to each other; that is, are measures designed to assess depression unrelated (or at least not strongly related) to scales intended to assess anxiety?

Examining first the issue of convergent validity, self-report scales generally have moderate to high convergent correlations, although there are small but systematic differences among the various types of scales. For example, convergent correlations between measures of immediate mood and mood or symptom scales assessing longer time frames (i.e., stait–trait correlations) average about .60 (range = .30 to .80), whereas the convergent correlations among longer-term symptom/syndrome measures (i.e., trait–trait correlations) are somewhat higher, averaging around .70 (range = .40 to .90) (e.g., see Dobson, 1985b).

We return later to these variations in convergent validity, but of greater concern at this point is the fact that the discriminant correlations between measures of anxiety and those of depression are disturbingly high. Two recent reviews (Dobson,1985b; Gotlib & Cane,1989), both based on large numbers of studies and diverse populations, have each concluded that existing self-report measures of anxiety and depression simply lack discriminative power; that is, measures of the two separate constructs correlate about as highly as measures of the same construct. Two explanations that have been offered to account for these findings are: (1) the presence of symptoms common to the two types of disorders, and (2) true empirical cooccurrence of the syndromes that is accurately reflected in the measures. However, counterarguments can be made which show that these explanations are, at best, incomplete. For example, measures with no overlapping items (e.g., the Costello-Comrey scales of Depression and Anxiety; Costello & Comrey, 1967) still correlate in the range of .40 to .60. Moreover, similar levels of correlation are seen in non-clinical populations with extremely low rates of disorder; thus, cooccurrence of the syndromes per se cannot account for the data.

The most plausible interpretation that has been made is that all these measures tap the common underlying construct of Negative Affectivity (trait NA; Watson & Clark, 1984), Neuroticism (Eysenck & Eysenck, 1968, 1975), or general psychological distress (Gotlib, 1984). In this view, a major aspect of both depression and anxiety is a fundamental predisposition to experience a wide variety of negative affective states. Trait NA has been shown to be a broad and pervasive personality disposition that has influences on mood, cognition, self-concept, and overall world view (Watson & Clark, 1984). Thus, correlations between symptom or syndrome measures of depression and anxiety may simply reflect the fact that both tap specific components of trait NA, while measures of state depression and anxiety may both reflect a general negative affective mood state.

Some investigators have taken this to mean that respondents fail to make precise distinctions between related affective states that have specific meanings to clinicians (e.g., Prusoff, Klerman, & Paykel, 1972). On this basis one might argue that the lack of discriminant validity of these measures is due to a basic limitation of self-report. If this were true, then one would expect relatively poor convergent correlations between self- and clinical measures of depression and anxiety, and that clinicians' ratings would display a better convergent/discriminant pattern. Let us examine these data next.

Self-report Versus Clinical Ratings

Before discussing any data based on clinical ratings, it is important to note that clinical ratings are themselves inferences that are, for the most part, ultimately based on patient self-report. In rare instances, the ratings are more broadly based on all available data, including interviews with significant others and psychiatric history, for example, but the primary source of information is inevitably the patient. What distinguishes standard clinical ratings from self-report, therefore, is not the informational source of the rating, but the fact that it is the clinician rather than the patient who weighs the data and determines the presence/absence or severity of each item rated.

Compared to the large number of self-report measures, the number and variety of established clinical rating scales for depression and especially anxiety are more limited, although the use of ad hoc measures is widespread (see Clark, 1989). The most widely used clinicians' measure for depression is the Hamilton Rating Scale for Depression (HRSD; Hamilton, 1960); the Hamilton Rating Scale for Anxiety (HRSA; Hamilton, 1959) is used less frequently. The Raskin Depression and Covi Anxiety Scales (see Lipman, 1982) are also relatively well-established. Unfortunately, few studies have used measures of both depression and anxiety, so conclusions regarding their interrelation must be extrapolated from incomplete data; on the other hand, those data that do exist are quite consistent.

Before one can examine the convergent/discriminant pattern for self-report versus clinical ratings, it is first necessary to establish the reliability of the latter. Unlike the self-report literature, where internal consistency and test-retest reliabilities are routinely reported, studies using clinical ratings have focused primarily on interrater reliability. For many years, the only reliable measures of anxiety and depression were global severity ratings, but with the development of specific diagnostic criteria, structured interviews, and standardized rating scales, high levels of reliability have become the norm for most measures, whether of mood, symptoms, syndromic severity, or diagnosis. In the DSM-III field trials, for example, the Phase Two kappa reliabilities for Major Affective and Anxiety Disorders were .80, and .72, respectively (American Psychiatric Association, 1980). We will restrict our examination to studies using measures with established reliability (See Clark, 1989, for an extended discussion of the issue of reliability in clinical ratings.)

Generally speaking, self-report and clinical measures of depression are strongly convergent. For example, we located 16 studies reporting correlations between the Beck Depression Inventory (BDI; Beck, Ward, Mendelson, Mock, & Erbaugh, 1961) and the Hamilton (HRSD), and computed a weighted mean r of .72 (total $n = 1492$). Similar correlations have been reported between the HRSD and the Carroll Rating Scale for Depression ($r = .71$, $n = 279$; Carroll, Feinberg, Smouse, Rawson, & Greden, 1981), the Center for Epidemiological Studies Depression Scale (CES-D; $r = .70$, $n = 406$; Weissman, Sholomskas, Pottenger, Prusoff, & Locke, 1977), and the newly developed Inventory to Diagnose Depression (IDD; $r = .80$ $n = 235$; Zimmerman, Coryell, Wilson, & Corenthal, 1986). It is noteworthy that the level of relation between the HRSD and these self-report scales is quite consistent, despite the fact that the latter have been variously designed to measure depression at the symptom, syndromal, or diagnostic levels.

Studies examining the convergent correlation of self-report and clinical measures of anxiety have reported a comparable level of convergence. For example, two studies have reported correlations between the State scale of the Spielberger State-Trait Anxiety Inventory (STAI-S; Spielberger, Gorsuch, & Lushene, 1970) and the Hamilton Anxiety scale of .75 ($n = 241$; Cohen et al., 1976) and .63 (n

= 70; Deluty, Deluty, & Carver, 1986). In their review, Watson and Clark (1984) concluded that there was a strong relation between self-report measures of trait NA and clinical ratings of anxiety, total pathology/adjustment, and so on, when reliable clinical measures were used (median $r = .59$). While convergent correlations of this level by no means indicate that self-report and clinical ratings are interchangeable, they do suggest that the poor discrimination between depression and anxiety seen in self-report data cannot be explained purely by the inadequacy of self-ratings.

In contrast to the many studies that have examined (and supported) the basic convergence of self-report and clinical measures of anxiety or depression, very few studies have considered the question of discriminative validity across these two types of measures. In a mixed sample of 29 patients and 25 normal controls, Zuckerman, Persky, Eckman, and Hopkins (1967) found no clear discriminant pattern between clinical ratings of anxiety and depression and two sets (state and trait) of corresponding self-report measures. Prusoff et al. (1972) assessed 147 depressed patients both at intake and at a 10-month followup using a semistructured clinical interview and two self-report checklists that measured a variety of pathological symptoms and mood, including anxiety and depression. Convergent correlations between corresponding symptom clusters were moderate at intake (range = .21 to .63, median = .46), and notably higher at follow-up (range = .60 to .74, median = .68), suggesting that better convergence is obtained when there is a greater range in the severity of manifest symptoms (at intake the patients were all quite severely disturbed, while at follow-up, some were markedly improved, while others were still ill). As for the discriminant correlations, most were nonsignificant at intake, so that a clear convergent/discriminant pattern could be seen. At follow-up, however, the level of discriminant correlations had also increased considerably (range = .34 to .70, median = .51). On the basis of the increased convergence with patient improvement, Prusoff et al. (1972) interpret their data as indicating that patients' self-reports are less accurate when they are more disturbed, but the fact that discrimination simultaneously deteriorated suggests that a more complex explanation is required.

Two studies have reported some success in discriminating anxiety and depression using both types of ratings. Beck (1967) reported a convergent correlation of .59 between his Depression Inventory and clinical ratings of depression in a sample of 606 patients, where the corresponding correlation with anxiety ratings was only .14. However, he had no self-report measure of anxiety, so it is impossible to examine the entire convergent/discriminant pattern. Vye (1986) reported on a small heterogeneous sample of patients with DSM-III anxiety ($n = 16$) or depressive ($n = 16$) disorders. The correlations between the BDI and clinician-rated depression and anxiety scales were .46 and .17 (ns), respectively, showing a good convergent/discriminant pattern. Unfortunately, the STAI-State

Anxiety scale showed exactly the same pattern, correlating .50 and .28 (ns), respectively, with the clinical measures of depression and anxiety, suggesting either some deficiency in the clinical ratings, an inappropriate labeling of the STAI, or both. Because no study has conclusively demonstrated a clear convergent/discriminant pattern for any set of self-report/clinician measures, we cannot at this point decide between these alternatives. However, the final type of data we will examine may shed some light on this issue.

Clinical Ratings of Depression and Anxiety

Clark (1989) reviewed studies reporting correlations between clinical ratings of depression and anxiety and uncovered an interesting pattern. First, in studies where ratings were made independently from diagnostic assignment, various measures of depression and anxiety showed moderate to high levels of correlation, depending in part on the degree of heterogeneity in the patient sample rated. For example, correlations between the HRSD and HRSA (Hamilton, 1959, 1960)—which, it is important to note, were intended as measures of syndromic severity, and were not constructed with regard to discriminant validity—ranged from .53 in a sample of 240 neurotic outpatients to .90 in a mixed sample of 70 psychiatric inpatients ($M = .68$). Under these same conditions (ratings made independently of the diagnostic process), scales that were developed with an eye to discriminant validity (e.g., via factor analysis) tended to be somewhat less correlated but were still substantially related, with coefficients ranging from .38 to .67 ($M = .46$). This pattern is clearly parallel to that seen in self-report, and must lay to rest any belief that the overlap seen in self-report is largely due to patients' inability to differentiate among the various negative affects. Rather, the most plausible interpretation is that anxiety and depression are both expressions of an underlying construct such as state or trait NA that is perceived by patients and clinicians alike.

However, Clark (1989) also found that if the ratings of anxiety and depression were made as part of the diagnostic process, rather than independently of it, the correlation between the two types of measures was significantly lower. That is, under circumstances where differentiating between anxiety and depression had important practical significance, as when assigning a diagnostic label with implications for treatment, clinicians apparently focused less on the absolute level of severity of the moods (or symptoms, or syndromes) and more on their relative levels. This, of course, forces ratings of depression and anxiety to be less highly correlated, or even negatively related. The effect of this process on the validity of the ratings, however, is unknown. A controlled outcome study in which assignment to treatment group is based on ratings made either independently of, or in connection with, the diagnostic process would provide a very useful contribution to our understanding of the relation between these syndromes.

Diagnostic, Pharmacological, Family, and Genetic Studies

The relation between anxiety and depression has been studied from other perspectives as well. It is not our intention to consider these in detail, but a summary will serve to demonstrate the scope of the problem. The interested reader is referred to Breier et al. (1985), and Clark (1989) for fuller discussions.

The diagnostic overlap between depression and anxiety is as pervasive as the correlation among measures. Although there are marked differences in the comorbidity rates depending on specific diagnoses, slightly over half of all patients with depression are also diagnosed as having an anxiety disorder, and vice versa. This occurs despite the tendency described earlier for clinicians to contrast depression and anxiety when making diagnostic decisions. Furthermore, various data indicate that the overlap does not simply result from one type of disorder consistently being "due to," or being an earlier manifestation of the other. For example, the percentage of patients who first manifest each type of disorder is roughly equivalent (Breier et al., 1984), and in a substantial proportion of patients, the anxiety and depressive episodes are temporally separate (Leckman, Merikangas, Pauls, Prusoff, & Weissman, 1983). Similarly, the existence of shared criteria may contribute to the observed comorbidity, but is insufficient to account for the data. For example, the anxiety disorder with the largest number of symptoms shared with depression is GAD, whereas agoraphobia shows the greatest prevalence of depression (72% compared with 38% for GAD; Clark, 1989).

Although there are as yet unexplained inconsistencies in the literature that render it impossible to calculate precise heritability estimates or to determine mode of transmission, the data support a genetic basis for Major Depression, Panic Disorder/Agoraphobia, and the personality dimension Negative Affectivity/Neuroticism (Breier et al., 1985; Carey & Gottesman, 1981; Jardine, Martin, & Henderson, 1984; Kendler, Heath, Martin, & Eaves, 1987; Weissman, 1985). In contrast, there does not appear to be familial transmission of GAD per se (Breier et al., 1985). Family and genetic studies of the relation between depressive and anxiety disorders provide somewhat less consistent data, but generally indicate that there is a familial relation between panic disorder and major depression (Clark, 1989). No other relations between specific types of anxiety and depression have been established, but several writers have suggested that the covariation of anxiety and depression is due to the same genetic diathesis that influences NA (e.g., Jardine et al., 1984; Kendler et al., 1987). Jardine et al. (1984) also found evidence for genetic variation specific to depressive symptoms. Investigations in this area are necessarily affected (and limited) by the (un)reliability of measures and methods of diagnosis, by the diagnostic system used, by the possibility of heterogeneity in the underlying genotypes, and by our imperfect understanding of the relation between genotypes and phenotypes (Carey, 1987). Clearly, this is an area in which much is as yet unknown.

There is strong evidence that tricyclic antidepressants and monoamine oxidase inhibitors are effective treatments for both panic disorder and major depression, and the antidepressant effects of these drugs appear to be distinct from their antipanic properties (Breier et al., 1985; Klein, 1981; Tuma & Maser, 1985). Moreover, neither of these drug classes is effective in treating GAD, while classical low potency benzodiazepines are effective for GAD but not for panic or major depression. Although there is some evidence that the newer high potency benzodiazepines are effective for all three disorders, the data regarding depression must be considered preliminary. Thus, drug studies again point to a specific relation between panic and depression, but they have not yet shed any further light on its precise nature. Furthermore, together with genetic studies, they indicate that GAD may not share the underlying diathesis that has been suggested for panic and major depression, although it may have links with each through trait NA (Clark, 1989).

Summary

From the foregoing review, one must conclude that the correlation found between measures of depression and anxiety is not a superficial one (e.g., due to unreliable scales or the inherent limitations of self-reports) that can be eliminated through simple methodological improvements. Rather, the overlap is pervasive and deeply rooted. It is seen in both self-report and clinicians' ratings, in measures of mood, symptoms, syndromes, and diagnoses, and likely has a biological basis. Even reliable measures of anxiety and depression that have been expressly developed to discriminate between them are moderately correlated. One notable exception to this is when circumstances encourage raters to contrast the two syndromes, in which case, the ratings are less strongly correlated, but of unknown validity. The most likely explanation for the observed correlation is that measures of both anxiety and depression are tapping aspects of state or trait NA, a broad and general mood and personality dimension characterized by the experience of various negative affective states.

Although the current state of assessment clearly leaves much to be desired, we can use these data to help improve it. First, we now have sufficient data for a thorough and systematic investigation of the properties of the various measures. Specifically, we can determine which scales within the overall matrix of anxiety and depression measures show the best convergent/discriminant pattern. Through an examination of the content of these identified scales, we can ascertain the particular symptoms or characteristics that are common to both types of disorders, or specific to one. We can then examine these characteristics in light of current theoretical conceptions of anxiety and depression, and adjust our measures, or our concepts, accordingly.

Second, progress has been made toward understanding the basic structure of mood and personality. Specifically, the existence of at least two broad affective dimensions—Positive Affect (PA) and Negative Affect (NA)—has been strongly supported (Tellegen, 1985; Watson & Tellegen, 1985). Although their names might suggest that they are opposite poles of the same dimension, PA and NA are in fact highly distinctive, and can be meaningfully represented as orthogonal (uncorrelated) factors. As mentioned earlier, these factors can be assessed either as transient mood states or as more stable affective traits or temperaments. We have already encountered the notion that trait NA (usually termed Negative Affectivity), is an important common component underlying the correlation between depression and anxiety. In the next sections, we will examine further evidence supporting this position, and then review research suggesting that the second dimension, trait PA, (i.e., Positive Affectivity), is an important factor distinguishing depression from anxiety.

COMMON AND DISTINCTIVE ASPECTS OF ANXIETY AND DEPRESSION

Basic Psychometric and Theoretical Issues

As already noted, studies examining the correlation between existing measures of depression and anxiety have found that the overall level of discrimination is poor. Particularly problematic is that the average convergent correlations among depression and anxiety measures are only slightly higher than the average discriminant correlation between them. However, there is considerable range (from .40 to .90) among both the convergent and discriminant correlations, suggesting that average figures may obscure meaningful differences between measures. If these ranges reflect systematic variation in the measures, then some scales may simply be poor measures of their intended construct (correlating moderately with measures of both constructs), while others may show a cleaner convergent/discriminant pattern.

Before proceeding further, however, it is necessary to specify the magnitude of depression-anxiety correlation that is optimally desirable from the standpoint of construct validity. The ideal level of relation is surely less than that usually observed, but neither would one expect (nor want) complete orthogonality. A number of characteristics (agitation/restlessness, difficulty concentrating, insomnia, and fatigability/loss of energy) appear as symptoms in both depressive and anxiety disorders. Thus, valid measures of depression and anxiety containing these symptoms will correlate in part due to item overlap, and discriminant correlations of .40, for example, may represent the true level of covariation. If so, then finding no correlation between symptom measures of depression and anxiety, however desirable from the point of view of discrimination, would itself be problematic.

As noted, however, there is great inconsistency in the use of the terms anxiety and depression, with some writers referring primarily to mood states, others to clinical symptoms, and still others to syndromes or diagnostic entities. Thus, the answer to the question of the ideal correlation will depend, in part, on the intended focus of a particular set of scales. Before we can determine the target correlation for measures of depression and anxiety, we must first clarify the nature of the relation between them both within and across these different levels of meaning. If depressed and anxious mood are, in fact, highly correlated, depressive and anxious symptoms somewhat less so, and the full syndromes/ diagnoses only moderately related, then correlations between measures of depression/anxiety at each of these levels should reflect these differences.

There is also the further complication that each of these broad categories subsumes specific diagnoses or subtypes that may also need to be distinguished. Data reviewed by Clark (1989), for example, revealed that the comorbidity of depressive and anxiety disorders varied widely depending on the particular diagnoses considered. Global measures of depression and anxiety are obviously unable to capture this variation. Gotlib and Cane (1989) analyzed a number of common self-report scales of depression and anxiety for the number of items measuring DSM-III Major Depression Disorder (MDD) and Generalized Anxiety Disorder (GAD). They found considerable variation in both the degree to which the scales assessed the symptoms of the intended disorder—as few as 32% of one scale's items tapped the desired construct, whereas up to 90% of another's did so— and also in the ratio of construct-related versus non-construct-related items on the various scales, ranging from scales containing a roughly even balance to scales comprised only of items appropriate to the intended construct. Of the scales they analyzed, they concluded that the BDI and CES-D most accurately represented MDD, while the STAI-S and Zung Anxiety Scale best captured GAD. Of importance here is that different conclusions might have emerged if the target diagnosis had been, for example, Panic Disorder, rather than GAD, or if they had analysed the data from the opposite direction, asking what percentage of the diagnostic criteria for each disorder were tapped by the various scales.

Analyses of Existing Measures of Depression and Anxiety

We use a combination of meta-analysis and content analysis to identify the constructs being measured by existing scales of depression and anxiety. Inspective of two major reviews of this area (Dobson, 1985b; Watson & Clark, 1984) and several studies not included in those reviews (Dobson, 1985a; Gotlib, 1984; Tanaka-Matsumi & Kameoka, 1986) revealed that ten scales—five purporting to measure "depression" and five "anxiety"—have been used sufficiently often to justify higher-order analyses: Beck Depression Inventory (BDI; Beck et al., 1961); Costello-Comrey scales for depression and anxiety (CC-D and CC-A; Costello & Comrey, 1967); Minnesota Multiphasic Personality Inventory Depression scale (MMPI-D; Hathaway & McKinley, 1942); a composite of the five top MMPI-based Anxiety/NA-markers identified by Watson and Clark (1984) (MMPI-NA); State-Trait Anxiety Inventory Trait Anxiety Scale (STAI-T; Spielberger et al., 1970); Institute for Personality and Ability Testing Anxiety Scale (IPAT; Krug, Scheier, & Cattell, 1976); Multiple Affect Adjective Check List Depression and Anxiety scales (MAACL-D and MAACL-A; Zuckerman & Lubin, 1965); and the Zung Self-rating Depression Scale (Zung-SDS; Zung, 1965).

The median correlation for each pair of scales was calculated from the values reported in the above studies. Because these median correlations are derived from diverse studies including both normal and patient populations, and ultimately are based on ns of hundreds, in some cases thousands of subjects, they likely represent reasonably precise estimates of the true correlations. On the other hand, we did not attempt an exhaustive search of the literature, so these correlations should not be taken as definitive.

A correlation matrix was constructed from these median coefficients, and subjected to a principal components analysis with varimax rotation. As expected, and consistent with previous studies and reviews, a large first factor accounted for most of the variance (68%). However, the second and third factors each accounted for sufficient variance (8% and 7%, respectively) that a second break in the scree was evident; in the interest of differentiation, we inspected these factors. The third factor clearly reflected method variance, as it was defined only by the two Adjective Checklist scales. We will therefore discuss the two-factor structure (shown in Table 2.1).

It is notable that the solution lacks simple structure—most of the scales have significant loadings (defined here as a loading of .30 or greater) on both factors—and we cannot extract two completely distinct dimensions from these data. Nevertheless, some of the scales more clearly defined one factor or the other. Two scales (one depression and one anxiety) were relatively pure markers of the first factor, while only the Costello-Comrey Anxiety scale (CC-A) both marked the second factor and had a low discriminant loading; two other scales that also marked the second factor had moderate loadings on the first factor.

Examining first the content of the first factor markers, the BDI taps a broad range of items generally considered diagnostic of major depressive disorder (e.g., sadness/unhappiness, loss of interest, guilt, suicidal tendencies, appetite disturbance), plus items that indicate general life dissatisfaction, hopelessness, or low self-esteem such as one might also see in other DSM-III-R diagnoses such as Dysthymia, Adjustment Reactions, Overanxious Disorder, Personality Disorder, and so on. It further assesses symptoms that are common to several depressive

TABLE 2.1
Varimax-Rotated Solution in a Meta-Analysis of Ten Self-report Measures of Anxiety and Depression

Scale	Factor 1	Factor 2
BDI	.85	.23
MMPI-NA[a]	.80	.27
CC-D	.79	.37
Zung-SDS	.78	.43
MAACL-D	.72	.35
MMPI-D	.70	.50
STAI-T	.69	.55
CC-A	.20	.90
IPAT	.45	.79
MAACL-A	.47	.68

Note. See text for full names of all scales.
[a] A composite of five MMPI-based Anxiety/NA markers identified by Watson and Clark (1984).

and anxiety disorders (e.g., irritability, poor concentration/indecisiveness, insomnia, fatigue). The five MMPI scales representing NA are quite heterogeneous in content, and contain many items similar to those in the BDI, plus others that more generally relate to anxiety (e.g., worry, brooding and other obsessive thinking, hypersensitivity).

In contrast, the only pure second factor marker, the CC-A, covers a very specific content domain—its nine items all assess whether the respondent has felt tense, nervous, easily upset or rattled, high-strung, jumpy or shaky, and oversensitive. Interestingly, these items reflect a highly specific mood state, rather than the broad range of affect, that comprise that general NA dimension. Thus, scales with widely varying content—both depressive and anxiety-related—all mark the large general factor, while the second factor identifies a distinctive subset of peculiarly anxious items. These data provide further evidence that the first factor is best identified as general distress of NA, and reinforce the earlier conclusion that the observed correlation between depression and anxiety is deeply rooted. However, these data also raise the question of why a parallel set of distinctively depressive items does not appear. Could it be simply that no one has constructed as scale as specific to depression as the CC-A is to anxiety, or is this unbalanced pattern somehow inevitable? What would be the item content of such a depression scale? We next examine other data that both replicate and extend this pattern.

Factor Analytic Studies

A number of studies have directly factor analyzed self- or clinical ratings of psychiatric symptoms. Those analyses that have included primarily a broad range of psychotic symptoms with smaller samples of depressive, anxiety, and other "neurotic" symptoms have tended to find a single neurotic factor comprising both depressive and anxiety symptoms (see Costello, 1970 for a review). However, those studies whose symptom lists were weighted more heavily toward neurotic symptoms have generally found separate depression and anxiety factors, or more rarely, a single bipolar factor (e.g., Derogatis & Cleary, 1977; Fleiss, Gurland, & Cooper, 1971; Lipman, Rickels, Covi, Derogatis, & Uhlenhuth, 1969; Roth et al., 1972). Two general patterns can be discerned. First, in many of these studies, the imbalance noted above is again evident: The "depression" factor is quite broad, encompassing many non-specific symptoms of distress in addition to more distinctively depressive symptoms, while the "anxiety" factor is more narrowly focused on panic or phobic symptoms, such as physiological signs of anxiety and shakiness/tension. We can illustrate this pattern using our own investigation of depressive and anxiety symptoms conducted as part of the Washington University Twin Series, a large study on the heritability of psychiatric features and disorders (Clark, Watson, & Carey, 1988). Subjects in the larger project were probands who were seen as either inpatients or outpatients, plus their participating cotwins. All subjects were interviewed by trained personnel using the Diagnostic Interview Schedule (DIS; Robins, Helzer, Croughan, & Ratcliff, 1981). Then, using information both from the DIS and other sources (including psychometric data), a team of clinical researchers diagnosed all subjects. Only those subjects from the larger project who had completed the research protocol by July, 1984, and who received a DSM-III diagnosis (some cotwins did not) are included in these analyses ($n = 90$ twin probands and 60 cotwins).

We performed a principal components analysis on all symptoms of anxiety or depression rated on Version 3.0 of the DIS. This includes symptoms of MDD, Dysthymia, Panic Disorder, Phobias, and Obsessive-Compulsive Disorder. GAD is not directly assessed in this version of the DIS, but 12 of the 19 symptoms of GAD are included as symptoms of another disorder. Inspection of the eigenvalues indicated a clear two-factor solution, which was then rotated using Varimax. Preliminary analyses indicated that the phobic and obsessive-compulsive symptoms did not contribute to either of the primary factors (only checking compulsions loaded as high as .30), so they were eliminated from further consideration. The first factor was defined by panic attacks and all related physiological symptoms (shaking, heart pounding, dizziness, etc.), while the second factor included all of the symptoms of a major depressive episode, feelings of hopelessness and chronic depression (from Dysthymia), and chronic nervousness (from GAD). The symptoms of GAD split between the two factors, with autonomic hyperactivity appearing on the first factor, and all others (e.g., restlessness, fatigability, insomnia) loading on the second factor. Thus our data follow the pattern previously described: The "depression" factor is actually a more general NA dimension, encompassing symptoms from several diagnoses, while the "anxiety" factor focuses more narrowly on panic symptoms. One would expect, therefore, that patients specifically diagnosed with anxiety disorders should score the highest on the "anxiety" factor, while patients without an

TABLE 2.2
Means of Four Patient Groups on Two Factors of Anxiety and Depression Symptoms

Type	Group No./Diagnosis	Factor 1 Mean	Factor 2 Mean
Pure	(1) Anxiety only	$.39^a$	$-.23^a$
Mixed	(2) Primary anxiety	$.31^{ab}$	$.92^{bc}$
Mixed	(3) Primary depression	$.05^{ab}$	$.79^{bc}$
Pure	(4) Depression only	$-.42^b$	$.31^{ab}$

Note. For Factor 1, $F(3,68) = 3.59$, $p < .02$. For Factor 2, $F(3,68) = 4.44$, $p < .01$.
Within a factor, individual group means with different superscripts are significantly different at the $p < .05$ level (corrected by Bonferroni for multiple comparisons). See text for discussion of other planned contrasts.

anxiety diagnosis should score the lowest. Mixed groups would fall somewhere in between, depending on the relative importance of anxiety disorders in their overall clinical picture. In contrast, if the depression factor is actually not specific to depression, but is instead a more general distress dimension, then patients with mixed anxious-depressive diagnoses should score the highest on this factor, while patients with specific depressive or anxiety disorders should score respectively lower.

To test these hypotheses, we computed factor scores for each subject on the two factors, and analyzed the scores of 69 subjects who had been diagnosed as having a depressive disorder, an anxiety disorder or both; patients with both types of disorders were further subdivided into those with primary anxiety versus those with primary depression. We computed an overall ANOVA for each factor, followed by single group contrasts, and several planned comparisons in which two or more of the subgroups were combined. For example, on the "anxiety" factor we compared patients with any anxiety disorder with patients with only depression. A significance level of $p < .05$ was used, corrected by Bonferroni for multiple comparisons.

The factor means are presented in Table 2.2. On the "anxiety" factor, a clear linear trend can be seen, with patients having only anxiety (Group 1) scoring the highest, and patients having only depression (Group 4) the lowest. One single group comparison reached statistical significance: Patients with only anxiety scored higher than patients with only depression. When patients with any anxiety disorder were combined (Groups 1, 2, and 3), they also scored significantly higher than patients having only depression. Finally, the comparison of those with pure and primary anxiety (Groups 1 and 2) versus those with pure and primary depression (Groups 3 and 4) showed a trend in the predicted direction ($p < .08$). These results support the idea that this is a rather specific factor, and that one will not score highly on it unless one has notable psychological and physiological manifestations of panic attacks.

In contrast, two single group comparisons were statistically significant on the depression factor: Those with both types of disorder (Groups 2 and 3) each scored significantly higher than those with no depression (Group 1). The pure depressives did not score significantly lower than either of these groups, but neither did they score significantly higher than the pure anxiety patients (Group 4 vs. Group 1). It is also interesting that of the mixed diagnostic groups, those with primary anxiety scored nonsignificantly higher than those with primary depression. As for the planned comparisons, patients with no depression (Group 1) did score significantly lower than those with any depression (Groups 2, 3, and 4), and patients with both types of disorder scored significantly higher than those with either pure anxiety or depression (Groups 2 and 3 vs. Groups 1 and 4). These results support the notion that this factor measures general NA rather than depression per se, (although the depressive aspect of NA is quite strongly represented), because patients with the greatest variety of neurotic symptoms had the highest scores on this factor, while those with specific depressive symptomatology scored somewhat lower, and those with no depression the lowest of all.

The second pattern that is seen with some frequency in symptom factor analyses, particularly in studies using variants of the Symptom Check List (SCL; originally developed by Parloff, Kelman, Frank, 1954) is a tripartite division of the items relevant to depression and anxiety. Rather than obtaining a single broad NA factor comprised of both general neurotic and more distinctively depressive symptoms, these studies find that these two components split into separate factors. The end result is three factors: a general "neurotic" factor, and two smaller specific depression and anxiety factors. The item content of the broad neurotic factor generally includes feelings of inferiority and rejection, oversensitivity to criticism, self-consciousness, and social distress; in some samples (e.g., Williams et al., 1968) the factor is even more general, and encompasses items reflecting both depressed and anxious mood. The specific anxiety factor is quite similar to those we have discussed before, focusing on feelings of tension, nervousness, shakiness, and panic (somatic items generally form a separate factor in these studies). Finally, for the first time, we see a specific depression factor. Items that consistently load on this factor include loss of interest/pleasure, anorexia, and crying easily; in addition, hopelessness, loneliness, suicidal ideation, and depressed mood were also included in several studies (e.g., Derogatis & Cleary, 1977; Lipman et al., 1969). It is notable that none of these items are criteria for any anxiety diagnoses. Thus, the imbalance seen previously, while persistent, is clearly not inevitable. We discuss possible reasons for this in a later section.

In this context it is important to recall our earlier discussion of the correlation between measures of depression and anxiety. Although the *factors* reviewed in this section are themselves orthogonal, complete independence is only obtained when the appropriate factor scoring weights are applied to the entire set of items, a procedure that is rarely performed in these studies. Instead, the most common practice is to sum the significant marker variables for each factor; the variables are simply unit-weighted, so that each item contributes equally to the score.

When this is done, the resulting factors are no longer orthogonal, but instead correlate in the .40 to .65 range reported previously. We are again confronted with the pervasive co-occurrence of symptoms in this realm. There is no doubt that clear *conceptual* distinctions can be made between many types of symptoms in this domain—for example, psychic anxiety can be defined independently of somatic anxiety, "worthlessness" and "guilt" do not mean the same thing, and even the layperson can describe depressed mood distinctively from anxious mood. Nevertheless, it is important to recognize is that these apparently distinct elements of distress are not *empirically* independent of each other. We must accept the fact of their cooccurrence and seek to understand its basis.

Implications for the Diagnosis of Anxiety and Depression

In addition to factor analytic studies, other evidence can be found to support a tripartite division of the symptoms of anxiety and depression. Clark (1989) found that only a small subset of anxiety-related symptoms reliably differentiated anxious from depressed patients: panic attacks, including the autonomic symptoms of panic, and agoraphobic avoidance. Similarly, the most differentiating depression symptoms were those generally associated with the depressive subsyndrome melancholic depression (e.g., profound loss of pleasure, early morning awakening). However, most symptoms reviewed failed to discriminate the two types of patients, primarily because they were highly prevalent in both groups. These symptoms may thus represent the non-specific NA component common to both depressive and anxiety disorders, while those symptoms that differed in frequency between the two types of patients, and that mark specific depression and anxiety factors in the factor analytic studies, may reflect their unique features.

Similarly, in his review of 13 factor analytic studies examining specific dimensions of depression, Beck (1972) noted three factors that appeared in all studies. One factor, marked by self-deprecation, low self-esteem, sad affect, self-blame, and so on, corresponds to the general NA dimension we have noted. A second factor, marked by apathy, emotional withdrawal, fatigue, loss of sexual interest, and lack of social participation, appears more specifically depressive. Somatic complaints and difficulties, which are also shared between anxiety and depression, comprised the third invariant factor. It is also noteworthy that most studies also found a specific anxiety factor, defined by such items as tension and agitation.

If this tripartite view of the components of depression and anxiety is correct, a complete assessment of the affective domain would necessarily require three separate measures—a general NA scale plus specific measures assessing "core anxiety" and "core depression." Neither the general NA measure nor the specific scales alone would completely assess either syndrome, but together they would be sufficient. Conceptualized in this way, depression and anxiety are like biological relatives who share a substantial portion of their makeup (NA) but who have notable individual aspects as well. To assess either of them, one would then require measures of both the common and unique elements.

It is also possible that attempts to differentiate anxiety and depression have failed in part because there is a sizable group of patients who cannot be neatly categorized as either anxious or depressed but who exhibit a wide variety of both types of symptoms. There has long been interest in differentiating subtypes of depression, and the most persistent classification scheme differentiates a more severe variety of depression (variously called *endogenous, psychotic, primary,* or *endogenomorphic depression*) from a less severe depression (variously termed *reactive, neurotic,* or *secondary depression*) (e.g., Fowles & Gersh, 1982; Kendell, 1977; Mendels & Cochrane, 1968). The corresponding distinction in DSM-III-R is between MDD with melancholia and MDD without melancholia/Dysthymia. Although subtyping in anxiety has received far less attention than in depression, a parallel distinction has been made, differentiating more severe anxiety (e.g., DSM-III-R's Panic Disorder, Agoraphobia) from milder forms (e.g., GAD, Overanxious Disorder). The critical variable in each case, however, is not severity per se, but rather the presence of a strong vegetative or physiological component (e.g., the distinct quality and diurnal variation in mood of MDD with Melancholia, or the sudden onset of autonomic symptoms in Panic Disorder) in the former subtypes, as opposed to more purely affective or psychological manifestations in the latter (nonmelancholic depression and GAD). The greater salience of physical symptoms in the former subtypes suggests that biological variables may play a more prominent etiological role, either through an underlying and perhaps specific genetic diathesis, or as a final common pathway for a variety of causal mechanisms.

The data presented here indicate that in their more purely affective forms, anxiety and depression may not be distinct entities, but may both, in fact, be variants of high NA. That is, the symptoms characterizing the more purely psychological forms of depression or anxiety are also less related to the distinctive cores of the disorders, whereas those reflecting the more strongly biological forms of depression and anxiety are also those most likely to differentiate the two groups.

THE STRUCTURE OF MOOD AND PERSONALITY

State and trait NA have already been introduced as a potential explanation for the observed relation between depression and anxiety. At this point it is important to examine these concepts within the broader framework of the structure of mood and personality. Recent research has produced strong evidence that two broad mood factors—Positive Affect (PA) and Negative Affect (NA)—are the dominant dimensions in self-reported mood, both in the United States and in other cultures (Watson, Clark, & Tellegen, 1984; Watson & Tellegen, 1985). Briefly, NA represents the extent to which a person is feeling upset or unpleasantly aroused versus peaceful, and encompasses a variety of aversive states including *distressed, upset, angry, guilty, afraid, disgusted,* and *worried;* low NA, on the other hand, is marked by such terms as *calm, relaxed,* and *at ease.* In contrast, PA reflects the extent to which a person feels a zest for life, and is most clearly defined by words expressing energy and pleasurable engagement such as *active, excited, delighted, interested, attentive, enthusiastic,* and *proud,* whereas low PA is best characterized by terms reflecting quiescence and fatigue, such as *still, quiet, tired, sluggish, drowsy,* and *dull.*

As mentioned earlier, these two mood dimensions are largely independent, and have distinctive relations with various daily events, external variables such as seasons or weather, and both biological and social rhythms (Clark & Watson, 1988, 1990; Watson, Clark, & Tellegen, 1988). More specifically, only PA is (positively) related to diverse measures of social activity, exercise and other physical activity, and reports of pleasant events, whereas NA alone is correlated with health complaints, perceived stress, concerns about relationships, hassles or irritants in daily life, and other unpleasant events (Clark & Watson, 1988, 1990; Watson, 1988). Furthermore, PA has been shown to have a pronounced circadian cycle, whereas NA does not (Clark, Watson, & Leeka, in press; Thayer, 1987). Finally, the two mood dimensions are differentially related to two major personality traits: State NA is associated with measures of trait NA (Costa & McCrae, 1980; Emmons & Diener, 1985; Tellegen, 1985; Watson & Clark, 1984) or Neuroticism (Eysenck & Eysenck, 1968, 1975); PA, on the other hand, is correlated with measures of Positive Affectivity (trait PA, Tellegen, 1982) or Extraversion (Eysenck & Eysenck, 1968, 1975). Individuals high in trait PA show temperamental characteristics of enthusiasm and vigor, but in addition to this core mood component, they also tend to be socially masterful, to be forceful leaders who enjoy being the center of attention, and to be achievement oriented—thus, they are willing to work hard to obtain their goals (Tellegen, 1985).

It is important to note that while most affective states are relatively pure markers of either PA or NA, a few are combinations of the two dimensions. Most notably, terms reflecting depressed mood (e.g., *sad, blue*) or interpersonal disengagement (e.g., *lonely, alone*) represent a mixture of relatively high NA and moderately low PA (Watson & Clark, 1984; Watson & Tellegen, 1985). These mood data suggest that whereas anxiety is essentially a state of high NA, depression is a more complex affect that includes a significant secondary component of low PA. Consistent with this idea, many existing measures of anxiety have been shown to be more-or-less pure measures of trait NA (Watson & Clark, 1984), whereas corresponding measures of depression, while strongly related to trait NA, also have a significant PA component (Watson & Kendall, 1989). This pattern was not seen in the factor analysis described previously, probably because no pure PA markers were included to define that factor. Nevertheless, it is consistent with the idea that a core set of symptoms specific to depression might be identified that would be quasi-independent of both general NA and of the specific anxiety cluster. In this regard it appears that the concept of PA might be usefully applied to the differential measurement of anxiety and depression.

We explored this issue in a study of the relation of trait measures of NA and PA to the depressive and anxiety disorders in the sample of probands and co-twins described earlier (Watson, Clark, & Carey, 1988). Briefly, trait NA was related to a very broad array of complaints, and was significantly associated ($p <$ .01) with the majority of anxiety symptoms, particularly those of panic; it was also correlated with 19 of 20 depressive symptoms. Trait PA, on the other hand, was much more strongly and consistently related to the depressive than the anxiety symptoms. Over 90% of the anxiety symptoms had non-significant correlations with trait PA, whereas more than half of the depressive symptoms were significantly related to it. Similarly, trait NA was correlated with the presence of both depressive and anxiety diagnoses, whereas trait PA was consistently related only to the depressive disorders. Thus, NA was nonspecific, and was most useful in indicating the general presence of a psychiatric disorder, whereas PA was specific to depression, further supporting its utility in differential diagnosis.

TOWARD A NEW MODEL FOR UNDERSTANDING ANXIETY AND DEPRESSION AND THEIR RELATION

One question that is yet unanswered is why it has been more difficult to obtain a pure or core depression factor than a specific anxiety factor. One answer may lie in the greater complexity of depression, so that the items included in many factor analyses have not been sufficiently heterogeneous to reveal its various facets. Moreover, while many researchers recognize at least two major subtypes of depression (e.g., psychotic vs. neurotic, endogenous vs. reactive, primary vs. secondary), the majority of research studies that have contrasted anxious with depressed patients have focused on only one of these depressive subtypes. Thus, studies that include patients with a greater variety of depressive illness, and that also include a diversity of items relating to depression, should find a pure depression factor more readily. This, of course, was the case in the factor analytic studies of depression reviewed by Beck (1972). All thirteen studies reported a specific depression factor whose markers are quite clearly manifestations of low PA (e.g., fatigue, emotional withdrawal, apathy, loss of interest).

Another answer lies in the discrepancy between the nature of PA and the way in which PA-related depression questions are phrased on existing measures. Among mood terms, there are many more descriptors of high than low PA, and most trait-PA items are also worded in the affirmative. Furthermore, the high PA terms tend to be purer markers of the underlying factor (Watson, Clark, & Tellegen, 1988). However, most symptom measures of depression focus to a large degree on the presence of clinical symptoms—which tends to link them with NA—rather than the loss of normal functions, which would emphasize their negative relation to PA. For example, the PA-related symptoms (such as "work and activities") on the HRSD all have, as their lowest (i.e., least depressed) rating, "no difficulty" or "absent," so the best one can do is not to show the symptom in question. If attention were instead shifted to assessing high PA, however, the "no difficulty" option might fall nearer the middle of the scale, with "superior functioning" as the high-end anchor, and greater differences among patients might be elicited. On the item "work and activities," the lowest score might then be "actively involved in work and leisure activities," with "no difficulty" or "normal involvement in work and activities," being the next higher score; degrees of impairment would obtain even higher scores. Similarly, on the BDI, rather than having "I am not particularly pessimistic or discouraged about the future" as the lowest score, this statement might better provide a midrange option, with a statement such as "I am quite excited about the future" as the zero response. If given the opportunity to express their high PA and capacity for positive engagement in this manner, patients who were primarily anxious, but not depressed, might appear significantly less depressed; depressed patients would, by contrast, appear particularly deficient.

In addition to these aspects of PA that seem immediately relevant to depression, consideration should also be given to other variables known to be specifically related to PA, particularly social engagement and mastery, and achievement orientation. Are these perhaps aspects of depression that have been understudied? Social withdrawal has long been recognized as an associated feature of depression (Goodwin & Guze, 1984), and evidence for social skills deficiency has been found in depressed patients (Lewinsohn, Shaffer, & Libet, 1969). Recall also that lack of social participation was a primary aspect of the low PA/core depression factor found in Beck's (1972) review. Yet none of the DSM-III-R (APA, 1987) criteria for depression refer specifically to this aspect of the disorder. It is certainly implied in the criterion "loss of interest or pleasure in activities," but it might be fruitful to consider withdrawal from social participation as a more central feature of the diagnosis. From the point of view of discrimination it is also important to note that, except for the self-imposed retirement of agoraphobic patients, and the specific disorder Social Phobia, social withdrawal is not a criterion of anxiety disorder, nor is it generally considered an associated feature.

Similarly, loss of motivation for work is more typically associated with depressive than anxiety disorders (Beck, 1967). Although not a separate criterion in DSM-III-R, it is implied by such symptoms as diminished interest or ability to think, and is included in many established measures of depression such as the BDI and HRSD. Interestingly, social withdrawal and decreased productivity were both specific DSM-III criteria for Cyclothymic and Dysthymic Disorder, but in DSM-III-R they have been eliminated without comment. However, because of the general association of these variables with depression, but not anxiety, and in light of the distinctive relation of social activity and achievement motivation with PA, it would seem that these topics merit further consideration.

With greater emphasis on the potential for positive functioning, especially in the areas of work and social activity, finer distinctions might be made not only between the depressive and anxiety disorders, but also among subtypes of depression. Particularly, patients with dysthymic disorder, while complaining loudly of their distress (high NA), would likely score somewhat higher on PA than those with severe melancholia. That is, while appearing equally or even more highly distressed, non-MDD patients might, nevertheless, report more positive experiences. It is an hypothesis that deserves attention.

Another aspects of PA that may have implications for depression is its diurnal variation. As mentioned earlier, PA has a pronounced daily cycle, with nearly all normal subjects reporting lower levels of PA early in the morning (Clark et al., in press; Thayer, 1987). Over the course of the day, PA rises to peak sometime between late morning and early evening (with considerable intra- and interindividual variation in peak time), but then reliably falls again to low levels late in the evening. In contrast, NA shows no consistent diurnal pattern, but exhibits, on the average, a flat curve over the course of the entire day (Clark et al., in press; Thayer, 1987). Similarly, although it is by no means inevitably present, a marked diurnal pattern with depression worse in the morning has long been noted in the mood of many patients with severe depression (Rosenthal & Klerman, 1966); in fact, it is one of the criteria for melancholia in DSM-III-R. The opposite pattern (depression worse in the evening) has been reported in patients with non-melancholic depression (Pilowsky, Levine, & Boulton, 1969). Similarly, worsening of depression in the evening was the most common pattern among normal college students who reported feeling depressed at least one day during a longitudinal study (Robbins & Tanck, 1987). In contrast, diurnal variation in anxiety has not been noted. The crucial point here is not the particular similarity or dissimilarity in the patterns of variation of PA and depression, but the fact that diurnal patterning is an important aspect of each, while it is not remarkable in either NA or anxiety. In the same vein, seasonal variation has been noted in both depression (Rosenthal et al., 1984) and PA (Smith, 1979), but not in either anxiety or NA. These data imply that the same or related functions, possibly biological in origin, influence intraindividual variation in both PA and depression, further suggesting a link between one of the two major mood/personality variables and its corresponding mood/syndrome/disorder.

CONCLUSION

Extensive data compel recognition that depression and anxiety show considerable overlap at every level that has been studied. However, a close examination of the evidence suggests that these correlations may stem from a shared underlying predisposition to experience negative affective states. State/trait NA, however, represent only one factor of a highly robust two-dimensional mood/personality structure; the second factor, composed of state/trait PA, has been largely neglected in research, and yet may offer us a new perspective on the differentiation of depression and anxiety. Specifically, a number of variables that are uniquely correlated with PA—social activity, energy level, achievement motivation, diurnal and seasonal variation—are also peculiarly relevant to depression, suggesting that this factor may play an important and distinctive role in depression.

Two issues seem particularly interesting for further research. First, alternative ways of assessing depression that focus more directly on the role of PA need to be explored. These should include both the core aspects of state PA itself (e.g., loss of enthusiasm, energy, delight), and also correlated variables such as decreased social interest/activities and low motivation for productive work. Second, evidence suggests that NA and PA may interact to produce various subtypes of anxiety and depression. For example, patients with purely high NA may suffer from a severe form of anxiety (i.e., with prominent physiological symptoms), those with moderate levels of high NA and low PA may represent a generalized anxious-depressed state in which affective distress is the most prominent symptom, while those with markedly low PA may suffer from melancholic depression. Further research investigating this model through various methods (e.g., family/genetic or controlled treatment studies) may prove fruitful.

ACKNOWLEDGMENTS

We are indebted to Irving I. Gottesman and Greg Carey for allowing us access to data from the Washington University Twin Series. This research was supported in part by National Institute of Mental Health Grant #MH14677.

REFERENCES

Akiskal, H. S., (1985). Anxiety: Definition, relationship to depression, and proposal for an integrative model. In A. H. Tuma & J. D. Maser (Eds.), *Anxiety and the anxiety disorders* (pp. 787–797). Hillsdale, NJ: Lawrence Erlbaum Associates.
American Psychiatric Association (1980). *Diagnostic and Statistical Manual of Mental Disorders, 3rd Edition*. Washington, D.C.: Author.
American Psychiatric Association. (1987). *Diagnostic and Statistical Manual of Mental Disorders, 3rd Edition-Revised*. Washington, D.C.: Author.
Beck, A. T. (1967). *Depression: Clinical, experimental, and theoretical aspects*. New York: Harper & Row.
Beck, A. T. (1972). The phenomena of depression: A synthesis. In D. Offer & D. X. Freedman (Eds.), *Modern psychiatry and clinical research* (pp. 136–158). New York: Basic Books.

Beck, A. T., Ward, C. H., Mendelson, M., Mock, J. E., & Erbaugh, J. K. (1961). An inventory for measuring depression. *Archives of General Psychiatry, 4*, 561–571.

Breier, A., Charney, D. S., & Heninger, G. R. (1984). Major depression in patients with agoraphobia and panic disorder. *Archives of General Psychiatry, 41*, 1129–1135.

Breier, A., Charney, D. S., & Heninger, G. R. (1985). The diagnostic validity of anxiety disorders and their relationship to depressive illness. *American Journal of Psychiatry, 142*, 787–797.

Carey, G. (1987). Big genes, little genes, affective disorder, and anxiety: A commentary. *Archives of General Psychiatry, 44*, 486–491.

Carey, G., & Gottesman, I. I. (1981). Twin and family studies of anxiety, phobic, and obsessive disorders. In D. F. Klein & J. Raskin (Eds.), *Anxiety: New research and changing concepts* (pp. 117–136). New York: Raven Press.

Carroll, B. J., Feinberg, M., Smouse, P. E., Rawson, S. G., & Greden, J. F. (1981). The Carroll Ratings Scale for Depression I. Development, reliability, and validation. *British Journal of Psychiatry, 138*, 194–200.

Clark, L. A. (1989). The anxiety and depressive disorders: Descriptive psychopathology and differential diagnosis. In P. C. Kendall & D. Watson (Eds.), *Anxiety and depression: Distinctive and overlapping features* (pp. 83–129). New York: Academic Press.

Clark, L. A., & Watson, D. (1988). Mood and the mundane: Relations between daily life events and self-reported mood. *Journal of Personality and Social Psychology, 54*, 296–308.

Clark, L. A., & Watson, D. (1990). *Predicting momentary mood: The role of ordinary life events and personality*. Manuscript submitted for publication.

Clark, L. A., Watson, D., & Carey, G. (1988). *Factors of symptom ratings in patients with depressive and/or anxiety disorders*. Unpublished raw data.

Clark, L. A., Watson, D., & Leeka, J. (in press). Diurnal variation in the positive affects. *Motivation and Emotion*.

Cohen, J., Gomez, E., Hoell, N. L., Kotin, J., Rickman, E. E., & Roessler, R. L. (1976). Diazepam and phenobarbital in the treatment of anxiety: A controlled multicenter study using physician and patient rating scales. *Current Therapeutic Research, 20*, 184–193.

Costa, P. T., & McCrae, R. R. (1980). Influence of extraversion and neuroticism on subjective well-being: Happy and unhappy people. *Journal of Personality and Social Psychology, 38*, 668–678.

Costello, C. G. (1970). Classification and psychopathology. In C. G. Costello (Ed.), *Symptoms of psychopathology* (pp. 1–26). New York: Wiley.

Costello, C. G., & Comrey, A. L. (1967). Scales for measuring depression and anxiety. *Journal of Psychology, 6*, 303–313.

Deluty, B. M., Deluty, R. H., & Carver, C. S. (1986). Concordance between clinicians' and patients' ratings of anxiety and depression as mediated by private self-consciousness. *Journal of Personality Assessment, 50*, 93–106.

Derogatis, L. R., & Cleary, P. A. (1977). Confirmation of the dimensional structure of the SCL-90: A study in construct validation. *Journal of Clinical Psychology, 33*, 981–989.

Derogatis, L. R., Klerman, G. L., & Lipman, R. S. (1972). Anxiety states and depressive neurosis. *Journal of Nervous and Mental Disease, 155*, 392–403.

Dobson, K. S. (1985a). An analysis of anxiety and depression scales. *Journal of Personality Assessment, 49*, 522–527.

Dobson, K. S. (1985b). The relationship between anxiety and depression. *Clinical Psychology Review, 3*, 307–324.

Emmons, R. A., & Diener, E. (1985). Personality correlates of subjective well-being. *Personality and Social Psychology Bulletin, 11*, 89–97.

Eysenck, H., & Eysenck, S. B. G. (1968). *Manual for the Eysenck Personality Inventory*. San Diego, CA: Educational and Industrial Testing Service.

Eysenck, H., & Eysenck, S. B. G. (1975). *Eysenck Personality Questionnaire*. San Diego, CA: Educational and Industrial Testing Service.

Fleiss, J. L., Gurland, B. J., & Cooper, J. E. (1971). Some contributions to the measurement of psychopathology. *British Journal of Psychiatry, 119,* 647–656.
Foa, E. B., & Foa, U. G. (1982). Differentiating depression and anxiety: Is it possible? Is it useful? *Psychopharmacology Bulletin, 18,* 62–68.
Fowles, D. C., & Gersh, F. (1982). Neurotic depression: The endogenous-neurotic distinction. In R. A. Depue (Ed.), *The psychobiology of the depressive disorders* (pp. 55–80). New York: Academic Press.
Goodwin, D. W., & Guze, S. B. (1984). *Psychiatric Diagnosis* (3rd Ed.). New York: Oxford University Press.
Gotlib, I. H. (1984). Depression and general psychopathology in university students. *Journal of Abnormal Psychology, 93,* 19–30.
Gotlib, I. H., & Cane, D. B. (1989). Self-report assessment of depression and anxiety. In P. C. Kendall & D. Watson (Eds.), *Anxiety and depression: Distinctive and overlapping features* (pp. 131–169). New York: Academic Press.
Hamilton, M. (1959). The assessment of anxiety states by rating. *British Journal of Medical Psychology, 32,* 50–55.
Hamilton, M. (1960). A rating scale for depression. *Journal of Neurology, Neurosurgery and Psychiatry, 23,* 56–62.
Hathaway, S. R., & McKinley, J. C. (1942). A multiphasic personality schedule (Minnesota): III. The measurement of symptomatic depression. *Journal of Psychology, 14,* 73–84.
Jardine, R., Martin, N. G., & Henderson, A. S. (1984). Genetic covariation between neuroticism and the symptoms of anxiety and depression. *Genetic Epidemiology, 1,* 89–107.
Johnstone, E. C., Owens, D. G. C., Firth, C. D., McPherson, K., Dowie, C., Riley, G., & Gold, A. (1980). Neurotic illness and its response to anxiolytic and antidepressant treatment. *Psychological Medicine, 10,* 321–328.
Kendell, R. E. (1976). The classification of depressions: A review of contemporary confusion. *British Journal of Psychiatry, 129,* 15–28.
Kendler, K. S., Heath, A. C., Martin, N. G., & Eaves, L. J. (1987). *Symptoms of anxiety and symptoms of depression.* Archives of General Psychiatry, 44, 451–457.
Klein, D. F. (1981). Anxiety reconceptualized. In D. F. Klein & J. Raskin (Eds.), *Anxiety: New research and changing concepts* (pp. 235–266). New York: Raven Press.
Klerman, G. L. (1977). Anxiety and depression. In G. D. Burrows (Ed.), *Handbook of studies on depression* (pp. 49–68). Amsterdam, The Netherlands: Elsevier.
Krug, S. E., Scheier, I. H., & Cattell, R. B. (1976). *Handbook for the IPAT Anxiety Scale.* Champaign, IL: Institute for Personality and Ability Testing, Inc.
Leckman, J. F., Merikangas, K. R., Pauls, D. L., Prusoff, B. A., & Weissman, M. M. (1983). Anxiety disorders and depression: Contradictions between family study data and DSM-III conventions. *American Journal of Psychiatry, 140,* 880–882.
Leckman, J. F., Weissman, M. M., Merikangas, K. R., Pauls, D. L., & Prusoff, B. A. (1983). Panic disorder increases risk of major depression, alcoholism, panic, and phobic disorders in affectively ill families. *Archives of General Psychiatry, 40,* 1055–1060.
Lewinsohn, P., Shaffer, M., & Libet, J. (1969). *A behavioral approach to depression.* Paper presented to the American Psychological Association. Miami Beach, FL.
Lewis, A. J. (1934). Melancholia: A clinical survey of depressed states. *Journal of Mental Science, 80,* 277–378.
Lipman, R. S. (1982). Differentiating anxiety and depression and anxiety disorders: Use of rating scales. *Psychopharmacology Bulletin, 18,* 69–77.
Lipman, R. S., Rickels, K., Covi, L., Derogatis, L. R., & Uhlenhuth, E. H. (1969). Factors of symptom distress. *Archives of General Psychiatry, 21,* 328–338.
Mapother, E. (1926). Discussion on manic-depressive psychosis. *British Medical Journal, 2,* 872–876.

Mendels, J., & Cochrane, C. (1968). The nosology of depression: The endogenous-reactive concept. *American Journal of Psychiatry Supplement, 124,* 1–11.

Mendels, J., Weinstein, N., & Cochrane, C. (1972). The relationship between depression and anxiety. *Archives of General Psychiatry, 27,* 649–653.

Parloff, M. B., Kelman, H. C., & Frank, J. D. (1954). Comfort, effectiveness and self-awareness as criteria of improvement in psychotherapy. *American Journal of Psychiatry, 3,* 343–351.

Pilowsky, I., Levine, S., & Boulton, D. M. (1969). The classification of depression by numerical taxonomy. *British Journal of Psychiatry, 115,* 937–945.

Pollitt, J., & Young, J. (1971). Anxiety state or masked depression: A study based on the action of monoamine oxidase inhibitors. *British Journal of Psychiatry, 119,* 143–149.

Prusoff, B. A., Klerman, G. L. & Paykel, E. S. (1972). Concordance between clinical assessments and patients' self-report in depression. *Archives of General Psychiatry, 26,* 546–552.

Robins, L., Helzer, J. E., Croughan, J., & Ratcliff, K. S. (1981). National Institute of Mental Health Diagnostic Interview Schedule: Its history, characteristics, and validity. *Archives of General Psychiatry, 38,* 381–389.

Robbins, P. R., & Tanck, R. H. (1987). A study of diurnal patterns of depressed mood. *Motivation and Emotion, 11,* 37–49.

Rosenthal, S. H., & Klerman, G. L. (1966). Content and consistency in the endogenous depressive pattern. *British Journal of Psychiatry, 112,* 471–484.

Rosenthal, N. E., Sack, D. A., Gillin, J. C., Lewy, A. J., Goodwin, F. K., Davenport, Y., Mueller, P. S., Newsome, D. A., & Wehr, T. A. (1984). Seasonal affective disorder: A description of the syndrome and preliminary findings with light therapy. *Archives of General Psychiatry, 41,* 72–80.

Roth, M., Gurney, C., Garside, R. F., & Kerr, T. A. (1972). Studies in the classification of affective disorders: Relationship between anxiety states and depressive illnesses-I. *British Journal of Psychiatry, 121,* 147–161.

Roth, M., & Mountjoy, C. Q. (1982). In E. S. Paykel (Ed.), *Handbook of affective disorders* (pp. 70–92). New York: Guilford Press.

Smith, T. W. (1979). Happiness: Time trends, seasonal variations, intersurvey differences, and other mysteries. *Social Psychology Quarterly, 42,* 18–30.

Spielberger, C. D., Gorsuch, R. L., & Lushene, R. E. (1970). *STAI-Manual for the State-Trait Anxiety Inventory.* Palo Alto, CA: Consulting Psychologists Press.

Tanaka-Matsumi, J., & Kameoka, V. A. (1986). Reliabilities and concurrent validities of popular self-report measures of depression, anxiety, and social desirability. *Journal of Consulting and Clinical Psychology, 54,* 328–333.

Tellegen, A. (1982). *A brief manual for the Differential Personality Questionnaire.* Unpublished manuscript, University of Minnesota.

Tellegen, A. (1985). Structures of mood and personality and their relevance to assessing anxiety, with an emphasis on self-report. In A. H. Tuma & J. D. Maser (Eds.), *Anxiety and the anxiety disorders* (pp. 681–706). Hillsdale, NJ: Lawrence Erlbaum Associates.

Thayer, R. (1987). Problem perception, optimism, and related states as a function of time of day (diurnal rhythm), and moderate exercise: Two arousal systems in interaction. *Motivation and Emotion, 11,* 19–36.

Tuma, A. H., & Maser, J. D. (Eds.). (1985). *Anxiety and the anxiety disorders.* Hillsdale, NJ: Lawrence Erlbaum Associates.

Vye, C. (1986, November). *Positive and Negative Affect and the differentiation of depression and anxiety.* Paper presented at the Association for the Advancement of Behavior Therapy Convention, Chicago, IL.

Watson, D. (1988). Intraindividual and interindividual analyses of Positive and Negative Affect: Their relation to health complaints, perceived stress, and daily activities. *Journal of Personality and Social Psychology, 54,* 1020–1030.

Watson, D., & Clark, L. A. (1984). Negative Affectivity: The disposition to experience aversive emotional states. *Psychological Bulletin, 96,* 465–490.
Watson, D., Clark, L. A., & Carey, G. (1988). Positive and Negative Affectivity and their relation to anxiety and depressive disorders. *Journal of Abnormal Psychology, 97,* 346–353.
Watson, D., Clark, L. A., & Tellegen, A. (1984). Cross-cultural convergence in the structure of mood: A Japanese replication and comparison with U.S. findings. *Journal of Personality and Social Psychology, 47,* 127–144.
Watson, D., Clark, L. A., & Tellegen, A. (1988). Development and validation of brief measures of Positive and Negative Affect: The PANAS Scales. *Journal of Personality and Social Psychology, 54,* 1063–1070.
Watson, D., & Kendall, P. C. (1989). Understanding anxiety and depression: Their relation to negative and positive affective states. In P. C. Kendall & D. Watson (Eds.), *Anxiety and depression: Distinctive and overlapping features* (pp. 3–26). New York: Academic Press.
Watson, D., & Tellegen, A. (1985). Toward a consensual structure of mood. *Psychological Bulletin, 98,* 219–235.
Weissman, M. M. (1985). The epidemiology of anxiety disorders: Rates, risks, and familial patterns. In A. H. Tuma & J. D. Maser (Eds.), *Anxiety and the anxiety disorders* (pp. 275–296). Hillsdale, NJ: Lawrence Erlbaum Associates.
Weissman, M. M., Sholomskas, D., Pottenger, M., Prusoff, B. A., & Locke, B. Z. (1977). Assessing depressive symptoms in five psychiatric populations: A validation study. *American Journal of Epidemiology, 106,* 203–214.
Williams, H. V., Lipman, R. S., Rickels, K., Covi, L., Uhlenhuth, E. H., & Mattsson, N. B. (1968). Replication of symptom distress factors in anxious neurotic outpatients. *Multivariate Behavioral Research 3,* 199–211.
Zimmerman, M., Coryell, W., Wilson, S., & Corenthal, C. (1986). Evaluation of symptoms of major depressive disorder: Self-report *vs.* clinical ratings. *Journal of Nervous and Mental Disease, 174,* 150–153.
Zuckerman, M., & Lubin, B. (1965). *The Multiple Affect Adjective Check List.* San Diego, CA: Educational and Industrial Testing Service.
Zuckerman, M., Persky, H., Eckman, K. M., & Hopkins, T. R. (1967). A multitrait multimethod measurement approach to the traits (or states) of anxiety, depression and hostility. *Journal of Projective Techniques and Personality Assessment, 31,* 39–48.
Zung, W. W. (1965). A self-rating depression scale. *Archives of General Psychiatry, 12,* 63–70.

3 Cross-Cultural Studies of Depression

Janis H. Jenkins
Case Western Reserve University

Arthur Kleinman
Byron J. Good
Harvard Medical School

CROSS-CULTURAL ASPECTS OF DEPRESSION: INTRODUCTION

In this chapter we examine key questions that arise from a cross-cultural approach to the study of depression. Several authors have noted that cross-cultural epidemiological data on depression share unsubstantiated assumptions about the cross-cultural validity of the concept depression and of associated epidemiological instruments (e.g., Marsella et al., 1985). Anthropological research suggests that models of depression based on studies of patients in Western psychiatric settings cannot be unquestioningly generalised to non-Western societies. Although some forms of depression may be found in all populations, it may not be valid to equate forms of the illness manifested primarily in psychological terms associated with strong feelings of guilt or remorse with illness experienced primarily in somatic terms.

Fundamental to the question of the cross-cultural validity of depression as a distinct psychiatric disorder is a critical appraisal of dichotomous mind-body approaches to psychological and somatic manifestations of depression. Contemporary DSM-III-R psychiatry defines depression as a mood disorder with associated somatic symptoms, and thus presupposes a dichotomous mind-body approach to psychological and somatic manifestations of depression. Insofar as this dichotomous approach distinguishes psyche and soma, it reproduces assumptions of Western thought and culture, which must from the outset be suspended in formulating a valid comparative stance.

Our review begins with consideration of cultural variation in dysphoric affect and the import of such variation for universalist definitions of depressive disorder. We examine cross-cultural evidence on somatic components of depression and explore the concept of somatization in relation to depression and the communication of distress. In the second part of our discussion, we review the evidence of cross-cultural variation in depressive symptomatology (Marsella et al., 1985). Observation of striking cultural and social class variations in symptoms is frequently used to support the view that culture affects the content but not the process or structure of psychopathology. We argue that culture is of profound importance to the experience of depression, the construction of meaning and social response to depressive illness within families and communities, the course and outcome of the disorder, and thus to the very constitution of depressive illness. This anthropological perspective is presented through examination of a series of theoretical, substantive, and methodological issues. In particular, we review the social and cultural contexts within which depression originates, examining the role of gender, social class, family relations, migration, political violence, and social change. Finally, we suggest directions for future research.

THE CULTURAL CONSTRUCTION OF EMOTION

Although the cross-cultural study of depression and depressive affect invariably presupposes a theory of emotion, it is by no means certain that emotions are constituted the same way in different cultures. We begin this section by briefly summarising an anthropological perspective on emotion, and then set forth issues central to the cross-cultural study of depression: (1) the ethnopsychology of emotion; and (2) culturally distinctive meanings associated with dysphoric emotions.

To the extent that emotions have been considered shared or common experiences of individuals across culturally distinct settings, they have generally been assumed similar on the basis of universal, innate human propensities (Ekman, 1982; Isard, 1977; Plutchik, 1980; Wierzbicka, 1986). If culture is acknowledged as a factor in emotional life, it is only as a second-order interpretation of such innate qualities (Levy, 1984). In addition, thought and emotion are cast as largely separate, mutually exclusive categories: "the cultural/ideational and individual/affective have been construed as theoretically, and empirically, at odds" (Rosaldo, 1984, p. 139). Against this common scholarly assumption we argue here for an approach to emotion as an essentially cultural integration of bodily experience and communication.

Given the (empirically unproven) assumption of biological similarity of emotional states, we need to consider cultural sources of similarity and variation. This point has been advanced by Geertz (1973), who asserted that "not only ideas, but emotions too, are cultural artifacts" (p. 81). Emotions can be considered as essentially cultural since no human response or experience occurs in the absence of culturally defined situations or meanings. It is particular situations or contexts that provide the basis for emotions and "the determination of when one ought to be angry, when sad, when sorry, when lonely, and how to act, is largely a cultural matter" (Myers, 1979, p. 349).

Anthropologists and cross-cultural psychologists have argued that affects are inseparable from cultural systems of meaning. Culture organizes the experience and interpretation of loss here as the sting of desperate grief, there as ambivalent silence, elsewhere as concatenations of feelings—guilt with sadness, rage with hopelessness, fear of sorcery with calm acceptance of fate—that hold special salience (and in some cases arguably may only be felt) in particular social systems. The documentation for this conclusion is impressive; the processes responsible for its occurrence and their implications for the epidemiology and phenomenology of depressive disorders are only now receiving serious attention (Geertz, 1980; Good & Good, 1982; Kleinman & Good, 1985; Lutz, 1985, 1988; Marsella, DeVos, & Hsu, 1985; Myers, 1979; Rosaldo, 1983; Schieffelin, 1983; Shweder & LeVine, 1984; White & Kirkpatrick, 1985).

THE ETHNOPSYCHOLOGY OF EMOTION

An essential step toward culturally informed models of depressive disorders is the investigation of indigenous or ethnopsychological models of dysphoric affects. Ethnopsychological themes include factors such as the relative egocentricity of the self; indigenous categories of emotion; the predominance of particular emotions within societies; the inter-relations of various emotions; identification of those situations in which emotions are said to occur; and ethnophysiological accounts of bodily experience of emotions. This constellation of sociocultural features will mediate how persons experience and express depression and other emotions.

Conceptions of emotion are embedded within notions of self, which have been characterized as varying along a continuum between "egocentric" and "sociocentric" (Shweder & Bourne, 1984). Individuals with a more sociocentric sense of self are considered to be more relationally identified with others than are individuals with a more *egocentric* sense of self, who view themselves as more or less unique, separate persons. The former have often been associated with non-Western cultural traditions, the latter with more industrialized nations (Geertz, 1984). The Pintupi aborigines of Australia provide an examplary case of a culture in which the conception of self is essentially kin-based (Myers, 1979). Similar claims of the primacy of family definitions of self have been made for Hispanic populations (Murillo, 1976). This tendency stands in notable contrast to middle class Caucasion Americans, for example, for whom self-identity, while family-related, is constituted more as a distinct individual who stands apart from others. While these characterizations of the self index general differences in broad cultural axes, it is important to note that as generalizations they oversimplify the construction of the self, failing to specify particular domains and settings across which selves may be differentially constituted within a culture.

An understanding of emotions as intrapsychic events, feelings or introspections of the individual is a specifically Western definition. A case contrast to emotion as introspective feeling state has recently been provided by Lutz (1985, 1988) in her studies of the Ifaluk of Micronesia. For the Ifaluk, cultural categories of thought and emotion are not strongly differentiated. Moreover, emotions are not located within persons, but in relationships between persons or within events and situations. *Metagu* (fear/anxiety), for example, is said to occur in response to a superior's justifiable *song* (anger) over the breach of a cultural taboo, the situation of being in an open canoe in shark-infested waters or the occurrence of ghost activity. (It is important to note, however, that emotion, for the Ifaluk *is* sometimes experienced and defined as "about our insides.") Dysphoria or depression may thus be experienced as a predominantly intra-psychic mood disorder of individuals in more social and contextual terms (Toussignant, 1984).

Differing cultural interpretations of self and emotion may therefore lead to one of the most important aspects of emotional life: variations in the qualitative features of bodily/emotional experience. Dysphoric affects cannot properly be considered as basically "the same" cross-culturally: there are culturally distinctive repertoires of distressing experience. For example, Ebigbo (1982, p. 29) found that "Mentally ill patients in Nigeria and indeed in West Africa very often complain of various types of somatic distress. These complaints are made independently of the diagnosis of the mental illness and whether or not it is very acute. Examples of such psychosomatic complaints are: heat in the head, crawling sensation of worms and ants, headache, heaviness sensation in the head, biting sensation all over the body, etc." Among a Mexican-descent population, Jenkins (1988a, 1988b) found that indigenously labeled conditions of *nervios* incorporate a variety of somatic complaints, including "brainache," or the sensation that the brain is "exploding" or "uncontrollable." These complaints stand in stark contrast to those commonly recognized among European and North American populations.

Emotion states not only vary in relation to self-concept, they are also elaborated in light of cultural knowledge. Entire domains of emotional life may be either culturally and experientially elaborated or unelaborated. This has been particularly documented for the emotion of anger. For example, while the Eskimos (Briggs, 1970) virtually never display anger, the Kaluli of New Guinea (Schieffelin, 1983) and the Yanomamo of Brazil (Chagnon, 1977) have highly elaborated, culturally sanctioned displays of anger. Among the Tahitians studied by Levy (1973), an important societal rule is the inhibition of anger. According to Levy these Society Islanders in fact seldom experience anger (Levy, 1973).

This is no less true of appropriate displays of profound sadness and sorrow, some cultures encourage such expressions (for example, Iranian culture) while others evidence little tolerance of these affects. Furthermore, within a culture, social class influences how particular emotions are communicated. Chinese villagers may express sadness publicly, but middle class, formally educated Chinese will not do so outside of close family relations. In addition to fundamental differences in cultural emphases on particular emotions, such states may also vary in affective intensity and meaning. Some societies (e.g., Amazonian Yanomamo) may foster intense emotional involvement, whereas others (e.g., the Javanese) may encourage inner states of "smoothness" and calm (Chagnon, 1977; Geertz, 1973).

Cross-cultural studies of the socialization of affect have documented that differences in emotional emphases are deeply rooted in the developmental makeup of cultural members (Ochs & Schieffelin, 1985). As noted by H. Geertz (1959), socialization of affect selects for a cultural repertoire or "vocabulary of emotion":

> Every cultural system includes patterned ideas regarding certain interpersonal relationship and certain affective states, which represent a selection from the entire potential range of interpersonal and emotional experiences. The child, growing up within the culture and gradually internalizing these premises, undergoes a process of socially guided emotional specialization. He learns, in a sense, a special vocabulary of emotion. (p. 225)

Cultural specialization in emotional life again raises the possibility of whether emotions, unknown to us, are part of the everyday experience of members of culturally distinct societies.

A common assumption is that depression can be conceived on a continuum, as mood, symptom, or disorder (see Kleinman & Good, 1985). That there is a clear cutoff point between normal dysphoria and pathological depression has never been definitively demonstrated for our own culture. There is even less empirical reason to believe that it is identical across cultures. Partly for this reason, indigenous concepts of dysphoric affect cannot be so neatly partitioned from psychiatric definitions of depressive disorder.

CULTURE AND DEPRESSIVE AFFECT

Dysphoria—sadness, hopelessness, unhappiness, lack of pleasure with the things of the world and with social relationships—has dramatically different meaning and form of expression in different societies (Kleinman & Good, 1985, p. 3). The suffering of individuals appears against the background of cultural images of suffering. Gaines and Farmer (1986) review the cultural system of meaning that identifies individuals who suffer as exemplary heroes in Mediterranean culture. Obeyesekere (1985) points out that suffering is a permanent positively valued feature of cosmology in Buddhist cultures. Good, Good, and Moradi (1985) demonstrate that suffering is a highly elaborated religious element associated with martyrdom and grief for Shi'ite Muslims. Tousignant (1984) and Jenkins (1988b) show that suffering is associated with a culturally profound sense of tragedy in Latin American cultures.

Different cultural traditions of suffering vary according to the salience of the "vocabulary of emotion" (Geertz, 1959), that is, whether notions of suffering are elaborated or unelaborated; expressed in secular or religious idioms; culturally valued or disvalued; relevant to the individual self or to broader social and historical contexts. While some cultures have no specific word for depression per se (Marsella, 1980), absence of a word or concept for an emotion does not preclude its presence. For example, some emotions may *elude* culture or be so deeply unconscious that they are not easily conceived or known (Obeyesekere, 1985). The cultural elaboration of depression may influence standards of individual social functioning in the face of suffering, where some may experience relatively higher levels of suffering and still perform occupational or interpersonal roles.

In the absence of a cultural concept of depression, depressive states can be studied as a feature of local forms of suffering. Indeed, some authors have documented a fundamental and pervasive "ethos of suffering" that permeates nearly every aspect of world view. "In highland Ecuador, *pena* refers to a state of mind characterized by a mixture of sadness and anxiety as well as to an illness state resembling depression . . . the ideology in which it is embedded serves to interpret a bodily problem at the same time as it reflects a more global attitude toward life . . . When misfortune abounds in the Sierra of Ecuador, life becomes a litany of *penas,* or sorrows" (Tousignant, 1984, p. 381). The ideology of *pena,* as with other Latin American attitudes toward suffering, cannot correctly be interpreted as a fatalistic resignation or submission; rather, it represents a cultural tradition of the recognition and existential working through of oppressive life circumstances.

From his ethnographic analysis of depressive moods in Sri Lanka, Obeyesekere (1985) elaborated an analytic conception of "the work of culture" to explain "the process whereby painful motives and affects such as those occurring in depression are transformed into publicly accepted sets of meanings and symbols" (Obeyesekere, 1985, p. 147). The cultural perception of chronic and pervasive suffering is expectable for any typical Buddhist. That one recognizes and accepts the inevitable condition of suffering is the first step toward the spiritual abandonment of suffering. Although suffering occupies a prominent part of life experience, it is nonetheless expected that a lay person take pleasure in everyday life. Suffering is, then, not an all-encompassing aspect of life in the sense of an ethos. Even so, Buddhist laymen may "generalize their despair from the self to the world at large and give it Buddhist meaning and significance" (Obeyesekere, 1985, p. 140).

The foregoing examples from Latin America and Sri Lanka provide a sharp contrast with an Anglo-American ethos concerning suffering. In the latter context, suffering is not an expectable or acceptable state of affairs. Rather, it is something to overcome through personal striving, volition, and the "pursuit of happiness." A strong contrast in willingness to endure suffering was observed by Jenkins (1988a), in her comparisons of Mexican-descent and Caucasion American families who were living with a family member afflicted with schizophrenic illness. Mexican families displayed more willingness to endure suffering associated with the problem and expressed sadness more frequently and profoundly than Caucasion Americans who more commonly voiced anger and frustration (Jenkins et al., 1986; Karno et al., 1987).

Empirical investigations of indigenous conceptions of depression—as symptom, mood, or syndrome—have been rare. A notable exception is the study by Manson, Shore, and Bloom (1985) of depression among the Hopi of the Southwestern United States. The authors documented five discrete depressive conditions recognized by the Hopi: worry sickness, unhappiness, heartbroken, drunken-like craziness (with or without alcohol), and disappointment-pouting. "Each of these categories of illness is associated with a cluster of cognitive, affective, and behavioral states" (p. 337). However, for the Hopi symptoms which would be subsumed under the single psychiatric diagnostic category of depression are parsed out among different illnesses, each with its characteristic etiology and treatment. The importance of examining the clinical relevance of such cultural differences in categories of illnesses has yet to be appreciated (Edgerton, 1966; Jenkins, 1988; Marsella, 1980; White, 1982).

SOMATIZATION AND DEPRESSION

Where standard criteria and diagnostic interviews of clinical depression (ICD-9 and DSM-III) are systematically used together, the prevalence rates of depression are found to vary greatly across cultures. For example, findings range from 4.6 to 6.5% in the North American Epidemiological Catchment Area studies (Myers et al., 1984; Robins et al., 1984) to .15 to 3.3% in various studies in India (Rao, 1973). Among the highest rates in the world are those reported for Africa: 14.3% for men and 22.6% for women in Orley and Wing's (1979) Uganda research. But these rates also disclose a particularly salient cross-cultural similarity: Most cases of depression world-wide are experienced and expressed in bodily terms of aching backs, headaches, constipation, fatigue and a wide assortment of other somatic symptoms that lead patients to regard this condition as a physical problem for which they seek out primary care assistance from general practitioners (be they traditional or cosmopolitan). Only in the contemporary West is depression articulated principally as an intrapsychic experience (e.g., "I feel blue"), and even in the West most cases of depression are still lived and coped with as physical conditions (e.g., "my back aches"). The term applied to this phenomenon is *somatisation:* the expression of interpersonal and personal distress—e.g., frustration, despair, major depressive disorder—in an idiom of bodily complaints (Kleinman, 1986, 1988a). Kirmayer (1985) shows that whether somatization is a sociolinguistic or psychophysiological process, or both, remains unclear. The practical significance of somatization for cross-cultural studies of depression is that the models of depression based on studies of inpatients and outpatients in Western psychiatric settings tend to emphasize a picture of depression that is not the main one in non-Western societies (where the vast majority of the world's population and most of the depressed live). In many societies and subcultures, rules of politeness, absence of psychological linguistic terms, expression of emotion in nonverbal modes or in formal aesthetic forms such as poetry, and understanding of depression as a bodily experience lead to symptom pictures that may include little or no psychologically minded expression of dysphoria.

For this reason, depression may not be diagnosed, and DSM-III and ICD-9 categories, if used in the strict sense without an appreciation for subtlety and metaphor, may lack validity in non-Western settings or among certain ethnic populations. The forms of somatization show local cultural patterns, with neurasthenic patterns of complain common in East and South Asia and becoming popular again in the West under the rubric of chronic fatigue syndrome. Heart distress in Iran (Good, 1977), dizziness in China (Kleinman, 1986; Ots, 1990), gastrointestinal complaints among Cambodian and Vietnamese refugees in North America, physical sensations of the loss of soul or vital essence in a number of societies (Shweder, 1985), are examples of local illness idioms, final common pathways that express distress and disorder of many types, including depression (see Carr & Vitaliano, 1985). Somatization in the non-Western world, moreover, is not infrequently associated with parasitic infections, anemia owing to malnutrition, and other intercurrent physiological pathologies so that the bodily idiom of distress has a ready-made physiological basis, and one that also contributes to the onset of depression. Indeed, this is also a significant problem for diagnosis (Weiss & Kleinman, 1987), inasmuch as the symptoms of many medical disorders (e.g., anorexia, sleep disturbance, reduced energy, motor retardation) overlap with the vegetative complaints of depression, rendering diagnosis uncertain.

Somatization may also shape the course and outcome of depressive disorder. Where somatization rates are highest, guilt, low self-esteem and suicide tend to be less frequent (see Kleinman's 1988a review of this issue, pp. 42–45). On the other hand, somatization of major depressive disorder has routinely been found to delay effective treatment for depressive disorders and to contribute to minimal utilization of outpatient and in-patient services (Katon, Kleinman, & Rosen, 1982). Anecdotal reports from clinicians suggest that somatization of depression may "protect" depressed patients from morbid preoccupation with emotional states and thus reduces the likelihood of depression becoming a way of life. To the best of our knowledge this potentially significant proposition has never been investigated. We turn our attention now to cross-cultural examination of social factors and the onset of depression. Most prominent among these are gender, social class, family relations, refugee/migrant status, and social change.

GENDER AND DEPRESSION

An overwhelming number of Western studies of depressive disorder report a significantly higher rate of depression among women than men (Blazer et al., 1985; Craig & Van Natta, 1979; Howell & Bayes, 1981; Redloff, 1985; Weissman & Myers, 1978). In a critical review of these studies, Weissman and Klerman (1981) conclude that socially inculcated gender differences in susceptibility to depression are real, that is, not based on endocrinological or genetic factors, differences in helpseeking or affective expression, or methodological artifact. For Western societies, they cite the often-quoted evidence showing greater depression among married females (vs. married males) as illustrative of the conflicts generated by the traditional female role (1981:184). The classic study of Broverman et al. (1970) documenting a strong gender differentiation in clinicians' mental health ideals has frequently been cited as evidence of the inherent conflicts posed by sex-role stereotypes in the United States (Broverman et al., 1970, p. 322). For example, healthy women are said to differ from healthy men by being more submissive, less independent, more emotional, and so forth.

Recent epidemiological evidence from the multi-site NIMH Epidemiological Catchment Area (ECA) studies confirms gender differences in the prevalence of affective disorders within the United States. From the cities of Baltimore, New Haven, and St. Louis, Robins and associates (1984) reported disorders that most clearly predominated in men were antisocial personality and alcohol abuse. Disorders that most clearly predominated in women were depressive episodes and phobias. This finding was true of all three East Coast ECA sites.

Further evidence of female psychiatric vulnerability comes from the work of Brown and Harris (1978), who found that depression was extremely common among London working class women. In addition, they identified a set of specific vulnerability factors characteristic of the life circumstances of depressed women. These include lack of employment outside the home; absence of an intimate or confiding relationship with a husband/boyfriend; three or more small children in the home; and loss of mother prior to age eleven. Howell and Bayes (1981) formulate a similar set of risk factors, including lack of outside employment, the presence of young children, being employed in addition to household and childcare responsibilities (resulting in fatigue), family moves that follow the husband's employment and result in her own unemployment and/or social isolation. Indeed, "because of the particular constellation of environmental circumstances that rather universally characterizes married women in this culture, we are often to some extent diagnosing a *situation* rather than a *person* when we diagnose a woman as depressed" (Howell, 1981, pp. 154–155, italics in original).

Weissman and Klerman (1981) report that "The evidence in support of these [gender] differential rates is best established in Western industrial societies. Further studies in non-Western countries . . . are necessary before any conclusions can be drawn as to the universality of this differential rate" (p. 184). Although much more research is needed to map out cultural dimensions of the role of gender in predisposing individuals to depression, these authors appear to have been unaware of a small but suggestive anthropological literature from which hypotheses can be drawn.

For Africa, the most important early work was conducted by M. J. Field. Based on her study of Ghanaians seeking help at healing shrines, she reported that "depression is the commonest mental illness of Akan rural women" (1960, p. 149). Women who have recourse to the healing shrines tend to be of an age at which they should be reaping the benefits and social prestige customarily accorded to senior wives, but in many cases their positions have been undermined by their husbands' introduction of younger wives into the household. A common presenting complaint of these women is self-accusation of witchcraft. Among the Akan, witchcraft is a detested and highly stigmatized behavior; thus self-accusation indicates extremely low levels of self-esteem and self-worth.

Abbott and Klein (1979) also document depression as more common among rural Kikuyu women than men in Kenya, linking it with women's low status and concomitant powerlessness. In this culture, residence is patrilocal, and land is predominantly owned and controlled by the patrilineage. "Cultural beliefs and values regarding women generally devalue them, characterizing them as less intelligent than men, as rightly under the domination of men, and as belonging only to the home, the domestic space. Women are to defer to men" (1979, p. 181). In addition, two thirds of the men have left the community to seek wage labor in cities and towns, leaving women with the burden of horticultural labor and family responsibility (1979, p. 164). Abbott and Klein find that the least modernized women are at the greatest risk for depression, seeming to belie the common notion that modern urban life is more conducive to mental disorder than traditional rural life. However, we would suggest that in a region so much under the hegemonic sway of wage labor economy that two thirds of the men are absent, the self-definition of women may have been sociohistorically recast as "backward," hence reinforcing their subordinate status.

More recently, Mitchell and Abbott (1987) reported on the patterning of symptoms of depression and anxiety among Kikuyu secondary school students. The authors found significant gender differences in the responses revealing that females reported more depressive symptoms than males. While the extent of the gender differences in depression was not as great as in the earlier study by Abbott and Klein (1979), they are nonetheless consistent in showing a greater female preponderance of depression. This finding was also recently reported in Kenya by Ndetei and Vadher (1982). The observation that depression is an extremely common disorder among African women has been supported by Orley and Wing (1979), who found higher rates among Ugandan female villagers than among working class women in London. Orley and Wing documented depressive disorder among 14.3% of male Ugandan villages and 22.6% of female villagers.

Ullrich (1987) observed depression to be extremely common among Havik Brahmin women in a south Indian village. Ullrich argues that the traditional cultural ideal of women predisposes them to depression. Indeed, Beck's triad of negative self-image, negative interpretation of life events, and negative view of the future is regarded as the cultural ideal for older women. Additional factors that may lead to depression among women in this setting include early marriage age (an associated loss of contact with close kin), poor marital relationships, and the perception of helplessness. With cultural changes and an increase in marriage age, educational level, and decision-making, however, it now appears that this cultural bias against women is no longer fully sanctioned in this contemporary Indian village.

A striking age-related finding in the study by Karno and colleagues (1987) identifies the group most vulnerable to depression as young (18–39 years-of-age) non-Hispanic White women: over 15% of this subgroup had suffered major depression. Such age-specific vulnerabilities to depression have been noted elsewhere (Hirshfeld & Cross, 1982). These younger age cohort of Caucasian American women in the ECA study suffer disproportionately from major depression relative to men in either ethnic group or women of Mexican-descent. These findings are particularly alarming, and as noted by the authors, require further explication. Such results sound a cautionary note against simplistic reasoning concerning presumed cumulative effects of ethnicity, socioeconomic status, and gender in the absence of sociodemographic data on age. The importance of age-specific data is further borne out by Karno and colleagues' (1987) findings that dysthymia was most prevalent (9.4%) among older women (+40 years of age) of Mexican descent. Although the Puerto-Rican study did not provide age-specific data, dysthymia was also noted to be highly prevalent among women (7.6%) relative to men (1.6%) (Canino et al., in press-b).

These age-related findings also raise the question of the relationship of traditional female roles and vulnerability to depression. Prudo, Harris, and Brown

(1984) found that the types of severe life events associated with depression varied with the degree of integration into traditional society. As among African women (Abbott & Klein, 1979; Field, 1960), Hispanic women have been identified as a population at high risk for the development of depressive disorders (Mendes de Leon, 1988; Richman, 1987; Torres-Matrullo, 1982; Vega et al., 1984; Zavalla, 1984). In the United States, this group has been considered particularly vulnerable by virtue of gender and ethnic minority status, and often, lower socioeconomic status as well (Mirande & Enriquez, 1979; Zavalla, 1984). From Los Angeles, a cross-cultural component of the Epidemiological Catchment Area survey (Karno et al., 1987) was designed to include Mexican-descent populations. Major depressive episodes showed:

> a surprising ethnicity effect among women, with non-Hispanic white women under 40 years of age showing 2.5 times the rate of Mexican-American women. These differences disappear in those over the age of 40. A strong trend is present for greater prevalence of total affective disorders on the part of young non-Hispanic white women compared with young Mexican-American women. Dysthymia shows a trend toward greater prevalence among Mexican women over 40 compared with their non-Hispanic white counterparts. (p. 699)

Recent lifetime prevalence data from epidemiological studies utilizing the Diagnostic Interview Schedule (DIS) confirm a gender vulnerability (Canino et al., in press-b; Karno et al., 1987). Among a Puerto Rican sample, Canino et al. (in press-b) found significantly higher depression and dysthymia among women. Gonzales (1978) found that Puerto Rican women who had been diagnosed as neurotic or depressive and were receiving treatment had sex-role orientations significantly more traditional than did comparison (normal healthy) housewives and students. Torres-Matrullo (1982) found a high incidence of symptoms of dependence among nonacculturated mainland Puerto Rican women. "Feelings of inferiority, low-self-esteem, psychosomatic complaints, and premature marriages and parenthood among Hispanic women have been regarded as resulting from the traditional female role" (Canino, 1982, p. 123). However, empirical research is necessary for a more sophisticated understanding of gender roles in Hispanic culture, since characterizations of women in the current literature are overly simplistic:

> It is questionable whether most functional Hispanic traditional women are as subjugated, passive, and dependent on the male as the literature depicts them to be. But the question still remains as to how can we explain the higher incidence of psychopathology found among traditional Hispanic women. Is it that the role per se induces psychopathology? Or is it that dysfunction occurs more often when the woman is in a societal and family context where the traditional role is not valued, but on the contrary, is maladaptive and conflictive? (Canino, 1982, p. 124)

In light of the foregoing cross-cultural studies, we can advance the hypothesis that epidemiological studies in the Third World will reveal a disparity between female and male rates of depression broadly similar to that documented in Western societies. This hypothesis is lent credence by the nearly universal structural subordination of women cross-culturally (Collier, 1987; Farnham, 1987; Lamphere, 1987; Rosaldo & Lamphere, 1974; Sanday, 1981). Nonetheless, overall rates are likely to vary for women relative to local factors such as child socialization practices, variations in control over resources, marriage patterns, and cultural ideology and value orientations surrounding gender relations. Moreover, there are exceptions. In one epidemiological survey, Carstairs and Kapur (1976) found a higher rate of depression among men than women in a rural region of southwestern India. However, in that matrilineal society there is considerable social dislocation due to newly legislated patrilineal inheritance patterns.

SOCIOECONOMIC STATUS AND DEPRESSION

Hirshfeld and Cross (1982) recently summarized the relationship of social class to depressive disorders in Western settings: "Whether defined by occupational, income, or educational level or a combination of these, there is strong evidence that rates of depressive symptoms are significantly higher in persons of lower SES than in persons of higher social class" (p. 39). Indeed, this association has been similarly reported by numerous investigators (e.g., Craig & Van Natta, 1979; Radioff, 1985; Weissman & Boyd, 1983). However, rates of unipolar depressive disorder have also been found to be exceptionally high among upper SES professional women (Welner, Marten, & Wochnick, 1977). Reviewing lifetime prevalence of depression in a community survey, Weissman & Myers (1978) similarly reported a vulnerability to depression among the upper social classes.

Studies of general psychiatric disability and unemployment have typically shown a strong relationship between economic conditions and admissions to treatment. Brenner (1973) conducted a survey of psychiatric hospitalizations in the United States between 1914 and 1967 to show that economic downturns were associated with increased rates of hospitalization. In an extensive review of research on schizophrenia and economic conditions, Warner (1985) cites evidence of the higher prevalence of schizophrenia found in lower social classes, except during times of full employment. He noted that outcomes, such as the degree of impairment in social functioning, are linked to the type of economic structures within social groups. During periods of unemployment in wage labor economies, for example, recovery is poor relative to patient outcomes within agrarian peasant societies. In light of current epidemiological data, similar hypotheses could also be advanced for depressive disorders.

As noted before, in London, England, Brown and Harris (1978) found that working class women had a rate of depression four times higher than middle-class women. Working class women were likely to suffer a depressive episode in the year prior to research contact if they had certain vulnerability factors (e.g., lack of a close confiding relationship with a husband/boyfriend; unemployment) and had experienced a severe life event (e.g., death in the family). Findings such as these raise the obvious question of whether qualitatively different life conditions may engender vulnerability to depressive disorders, and thereby account for the association between SES and depression.

Brown and Harris (1978) lay the groundwork for empirical investigation of this issue by elaborating research methods to document life events and life difficulties. They begin with the caveat that there is ". . . nothing to suggest there is any difference in the appraisal of adversity in the differing social classes in Camberwell . . . working-class women simply have more" (p. 191). (Similar observations about the cumulative and "objective" effects of oppressive life circumstances among the poor have been reported by other investigators [Hirschfeld & Cross 1982]). In addition, because their material conditions are more tenuous than their middle-class counterparts, they suffer more in response to loss or disappointment. Brown and Harris pinpoint the subgroup of lower SES women with children living at home as experiencing the greatest number of *severe* life events. Examples of such events include learning that a husband has cancer, losing a job at short notice, son killed while at play, evicted by landlord, being forced to have an unwanted abortion because of poor housing conditions, overdose taken by schoolage daughter. For chronic depressive conditions, the higher rates of depression for working class women hold across all life stages, and are not restricted to those with children living at home.

This work suggests that attention to adverse life events may contribute a valuable element of specificity to broad-based findings about social class and vulnerability to depression. Studies which have begun to follow this lead include a comparison of depressed and normal controls in Kenya that found significantly more life events among depressed patients in the 12 months preceding onset (Vahder & Nedetei, 1981). In an independent line of research Paykel (1978) has also documented the precipitation of clinical depression by stressful life events. Brown and his colleagues have continued to increase the specificity of the relation between particular types of severe life events and characteristics of women at risk (Brown, Bifulco, & Harris, 1987; for a methodological critique of Brown's earlier work see Tennant & Bebbington, 1978).

Consistent with the approach adopted by meaning-centered medical anthropology (Good & Good, 1982) is the finding that the most important aspect of life events is the meaning attributed to specific and cumulatively distressing life circumstances. Rather than the impact of change per se being deleterious to one's mental health, it is the personally incorporated cultural meanings of those events that appears to be of crucial importance (Brown, 1974; Brown & Harris, 1978;

Day et al., 1987). Moreover, social supports have routinely been shown to be less available and more fragile for lower socioeconomic persons. Inasmuch as this feature of the social environment also predicts for depressive onset, comparative studies of the meaning of supports would seem to be another avenue for future cross-cultural research. From the anthropological standpoint, stressors and supports are systematically bound together within local social systems. These systems may protect individuals (and categories of individuals) from major social pressures or may render them particularly vulnerable to forces of deprivation, oppression, or loss (Kleinman, (1986), forces which can create local vicious cycles of demoralization and defeat. The anthropological perspective calls for a different methodology for measuring stress and support, one that takes into account the ethnographic description of the changing social contexts within which events are perceived, experienced, and managed.

Relatively scant attention, on the whole, has been allotted to the question of socioeconomic status and depression cross-culturally. This is in part due to the difficulty of obtaining valid indicators of social stratification and class variation, on the one hand, and the paucity of cross-cultural studies on depression, on the other. However, these studies consistently report that the least educated have higher depression scores (e.g., Abbott & Klein, 1979; Vega et al., 1984; Zavalla, 1984). Moreover, the other major component of social class, employment, is also linked to depressive illness (Dressler, 1986; Ndetei & Vadher, 1982). Dressler and Badger (1986) found that among Blacks in the southern United States unemployment was significantly related to higher depressive symptomatology, independent of other demographic factors or stressful life circumstances. These findings support the general conclusion that unemployment engenders a substantial risk for the development of depression.

DEPRESSION AMONG REFUGEES AND IMMIGRANTS

Recently, there has been a proliferation of studies of the relation between political exile and depressive disorders. Depressive illness is apparently quite common among Southeast Asian refugees (Beiser, 1985; DeLay & Faust, 1987). In a survey of 97 Hmong adult refugees in the U.S., Westermeyer (1988) found a very high rate of psychiatric and social disorder that included major depressive illness. A group that was found to be particularly vulnerable to depression was unmarried Laotian and Vietnamese refugees, who showed high levels of depression in the 1–12 months following their arrival. Other investigators have also found depression to be extremely common among Vietnamese refugees in primary clinic settings.

In an Indochinese clinic population in the United States, many of the patients had concurrent diagnoses of major affective disorders, posttraumatic stress disorder, and medical and social disabilities resultant from a history of trauma and torture (Mollica, Wyshak, & Lavelle, 1987, p. 1567). The most vulnerable subgroup identified by these investigators was unmarried women. These women, typically the victims of rape and torture in the natal countries, suffered the most severe psychiatric and social impairment.

A protective factor identified for Indochinese refugees in the U.S. is living arrangements with families of similar cultural background: refugees in these settings were found to be significantly less depressed and had better school performance than those who lived in foster homes with Caucasian families or in group homes. Beiser (1988) investigated the issue of whether resettlement in Canada is associated with an increased risk for depression among Southeast Asian refugees, and found that better mental health was enjoyed by refugees the longer they remained in Canada. Length of time after displacement was also found to be associated with decreased symptom levels in a study of Iranian immigrants to the United States (Good, Good, & Moradi, 1985).

In Africa, the prevalence of depressive symptomatology among Namibian refugees residing in a sub-Saharan host country was quite high (Shisana & Celentano, 1985). These authors also found that social support helped to ameliorate the effects of chronic stress, as represented by the length of time in exile, but that depressive symptomatology was to be understood as directly associated with difficulties incurred by the problems posed by the stressors of adaptation and acculturation.

Vega et al. (1986) conducted a large survey of immigrant Mexican women in southern California. Using the Center for Epidemiological Studies Depression checklist (CES-D), they determined that there was an inverse association between CES-D scores and number of years in the United States. Depression has also been reported as extremely common among Mexican immigrants in Northern California, and has been linked to the difficulties associated with living conditions that include racism, unemployment, crowded and unsanitary living situations, and nondocumented legal status (Ring & Munoz, 1987).

In a study of Iranian immigrants to the United States Good, Good, and Moradi (1985) document the interplay of cultural themes, sociopolitical events, and depressive disorder. Iranians interpret and communicate depressive symptoms in relation to elements already thematized in Iranian culture: sadness and grief are essential qualities of life elaborated in Shi'ite religious culture and popular literature, insecurity and mistrust are common interpersonal themes especially with regard to interpersonal relations and marital fidelity; uncontrolled anger is a culturally marked and stigmatized sign of depression; and emotional "sensitivity" acquired through early childhood experience is a common personality self-attribution. The experience of depression consequent to political deracination is shaped by these four cultural themes.

A factor analytic study of psychiatric symptom levels assessed with the Brief Symptom Index (BSI) in a nonclinical population of Jewish Iranian women immigrants suggested the presence of a distinctly Iranian depressive syndrome, the symptoms of which cross-cut the pre-established categories of the Western-based epidemiological instrument. Based on cross-sectional analysis, reported symptom levels peak at 2 years postmigration and decline thereafter, a time frame which the authors suggest is typical of a grieving process and indicates that the culturally elaborated grieving process remains intact for these immigrants. Among types of losses reported, including loss of wealth, home, and one's "very life," the lowest symptom levels were found among those emphasizing loss of friends. In line with their association of the grieving process with adjustment to the immigrant experience, Good, Good, and Moradi (1985, p. 413) suggest that "the ability to have and to mourn the loss of close friendships is a mark of a healthier immigrant" (see also Good & Good, 1988). However, longitudinal studies are necessary to separate adaptation processes from cohort effects.

Research is only now becoming available on depression among political refugees from Central America (Williams, 1987), especially El Salvador and Guatemala (Guarnaccia & Farias, 1988; Jenkins, 1989), and much more attention will need to be paid to this topic as these groups continue to enter the United States. In the clinical/research experience of the first author (JJ) and her Latino colleagues from a specialty Latino clinic in a Boston area hospital, depression, among other psychiatric disorders (e.g., dysthymia, panic disorders and posttraumatic stress syndromes) is very frequent, and is apparently due to the after effects of political violence and inhospital life conditions in American urban settings. While forced uprooting and difficulties of acculturation are sources of distress, political oppression and turmoil also clearly have an effect independent of migration.

DEPRESSION AND FAMILY FACTORS

While the influence of early developmental experience for subsequent onset of depression has long been presumed in psychoanalytic circles (e.g., Arieti, 1959; Robertson, 1979), empirical evidence for Western or cross-cultural examination of such theories has been lacking. In a recent review Campbell (1986, p. 47) notes the surprising paucity of research on the family and depressive disorders. Nonetheless, there have been hypotheses concerning the etiology of depression in relation to cultural variations in socialization practices and family structure. Several family contextual factors have been examined, including number of primary caretakers (for presumed minimization of child frustration), family cohesiveness and extended networks, values orientations, and self-structures (Engelsman, 1982). Eaton and Weil (1955) have linked family cohesiveness and patriarchal structure to rates of depression.

In a recent study by Weissman and colleagues (1984), depressive illness was found to be three times more likely among children who had parents with major depression. As noted by Campbell (1986), "the extent to which the increased depression is due to genetics versus the family environment has not been determined and requires adoption studies similar to those used in schizophrenia" (p. 48). And, as with studies of schizophrenic disorders, identification of specific family factors that are of etiological significance is problematic in depression research. A major dilemma is the difficulty of identifying factors that reliably distinguish between "disturbed" and "normal" families. For example, in a study of child rearing behavior in Swedish and Dutch samples, Arrindell et al. (1986) found family "rejection" and "emotional warmth" to be similarly present among families of depressed patients and healthy controls.

On the other hand, several investigators have found major differences in the qualitative features of family life that may lead to psychiatric vulnerability. Zavalla (1984) has documented significant differences in negative parental experiences among depressed Mexican-descent women. Mothers were reported to have been indifferent, strict, or authoritarian by 33% of her sample of depressed women (which contradicts the culturally prescribed ideal of Mexican mothers as warm, indulgent, and protective). In her sample of depressed women, 42% reported their fathers as indifferent, strict, authoritarian, and abusive. In Zavalla's thoroughgoing investigation of psychosocial and sociodemographic factors related to depression, reports of negative child-rearing experiences emerges as the most significant factor for the development of clinical depression. Parker (1983) found that a sample of depressed patients considered their parents to be aloof, controlling, and overprotective compared to controls or other illness groups.

The clinical and research experience of numerous cross-cultural investigators has led them to assign dysfunctional family dynamics an instrumental role in the genesis of disorder (e.g., Campbell, 1986; Rogler & Hollingshead, 1965; Scheper-Hughes, 1979). For ethnic minority groups, family dysfunction is complicated by acculturation pressures. Canino (1982) links these two factors, and argues that acculturation pressures among dysfunctional Puerto Rican families are more likely to compound one another in ways that are less disruptive among more high functioning families.

This line of investigation has been criticized with regard to the validity of subjective, retrospective accounts by persons who are (by selection criteria) troubled with psychiatric illness. Formidable as these difficulties are, however, the methodological dilemma posed should not result in either the dismissal or eclipse of life history materials for the role of psychocultural and family factors in the development of affective disorders. Among the methods to improve the reliability of patient reports are corroborative evidence obtained from other sources, such as family members, and school and medical records (Brown, 1981).

Marital discord has been widely acknowledged as a vulnerability factor for depression, particularly in women. Brown and Harris (1978) identified the lack of a confiding relationship with a husband or boyfriend as particularly important. Paykel et al. (1969) noted that the onset of a depressive episode is frequently preceded by an increase in arguments with a spouse. Indeed, during an active illness episode, depressed women report a variety of interpersonal difficulties with families, including arguments and quarrels (Weissman & Paykel, 1974). Thus gender variation in the prevalence of depressive disorder appears to be related to qualitative features of marital or family life, such as intimacy (Brown & Harris, 1978; Vega et al., 1984).

However, since the etiological relevance of family factors remains unsubstantiated, some researchers have turned their attention instead to an examination of how such features may affect the course and outcome of psychiatric disorder. This shift in emphasis began with psychosocially and cross-culturally oriented schizophrenia research. In the late 1950s, Brown and his colleagues developed a methodology for assessing particular aspects of the family emotional environment and observed how these affected the course of illness. This line of investigation, which has come to be known as "expressed emotion" (EE) research, focuses on family response to and attitudes toward a relative who had been hospitalized for an acute psychotic episode. The EE index measures criticism, hostility, and emotional overinvolvement expressed about the patient by close family members. Brown, Birley, and Wing (1972) found that high levels of criticism and overinvolvement were associated with poor prognosis, and that high EE predicted schizophrenic relapse none months subsequent to hospital discharge.

This British study was replicated among English-speaking populations in the United Kingdom (Vaughn & Leff, 1976) and the United States (Vaughn et al., 1984), and among Mexican immigrants to the United States (Karno et al., 1987). Results of the Mexican study confirmed the significance of "expressed emotion" (EE) to outcome, and that EE could be employed in a culturally meaningful way in Spanish within a distinctively different cultural context (Jenkins, Karno, & de la Selva, in press). This cross-cultural validation, however, required adaptation of the scales to culturally appropriate expressive styles and values of interpersonal relations within families.

In the English replication by Vaughn and Leff (1976), EE research was extended to a sample of "neurotic depressed" patients. The average number of critical comments for this group of relatives was the same as for schizophrenic patients, indicating that there were no illness-specific family response styles (Leff & Vaughn, 1985). However, it was discovered that depressed patients relapsed at a significantly lower threshold of criticism than the schizophrenic sample. Thus it appears that depressed patients are even more sensitive to negative affects than are their schizophrenic counterparts. A more recent study of 39 depressed patients found that negative expressed emotion on the part of spouses significantly predicted the course of illness: 59% of the patients with high EE spouses relapsed, whereas *no* patients living with low EE spouses did so (Hooley, Orley, & Teasdale, 1986). These results provide further support for those originally obtained by Vaughn and Leff (1976). EE research has been extended to families of schizophrenic patients in India, but we are not aware of cross-cultural studies of EE among the families of depressed patients.

A much neglected area of research into psychiatric disorder and familial relationships concerns how the illness comes to affect the family (Good, Good, & Burr, 1983; Jenkins et al., 1986; Jenkins, 1988a, 1988b; Kleinman, 1980, 1988). Sartorius (1979) has estimated that over 100 million persons in the world suffer from depression and that perhaps three times that many persons are affected by their suffering. Coyne and his colleagues (1987) have summarized a wide range of literature on the role of close relationships in the etiology, course, and outcome of depression, and the negative impact of depression on close relationships:

> Interactions between depressed persons and their relatives are negative and conflictual. It seems such a familial environment would take its toll on relatives as well as on depressed persons. A depressed family member may provide a major source of stress and a loss of social support, which could trigger a disturbance in vulnerable persons. Indeed, there is evidence that spouses of depressed persons often have family histories of psychiatric disturbance and thus may be prone to affective disturbance (p. 347).

To date, there is no evidence to support a generalization of this conclusion, since the cross-cultural study of family and community response to depressive disorders is a neglected area of inquiry. Among areas that must be documented before generalizations can be made are culturally based conceptions of depression, criteria by which depression is indigenously recognized and identified, and explanatory models of depressive illness. Likewise, documentation of cultural coping responses is contingent on community resources, the structure of interpersonal social networks, and intrafamilial styles of expressed emotion.

DEPRESSION AND SOCIAL CHANGE

Tsung-Yi Lin and his colleagues in Taiwan have demonstrated that rapid urbanization, industrialization and related social changes in that society from the late 1940s to the middle 1960s were accompanied by escalating rates of depression and anxiety disorders (Lin et al., 1969). Yeh et al. (1987) found that this increase persisted and even worsened in the 1970s and '80s. Leighton and his coworkers (1963) in the celebrated Sterling County Study showed that the social breakdown of a community correlated with measured rates of mental distress, including depression and anxiety complaints. These epidemiological studies are complemented by ethnographic and historical accounts of increased hopelessness, despair and demoralization in the wake of community changes that place large numbers of persons under the severest pressures of economic dislocation, unemployment, lack of resources and supports, intensified oppressive relationships and dependency (see, for example, Warner, 1985). Brenner (1981) has shown, as already noted, that economic depressions forecast increases in mental hospitalization and suicide, indirectly indicating that depressive conditions are very likely more frequent. Kleinman (1986), studying the survivors of the Great Proletarian Cultural Revolution in China, found that, among vulnerable individuals, macrosocial calamity frequently provoked depressive conditions, especially in local settings where victims were least protected by the community. All of these indicators register the relationship of depressive disorders to major social historical transformation. That these changes are most commonly not examined in clinical and epidemiological research suggests that a more fundamental large-scale social impact may be significant in the onset of depression and its recurrence than has heretofore received study.

METHODOLOGICAL PROBLEMS IN CROSS-CULTURAL RESEARCH ON DEPRESSION

Psychiatric epidemiology relies on instruments to elicit self reports of symptoms and on standardized clinical interviews, nearly all developed in Western cultural settings and with North American and European patient populations. Given the variability of depressive symptoms and disorders cross-culturally, the use of standard instruments must evoke strong methodological caution. Whereas both validity and reliability have been of great concern in Western psychiatric research, with instruments growing out of wide clinical experience, cross-cultural research has focused almost exclusively on the reliability of research methods. When instruments developed for use in the West are directly translated for use in non-Western settings, several methodological difficulties are hidden, however careful the translation. These may be summarized as five problems of cross-cultural method (see Good & Good, 1986).

1. The Problem of Normative Uncertainty. All psychiatric ratings are ultimately grounded in culturally specific and locally defined judgments about normal and abnormal behavior. Interpretations of individual symptoms or behaviors, of level and duration of symptoms, and of scalar values all require assumptions be made about what is abnormal for a particular culture.

Cross-cultural and cross-group comparisons of symptom checklist data raise particular problems. For example, researchers have consistently found higher levels of psychological symptoms among Puerto Ricans than other American populations (Dohrenwend & Dohrenwend, 1969; Srole et al., 1962). Still unresolved is whether levels of psychiatric illness are actually higher among Puerto Ricans or whether this represents culturally prescribed differences in communicating symptoms. Many researchers (e.g., Haberman, 1976) have concluded the latter, that is, that differences reflect culturally patterned variations in ways of *expressing* distress rather than actual degree of pathology. Such problems bedevil interpretations not only of cross-cultural data, but also comparisons between men and women and among ethnic groups. Researchers often elect either to compare scores derived from standard psychometric instruments administered across groups directly, assuming comparability of scores, or, alternatively, to develop norms and compare groups controlled for differences in norms.

Diagnostic judgments face similar problems. Not only is symptom (dysphoria, loss of energy, feelings of worthlessness) grounded in judgments about normality, so also are determinations of threshold and duration. The distinction between dysthymia and major depression is a case in point. The two are currently distinguished by duration and number of symptoms. To count as dysthymia an illness must be "not of sufficient severity and duration to meet criteria for a major depressive episode (although major depressive episode may be superimposed on dysthymia). Clear "cutoff points" between normal dysphoria and pathological depression or between dysthymia and major depression have never been definitively demonstrated within our own culture. Assuming that such a threshold exists in principle, there seems little empirical reason to believe that it is the same across cultures, since cultures incorporate dysphoria into normative behavior in varying ways (Good, Good & Moradi, 1985; Jenkins, 1988a, 1988b; Manson et al., 1985; Obeyesekere, 1985; Toussignant, 1984).

2. The Problem of Centricultural Bias. Wober (1969) has labeled those research strategies that begin with a research instrument developed and validated exclusively in one culture and directly translate them into languages for use in other cultures as "centricultural." Difficulties associated with the centricultural approach can be illustrated by cross-cultural variation in the content of symptoms. For example, the Yoruba literature (Murphy, 1982) indicates that anxiety disorders are associated with three primary clusters of symptoms: worries about fertility, dreams of being bewitched, and bodily complaints (Collis, 1966; Jegede, 1978). As noted earlier, research by an Ibo psychologist indicates that a rich somatic vocabulary is typical of Nigerian psychiatric patients (Ebigbo, 1982). For instance, patients commonly complain that "things like ants keep on creeping in various part of my brain," or "it seems as if pepper were put into my head," in a manner that would be interpreted in nearly any North American patient as psychotic.

Such differences in symptoms raise two very clear difficulties for research following the centricultural approach to translating diagnostic criteria and epidemiological instruments. First, a wide range of symptoms typical of a particular culture may simply be omitted from consideration because they are not present for the development of the criteria. Second, differences in content and duration of symptoms of diagnostic significance across cultures are ignored. Simple translation of those symptoms found to result in valid diagnosis among particular

American populations does not ensure the validity of these symptoms as criteria among other cultures.

3. The Problem of Indeterminacy of Meaning. The most typical approach to the translation of psychiatric diagnostic criteria is to locate *semantic equivalents.* Items are translated from English into a non-Western language, then back-translated into English to check for accuracy in translation, and finally administered to bilingual subjects. As Good and Good (1986) note, "Such a method assumes the existence of objective and universal referents, which may be represented by different symbolic forms in different cultures." However, most psychiatric symptoms have no such extracultural referents. Guilt, shame, and sinfulness, which could be combined as a single item on the DIS, had to be carefully distinguished for Hopi Indians (Manson et al., 1985, p. 341). Even seeming physiological symptoms, such as 'heart palpitations,' belong to extraordinarily different semantic and phenomenological domains across cultures (see Good 1977), rendering determination of equivalence of meaning extremely difficult.

4. The Problem of Narrative Context. As we have noted, peoples express symptoms differently across cultures. However, this same point also applies across specific intracultural *contexts.* Thus, how a patient presents his or her problem in a clinical office consultation with a physician might be quite a different representation than is conveyed at home to a close relative or friend. For this reason, the sampling of patients' complaints in different contexts—at home, with primary care practitioners, with native healers, in a church healing ritual— may well give a very different picture of a patient's symptoms, accounting for disagreements in reports of such phenomena as somatization (Cheung 1982, 1984; Good & Good 1988; Jenkins 1988b; Kleinman 1986).

5. The Problem of Category Validity. We have raised the problem of whether depressive disorders can be identified through the use of universal categories. While we have little doubt that some forms of depression are found in all populations, at issue are such questions as whether some forms of the illness, experienced primarily in psychological terms associated with strong feelings of remorse and guilt, are to be equated with that experienced primarily in sociosomatic terms (Kleinman & Good, 1985). The problems raised about norms and equivalence of meaning thus point to more fundamental questions about mapping even culturally appropriate symptoms onto universal categories. Only research that directly examines this issue can tell us whether particular categories are universal or whether seeming universality is produced as an artifact of research and clinical method.

In the limited space available we can only briefly refer to several efforts to develop or revise psychiatric research instruments for cultural validity. Mollica, Wyshak, de Marneffe, & LaVelle (1987, p. 497) developed and validated a

Cambodian, Laotian, and Vietnamese version of the Hopkins Symptom Checklist-25. This abbreviated assessment instrument provides an effective screening method for symptoms of depression and anxiety, and was found to be particularly useful in evaluating trauma victims. The Beck Depression Inventory has been validated for use in Arabic (West, 1985) although the mistake must not be made of assuming that such an instrument will be valid in all Arabic cultures.

Researchers attempting to develop a Hispanic variant of the Diagnotic Interview Schedule (DIS) were able to obtain useful results with a somewhat modified translation among Mexicans (Karno et al., 1987), but found it necessary to prepare substantially different version for Puerto Ricans (Canino et al., in press-a) due to ethnic variations in Spanish vocabulary and usage, as well as cultural norms concerning inquiries into sexual behavior. Manson and colleagues (1985) developed a Hopi translation of the DIS based on a three-stage process of eliciting culturally meaningful mental illness categories and identifying their criterial symptoms, developing a Hopi diagnostic interview, and translating relevant portions of the DIS to be combined with the indigenous categories in a new instrument. Given the cultural specificity of somatic symptomatology among Nigerians, Ebigbo (1982) found it necessary to develop a culture-specific screening scale for psychiatric assessment. Fava (1983) conducted a study to validate an Italian language version of the CES-D, and concluded that it could sensitively discriminate between depressed patients and normals. These studies, though preliminary in several instances, represent a significant methodological advance over literal translation of research instruments, by taking into account cultural differences in the experience and presentation of depressive symptomatology. Valid cross-cultural research requires that such methodological adaptations should be actively pursued. Given the current investment in translating instruments such as the DIS for cross-cultural epidemiological studies, collaboration between anthropologists, local clinicians, and epidemiologists and new standards for cross-cultural epidemiological research are urgently needed in the field.

DIRECTIONS FOR FUTURE RESEARCH

In light of the methodological discussion, we suggest that cross-cultural research on depression emphasize the relationship of depression to the local context to assure cultural validity. The examination of cultural contexts is the domain of ethnographic research. Although the specific methods of ethnography are too diverse to summarize here, in general terms, ethnography is concerned with the description of patterns of shared cultural meaning, behavior, and experience. Ethnographic methods range from observational analysis to detailed interview data and can be applied in the domains of public culture and individual or family settings. The medical ethnographer observes individuals not just in the role of patient but in that of spouse, parent, worker, neighbor, and so forth. The ethnographer may therefore spend many hours conducting these observations of individuals in different situations and settings. An ethnographic approach to the contextualization of variables (e.g., life events, expressed emotion, explanatory models) can be of value in examining the complexity of the social origins and consequences of depression. For example, while we have substantial evidence that "expressed emotion" is associated with the course and outcome of depression (Karno et al., 1987; Vaughn & Leff, 1976; Vaughn et al., 1984), we know relatively little about how or why this factor mediates illness careers. Ethnographic observational data of everyday family life may contribute toward the specification of these relationships in culturally meaningful terms (Jenkins, Karno, & de la Selva, in press).

Another advantage of ethnographic methods is their ability to establish the validity of analytic categories where what is taken for granted in the social life of subjects—cultural assumptions and ground rules—challenges the conceptual underpinnings of those categories. The difficulty with these approaches is that close reading of cultured meaning and behavior precludes extensive surveys, random sampling, and large sample sizes, all of which are necessary for reliable testing of hypotheses. The complementarity of these approaches is fundamental, and no researcher attempting cross-cultural studies in mental health should exclude an ethnographic component of research.

The foregoing discussion also suggests that much more attention must be given to the intricacies of personal relations in cultural context. As we have seen, the work of Brown and his colleagues has demonstrated the importance of social response—"expressed emotion"—to schizophrenic and depressive outcomes. A series of interrelated hypotheses suggested by this work might be as follows. If someone is considered (by self *and* others) as worthless, lacking in energy, excessively worrying, it may be particularly debilitating, for "if one takes this behavior personally or otherwise becomes emotionally overinvolved, the burden . . . can be aggravated" (Coyne et al., 1987, p. 351). If, however, depressive symptoms and social response are not influenced by cultural frameworks of personal blame or fault, then outcome is likely to be more favorable. Again, if the illness behavior is somatized and the illness conception does not incorporate personality attributions about either the afflicted or affected, course of illness and social response of kin groups may be less debilitating or distressing (Kleinman, Good, & Guarnaccia, 1986). Testing these hypotheses requires careful documentation of cultural meanings as they are brought into play in particular interactive settings.

Cross-cultural variations in notions of the self may also be associated with the course of depressive disorders (Marsella, 1980). Major differences in sociocentric versus egocentric orientations to the self, accompanied by respective kin-group or individualistic values, may temper the process of self-identification with dysphoric affects and bodily states. On the one hand, it could be hypothesized that a more sociocentric sense of self would provide protection from a near complete ego-identification with depressive states. On the other hand, it could also be that a more relationally identified sense of self could predispose to greater susceptibility to others' troubles and difficulties. Such hypotheses have been advanced for women's mental health status, but as of yet have not been adequately tested. More specific understandings of vulnerability of women to stress and depressive illness are required. As noted earlier, future research that seeks to examine the interactive processes and contextual specificities of depressive disorder can be productively pursued through ethnographic techniques.

In conclusion, we agree with Marsella et al. (1985) "that cultural factors constitute an important context for all aspects of depressive experience and disorder and they must be considered if an accurate understanding of depression is to be achieved" (p. 300). Likewise, we concur with Sartorius (1986), who calls for a more central role for comparative research in determining the nature of depression: "Properly conducted cross-cultural research can yield results which can help to resolve the conundrum of depression and respond to the challenge which depression poses to the society, to public health authorities, and to the individuals who suffer from it" (p. 6). Such research is critical to resolving the dual shortcomings in current literature on this subject, in which depression is not granted an ontological status on a par with physical diseases by anthropologists, and is stripped of personal and cultural meanings by biological psychiatrists.

REFERENCES

Abbott, S., & Klein, R. (1979). Depression and anxiety among rural Kikuyu in Kenya. *Ethos, 7,* 161–188.

Arieti, S. (1959). Manic depressive psychosis. In S. Arieti (Ed.), *Symptoms of psychopathology: A handbook.* New York: Wiley.

Arrindell, W., Perris, C., Perris, H., Eisemann, M., Van-der Ende, J., & Von-Knorring, L. (1986). Cross-national invariance of dimensions of parental rearing behaviour: comparison of psychometric data of Swedish depressives and healthy subjects with Dutch target ratings on the EMBU. *British Journal of Psychiatry, 148,* 305–309.

Beiser, M. (1985). A study of depression among traditional Africans, urban North Americans, and Southeast Asian refugees. In A. Kleinman & B. Good, (Eds.), Culture and Depression: *Studies in the anthropology and cross-cultural psychiatry of affect and disorder.* Berkeley: University of California Press.

Beiser, M. (1988). Influences of time, ethnicity, and attachment on depression in Southeast Asian refugees. *American Journal of Psychiatry, 145*(1), 46–51.

Blazer, D., George, L. K., Landerman, R., Pennybacker, M., Melville, M., Woodbury, M., Manton, K., Jordan, K., & Locke, B. (1985). Psychiatric disorders: A rural/urban comparison. *Archives of General Psychiatry, 42,* 651–656.

Brenner, R. (1981). *Mental illness and the economy.* Cambridge, MA: Harvard University Press.

Briggs, J. (1970). *Never in anger: Portrait of an Eskimo family.* Cambridge, MA: Harvard University Press.

Broverman, I., Vogel, S. R., Broverman, D. M., Clarkson, F. E., & Rosenkrantz, P. S. (1970). Sex-role stereotypes and clinical judgments of mental health. *Journal of Consulting and Clinical Psychology, 34*(1), 1–7.

Brown, G. W. (1974). Meaning, measurement and stress of life events. In B. S. Dohrenwend & B. P. Dohrenwend, (Eds.), *Stressful life events: Their nature and effects.* New York: Wiley.

Brown, G. W. (1981). Life Events, psychiatric disorder and physical illness. *Journal of Psychosomatic Research, 25*(5), 461–473.

Brown, G. W., Bifulco, A., & Harris, T. (1987). Life Events, vulnerability and onset of depression: Some refinements. *British Journal of Psychiatry, 150,* 3–42.

Brown, G., & Harris, T. (1978). *Social origins of depression: A study of psychiatric disorder in women.* London: Tavistock.

Brown, G., Birley J., & Wing, J. (1972). Influence of family life on the course of schizophrenic disorders: a replication. *British Journal of Psychiatry, 121,* 241–258.

Campbell, T. (1986). Family's impact on health: A critical review and annotated bibliography. U.S. Department of Health and Human Services, Public Health Service, National Institute of Mental Health. Rockville, Maryland.

Canino, G. (1982). The Hispanic woman: Sociocultural influences on diagnoses and treatment. In R. Becerra, M. Karno, & J. Escobar. (Eds.), *Mental health and Hispanic Americans.* New York: Grune & Stratton.

Canino, G., Bird, H.,Shrout, P., Rubio-Stapec, M.,Bravo, M.,Martinez, R., Sesman, M., Guzman, A., Guevara, L., & Costes, H. (in press-a). The Spanish DIS: reliability and concordance with clinical diagnoses in Puerto Rico. *Archives of General Psychiatry.*

Canino, G. J., Bird, H., Shrout, P., Rubio, M., Bravo, M., Martinez, R., Sesman, M., & Guevara, L. (in press-b). The prevalence of specific psychiatric disorders in Puerto Rico. *Archives of General Psychiatry.*

Carr, J. E., & Vitaliano, P. P. (1985). The theoretical implications of converging research on depression and the culture-bound syndromes. In A. Kleinman & B. Good, (Eds.), Culture and depression: *Studies in the anthropology and cross-cultural psychiatry of affect and disorder.* Berkeley: University of California Press.

Carstairs, G. M., & Kapur, R. L. (1976). *The great universe of Kota: Stress, change and mental disorder in an Indian village.* Berkeley: University of California Press.

Chagnon, N. (1977). *Yanomamo: The fierce people.* New York: Holt, Rinehart & Winston.

Cheung, F. M. (1982). Psychological symptoms among Chinese in urban Hong Kong. *Social Science and Medicine, 16,* 1339–1344.

Cheung, F. M. (1984). Preferences in help-seeking among Chinese students. *Culture, Medicine, and Psychiatry, 8,* 371–380.

Collier, J. (1987). *Marriage and inequality in classless societies.* Stanford, CA: Stanford University Press.

Collis, R. (1966). Physical health and psychiatric disorder in Nigeria. *Transactions of the American Philosophical Society, 56*(4), 1–45.

Coyne, J., Kessler, R., Tal, M., Turnbull, J., Wortman, C., & Greden, J. (1987). Living with a depressed person. *Social Science and Medicine, 55*(3), 347–352.

Craig, T., & Van Natta, P. (1979). Influence of demographic characteristics on two measures of depressive symptoms: The relation of prevalence and persistence of symptoms with sex, age, education, and marital status. *Archives of General Psychiatry, 36,* 149–154.

Day, R., Nielsen, J., Korten, A., Ernberg, G., Dube, K., Gebhart, J., Jablensky, A., Leon, C. A., Marsella, A., Olatawura, M., Sartorius, N., Stromgren, E., Takahashi, R., Wig, N., & Wynne, L. C. (1987). Stressful life events preceding the acute onset of schizophrenia: A cross-national study from the World Health Organization. *Culture, Medicine, and Psychiatry, 11*(2), 123–206.

DeLay, P., & Faust, S. (1987). Depression in Southeast Asian refugees. *American Family Physician, 36*(40), 179–184.

Dohrenwend, B. P., & Doh renwend, B. S. (1969). *Social status and psychological disorder: A causal inquiry.* New York: Wiley Interscience.

Dressler, W. (1986). Unemployment and depressive symptoms in a southern black community. *Journal of Nervous and Mental Disorders, 174*(11), 639–645.

Dressler, W., & Badger, L. (1986). Epidemiology of depressive symptoms in black communities: A comparative analysis. *Journal of Nervous and Mental Disorders, 173*(4), 212–220.

Eaton, J., & Weil, R. (1955). *Culture and mental disorders.* New York: Free Press of Glencoe.

Ebigbo, P. (1982). Development of a culture specific (Nigeria) screening scale of somatic complaints. *Culture, Medicine, and Psychiatry, 6,* 29–44.

Edgerton, R. (1966). Conceptions of psychosis in four East African societies. *American Anthropologist, 68,* 408–425.

Ekman, P. (1982). *Emotion in the human face.* New York: Cambridge University Press.

Engelsmann, F. (1982). Culture and depression. In I. Al-Issa, (Ed.), *Culture and psychopathology.* Baltimore: University Park Press.

Farnham, C. (1987). The same or different? In C. Farnham, (Ed.), *The impact of feminist research in the academy.* Indiana University Press.

Fava, G. (1983). Assessing depressive symptoms across cultures: Italian validation of the CES-D self-rating scale. *Journal of Clinical Psychology, 39*(2), 249–251.

Field, M. J. (1960). *Search for security: An ethnopsychiatric study of rural Ghana.* Evanston, IL: Northwestern University Press.

Gaines, A., & Farmer, P. (1986). Visible saints: Social cynosures and dysphoria in the Mediterranean tradition. *Culture, Medicine, and Psychiatry, 10*(4), 295–330.

Geertz, C. (1984). "From the native's point of view": On the nature of anthropological understanding. In R. Shweder & R. LeVine, (Eds.), *Culture theory: Essays on mind, self, and emotion.* New York: Cambridge University Press.

Geertz, C. (1973). *The interpretations of cultures.* New York: Basic Books.

Geertz, C. (1980). *Negara: The theatre state in nineteenth-century Bali.* Princeton, NJ: Princeton University Press.

Geertz, H. (1959). The vocabulary of emotion: A study of Javanese socialization processes. *Psychiatry, 22*(3), 225–237.

Gonzales, L. G. (1978). *Relacion entre vision hacia los roles sexuales, actualizacion personal y problemas de salud mental en tres grupos de mujeres.* Tesis de maestria, Universidad de Puerto Rico, Departamento de Psicologia.

Good, B. (1977). The heart of what's the matter. *Culture, Medicine, and Psychiatry,* 25–38.

Good, B., & Good, M.-J., (1982). Toward a meaning-centered analysis of popular illness: categories "fright illness" and "heart distress" in Iran. In A. Marsella & G. White, (Eds.), *Cultural conceptions of mental health and therapy.* Boston: D. Reidel.

Good, B., & Good, M.-J., (1986). The cultural context or diagnosis and therapy: a view from medical anthropology. In M. Miranda & H. Kitano, (Eds.), *Research and practice in minority communities.* Medical Health. Washington, U.S. Government Planning Office, NIMH.

Good, M.-J., & Good, B. (1988). Ritual, the state, and the transformation of emotional discourse in Iranian society. *Culture, Medicine and Psychiatry, 12,* 43–63.

Good, B. J., Good, M.-J., & Burr, B. D. (1983). Impact of Illness on the Family: Disease, Illness, and the Family Trajectory. In R. B. Taylor, (Ed.), *Family medicine: Principles and practice* (2nd ed.). New York: Springer-Verlag.

Good, B., Good, M.-J., & Moradi, R. (1985). The interpretation of Iranian depressive illness and dysphoric affect. In A. Kleinman & B. Good (Eds.), *Culture and depression: Studies in the anthropology and cross-cultural psychiatry of affect and disorder.* Berkeley: University of California Press.

Guarnaccia, P., & Farias, P. (1988). The Social Meanings of *nervios*. A case study of a Central American woman. *Social Science and Medicine, 26,* 1223–1232.

Haberman, P. W. (1976). Psychiatric symptoms among Puerto Ricans in Puerto Rico and New York City. *Ethnicity, 3,* 133–134.

Hirschfield, R. M., & Cross, C. (1982). Epidemiology of affective disorders: Psychosocial risk factors. *Archives of General Psychiatry, 39,* 35–46.

Hooley, J., Orley, J., & Teasdale, J. (1986). Levels of expressed emotion and relapse in depressed patients. *British Journal of Psychiatry, 148*, 642–647.

Howell, E. (1981). The influence of gender on diagnosis and psychopathology. In E. Howell & M. Bayes (Eds.). *Women and mental health*. New York: Basic Books.

Izard, C. (1977). *Human emotions*. New York: Plenum Press.

Jegede, R. O. (1978). Outpatient psychiatry in an urban clinic in a developing country. *Social Psychiatry, 13*, 93–98.

Jenkins, J. H. (1988a). Conceptions of schizophrenia as a problem of nerves: a cross-cultural comparison of Mexican-Americans and Anglo-Americans. *Social Science and Medicine, 26*(12), 1233–1244.

Jenkins, J. H. (1988b). Ethnopsychiatric Interpretations of Schizophrenic Illness: The problem of *nervios* within Mexican-American Families. *Culture, Medicine, and Psychiatry, 12*(3), 303–331.

Jenkins, J. H. (1989). *Neither here nor there: Depression and trauma among Salvadoran women refugees*. Paper presented at the annual meeting of the American Anthropological Association, Washington, D.C.

Jenkins, J. H., & Karno, M. (in press). Inside the black box called "expressed emotion": A theoretical analysis of the construct in psychiatric research.

Jenkins, J. H., & Karno, M., & de la Selva, A. (in press). *Expressed Emotion among Mexican-descent families: Cultural adaptation and principal findings*.

Jenkins, J. H., Karno, M., de la Selva, M., & Santana, F. (1986). Expressed emotion in cross-cultural context: Familial responses to schizophrenic illness among Mexican-Americans. In M. J. Goldstein, I. Hand & K. Hahlweg, (Eds.), *Treatment of schizophrenia: Family assessment and intervention*. New York: Springer-Verlag.

Jenkins, J. H., Karno, M., de la Selva, A., Santana, F., Telles, C., Lopez, S., & Mintz, J. (1986). Pharmacotherapy, expressed emotion and schizophrenic outcome. *Psychopharmacology Bulletin, 22*(3), 621–627.

Karno, M. et al. (1987). Lifetime prevalence of specific psychiatric disorders among Mexican American and non-Hispanic whites in Los Angeles. *Archives of General Psychiatry, 44*, 695–701.

Karno, M., Jenkins, J. H., de la Selva, A., et al. (1987). Expressed emotion and schizophrenic outcome among Mexican-American families. *Journal of Nervous and Mental Disorders, 175*(3), 143–151.

Katon, W., Kleinman, A., & Rosen, G. (1982). The prevalence of somatization in primary care. *Comprehensive Psychiatry, 25*(2), 208–215.

Kirmayer, L. (1985). Culture, affect, and somatization. Parts 1 and 2. *Transcultural Psychiatric Review, 21(3)*, 159–218 & (4), 237–262.

Kleinman, A. (1980). *Patients and healers in the context of culture: An exploration on the borderland between anthropology, medicine, and psychiatry*. Berkeley: University of California.

Kleinman, A. (1986). *Social origins of distress and disease: Depression, neurasthenia, and pain in modern China*. New Haven: Yale University Press.

Kleinman, A. (1988a). *Rethinking psychiatry*. New York: Free Press.

Kleinman, A. (1988b). *The illness narratives*. New York: Basic Books.

Kleinman, A., & Good, B. (1985). Epilogue. In A. Kleinman & B. Good (Eds.), *Culture and depression: Studies in the anthropology and cross-cultural psychiatry of affect and disorder*. Berkeley: University of California Press.

Kleinman, A., Good, B., & Guarnaccia, P. (1986). *Critical review of selected cross-cultural literature on depressive and anxiety disorders:* Final report under a contract for NIMH.

Lamphere, L. (1987). Feminism and anthropology: The struggle to reshape our thinking about gender. In C. Farnham, (Ed.), *The impact of feminist research in the academy*. Bloomington: Indiana University Press.

Leff, J., & Vaughn, C. (1985). *Expressed emotion in families: Its significance for mental illness.* New York: The Guilford Press.

Leighton, D. C., Harding, J. S., Macklin, D. B., MacMillan, A., & Leighton, A. (1963). *The character of danger.* New York: Basic Books.

Levy, R. (1973). *Tahitians: Mind and experience in the Society Islands.* Chicago: University of Chicago Press.

Levy, R. (1984). Emotion, knowning, and culture. In R. Shweder & R. LeVine, (Eds.). *Culture theory: Essays on mind, self, and emotion.* New York: Cambridge University Press.

Lin, T.-Y., et al. (1969). Mental disorders in Taiwan: 15 years later. In W. Caudill & T.-Y. Lin, (Eds.). *Mental health in Asia and the Pacific.* Honolulu: East-West Center Press.

Lutz, C. (1985). Depression and the translation of emotional worlds. In A. Kleinman & B. Good (Eds.), *Culture and depression: Studies in the anthropology and cross-cultural psychiatry of affect and disorder.* Berkeley: University of California Press.

Lutz, C. (1988). *Unnatural Emotions: Everyday sentiments on a Micronesian atoll and their challenge to Western theory.* University of Chicago Press.

Manson, S., Shore, J., Bloom, J. (1985). The depressive experience in American Indian communities: A challenge for psychiatric theory and diagnosis. In A. Kleinman & B. Good (Eds.), *Culture and depression: Studies in the anthropology and cross-culture psychiatry of affect and disorder.* Berkeley, University of California Press.

Marsella, A. (1980). Depressive experience and disorder across cultures. In H. Triandis & J. Draguns, (Eds.), *Handbook of cross-cultural psychology. Vol. V. (Psychopathology).* Boston: Allyn and Bacon.

Marsella, A., Sartorius, N., Jablensky, A., & Fenton, F. (1985). Cross-cultural studies of depressive disorders: An overview. In A. Kleinman & B. Good (Eds.), *Culture and depression: Studies in the anthropology and cross-cultural psychiatry of affect and disorder.* Berkeley: University of California Press.

Marsella, A., DeVos, G., & Hsu, F. (Eds.). (1985). *Culture and self: Asian and Western Perspectives.* New York: Tavistock Publications.

Mendes de Leon, C-F. (1988). Depressive symptoms among Mexican Americans: a three-generation study. *American Journal of Epidemiology, 127*(1), 150–160.

Mirande, A., & Enriquez, E. (1979). *LaChicana: The Mexican-American woman.* University of Chicago Press: Chicago.

Mitchell, S., & Abbott, S. (1987). Gender and symptoms of depression and anxiety among Kikuyu secondary school students in Kenya. *Social Science and Medicine, 24*(4), 303–316.

Mollica, R., Wyshak, G., & Lavelle, J. (1987). The psychosocial impact of war trauma and torture on Southeast Asian refugees. *American Journal of Psychiatry, 144*(12), 1567–1572.

Mollica, R., Wyshak, G., de Marneffe, D., Khuon, F., Lavelle, J. (1987). Indochinese versions of the Hopkins symptom checklist-25: A screening instrument for the psychiatric care of refugees. *American Journal of Psychiatry, 144*(4), 497–500.

Murillo, N. (1976). The Mexican-American family. In *Chicanos: Social and psychological perspectives.* St. Louis: C. V. Mosby Co.

Murphy, H. B. M. (1982). *Comparative psychiatry: The International and Intercultural Distribution of Mental Illness.* New York: Springer-Verlag.

Myers, F. (1979). Emotions and the self: A theory of personhood and political order among Pintupi Aborigines. *Ethos, 7*(4), 343–370.

Ndetei, D., & Vadher, A. (1982). A study of some psychological factors in depressed and nondepressed subjects in a Kenyan setting. *British Journal of Medical Psychology, 55*(3), 235–239.

Obeyesekere, G. (1985). Depression, Buddhism, and the work of culture in Sri Lanka. In A. Kleinman & B. Good (Eds.), *Culture and depression: Studies in the anthropology and cross-cultural psychiatry of affect and disorder.* Berkeley: University of California Press.

Ochs, E., & Schieffelin, B. (1984). Language acquisition and socialization: three developmental stories and their implications. In R. Shweder & R. LeVine, (Eds.), *Culture theory: Essays on mind, self, and emotion.* New York: Cambridge University Press.

Orley, J., & Wing, J. K. (1979). Psychiatric disorders in two African villages. *Archives of General Psychiatry, 36,* 513–557.

Ots, T. (in press). The angry liver, the anxious hear, and the depressed spleen: Somatization, the role of emotions, and the language of physical symptoms in traditional Chinese medicine. *Culture, Medicine, and Psychiatry.*

Parker, G. (1983). Parental "affectionless control" as an antecedent to adult depression: A risk factor delineated. *Archives of General Psychiatry, 40,* 956–960.

Paykel, E. (1978). Contribution of life events to causation of psychiatric illness. *Psychological Medicine, 8,* 245–254.

Paykel, E., Myers, J., Dienelt, M., et al. (1969). Life events and depression: A controlled study. *Archives of General Psychiatry, 21,* 753–760.

Plutchik, R. (1980). A language for the emotions. *Psychology Today, 13*(9), 68–78.

Prudo, R., Harris, T. & Brown, G. (1984). Psychiatric disorder in a rural and an urban population: Social integration and the morphology of affective disorder. *Psychological Medicine 14*(2), 327–345.

Radloff, L. (1985). Risk factors for depression: What do we learn from them? In *Essential papers on depression.* New York University Press.

Rao, A. V. (1973). Depressive illness and guilt in Indian Culture. *Indian Journal of Psychiatry, 15,* 231–236.

Richman, J. (1987). Societal sex role changes and ethnic values: Psychological issues for Hispanic women. In M. Gaviria & J. Arana., (Eds.). *Health and Behavior: Research Agenda for Hispanics.* The Simon Bolivar Research Monograph Series No. 1. University of Illinois at Chicago.

Ring, J., & Munoz, R. (1987). *The Mexican immigrant and depression: perspectives on treatment and prevention.* Paper presented at the First Binational conference on Mexico-U.S. migration. Guadalajara, Mexico.

Robertson, B. M. (1979). The psychoanalytic theory of depression. *Canadian Journal of Psychiatry, 24*(4), 341–352 & 24(6), 557–574.

Robins, L., Helzer, J., Weissman, M., Orvaschel, H., Gruenberg, E., Burke, J., & Regier, D. (1984). Lifetime prevalence of specific psychiatric disorder in three sites. *Archives of General Psychiatry, 41,* 949–958.

Rogler, L. H., & Hollingshead, A. B. (1965). *Trapped: Families and schizophrenia.* New York: Wiley.

Rosaldo, M. (1983). The shame of headhunters and the autonomy of self. *Ethos, 11*(3), 135–151.

Rosaldo, M. (1984). Toward an anthropology of self and feeling. In R. A. Shweder & R. A. LeVine, (Eds.), *Culture theory; Essays on mind, self, and emotion.* New York: Cambridge University Press.

Rosaldo, R., & L. Lamphere, (Eds). (1974). *Women, culture, and society.* Stanford: Stanford University Press.

Sanday, P. (1981). *Female power and male dominance.* Cambridge, England: Cambridge University Press.

Sartorius, N. (1986). Cross-Cultural research on depression. *Psychopathology. 19 Suppl. (Review), 2,* 6–11.

Sartorius, N. (1979). Research on affective psychoses within the framework of the WHO programme. In M. Schou & E. Stromgren, (Eds.), *Origin, prevention and treatment of affective disorders.* London: Academic Press.

Scheper-Hughes, N. (1979). *Saints, scholars, and schizophrenics: Mental illness in rural Ireland.* Berkeley: University of California Press.

Schieffelin, E. (1983). Anger and shame in the tropical forest: On affect as a cultural system in Papua, New Guinea. *Ethos, 11*(3), 181–191.

Shisana, O., & Celentano, D. (1985). Depressive symptomatology among Manibian adolescent refugees. *Social Science and Medicine, 21*(11), 1251–1257.

Shweder, R. (1985). Menstrual pollution, soul loss, and the comparative study of emotions. In A. Kleinman & B. Good (Eds.), *Culture and depression: Studies in the anthropology and cross-cultural psychiatry of affect and disorder.* Berkeley: University of California Press.

Shweder, R., & Bourne, E. (1984). Does the concept of the person vary cross-culturally? In *Culture theory: Essays on mind, self, and emotion.* New York: Cambridge University Press.

Shweder, R., & LeVine, R. (Eds.). (1984). *Culture theory: Essays on mind, self, and emotion.* New York: Cambridge University Press.

Srole, L., Langer, T., Michael, S., et al. (1962). *Mental health in the metropolis: The midtown Manhattan study.* New York: McGraw-Hill.

Tennant, C., & Bebbington, P. (1978). The social causation of depression: a critique of the work of Brown and his colleagues. *Psychological Medicine, 8*, 565–575.

Torres-Matrullo, C. (1982). Cognitive therapy of depressive disorders in the Puerto Rican female. In R. Becerra, M. Karno, & J. Escobar, (Eds.), *Mental health and Hispanic Americans: Clinical perspectives.* New York: Grune and Stratton.

Toussignant, M. (1984). *Pena* in the Ecuadorian Sierra: A Psychoanthropological analysis of sadness. *Culture, Medicine, and Psychiatry, 8*, 381–398.

Ullrich, H. (1987). A study of change and depression among Havik Brahmin women in a south Indian village. *Culture, Medicine, and Psychiatry, 11*(3), 261–287.

Vahder, A., & Nedetei, D. M. (1981). Life events and depression in a Kenyan setting. *British Journal of Psychiatry, 139*, 134–37.

Vaughn, C., & Leff, J. (1976). The influence of family and social factors on the course of psychiatric illness. *British Journal of Psychiatry, 129*, 125–137.

Vaughn, C., Snyder, K., Jones, S., Freeman, W., & Falloon, I. (1984). Family factors in schizophrenic relapse: a California replication of the British research on expressed emotion. *Archives of General Psychiatry, 41*, 1169–1177.

Vega, W., Kolody, B., Valle, R., & Hough, R. (1986). Depressive symptoms and their correlates among immigrant Mexican women in the United States. *Social Science and Medicine, 22*(6), 645–652.

Vega, W., Warheit, G., Buhl-Auth, J., Meinhardt, K. (1984). The prevalence of depressive symptoms among Mexican Americans and Anglos. *American Journal of Epidemiology, 120*(4), 592–607.

Warner, R. (1985). *Recovery from schizophrenia: Psychiatry and political economy. London:* Routledge and Kegan Paul.

Weiss, M., & Kleinman, A. (1987). Psychosocial and cross-cultural issues in depression: A prolegomenon for culturally informed research. In P. Dassen, N. Sartorius, et al., (Eds.), *Psychology, culture and health:* Toward applications. Beverly Hills, CA: Sage.

Weissman, M., & Boyd, J. (1983). The epidemiology of bipolar and nonbipolar depression: rates and risks. In J. Angst (Ed.), *The origins of depression: Current concepts and Approaches.* New York: Springer-Verlag.

Weissman, M., & G. Klerman. (1981). Sex differences and the epidemiology of depression. In E. Howell & M. Bayes, (Eds.), *Women and mental health.* New York: Basic Books.

Weissman, M., & Myers, R. (1978). Affective disorders in a U.S. urban community: the use of research diagnostic criteria in an epidemiological survey. *Archives of General Psychiatry, 335*, 1302–1311.

Weissman, M., & Paykel, E. (1974). *The depressed woman: A study of social relationships.* Chicago: University of Chicago Press.

Weissman, M. M., Prusoff, B., Gammon, G. D., Merikangas, K., Leckman, J., & Kidd, K. K. (1984). Psychopathology in children (ages 6–18) of depressed and normal parents. *Journal of the American Academy of Child Psychiatry, 23*, 78–84.

West, J. (1985). An Arabic validation of a depression inventory. *International Journal of Social Psychiatry, 31*(4), 282–84.

Westermeyer, J. (1988). DSM-III psychiatric disorders among Hmong refugees in the United States: a point prevalence study. *American Journal of Psychiatry, 145*(2), 197–202.

White, G. (1982). The ethnographic study of cultural knowledge of "mental disorder." In A. Marsella & G. White (Eds.), *Cultural conceptions of mental health and therapy*. Dordrecht, Holland: D. Reidel.

White, G., & Kirkpatrick, J. (1985). *Person, self, and experience: Exploring Pacific ethnopsychologies*. Berkeley: University of California Press.

Wierzbicka, A. (1986). Human emotions: Universal or culture-specific? *American Anthropologist, 88*(3), 584–594.

Williams, C. (1987). *An annotated bibliography on refugee mental health*. U.S. Department of Health and Human Services. National Institute of Mental Health. U.S. Government Printing Office, Washington, D.C.

Wober, M. (1969). Distinguishing multi-cultural from cross-cultural tests and research. *Perceptual and Motor Skills, 28*, 488.

Yeh, E. K., et al. (1987). Social changes and prevalence of specific mental disorders in Taiwan. *Chinese Journal of Mental Health, 3*(1), 31–42.

Zavalla, I. (1984). *Depression among women of Mexican descent*. Unpublished doctoral dissertation, University of Massachusetts, Department of Psychology.

4 Life Stress and Depression

Scott M. Monroe
University of Pittsburgh

Richard A. Depue
University of Minnesota

> *I hesitate to refer to such banalities as mental stresses in these days when the quest for the obscure and the terror of the obvious has become a cult.*
> —Mapother (1926)

Life stress, or closely allied concepts, have long been associated with depression. Described under varied labels such as pressure, strain, tension, turmoil, conflict, reactivity, reaction sets, and so on, the idea encompasses psychosocial circumstances thought to instigate the onset of at least some forms of the disorder. To explain such psychopathology, then, conceptual models typically have contained some representation of this tension between person and social circumstances. The relative importance of life stress in these descriptive frameworks, however, has been a topic of enduring dispute. As illustrated by Edward Mapother's remarks from over a half a century ago on "mental stresses" and mood disorders, these concepts have cycled through successive eras of attempts to understand the genesis of depression.

Contemporary viewpoints on life stress and depression reflect this controversial heritage. Reviews of recent research typically suggest a general association exists between the two (Brown & Harris, 1986; Lloyd, 1980; Monroe & Peterman, 1988; Paykel, 1982). Yet, while many authorities conceptualize stress as a central determinant of the disorder (Brown & Harris, 1978, 1986; Cooke & Hole, 1983; Finlay-Jones, 1981; Katschnig, 1986a), others relegate stress to a more peripheral role in the complex of factors that lead to depression (e.g., Clayton, 1986; Tennant, 1983; Tennant, Bebbington, & Hurry, 1981a). These differing contentions may well be attributable to two concerns. First, approaches to research in this area over the past 2 decades have adopted several different conceptual and measurement viewpoints in relation to life stress. Second, the complex temporal interplay between stress and depression over time precludes simple summary analyses of cause and effect. These two concerns serve as the foci for the present chapter, in which we (a) outline the historical underpinnings of present conceptual and methodological controversies; (b) elaborate the contemporary counterparts of these divided opinions; and (c) discuss recent work with explicit attention to procedural limitations and their implications for research and theory on the relations between life stress and depression. Our goal is to distinguish the "banalities" that may accompany empirical research on as complex a construct as life stress from the more theoretically fertile components of the concept. This, it is hoped, will provide for a broader understanding of the role that life stress may play in depression: the inception, termination, and recurrence of the disorder over an individual's lifetime.

HISTORICAL BACKGROUND

Given the tendency of people to associate changes in daily moods and behaviors with ambient social circumstances, people have commonly explained more extreme and unusual emotional disturbances as a result of more severe and distinctive psychosocial circumstances. This is, of course, a core premise of the stress model. Yet the history behind the idea, and the continuing controversy it has engendered with respect to depression, are virtually as old as the earliest written accounts of the disorder.

Depression Without Stress

Since antiquity, accounts of depression have referred to the symptoms of "sadness without reason" as one frequent feature of the disorder (Klibansky, Panofsky, & Saxl, 1979). More recently, Kraepelin (1928) and his contemporaries characterized such forms of depression as being mostly "*independent of external influences*" (p. 181). The meaning of such statements is that depression can occur in the absence of environmental circumstances that are commonly believed to be of causal importance. This view of depression—arising independent of environmental stressors—subsequently lead to the concept of classical endogenous depression (i.e., a form of depression unrelated to stress; possessing distinctive symptoms; and assumed to be due to biological factors; see Jackson, 1986, pp. 315–317).

The endogenous perspective, then, is based on observations that many depressions seem to arise within relatively benign psychosocial contexts. Note also that while some writers endorsed a clear-cut disjunction between the onset of depression and associated social circumstances, others acknowledged a partial relation by noting the disproportionate nature of the misery relative to environmental conditions. Both varieties of depression onset were incongruent with explanatory models based on mood regulation caused by social circumstances, and instead typically were accounted for by biological theories of etiology.

On the other hand, psychological factors have long been popular explanations for depression. Rufus of Ephesus, whose writings date to the second century A.D. and were highly influential for over 1500 years, believed that the activity of the mind was a direct cause of depression (Klibansky et al., 1979). According to Pinel (1806), exciting causes could include "very vivid affections of the mind, such as ungovernable or disappointed ambition, religious fanaticism, profound chagrin, and unfortunate love" (p. 113). Other commonly cited psychosocial themes in the history of depression included "losses, disappointments, failures, and excessive mental activity" (Jackson, 1986, p. 315–317). Once again, however, the "disproportionate" nature of these reactions to the various adversities was often mentioned, and the similarity in the syndromes between stress "provoked" and "unprovoked" depressions was noted or implied.

Some depressions, then, apparently rose out of innocuous psychosocial circumstances. Some apparently arose out of understandable adversities. And many arose out life conditions that were ambiguous with respect to their psychosocial plausibility. Yet despite ostensibly different origins or immediate precipitants, depressions appeared to have widely overlapping clinical form. One of the most enduring and puzzling paradoxes of mood disorders research was thereby posed: How is it that for some individuals depression seems to arise "out of the blue," and for others it seems to originate, at least partly, out of psychosocial adversities?

Models of Stress-Depression Interactions

The paradox of depression—that life stress may be significantly related to some depressions but not to others—usually has been explained in two ways. The first is a unified perspective, wherein the same, or fundamentally similar, depressive syndromes occur as the result of diverse psychosocial and biological mechanisms. That is, diverse conditions—separate and/or together—lead to alterations in a common pathophysiology that results in depression. Such an integrated conceptualization was characteristic of historical explanations of depression (see Jackson, 1986). The contemporary counterpart of this viewpoint postulates that many different factors suspected of bringing about depression are integrated within a collective framework through their varying, yet often united, influences upon a final common pathway (e.g., Akiskal, 1979).

The second approach to resolving the paradox has been to propose two or more distinct disorders that are phenotypically similar, yet derive from fundamentally different etiologies. Life circumstances could play a role, or different roles, in one or more of the postulated subtypes of depression. The inception of such ideas once again can be traced far back to earlier times, wherein variants of depression were believed to exist (e.g., acquired versus innate forms of the disorder; Klibansky et al., 1979). Again, contemporary models of depression often posit two or more subtypes of depression, with life stress playing different roles in the onset of the respective subtypes (e.g., Klein, 1974; Willner, 1985).

A vast array of diagnostic subtypes and classification schemes for depression have evolved as a result of this second approach (see Lewis, 1934). In structuring these nosological systems, life stress has often been invoked as a central feature by both its presence and its absence. In particular, such classifications as psychogenic, reactive, situational, and neurotic have all been used to imply an important contribution by psychosocial factors to the development of particular subtypes of depression; endogeneity, melancholia, and psychotic have referred to subtypes often conceived as unrelated to life stress and originating from biologic susceptibilities. Much of contemporary research on mood disorders is directed toward a finer analysis of such subgroup distinctions, with one goal being a better grasp of how life stress may fit into—and help define by its presence, absence, or partial involvement—such distinctions (Depue, 1979; Depue & Monroe, 1978, 1983, 1986).

Life stress, then, could be an essential factor, an element of variable magnitude, or an unrelated component in the etiology of any particular depression or in the etiology of any particular depressive subtype. Such flexible formulations initially appear satisfying: they are capable of reconciling disparate observations into a common explanatory framework. Yet they may also possess a potential elusiveness regarding the role of stress in depression, for they can conspire against falsification of stress theory. For instance, when stress exists prior to depression onset, it is attributed at least partial etiological significance. When stress is *not* apparent before the disorder develops, either (a) other etiologic agents are invoked, or (b) other subtypes of depression are postulated.

The problem is that multifactorial models and multiple subtypes of the disorder create a cloud of alternative explanations that can obscure the true role of stress. This is particularly so when research practices do not take care to specify the conditions under which stress is and is not operative. In both instances, the circumstances under which stress is more or less likely to lead to depression should be clearly defined before the fact. This means that the alternative etiologic influences, and/or respective subtypes of disorder, should be specified *a priori* (e.g., stress is less influential for individuals with biological markers, such as reduced REM latency, or for individuals with strong family history of depression; cf. McGuffin, Katz, & Bebbington, 1988; Kupfer, 1986). *Post hoc* speculation on etiology and classification must be avoided, for stress is too easily invoked or discarded within such loose conceptual schemes.

As currently conceptualized, the role of stress in depression can lend itself to rather evasive hypotheses. Ambiguity in theory is further complicated by challenges in operationalizing the family of concepts comprised by life stress. In fact, the predicament with current theory may be traced in part to the diverse connotations associated with stress, and the implications of these connotations for defining and measuring the construct. We outline the sources of this important concern next.

Life Stress: Incarnations and Connotations

Over the centuries during which the term stress has been part of the English vocabulary, its semantics have varied. According to some sources, stress was used in the 14th century to indicate hardship, adversity, or affliction (Lazarus & Folkman, 1984; Lumsden, 1981). In the 15th century, stress became a shortened version of "distress" (Rees, 1976). Since these times, many additional terms have been invoked that connote some form of tension between the individual and his or her life's challenges, often also incorporating some notion of subjective discomfort (Cooper, 1986; Hinkle, 1977; Mason, 1975a, 1975b; Selye, 1976). The longevity of these concepts—albeit protean in form, variable in popularity, and rich in meanings—is in itself a curiosity. What is it about this network of associated ideas, all united ultimately within some notion of tension between the person and aspects of the environment, that accounts for their enduring explanatory appeal?

A few points merit attention with respect to the persistence of stress as a concept. First is the perception of the ubiquitousness of stress. Second is the ease with which stress lends itself to ready explanations of all sorts of ills. As Rosen (1957) reminds us, John Hawkes' comments in 1857 have a surprisingly modern tone:

> I doubt if ever in the history of the world, or the experiences of past ages, could show a larger amount of insanity than that of the present day. It seems, indeed, as if the world was moving at an advanced rate of speed proportionate to its approaching end; as though, in this rapid race of time, increasing with each revolving century, a higher pressure is engendered on the minds of men and with this; there appears a tendency among all classes constantly to demand higher standards of intellectual attainment, a faster speed of intellectual travelling, greater fancies, greater forces, larger means than are commensurate with health.

A century later, yet before the proliferation of research on stress began in the late 1960's, Garmany (1958) warned:

> The problem is one of exceptional difficulty because of the universal human tendency to seek causes for the effects it witnesses. Thus it happens that both the patient with the endogenous depression and his relatives may produce all kinds of apparent aetiological factors, many of which are really the results or content of the illness rather than its cause.
>
> Life is full of troubles, and it is statistically not unlikely that, whenever an

endogenous depression begins, some traumatic incident will have preceded it, so that the one is regarded as the result of the other (p. 342).

These quotations reflect alluring aspects of the concept of stress, easily obscured by its apparently obvious meaning. The intuitive appeal of the idea conceals the variety of connotations subsumed by the term, some of which may be informative, some of which may be only superficially seductive. Three points are most relevant. First, stress is readily perceived, given life's continuous demands and vicissitudes. Since people tend to search for causes to explain the experiences in their lives, and it is easy to ascribe causality to those circumstances that simply precede the situation to be explained, stress is a readily available explanatory concept. Second, the perceived pervasiveness of stress conveniently couples with the persuasiveness of its plausibility. As a culturally sanctioned justification for a variety of ills, stress easily can become a false but subjectively satisfying refuge. Finally, and perhaps most importantly, if stress did not exist prior to a depression, considerable stress exists during or after its onset. The symptoms of depression almost invariably create additional stressors (e.g., lack of concentration and energy commonly results in work stress, irritability and social withdrawal result in interpersonal difficulties). Depression, simply put, is stressful. This confounding can be compounded further, for the transition into a depressive state can be relatively insidious. Over time, stress can be a cause, correlate, or consequence of depression (Monroe & Steiner, 1986).

The concept of stress, then, possesses a variety of meanings, some of which may too easily play into human tendencies to explain away emotional ills (Brown, 1974). This underscores the need to carefully define the construct in a manner that leads to adequate measurement procedures that avoid, or control for, such tendencies. These issues are elaborated next.

CONCEPTUAL AND MEASUREMENT ISSUES IN LIFE-STRESS RESEARCH

Despite long-standing speculation on the implications of life's adversities for health and well-being, only in relatively recent times have operational definitions of stress permitted more systematic testing of the premises of the construct. A major concern is how adequately these approaches control for the potential confounding between stress as a cause, consequence, or correlate of depression.

Definitional and Conceptual Issues

The potential breadth of the stress concept precludes uniformity of opinion. Virtually any life experience can be construed under its heading. Indeed, the definition of stress offered by Hans Selye, the founding father of the modern physiological stress tradition, is "the nonspecific response of the body to any demand made upon it" (Selye, 1976). A consonant extension of this definition to human study was provided by the early advocates of life events research, wherein any experience that entailed change or "readjustment" was included in the life events checklist (Holmes & Rahe, 1967). Pursuant to these initial attempts to specify what is "stress," a number of definitions have appeared in the literature (see Lazarus & Folkman, 1984). Recent efforts to unite these varied viewpoints, however, have led to concepts and definitions of stress that may be ill-suited for research on the psychosocial conditions leading to depression.

Definitional Diversity and Conceptual Diffusion. Despite intense interest in stress over the past 2 decades, little consensus has been reached on basic definitional issues (Elliot & Eisdorfer, 1982; Lazarus & Folkman, 1984). Viewpoints on this topic vary along many dimensions, including the types of experiences that constitute stressful encounters (e.g., undesirable events versus changes in routine), temporal parameters (e.g., acute events, chronic conditions, intermittent stressors), and frequency-severity differences (e.g., infrequent major severe events versus common daily hassles; Kanner, Coyne, Schaefer, & Lazarus, 1981). Oftentimes it is assumed that since diverse conditions *can* increase the vague subjective sense of what is stressful, it follows that more encompassing definitions, incorporating many different sources and dimensions of stress, constitute better representations of the concept.

There is good reason to question such thinking, at least with respect to understanding the psychosocial antecedents of depression. The objectives of general definitions of stress may conflict with the objective of defining the conditions that lead to depression. Comprehensive definitions of the stress concept could obscure underlying dimensions of adversity that are especially relevant for the development of depression. The disorder of depression represents a relatively specific psychobiologic syndrome. Its evolutionary heritage may be due to the adaptive advantages of the response pattern in the face of relatively specific environmental threats (e.g., withdrawal of primary attachment bonds, or conservation/withdrawal responses under uncontrollable threatening conditions; Bowlby, 1969; Klerman, 1987; Schmale, 1973). Many depressions may reflect a derailment of such mechanisms for abetting survival; if so, it is likely that the eliciting conditions could possess important similarities. One must avoid "diluting" of the definition of stress by the overinclusion of intuitively appealing, yet conceptually disjointed, aspects of the concept. At a theoretical level, then, there may be important differences between the nonspecific concepts used in general stress research and the more theoretically precise concepts used in depression research (Depue & Monroe, 1986).

Additivity and Specificity of Stressors. Another way of viewing the foregoing discussion on definitions of stress concerns the issue of additivity, which in turn reflects underlying conceptualizations of the specificity of stress-disorder interactions. That is, do diverse life experiences summate in their impact, or are particular environmental conditions more directly relevant for precipitating specific disorders? Within the life events literature, this issue usually has been restricted to whether or not life events are cumulative in their effects (i.e., many low-level events possess the equivalent impact of one or two major events) (see Brown & Harris, 1986). In many of the recent approaches to investigating life stress in depression, definitions of life stress have expanded from cumulative totals of acute major life events to include such other facets of stress as minor daily hassles and chronic problems. Under such definitional guidelines, individuals can attain comparable stress levels via quite different forms of adaptive demands. Thus, for example, the stress rating for someone with a variety of small-scale, minor annoyances could be equated with an individual with one major, devastating experience.

Comprehensive, cumulative definitions of stress most likely merge dimensions of differential importance for depression. This probability is strongly supported by the available empirical evidence. In contrast to totals of diverse life events, major events that signify serious losses or exits from one's social field have been found to be relatively specific to and strongly associated with the onset of depression (Brown & Harris, 1986; Cooke & Hole, 1983; Paykel, 1982). The refinement of concepts and the assessment of stress in terms of conceptual relevance for depression, rather than in terms of breadth of coverage for subjectively appealing notions of stress, appears a more advantageous approach.

The net result of a diffuse definitional approach to stress for the existing literature is difficult to evaluate. On the one hand, it might simply lead to vague definitions and operationalization of the construct which lack the requisite theoretical specificity for enhancing understanding of the dynamics of depression onset. But more perniciously, it could result in capitalizing on the ambiguities of stress and thereby in leading to illusory associations with depression. This issue becomes particularly problematic when one examines the existing traditions for translation of definitions into measures of life stress. As we see next, nonspecific definitional approaches may be fused with operational practices that together increase the probability of producing spurious correlations with depression.

Measurement Issues

As one would expect from the many approaches to conceptualizing and defining stress, many different procedures have been developed for its measurement. It is difficult, in fact, to evaluate definitions of stress in isolation from their operational counterparts. Yet there are trends in operationalization that have important implications for understanding the adequacy of stress measurement in research on depression, and for interpreting the relevant literature.

Standardization Considerations. A major concern in the operationalization of stress involves the reference point for defining what is stressful. Some investigators advocate a respondent-based approach, others advocate an investigator-based approach (Brown, 1981). The former is predicated on the idea that the individual (i.e., the respondent) is the one most qualified to report on what circumstances are personally stressful, and how stressful they are. Definitions of stress within such systems, consequently, are based on subjects' perceptions of their psychosocial circumstances. Self-report life event checklists are the typical medium used with these approaches.

The alternative viewpoint is that, while it may be true that the individual has the best access to such information, there are complicating considerations that render reliance upon the subject's perception of stress quite problematic. Subjects bring to the assessment situation a variety of idiosyncratic views that can distort the measurement process (Brown, 1981). Much room for interpretation is left to the judgment of the respondent in determining whether or not their recent experiences conform to the experiences that are being assessed by the investigator. For example, two people could endorse "serious illness in a close family member" despite great differences in the objective events. For a particular anxious person, the response could reflect a child's one-day bout with the flu, whereas for another, it may reflect a spouse's recent heart attack. The result is that one obtains considerable variability in the rating of "objective" experiences within ostensibly specific event categories (Brown & Harris, 1978; Dohrenwend, Link, Kern, Shrout, & Markowitz, 1987).

The cornerstone of measurement for investigator-based procedures, then, is a semistructured interview containing explicit probes to fully detail the nature of the life events and conditions to which the subject is exposed. Upon gathering sufficient details about the events, operational criteria and systematic guidelines are applied by trained raters to formalize and standardize which experiences count as events within the system, and which events do not. Several research groups have developed such procedures (see Brown & Harris, 1978; Dohrenwend et al., 1987; Paykel, 1982). And it is noteworthy that these types of assessments do not necessarily preclude a sensitivity to the meaning of different events for particular individuals. Brown and Harris (1978), developers of the Bedford College Life Events and Difficulties Schedule (LEDS), have also developed the "contextual" rating system, in which the meaning of events is taken into account for the particular person based on his or her life circumstances (not based on the individual's self report or his/her reaction to the event). For example, the birth of a child would be likely to have a very different meaning for an affluent women in a satisfying marriage compared to an impoverished woman in an abusive marriage. Such procedures help to bridge the gap between the conservative (but general) normative scaling of life events and the more sensitive (but confounded) subjective scaling of life events (see Brown & Harris, 1978, 1986).

Without such procedures for clarifying and classifying the circumstances of individuals' lives, the meaning of the measure of stress can be too easily lost. It becomes an uninterpretable mixture of the attributes of the individual (e.g., perceptual influences) and of his or her social environment (e.g., the external demands for adaption). There is no basis for determining the relative importance of stress versus perception or their interactions in the resulting definition and measure. These concerns do not represent infrequent or innocuous problems. Recent research bears out the empirical reality of this serious limitation of procedures based on life event checklists (Dohrenwend et al., 1987).

Additivity and Specificity Revisited. The aforementioned concerns with additivity and specificity take on new dimensions when considering stress measurement issues. The first concern is methodological, and pertains to the continuing theme of controlling for the potential confounding between stress and depression. In a probability sense, the minor events and chronic stressors—so common and prevalent—often account for the majority of the variance in individuals' scores on comprehensive measures of stress (i.e., major impact events typically are not of great frequency; Depue & Monroe, 1986). In other words, it is very probable that most individuals who report high stress experience primarily hassles and/or chronic stressors, not necessarily major acute events. Yet it is the hassles and chronic stressors that may be most suspect in terms of confounding with depression. Operationally, one must ensure that actual changes occurred in such conditions prior to disorder onset. That is, an eminently viable alternative interpretation is that the insidious onset of depression led to altered perceptions of increased life stress. These may be the kinds of conditions that, as Garmany (1958) noted 30 years ago, are ripe for the ". . . universal human tendency to seek causes for the effects it witnesses" (p. 342).

The second concern has to do with the adequacy of the measurement system for providing the necessary conceptual breadth to investigate specificity hypotheses (i.e., do particular characteristics of stressful conditions lead to specific types of disorders?). Thus, if particular disorders are suspected to be at least in part related to different types of antecedent stress, the assessment procedures must be sufficiently flexible to adequately portray the dimensions of theoretical relevance. Given a foundation of consensually defined events (i.e., events defined by operational criteria and explicit inclusion and exclusion rules), those employing investigator-based methods have delineated rating procedures designed to specify and refine particular qualities of stressful encounters. Considerable evidence indicates that it is only experiences associated with particular qualities that are most likely to precede a depressive episode, not simply high levels of nonspecific stress. These types of events appear to be highly unpleasant, and often are related to loss of relationships, valued goals, or even cherished ideas (Brown & Harris, 1986).

Psychometric Issues. Since the early work on life events based on life event checklists, considerable attention has been focused on the reliability of life stress measures. Early investigations indicated that self-report checklists, characteristic of respondent-based approaches, suffered from unacceptably poor test-retest reliability. The major limitation, it appeared, was in the fall-off, or forgetting, of reported events given increasing intervals of retrospective recall (Monroe, 1982a, 1982c; Paykel, 1983). In contrast, there is substantial support for the reliability of particular investigator-based procedures. Even over protracted periods of recall, LEDS possesses quite acceptable psychometric characteristics (Brown & Harris, 1986).

Recent Developments. More recent innovations in the measurement of stress attempt to address the complexity of the implications of events and ongoing adversities for one another. That is, different combinations of stress may create different degrees of vulnerability to depression. In particular, it is likely that ongoing difficulties—the chronic stressors in people's lives—both (a) set the stage for major negative life events to occur and (b) are especially sensitive areas of influence for the person. For example, ongoing relationship problems are highly correlated with major events such as break-up, divorce, infidelity, and so on. It may be that events that arise from, or have implications for, ongoing adversities create greater susceptibility. The matching of acute events with ongoing problems, wherein further aspects of the likely meaning of the event for the person are incorporated, may lead to experiences that are synergistically stressful (Brown & Harris, 1986). These recent developments in a sense represent attempts to put the "life" back into the standard, but still incomplete, picture of stress as decomposed into discrete events and difficulties. The potential is that one may gain a more complete representation of individual differences in life stress, replicable across both individuals and investigators.

Summary and Conclusions. Although the majority of research on life stress and depression has been performed with life event checklists, there are many reasons why such approaches are likely to prove inadequate to the task of unraveling the complex network of associations that may link stress with depression. Although there remains disagreement in the field (e.g., Oei & Zwart, 1986; Zimmerman, Pfohl, & Stangl, 1986), a consensus appears to be emerging that the more sophisticated, interview-based life stress measures provide the soundest foundation on which to build an understanding of the important theoretical associations between stress and depression (Bebbington, 1986; Brown & Harris, 1986; Katschnig, 1986b).

LIFE STRESS AND THE ONSET OF DEPRESSION: INTEGRATIVE MODELS AND SUBTYPE DISTINCTIONS

An extensive research literature documents the general association between measures of life stress and depression. Investigations range from simple cross-sectional studies correlating life events with depressive symptoms, through prospective inquiries employing more sophisticated assessments of life events and for diagnosing depression. Although there appears to be an overall consensus that life stress can play a role in the development of a depressive episode, controversy remains concerning the specific implications and importance of stress as a causal agent (cf. Lloyd, 1980; Katschnig, 1986a). It is most useful to evaluate such questions within the context of the two approaches to explaining the relations between life stress and depression: the integrated or unitary model, and the subgroup distinctions model.

Unitary Models: Magnitude of Effect

The major issue for the unitary model is the magnitude of the contribution of life stress to the onset of the depression. This question concerns the relative importance of life stress in the etiologic network of factors responsible for bringing about an episode of depression. Stress alone appears not to be a sufficient causal factor, and in at least some instances it may not even be a necessary ingredient, for the onset of the disorder.

The most common approach has been to pose the question in terms of traditional statistical measures of association, such as magnitude of effect. Indeed, one of the major criticisms of the life stress perspective on depression has been that there is only a relatively minor degree of association as typically indexed by such statistical measures (e.g., only about 10% of the variance in depression accounted for by life stress, most commonly with stress assessed by self-report checklist procedures). This problem may not be so much the predictive utility of stress, but rather the adequacy of fit between statistical index and the phenomenon measured. Although life stress may lead to depression in some instances, in the majority of cases it does not (e.g., only one in five women who experience severe events develop depression; Brown & Harris, 1978). As Brown and Harris (1986) and others (Cooke & Hole, 1983; Finlay-Jones, 1981) have effectively argued, other indices of association than magnitude of effect may better represent the degree of influence of stress on the development of depression.

An example from another area of research depicts this issue. Although most cases of lung cancer are associated with smoking, less than 1% of the variance is explained by the magnitude of effect statistical index (Brown & Harris, 1978; Cooke & Hole, 1983). The issue is that the majority of individuals who smoke do not develop lung cancer, yet those who do develop the disease are disproportionately likely to be smokers. Put differently, since most people do not develop the disease, the overall association between the risk factor and the disorder is attenuated, and masks the significance of the risk factor as a causal agent within the subgroup of individuals that do become ill. When more appropriate measures of association are applied to take into account the fact that the majority of people do not develop the disorder, over 80% of onsets of depression in community samples may be related to life stress agents (allowing for the chance association between events and depression) (Brown & Harris, 1986). The possibility exists that with additional refinement of life stress measures and the incorporation of other risk indices into the model, the strength of prediction may be further enhanced (see Brown, Bifulco, & Harris, 1987; Brown, Bifulco, Harris, & Bridge, 1986).

Within this viewpoint, the difficulties in reconciling findings on life stress and depression may not be as penetrating a problem as it first appears. Life stress may figure prominently in the onset of depression for most cases. Episodes of disorder "without apparent cause" (i.e., stressful events) may be relatively rare, or may occur in the context of distinctly different psychopathologies (e.g., bipolar disorder). Also, cases of "out of the blue" depression may be especially compelling in presentation, and may command a disproportionate degree of attention compared to cases in which the onset of depression appears to make sense in terms of antecedent stressors. Furthermore, individuals with depression for whom life stress does not appear to be a viable explanation may have an enhanced likelihood of entry into treatment systems, for such conditions may be more mysterious and more readily seen within the province of problems requiring medical attention. Overall, this suggests that either selective attention (i.e., depressions without antecedent stress are more memorable) or sampling bias (i.e., depressions without antecedent stress are more likely to be referred for help) could inflate the perceived importance and/or perceived incidence of unprecipitated depressions.

On the other hand, as previously noted incidences of "sadness without reason" depression may be underestimated due to the ubiquitousness of stress and its explanatory availability. Although this would appear to be less likely in the research employing life event assessments with explicit, investigator-based criteria for defining events and their dimensions, it could represent a very serious problem when less sophisticated, yet still commonly used, respondent-based (i.e., self-report) assessment techniques are used. A major agenda for future work would be to work toward a better understanding of the relative incidence of depressions defined in terms of the presence or absence of psychosocial antecedents, particularly across the ranges of samples commonly investigated (e.g., community versus treatment samples). As we see next, however, efforts to date directed toward this goal have not produced clear results.

Subtype Distinction Models: Construct Validation

Considerable effort has been directed toward understanding the implications of life stress for subtyping of depressive episodes. Two major approaches have been adopted. First and most traditionally, subgroups have been formed based on symptomatic distinctions and investigated in relation to life stress (or, conversely, depressed individuals with and without prior life stress are compared along a variety of symptom dimensions). Second, and more recently, other variable domains have been included, enlarging the approach for detecting and validating potential differences between different types of depression. In particular, two developments in recent research are noteworthy: the importance of differences between subtypes over time in clinical presentation, and the importance of biological differences between subgroups.

Symptomatic Distinctions. Most efforts have been directed toward understanding the heterogeneity of depressive symptoms and clinical presentations in relation to the presence or absence of life stress. Three overlapping literatures bear on this issue: (a) comparisons of groups with and without prior life stress with respect to severity of symptoms; (b) comparisons of individuals with and without prior life stress with respect to patterning of symptom profiles; and conversely, (c) comparisons of different symptom profiles of depressed patients (e.g., endogenous versus nonendogenous) with respect to antecedent life stress.

The most elemental subgroup distinction concerns differentiation of minor affective disturbances from depressive episodes of more severe, clinical proportions. Some investigators contend that the dominant influence of life stress may be restricted to the realm of more minor, transient affective problems (e.g., Bebbington, 1986; Bebbington et al. 1988; Bebbington, Tennant, & Hurry, 1981b). From this point of view, life stress plays but a minor role, if any, in the development of the more severe, disabling forms of depression. Although recent work has demonstrated that stressors are important for the development of minor affective disorders, other studies strongly suggest that such conditions are also significantly related to the onset of relatively severe, debilitating levels of depression as well (Brown, Craig, & Harris, 1985; Brown & Harris, 1986; Brugha & Conroy, 1985; Perris, 1984b).

Others have suggested that the presence or absence of prior life stress is associated with specific symptomatic, distinctly qualitative, differences in the disorder. This is perhaps the most entrenched and traditional viewpoint: depressions associated with life stress are essentially different from those not so related. The variable domain explored for documenting such hypothetical differences previously has been confined largely to presenting signs and symptoms. There are two sides to the issue. First, do the symptom profiles of individuals with stress differ from those without such circumstances? (For example, traditionally the endogenous form of depression was viewed as either unrelated to pre-existing stress or as not reactive to concurrent stress; Fowles & Gersh, 1979). Or, turning the question around, do different phenotypic expressions of depression suggest differences in previous life stress? In keeping with this latter notion, more recent research practices have been to define endogeneity strictly in terms of a particular type of symptom pattern. Both of these questions reflect traditional subtype explanations of the role of life stress and depression. That is, some depression arise owing to internal causes, some owing to external causes, and if one observes the two closely enough they may be distinguishable in terms of the current symptom picture of the patient.

There is reliable information from multivariate studies indicating a relatively distinctive endogenous subgroup in terms of a particular symptom profile. Yet the bulk of existing research suggests that life stress *also* is related to such forms of depression (Bebbington et al., 1988; Katschnig, Pakesch, Egger-Zeidner, 1986). Viewing the question the other way around, individuals who experience life stress prior to their depression have not been differentiated reliably nor persuasively in terms of their presenting clinical picture from patients for whom no antecedent stressors can be documented. Such null results might be explained owing to poor procedures for operationalizing life stress and/or defining and diagnosing subgroups in the earlier investigations on the topic (e.g., Leff, Roatch, & Bunney, 1970; Thomson & Hendrie, 1972). More recent inquiries, however, employing adequate assessment procedures for life stress and diagnostic practices for examining subgroup distinctions, reinforce the conclusions of earlier work that at least the majority of endogenous subtypes are associated with antecedent life stress (e.g., Brown & Harris, 1978; Bebbington et al., 1988; Dolan et al., 1985; Hirschfeld, 1981; Hirschfeld, Klerman, Andreasen, Clayton, & Keller, 1985; Roy et al. 1986). Yet potentially important exceptions exist. For example, Roy, Breier, Doran, & Pickar (1985) found higher totals of life events preceding depression onset for melancholic versus nonmelancholic DSM-III major depressives. Other investigators, too, have documented differences between diagnostic subgroups of depressives in relation to life events, although overall such studies reveal "a tendency to weak relationships and patchiness" of positive results mixed with negative findings (Paykel, Rao, & Taylor, 1984, p. 566). (See also Bebbington et al., 1981; Brown, this volume; Cooke, 1980, 1981; Matussek & Wiegand, 1985; Roy, 1987; for an insightful and thorough review of the topic, see Katschnig et al., 1986.)

Such discrepancies likely follow from the diversity of measures employed to assess life stress and to define depressive subtypes, as well as from differences in sample characteristics (e.g., inpatients, outpatients, and untreated cases in the community). For instance, although employing investigator-based procedures, many recent studies have operationalized life stress in different ways. Some studies focus primarily on life event totals compared across patient subgroups (yet still vary in the use of overall event scores versus limiting totals to undesirable event scores; e.g., Roy et al., 1985, 1986), while other studies focus on proportions of patients in the respective subgroups with single events of severe impact (e.g., one major event or a serious ongoing difficulty; e.g., Brown & Harris, 1978; Dolan et al., 1985). Given such operational inconsistency and multiple methods of indexing life stress, the likelihood of producing false positive findings is increased. Furthermore, although diagnoses may frequently be based on acceptable diagnostic procedures, the terms "endogenous," "melancholic," and "psychotic" are often used somewhat cavalierly and interchangeably. Consequently, subtype distinctions are often made across studies using similar surface terminology yet employing alternative operational systems that produce very different underlying categories of patients (see Katschnig et al., 1986).

Overall, the bulk of evidence and reviews suggest that life stress is related to *both* endogenous and nonendogenous, or both melancholic and nonmelancholic, subtypes of depression. Yet, the recent reports suggesting subgroup or symptomatic differences between individuals who do and do not experience life stress prior to an episode of depression cannot be ignored. Given the diversity of approaches used by investigators, it may be premature to accept a 'majority' view, particularly when it is based on mostly null findings. One goal of the next generation of research should be to strive toward maximizing comparability of event measures and diagnostic formulations with preceding research to establish appropriate bases for comparison (see Brown & Harris, 1986).

Clinical Course Differences. A longitudinal perspective focused on individual differences in the course of depression may provide useful data. Do depressions that apparently arise consequent to life stress follow a different clinical course compared to those depressions that apparently arise unrelated to stress? Since ethical concerns and clinical demands typically preclude research on the natural course of depression, research typically has been based largely upon differences in the clinical course of individuals receiving various forms of treatment.

Some research suggests that life stress differentially predicts the resolution of a depressive episode. Life events preceding treatment entry significantly predicted subsequent depressive symptomatology and clinical outcome over a 6-month follow-up period, with the greater the number of events, the greater the likelihood of enhanced recovery (Monroe, Bellack, Hersen, & Himmelhoch, 1983). This effect was primarily attributable to patients who initially evidenced endogenous depression profiles: Women with endogenous symptoms and increased life stress prior to treatment entry were found to have the best clinical outcome and follow-up status (Monroe, Thase, Hersen, Bellack, & Himmelhoch, 1985).

Expanding on this general finding, it is worthwhile to speculate that specific types of events are related to the clinical course of the episode. Recent reports by Parker and colleagues suggest that, in particular, one type of life event predicts a more favorable resolution of depression (as well as predicting certain specific symptoms) (Parker & Blignault, 1985; Parker, Tennant, & Blignault, 1985; Parker, Blignault, & Manicavasagar, 1988). In both treated and untreated samples improvement was predicted by the presence of a break-up of an intimate relationship in the preceding 12 months. Such depressions were also more commonly associated with weight loss, and possibly other symptoms often associated with endogenous forms of depression (Parker et al., 1988).

Finally, some forms of prior life stress may predict a more favorable clinical course, while other forms of concurrent life stress may predict the maintenance and remission of more chronic forms of depression. Brown, Adler, and Bifulco (1988) recently found changes in life events and difficulties were related to recovery from chronic depression. Furthermore, Miller et al. (1987) reported that the duration of psychiatric illness was longer when antecedent stressors had uncertain outcomes (i.e., heart attacks to spouse, stormy relationship with boyfriend); the duration of episodes was shortened when antecedent stressors were characterized as restricted in their impact (i.e., many health conditions, burglaries, and other minor situations). Again, such research suggests the need for greater theoretical precision in the delineation of particular dimensions of importance both in terms of stress and depression that may underlie the general association between the two (cf. Hirschfeld et al., 1986).

Biological Differences. A number of biological parameters have been reported to distinguish between subgroups of depressed patients. These measures commonly are associated with the integrity of CNS neuroregulatory activity, either via the assessment of metabolites of major brain neurotransmitter systems or of "downstream" neuroendocrine functioning (under the control of CNS regulation). Individual differences between major depressives with respect to these biological tests suggest biological distinctions in etiology (i.e., such differences distinguish biologically distinct subgroups). Although the underlying basis for such findings remains in dispute (i.e., whether or not such distinctions reflect true etiologic heterogeneity or reflect other individual difference dimensions of less relevance to etiology), reliable results in subgrouping individuals with major depression have been attained for certain indices. Such thinking naturally complements distinctions based on differences in the existence or absence of antecedent life stress. For example, subgroups of depressives evidencing biologic dysregulation in brain neurotransmitter functioning may exhibit less antecedent life stress than subgroups of depressives without such biologic concomitants. It is not surprising that recent investigations have combined the two approaches in order to clarify issues relevant to the relationship of life stress to depression.

Perhaps the most extensively investigated neurobiologic system has been the hypothalamic-pituitary-cortical (HPA) axis. Many studies indicate that approximately 50% of patients with endogenous major depression (defined by symptomatic criteria) exhibit hypersecretion of cortisol which, for the majority of patients, reverts to normal upon recovery. The dexamethasone suppression test (DST) has become one of the most reliable and replicable tests of such overactivity of the HPA axis (Lesser et al., 1983). Of the available work on this interesting topic, Lesser et al. (1983) and Dolan et al. (1985; see also Calloway et. al., 1984a) could *not* distinguish DST suppressors from nonsuppressors according to antecedent life stress. In contrast, Roy et al. (1986) found that patients with an undesirable life event responded to the DST normally compared to the abnormal DST response of patients with an undesirable life event (i.e., life stress and the HPA axis dysfunction designated two different subgroups; $p < .06$). Investigators have also reported other biologic indices to differentiate depressions in relation to life stress (e.g., urinary free cortisol and free thyroxin in Calloway et al., 1984b; dopamine metabolite homovanillic acid and serotonin metabolite 5-hydroxyindoleascetic acid in the Roy et al., 1986; platelet MAO activity, Perris, von Knorring, Oreland, & Perris, 1984).

At the present stage of research, it appears premature to derive any conclusions. Discrepancies between the few existing studies could again be due to differences in assessing and quantifying life stress, or in the sampling of patients. Furthermore, considerable controversy exists in terms of the underlying meaning of differences in the DST results (e.g., whether or not the test distinguishes biologically different depressive disorders). Yet there are interesting leads that may suggest other lines of inquiry (e.g., individual differences in life stress and other biologic distinctions, such as shortened REM sleep latency; Kupfer, 1986). As knowledge of the meaning of many of the biologic markers evolves, a better understanding of the implications of such work for understanding life stress and depression may emerge.

CONCURRENT LIFE STRESS: EXACERBATION, REMISSION, RELAPSE, AND RECURRENCE

The most common view of life stress emphasizes its role in the onset, or etiology, of an episode of the disorder. As suggested in the previous section, antecedent stress also may be related to the clinical course of depression. Yet more recently, concurrent life stress also has been viewed as potentially influential for the clinical course of depression, both within particular episodes (e.g., exacerbation and remission of an episode) as well as over the lifetime course of the individual, potentially influencing subsequent occurrences of the disorder (Brown & Harris, 1978, 1986; Depue & Monroe, 1983, 1986; Monroe, 1982b; Monroe et al., 1983). Despite the notion that depressions often autonomously "run their course," considerable variability exists across patients with respect to the severity, duration, and recurrence of depressive episodes. Concurrent life stress may play an important, albeit complex, intra- and inter-episode role in accounting for such individual differences.

The strength of this viewpoint again derives from its intuitive plausibility. Individuals who not only are depressed, but who are additionally beset by other life stressors, may find it especially difficult to cope. Such external demands could exacerbate the disorder in terms of severity, symptom profile, and/or duration. The weakness of this perspective is the difficult methodological issues it raises. By definition these individuals are depressed, and the events that befall them may be at least in part a consequence of their pathology. People with more severe forms of depression may simply suffer greater psychosocial turbulence as a consequence of the degree of pathology from which they suffer (rather than as a cause of the severity). In this respect it will prove useful to distinguish events that are a consequence of the person's depression from those that are clearly independent. It is likely, though, that many such determinations may be difficult to make. Under such conditions, it might be useful to at least stratify people according to severity of symptoms in order to understand the differential importance of stress versus the severity of disorder in predicting subsequent course. Nonetheless, it seems imprudent at the present stage of knowledge to assume that such stressors are *necessarily,* or only, artifactual consequences or tautological outgrowths of increased illness severity (Monroe & Peterman, 1988). Once again, the problem of separating the relevant from the artifactual connotations and consequences of life stress is of importance.

A number of definitional issues arise with such research that are essential for establishing standardized procedures. In particular, consistent definitions and criteria are required for such concepts as remission, relapse, and recurrence. These entail both severity and duration criteria. For example, for remission standards of required levels of symptomatology as well as duration of sustained improvement are necessary. The issues of relapse and recurrence build upon such definitional foundations. Relapse (in the sense of a re-emergence of symptoms associated with the index episode), for instance, can only occur following remission. Yet within a depressive episode the course of depressive symptoms is often quite variable, periods of suffering may be punctuated with brief respites of normal mood and behavior. Definitions of relapse, then, require similar considerations to those associated with definitions of recovery: What degree of symptomatic relief is required, and over what sustained period of time, are needed to separate a lack of recovery from a relapse? Lastly, recurrence (in the sense of the re-emergence of symptoms in a new episode) requires similar considerations in conceptualization and operational definition. For example, standards and criteria must be adopted to distinguish between the theoretically different considerations of relapse and recurrence. As will be apparent, unfortunately little consistency exists with respect to such matters, thereby compromising the interpretability of existing work.

Clinical Course of a Depressive Episode

Many attributes of the course of an episode of depression are of theoretical interest with respect to the implications of life stress. Exacerbation of depressive symptoms within an episode, maintenance of symptoms and remission, as well as relapse represent important domains of individual differences in depression. Compared to the literature bearing on the onset question of life stress and depression, however, the literature on these issues is relatively small. Nonetheless, the literature suggests that life stress may figure in predicting changes in the clinical course of a depressive episode.

Exacerbation of Symptoms. In a study employing careful measures of life stress and changes in affective functioning, Brown and Harris (1978) found that the natural course of depressive symptoms was related to concurrent life events. In particular, events rated as severely threatening—the same types of events that predicted onset—also predicted significant increases in within-episode symptomatology. Importantly, this association held once illness-related events were excluded from the analyses (i.e., events that appeared to be a consequence of the depressive illness). They concluded that "severe events are apparently capable of bringing about a marked worsening of an established depression" (Brown & Harris, 1978, p. 209). Unfortunately, little additional research is available on this particular issue.

Remission. Other inquiries have not directly addressed exacerbations of symptoms, but rather have focused on the related concerns of maintenance of symptoms and remission. Consonant findings to those of Brown and Harris were reported in a study of treatment response by Lloyd, Zisook, Click, and Jaffe (1981). After 2 weeks, patients evidencing a relatively poor outcome were found to have almost three times as many concurrent life events compared to the improved patients. In contrast, Monroe et al. (1983) did not find events occurring during treatment or the 6-month subsequent follow-up period to be related to final follow-up status. These discrepancies in findings are likely attributable to differences in the time periods over which the effects of stress were examined.

Work has been undertaken on the implications of life events in relation to the remission of disorder. Instead of viewing life stressors as retarding remission, other concurrent psychosocial conditions may foster a more rapid recovery. Tennant, Bebbington, and Hurry (1981b) found that events occurring after the onset of disorder, yet effectively "neutralizing" previous stressors, were related to a more favorable outcome. In a similar vein, Parker et al. (1985) reported that both positive life events, and neutralizing events, predicted improvement for nonendogenous depressives receiving treatment. Others have found conditions that neutralize stressful events or terminate ongoing stressors to predict favorable outcomes (Miller et al., 1987).

Relapse. Preliminary evidence suggests that life stress may increase the likelihood of relapse. After 4–6 weeks of treatment with medications, patients evidencing at least a 50% reduction in symptoms were followed over time in a maintenance treatment comparison of the efficacy of medications versus psychotherapy (Paykel & Tanner, 1976). Relapse was defined as a return of symptoms to pretreatment entry criteria for a 1-month period ("with a shorter time at a higher symptom level being accepted if clinical prudence necessitated it" p. 482). Life events were assessed with a semistructured interview. Compared to controls, individuals who relapsed were found to report more events in the preceding 3-months, and especially so for the month immediately prior to relapse. In contrast, Mendlewicz, Charon, and Linkowski (1986) reported that concurrent life events during a 12-month follow-up period were not predictive of relapse. Yet in this latter study no duration criteria were cited for sustained improvement, and it is unclear how well timing of events and relapse was handled. Clearly the differences may be attributable to discrepancies in the definitions surrounding recovery and relapse.

Lifetime Course of Disorder

It is well known that individuals who have suffered from a diagnosable depression are at increased risk for subsequent episodes of the disorder. Estimates vary, but approximately 40–50% of individuals who experience an episode of depression may experience one or more recurrences (Klerman, 1978). More recently, attention to the lifetime course of psychopathology has suggested that these individuals also possess heightened vulnerability to episodes of anxiety disorders. These expanded temporal perspectives on interactions between life stress and psychopathology renew and amplify the concern for clarifying cause and effect relations to a new level of analysis.

Recurrence of Depression. There are important reasons why distinctions should be made between individuals who experience one episode of depression and those who have repeated experiences with the disorder. Conceptually, severe psychosocial circumstances may be very influential in the early phases of the lifetime course (i.e., first or second episode). Yet once an individual has experienced depression, there may be psychobiologic alterations that increase susceptibility and decrease the degree of stress necessary to cause a subsequent episode. Thus, individuals who have suffered a depression may be more sensitive to stressors, or more prone to experience "sadness without cause" in subsequent episodes. Within such a model, stress could be crucial at particular points in time in the lifetime progression of the disorder, yet not at others. For example, normatively severe stressors may be essential for early episodes of the disorder. Less severe, yet still relatively stressful events, may be important for subsequent depressions, or stress may be comparatively inconsequential at later stages. As most studies of onset of depression in relation to life stress have not not taken into account prior history of depression, existing evidence confounds information on the importance of life stress for first episodes of depression with the implications of life stress for recurrences of the disorder.

Early research addressing this issue suggested that initial episodes of depression were more frequently precipitated by life events than later episodes (Angst, 1966). Recently, this idea has been tested more formally. Perris (1984a) found that although patients with recurrent depression tended to experience fewer events compared to patients with first episodes, the differences were small. In contrast, Ezquiaga, Gutierrez, and Lopez (1987) compared life events occurring for patients with an initial or second episode of depression to events occurring for patients with later episodes. They found life events to be more common prior to the earlier episodes relative to the later ones. Furthermore, the frequency of events preceding the later episodes did not differ from those of a normal control group. Dolan et al. (1985) also found similar results using the LEDS methodology.

Overall, such findings are compatible with the notion that life stress may be more influential for earlier episodes of depression. An alternative interpretation, however, is that many individuals destined to repeated depressions suffer from a distinctively different form of disorder, one that possesses origins essentially autonomous of psychosocial processes. Future investigations directed toward within individual analyses over repeated episodes would be useful for beginning to distinguish between these rival interpretations.

Other, more subtle, concerns reflect upon the validity of such associations. Most important is the continuing theme of causes, correlates, and consequences. Given a prior history of depression, one must be concerned with the possibility that residual symptoms artifactually predict recurrence. Yet alternatively, and most importantly from a life stress perspective, socioenvironmental consequences of prior illness may represent one mechanism explaining why some depressions can become a recurrent problem. For example, someone with a prior episode may experience changes in his or her social environment as a consequence of the illness (such as work demotions or marital conflict). While such changes could be thought to simply reflect a more virulent form of the disorder (that has a high likelihood of recurrence irrespective of the psychosocial changes), they could also represent a means via which vulnerability to future episodes is translated. Once again, the investigations noted on life stress have not taken such possibilities into account, so there is very little understanding of the complexities involved in the longitudinal interactions between life stress and depression.

Comorbidity of Anxiety and Depression. The presence of anxiety and depression concurrently in the diagnostic picture has long been noted (Slater & Slater, 1944). Taking into consideration the issue of enduring vulnerability and recurrence, however, opens up another avenue of inquiry that may contribute to an understanding of the relations between depression and stress. In particular, over an afflicted individual's life, there may not only be repeated episodes of depression, but there also may be episodes of anxiety disturbances. Investigating the longitudinal course highlights the frequent "crossing over" from one disorder to the other with the passage of time. As Tyrer (1985) recently indicated, over time these people "pass, chameleon-like, through different diagnostic hues depending upon the nature of the stresses they encounter" (p. 687).

Especially important are the findings from recent research that indicates the temporal independence for some individuals between relatively severe episodes of depressive and anxiety disorders (Breier, Charney, & Heninger, 1984, 1985). Put differently, individuals who display the features of one syndrome appear to be at increased risk for the other, yet can manifest intermorbid periods of relatively normal functioning. These results are complemented by research on family studies, wherein comorbidity of anxiety and depression of the proband predicts increased rates of lifetime major depression and anxiety disorders among family members (Leckman, Weissman, Merikangas, Pauls, & Prusoff, 1983; Van Valkenburg, Akiskal, Puzantian, & Rosenthal, 1984). Furthermore, recent genetic research suggests that while the propensity to experience psychiatric symptoms is under genetic influence, the qualities that determine the anxiety or depressive phenotype are under environmental control (Kendler, Heath, Martin, & Eaves, 1987).

These discoveries are compatible with the idea that particular dimensions of life stress may be specifically related to particular forms of psychological disorder. Complementary results from the life stress literature have been provided by Brown and colleagues. Life events that signified loss were found to occur much more frequently before the onset of depression; life events that signified danger before the onset of anxiety disorders; and life events that signified both a loss and danger before the onset of mixed cases of anxiety and depression (e.g., Finlay-Jones & Brown, 1981). Once again, there is support for the specificity premise of specific stressors and specific disorders, at least with respect to anxiety and depression (see also Prudo, Harris, & Brown, 1984).

It is interesting to again speculate on the nature of the longitudinal relationships between life stressors and the expression of these forms of psychopathology. Linear concepts of causes, correlates, and consequences may give way to more complicated modes of interactions between social factors and biology. For example, disruption of interpersonal relationships or work effectiveness consequent to a depressive episode could create social conditions that subsequently increase the likelihood of other severe stressors occurring that could bring about later episodes of anxiety disturbances (e.g., danger conditions for loss of important relationships or employment). Multiple risk conditions may not simply merge coincidentally, they may gravitate interactively over time in a manner that eventually brings about the necessary and sufficient conditions for episode onset. The arbitrary nature of assigning causal pre-eminence to one set of factors at the expense of the others should be emphasized. Given complicated transactions over extended periods of time between the individual and environment, it would seem premature to summarily dismiss consequences of prior pathology that result in life stress. Such factors may represent one necessary, yet alone insufficient, component of an evolving set of circumstances that ultimately lead to, and coalesce in, disorder onset (Monroe, 1990).

CONCLUDING REMARKS

Our goal in this chapter has been to characterize the research literature on life stress and depression in relation to (a) the diversity of concepts and measures for describing life stress, and (b) the variety of associations that are involved when the multi-faceted concept of stress is studied in relation to depression, especially when such interactions are traced over time. Critical analysis of the simple idea that life stress can lead to depression quickly expands to an awareness of the complicated web of possibilities underlying the surface of the notion. Some of these relationships may be very important for developing theory on depression, whereas other relationships may be very misleading. Our goal for the remaining discussion is to briefly address other considerations that require attention for deriving more comprehensive models describing how stress may lead to depressive episodes.

Viewpoints differ on the etiologic importance of life stress for depression. But there appears to be consensus that if life stress is an important operative element, other psychosocial (as well as biological) vulnerabilities are required to precipitate a depressive episode. This is because even with the best of measures available, it seems clear that the majority of individuals under severe stress do not develop a depressive disorder. Social support is perhaps the most widely-recognized and researched condition believed to moderate the impact of life stress. That is, individuals exposed to severely stressful circumstances may be buffered from adverse psychiatric consequences through the benefits afforded by such relationships (Brown & Harris, 1986; Cohen & Wills, 1985). Yet there are a variety of other psychosocial (e.g., Brown & Harris, 1986) and biological (e.g., Perris et al., 1984) factors that my influence the likelihood of developing depression. While increasing the explanatory potential of life stress, such developments also expand the conceptual and analytic requirements for understanding the nature of associations between stress, depression, and the implicated moderator variables (Monroe & Steiner, 1986; Thoits, 1982). Once again, distinguishing between processes that confound components in the model from processes that are part of an essential developmental sequence will prove to be an important and challenging undertaking.

The major emphasis in the literature on stress and depression has been in relation to *changes* in affective functioning, *episodes* of disorder. It is such dramatic transitions from relatively normal feelings and behavior into the profound miseries of depression that have captured the minds (and hearts) of investigators. The prototypical model of depression has emphasized the dramatic nature and degree of change across the spheres of the individual's psychic, behavioral, and biological existence. Yet it is unclear how representative this viewpoint is for the onset of depression for the majority of afflicted individuals. Behind the extreme transitions may be a backdrop of ongoing distress and chronic, yet lower level, suffering. These milder forms of impairment may be influential in creating socioenvironmental circumstances with high potential to bring about serious forms of stress, which in turn may result in a dramatic, severe depressive episode. It may be out of such emotional breeding grounds that many severe episodes of depression arise (Brown et al., 1986).

Awareness of the chronic dimension of depression has increased over the past few years, along with the attendant heightened risk for major episodes of depression (Keller, Lavori, Endicott, Coryell, & Klerman, 1983). Under such circumstances, the analysis of stress-disorder interactions over prolonged periods of time becomes yet more complex. Although such conditions pose additional challenges for methodology and research design, psychopathologists can no longer afford to ignore the potential explanatory power of more integrative, longitudinal models. It may be through research on such complicated contexts that investigators dispense with the "banalities" associated with the concept of stress, and progress to understanding what aspects of life's misfortunes, for whom and under what circumstances, can lead to depression.

ACKNOWLEDGMENTS

The authors appreciate the helpful comments provided by Professors Joseph Becker and George Brown.

The authors gratefully acknowledge the support of NIMH grants 39139 (Dr. Monroe) and 37195 (Dr. Depue).

REFERENCES

Akiskal, H. S. (1979). A biobehavioral approach to depression. In R. A. Depue (Ed.)., *The psychobiology of the depressive disorders: Implications for the effects of stress*. New York: Academic Press.

Angst, J. (1966). *Atiologie und Nosologie endogener depressiver Psychosen*. Berlin: Springer-Verlag.

Bebbington, P. (1986). Establishing causal links—recent controversies. In H. Katschnig (Ed.), *Life events and psychiatric disorders: Controversial issues* (pp. 188–200). Cambridge, England: Cambridge University Press.

Bebbington, P. E., Brugha, T., MacCarthy, B., Potter, J., Sturt, E., Wykes, T., Katz, R., & McGuffin, P. (1988). The Camberwell Collaborative Depression Study: I. Depressed probands: Adversity and the form of depression. *British Journal of Psychiatry, 152*, 754–765.

Bebbington, P. E., Tennant, C., & Hurry, J. (1981). Life events and the nature of psychiatric disorder in the community. *Journal of Affective Disorders, 3*, 345–366.

Bowlby, J. (1969). *Attachment.* New York: Basic Books.
Breier, A., Charney, D. S., & Heninger, G. R. (1984). Major depression in patients with agoraphobia and panic disorder. *Archives of General Psychiatry, 41,* 1129–1135.
Breier, A., Charney, D. S., & Heninger, G. R. (1985). The diagnostic validity of anxiety disorders and their relationship to depressive illness. *American Journal of Psychiatry, 142,* 787–797.
Brown, G. W. (1974). Meaning, measurement, and stress of life events. In B. S. Dohrenwend & B. P. Dohrenwend (Eds.), *Stressful life events: Their nature and effects.* New York: Wiley.
Brown, G. W. (1981). Life events, psychiatric disorder, and physical illness. *Journal of Psychosomatic Research, 25,* 461–473.
Brown, G. W., Adler, Z., & Bifulco, A. (1988). Life events, difficulties and recovery from chronic depression. *British Journal of Psychiatry, 152,* 115–128.
Brown, G. W., Bifulco, A., & Harris, T. O. (1987). Life events, vulnerability and onset of depression: Some refinements. *British Journal of Psychiatry, 150,* 30–42.
Brown, G. W., Bifulco, A., Harris, T., & Bridge, L. (1986). Life stress, chronic subclinical symptoms and vulnerability to clinical depression. *Journal of Affective Disorders, 11,* 1–19.
Brown, G. W., Craig, T. K. J., & Harris, T. O. (1985). Depression: Distress or disease? Some epidemiological considerations. *British Journal of Psychiatry, 147,* 612–622.
Brown, G. W., & Harris, T. (1978). *Social origins of depression.* New York: Free Press.
Brown, G. W., & Harris, T. (1986). Establishing causal links: The Bedford College studies of depression. In H. Katschnig (Ed.), *Life events and psychiatric disorders: Controversial issues* (pp. 107–187). Cambridge, England: Cambridge University Press.
Brugha, T. S., & Conroy, R. (1985). Categories of depression: Reported life events in a controlled design. *British Journal of Psychiatry, 147,* 641–646.
Calloway, S. P., Dolan, R. J., Fonagy, P., De Souza, F. V. A., & Wakeling, A. (1984a). Endocrine changes and clinical profiles in depression: I. The dexamethasone suppression test. *Psychological Medicine, 14,* 749–758.
Calloway, S. P., Dolan, R. J., Fonagy, P., De Souza, V. F. A., & Wakeling, A. (1984b). Endocrine changes and clinical profiles in depression: II. The thyrotropin-releasing hormone test. *Psychological Medicine, 14,* 759–765.
Clayton, P. J. (1986). Prevalence and course of affective disorders. In A. J. Rush & K. Z. Altshuler (Eds.), *Depression: Basic mechanisms, diagnosis, and treatment* (pp. 32–44). New York: The Guilford Press.
Cohen, S., & Wills, T. A. (1985). Stress, social support, and the buffering hypothesis. *Psychological Bulletin, 98,* 310–357.
Cooke, D. J. (1980). Conceptual and methodological considerations of the problems inherent in the specification of the simple event-syndrome link. In I. G. Sarason & C. D. Spielberger (Eds.), *Stress and anxiety* (Vol. 7, pp. 139–157). Washington, D.C.: Hemisphere.
Cooke, D. J. (1981). Life events and syndromes of depression in the general population. *Social Psychiatry, 16,* 181–186.
Cooke, D. J., & Hole, D. J. (1983). The aetiological importance of stressful life events. *British Journal of Psychiatry, 143,* 397–400.
Cooper, B. (1986). Mental disorder as a reaction: the history of a psychiatric concept. In H. Katschnig (Ed.), *Life events and psychiatric disorders: Controversial issues* (pp. 1–32). Cambridge, England: Cambridge University Press.
Depue, R. A. (1979). (Ed.), *The psychobiology of the depressive disorders: Implications for the effects of stress.* New York: Academic Press.
Depue, R. A., & Monroe, S. M. (1978). Learned helplessness in the perspective of the depressive disorders: Conceptual and definitional issues. *Journal of Abnormal Psychology, 87,* 3–20.
Depue, R. A., & Monroe, S. M. (1983). Psychopathology research. In M. Hersen, A. E. Kazdin, & A. S. Bellack (Eds.), *The clinical psychology handbook, Vol. 1: The foundations* (pp. 239–264). New York: Pergamon Press.

Depue, R. A., & Monroe, S. M. (1986). Conceptualization and measurement of human disorder in life stress research: The problem of chronic disturbance. *Psychological Bulletin, 99,* 36–51.
Dohrenwend, B. P., Link, B. G., Kern, R., Shrout, P. E., Markowitz, J. (1987). Measuring life events: The problem of variability within categories. In B. Cooper (Ed.), *Psychiatric epidemiology* (pp. 103–119). London: Croom Helm.
Dolan, R. J., Calloway, S. P., Fonagy, P., De Souza, F. V. A., & Wakeling, A. (1985). Life events, depression and hypothalamic-pituitary-adrenal axis function. *British Journal of Psychiatry, 147,* 429–433.
Elliot, G. R., & Eisdorfer, C. (1982). (Eds.), *Stress and human health.* New York: Springer.
Ezquiaga, E., Gutierrez, J. L. A., & Lopez, A. G. (1987). Psychosocial factors and episode number in depression. *Journal of Affective Disorders, 12,* 135–138.
Finlay-Jones, R. (1981). Showing that life events are a cause of depression - A review. *Australian and New Zealand Journal of Psychiatry, 15,* 229–238.
Finlay-Jones, R., & Brown, G. W. (1981). Types of stressful life event and the onset of anxiety and depressive disorders. *Psychological Medicine, 11,* 803–815.
Fowles, D. C., & Gersh, F. S. (1979). Neurotic depression: The endogenous-neurotic distinction. In R. A. Depue (Ed.), *The psychobiology of the depressive disorders: Implications for the effects of stress.* New York: Academic Press.
Garmany, G. (1958). Depressive states: Their aetiology and treatment. *British Medical Journal, xx,* 341–344.
Hawkes, J. (1857). On the increase of insanity. *Journal of Psychological Medicine and Mental Pathology, 10,* 508–521.
Hinkle, L. E., Jr. (1977). The concept of "stress" in the biological and social sciences. In Z. J. Lipowski, D. R. Lipsitt, & P. C. Whybrow (Eds.), *Psychosomatic medicine: Current trends and clinical applications.* New York: Oxford University Press.
Hirschfeld, R. M. A. (1981). Situational depression: Validity of the concept. *British Journal of Psychiatry, 139,* 297–305.
Hirschfeld, R. M. A., Klerman, G. L., Andreasen, N. C., Clayton, P. J., & Keller, M. B. (1985). Situational major depressive disorder. *Archives of General Psychiatry, 42,* 1109–1114.
Hirschfeld, R. M. A., Klerman, G. L., Andreasen, N. C., Clayton, P. J., & Keller, M. B. (1986). Psychosocial predictors of chronicity in depressed patients. *British Journal of Psychiatry, 148,* 648–654.
Holmes, T. H., & Rahe, R. H. (1967). The social readjustment rating scale. *Journal of Psychosomatic Research, 11,* 213–218.
Jackson, S. W. (1986). *Melancholia and depression: From Hippocratic times to modern times.* New Haven, Connecticut: Yale University Press.
Kanner, A. D., Coyne, J. C., Schaefer, C., & Lazarus, R. S. (1981). Comparisons of two modes of stress measurement: Daily hassles and uplifts versus major life events. *Journal of Behavioral Medicine, 4,* 1–39.
Katschnig, H. (1986a). (Ed.) *Life events and psychiatric disorders: Controversial issues.* Cambridge, England, Cambridge University Press.
Katschnig, H. (1986b). Measuring life stress - a comparison of the checklist and panel technique. In H. Katschnig (Ed.), *Life events and psychiatric disorders: Controversial issues* (pp. 74–106). Cambridge, England: Cambridge University Press.
Katschnig, H., Pakesch, G., & Egger-Zeidner, E. (1986). Life stress and depressive subtypes: a review of present diagnostic criteria and recent research results. In H. Katschnig (Ed.), *Life events and psychiatric disorders: Controversial issues* (pp. 201–245). Cambridge, England: Cambridge University Press.
Keller, M. B., Lavori, P. W., Endicott, J., Coryell, W., & Klerman, G. L. (1983). "Double depression": Two-year follow-up. *American Journal of Psychiatry, 140,* 689–694.
Kendler, K. S., Heath, H. C., Martin, N. G., & Eaves, L. J. (1987). Symptoms of anxiety and

symptoms of depression: Same genes, different environments? *Archives of General Psychiatry, 44,* 541–457.

Klein, D. (1974). Endogenomorphic depression: a conceptual and terminological revision. *Archives of General Psychiatry, 31,* 447–454.

Klerman, G. (1978). Long-term maintenance of affective disorders: In M. A. Lipton, A. Di Mascio, & K. F. Killam (Eds.), *Psychopharmacology: A generation of progress* (pp. 1303–1311) New York: Raven Press.

Klerman, G. L. (1987). The nature of depression: Mood, symptom, disorder. In A. J. Marsella, R. M. A. Hirschfeld, & M. Katz, *The measurement of depression* (pp. 3–19). New York: Guilford.

Klibansky, R., Panofsky, E., & Saxl, F. (1964). *Saturn and melancholy: Studies in the history of natural philosophy, religion, and art.* New York: Basic Books.

Kraepelin, E. (1921). *Manic-depressive insanity and paranoia.* Edinburgh: E. & S. Livingstone.

Kupfer, D. J. (1986). The sleep EEG in diagnosis and treatment in depression. In A. J. Rush & K. Z. Altshuler (Eds.), *Depression: Basic mechanisms, diagnosis, and treatment* (pp. 102–125). New York: The Guilford Press.

Lazarus, R. S., & Folkman, S. (1984). *Stress, appraisal, and coping.* New York: Springer.

Leckman, J. F., Weissman, M. M., Merikangas, K. R., Pauls, D. L., & Prusoff, B. A. (1983). Panic disorder and major depression: Increased risk of major depression, alcoholism, panic and phobic disorders in families with depressed probands with panic disorder. *Archives of General Psychiatry, 40,* 1055–1060.

Leff, M. J., Roatch, J. F., & Bunney, W. E. (1970). Environmental factors preceding the onset of severe depressions. *Psychiatry, 33,* 293–311.

Lesser, I. M., Rubin, R. T., Finder, E., Forster, B., & Poland, R. E. (1983). Situational depression and the dexamethasone suppression test. *Psychoneuroendocrinology, 8,* 441–445.

Lewis, A. J. (1934). Melancholia: A historical review. *Journal of Mental Science, 80,* 1–42.

Lloyd, C. (1980). Life events and depressive disorder reviewed: II. Events as precipitating factors. *Archives of General Psychiatry, 37,* 542–548.

Lloyd, C., Zisook, S., Click, M., Jr., & Jaffe, K. E. (1981). Life events and response to antidepressants. *Journal of Human Stress, 7,* 2–15.

Lumsden, D. P. (1981). Is the concept of "stress" of any use, anymore? In D. Randall (Ed.), *Contributions to primary prevention in mental health: Working papers.* Toronto: Toronto National Office of the Canadian Mental Health Association.

Mapother, E. (1926). Discussion on manic-depressive psychosis. *British Medical Jourral, 2,* 872–879.

Mason, J. W. (1975a). A historical view of the stress field: Part I. *Journal of Human Stress, 1,* 6–12.

Mason, J. W. (1975b). A historical view of the stress field: Part II. *Journal of Human Stress, 1,* 22–36.

Matussek, P., & Wiegand, M. (1985). Partnership problems as causes of endogenous and neurotic depressions. *Acta Psychiatrica Scandanavica, 71,* 95–104.

McGuffin, P., Katz, R., & Bebbington, P. (1988). The Camberwell Collaborative Depression Study: III. Depression and adversity in the relatives of depressed probands. *British Journal of Psychiatry, 152,* 775–782.

Mendlewicz, J., Charon, F., & Linkowski, P. (1986). Life events and the dexamethasone suppression test in affective disorders. *Journal of Affective Disorders, 10,* 203–206.

Miller, P. McC., Ingham, J. G., Kreitman, N. B., Surtees, P. G., & Sashidharan, S. P. (1987). Life events and other factors implicated in onset and in remission of psychiatric illness in women. *Journal of Affective Disorders, 12,* 73–88.

Monroe, S. M. (1982a). Assessment of life events: Retrospective versus prospective strategies. *Archives of General Psychiatry, 39,* 606–610.

Monroe, S. M. (1982b). Life events and disorder: Event-symptom associations and the course of disorder. *Journal of Abnormal Psychology, 91*, 14–24.

Monroe, S. M. (1982c). Life events assessment: Current practices, emerging trends. *Clinical Psychology Review, 2*, 435–453.

Monroe, S. M. (1990). Symptom comorbidity in anxiety and depression: Psychosocial factors. In J. D. Maser & C. R. Cloninger (Eds.), *Comorbidity in anxiety and mood disorders*. Washington, D.C.: American Psychiatric Press.

Monroe, S. M., Bellack, A. S., Hersen, M., & Himmelhoch, J. M. (1983). Life events, symptom course, and treatment outcome in unipolar depressed women. *Journal of Consulting and Clinical Psychology, 51*, 604–615.

Monroe, S. M., & Peterman, A. M. (1988). Life stress and psychopathology. In L. H. Cohen (Ed.), *Research on stressful life events: Theoretical and methodological issues* (pp. 31–63). New York: Sage.

Monroe, S. M., & Steiner, S. C. (1986). Social support and psychopathology: Interrelations with preexisting disorder, stress, and personality. *Journal of Abnormal Psychology, 95*, 29–39.

Monroe, S. M., Thase, M. E., Hersen, M., Bellack, A. S., & Himmelhoch, J. M. (1985). Life events and the endogenous-nonendogenous distinction in the treatment course of depression. *Comprehensive Psychiatry, 26*, 175–186.

Oei, T. I., & Zwart, F. M. (1986). The assessment of life events: Self-administered questionnaire versus interview. *Journal of Affective Disorders, 10*, 185–190.

Parker, G., & Blignault, I. (1985). Psychosocial predictors of outcome in subjects with untreated depressive disorder. *Journal of Affective Disorders, 8*, 73–81.

Parker, G., Blignault, I., Manicavasagar, V. (1988). Neurotic depression: Delineation of symptoms profiles and their relation to outcome. *British Journal of Psychiatry, 152*, 15–23.

Parker, G., Tennant, C., & Blignault, I. (1985). Predicting improvement in patients with nonendogenous depression. *British Journal of Psychiatry, 146*, 287–293.

Paykel, E. S. (1982). Life events and early environment. In E. S. Paykel (Ed.), *Handbook of affective disorders* (pp. 146–161). New York: Guilford.

Paykel, E. S. (1983). Methodological aspects of life event research. *Journal of Psychosomatic Research, 27*, 341–352.

Paykel, E. S., Rao, B. M., & Taylor, C. N. (1984). Life stress and symptom pattern in out-patient depression. *Psychological Medicine, 14*, 559–568.

Paykel, E. S., & Tanner, J. (1976). Life events, depressive relapse and maintenance treatment. *Psychological Medicine, 6*, 481–485.

Perris, H. (1984a). Life events and depression: Part 2. Results in diagnostic subgroups, and in relations to the recurrence of depression. *Journal of Affective Disorders, 7*, 25–36.

Perris, H. (1984b). Life events and depression: Part 3. Relation to severity of the depressive syndrome. *Journal of Affective Disorders, 7*, 37–44.

Perris, H., von Knorring, L., Oreland, L., & Perris, C. (1984). Life events and biological vulnerability: A study of life events and platelet MAO activity in depressed patients. *Psychiatry Research, 12*, 111–120.

Pinel, P. (1806/1962). *A treatise on insanity, in which are contained the principles of a new and more practical nosology of maniacal disorders* (Translated by D. D. Davis). New York: Hafner.

Prudo, R., Harris, T., & Brown, G. W. (1984). Psychiatric disorder in a rural and an urban population, 3: Social integration and the morphology of affective disorder. *Psychological Medicine, 14*, 327–345.

Rees, W. L. (1976). Stress, distress, and disease. *British Journal of Psychiatry, 128*, 3–18.

Rosen, G. (1957). Social stress and mental disease from the eighteenth century to the present: Some origins of social psychiatry. *The Milbank Memorial Fund Quarterly, xx*, 5–32.

Roy, A. (1987). Five risk factors for depression. *British Journal of Psychiatry, 150*, 536–541.

Roy, A., Breier, A., Doran, A. R., & Pickar, D. (1985). Life events in depression: Relationship to subtypes. *Journal of Affective Disorders, 9,* 143–148.

Roy, A., Pickar, D., Linnoila, M., Doran, A. R., & Paul, S. M. (1986). Cerebrospinal fluid monoamine and monamine metabolite levels and the dexamethasone suppression test: Relationship to life events. *Archives of General Psychiatry, 43,* 356–360.

Schmale, A. H. (1973). Normal grief is not a disease. In I. K. Goldberg, S. Maltiz, & A. H. Kutscher (Eds.), *Psychopharmacological agents for the terminally ill and bereaved.* New York: Columbia University Press.

Seyle, H. (1976). *The stress of life* (2nd ed.). New York: McGraw-Hill.

Slater, E., & Slater, P. (1944). A heuristic theory of neurosis. *Journal of Neurological Psychiatry, 7,* 49–55.

Tennant, C. (1983). Life events and psychological morbidity: the evidence from prospective studies (Editorial). *Psychological Medicine, 13,* 483–486.

Tennant, C., Bebbington, P., & Hurry, J. (1981a). The role of life events in depressive illness: Is there a substantial causal relation? *Psychological Medicine, 11,* 379–389.

Tennant, C., Bebbington, P., & Hurry, J. (1981b). The short-term outcome of neurotic disorders in the community: the relation of remission to clinical factors and to neutralizing life events. *British Journal of Psychiatry, 139,* 213–220.

Thoits, P. A. (1982). Conceptual, methodological, and theoretical problems in studying social support as a buffer against life stress. *Journal of Health and Social Behavior, 23,* 145–159.

Thomson, K. C., & Hendrie, H. C. (1972). Environmental stress in primary depressive illness. *Archives of General Psychiatry, 26,* 130–132.

Tyrer, P. (1985). Neurosis divisible? *Lancet, 1,* 685–688.

Van Valkenburg, C., Akiskal, H. S., Puzantian, V., & Rosenthal, T. (1984). Anxious depressions: Clinical, family history, and naturalistic outcome - Comparisons with panic and major depressive disorders. *Journal of Affective Disorders, 6,* 67–82.

Willner, P. (1985). *Depression: A psychobiological synthesis.* New York: Wiley.

Zimmerman, M., Pfohl, B., & Stangl, D. (1986). Life events assessment of depressed patients: A comparison of self-report and interview formats. *Journal of Human Stress, 11,* 13–19.

5 Interpersonal Aspects of Depression from Psychodynamic and Attachment Perspectives

Joseph Becker
University of Washington, Seattle

Karen Schmaling
National Jewish Center for Immunology and Respiratory Medicine and University of Colorado

Even most biologically oriented investigators acknowledge that psychosocial factors probably play a significant role in aspects of the etiology, onset, course, and outcome of affective disorders. But as yet we lack definitive evidence for the relative weight of genetic and social environmental factors in the etiology of affective disorders. In summarizing the relevant genetic data, Wender, Kety, Rosenthal, et al. (1986) cite convergent evidence that is strongly suggestive of a significant genetic contribution to bipolar affective disorder and to severe, recurrent unipolar major depressive disorder. However, findings such as those by Frank, Kupfer, and Perel (1989) who found that once a month maintenance sessions of interpersonal psychotherapy (Klerman, Weissman, Rounsaville, & Chevron, 1984) substantially reduced the rate of recurrence of unipolar major depression in recovered patients who were at high risk for recurrences, and of those by Miklowitz, Goldstein, Nuechterlein, et al. (1988) on the relationship of expressed emotion to frequency and severity of bipolar episodes indicate that psychosocial factors play a significant role even in genetically loaded affective disorders.

At present, it seems probable that psychosocial factors play a significant role in the etiology of minor affective disorders, in the precipitation of minor and major affective disorders, and in the maintenance, severity, and relapse rates of these disorders. However, it should be noted that the likelihood of a significant genetic component even in such relatively mild forms of depression as dysthymia has received increased support (Akiskal, Rosenthal, Haykal et al., 1980; Klein, Clark, Dansky & Margolis, 1988).

In the absence of both good longitudinal data on the interpersonal aspects of persons at high risk for nonbipolar mood disorders and of systematic cross-sectional data, we review literature of widely varying objectivity. Recently, Barnett and Gotlib (1988) reviewed content which somewhat overlaps our own, but they confined themselves to studies that are reasonably rigorous and relevant to prevailing social learning and cognitive theories of depression. Because their review indicated rather limited progress in our understanding of the psychosocial and interpersonal aspects of depression it seemed worthwhile in this review to include some less rigorous, more speculative perspectives. Our review of social learning and cognitive theories and research are mostly contained in the chapter which follows.

Thus far, only psychodynamic investigators have observed persons with affective disorders intensively and over prolonged time periods. A review of psychodynamic formulations also provides historical perspective on how interpersonal aspects of mood disorders have been conceptualized. As will become apparent, many aspects of contemporary nonpsychodynamic models of depression were anticipated in the psychodynamic literature. There appears to be a growing coalescence of these perspectives (Horowitz, 1988). Perhaps some of the astute clinical observations contained in the psychodynamic literature may yet stimulate additional fertile, testable hypotheses. In order to facilitate an historical perspective, these papers are reviewed roughly in the order of their publication.

INTERPERSONAL ASPECTS OF PSYCHODYNAMIC THEORY

Classical Psychoanalysis

Classic psychoanalytic papers dealt mostly with severe mood disorders and emphasized intrapsychic rather than interpersonal or broader ecological phenomena. The intrapsychic aspects of this literature (Becker, 1974; Mendelson, 1974), indicate that persons who are prone to severe depressive disorders are afflicted by so called instinctual fixations acquired during the late oral and early anal developmental stages. These fixations are caused by excessive indulgence, deprivation, or a mixture of the two that result from interpersonal interactions and/or their interactions with predisposing genetic and constitutional factors. Later in life, when depression prone persons are faced with severe loss or disappointment they tend to partially regress toward the developmentally earlier modes of relating and experiencing that characterize these fixation stages (Erickson, 1963). The probable role of biogenetic factors in many depressions was generally acknowledged.

According to Abraham's 1911 and 1916 papers (1945) interpersonal relations associated with such early developmental fixations are intensely ambivalent, with the hostile component largely out of awareness. The intensity of depression is directly proportional to the intensity of repressed hatred. He contended that

". . . hate paralyzes love," which accounts for the frequent depressive complaint of a diminished capacity to love. The interpersonally annoying quality of depressive symptoms derives from the repressed hostility. Because of their impaired reality-testing, depressives tend to equate thought with action and to therefore experience intense guilt for harboring destructive impulses toward others (see Feather & Rhoades, 1972 for a psychodynamic/cognitive-behavioral treatment approach related to such false equivalencies). Furthermore, Abraham speculated that depressives project much of their repressed hatred, thus they tend to believe that others hate them because of their inherent, hence inescapable, deficits.

Abraham (1924) partly ascribed the depressives' fixations to severe injuries to their self-esteem that resulted from multiple disappointments in their early parental relations. Because the love objects of adults tend to be partly identified with the adult's own parents, the hostility of adult depressives toward their current significant others partly reflects their earlier dissatisfying relations with their parental figures. In the depression prone, this partial identification of current with past significant others becomes even more pronounced after disappointment-induced regression.

In terms of character structure and related interpersonal patterns, Abraham contended that when not depressed, the depression-prone relate to others in an obsessional manner (i.e., they are controlling, obstinate, and defiant). He contended that successful treatment outcomes could result from changing their distorted thinking during remissions.

In his classic paper "Mourning and Melancholia" Freud (1917) noted the disparity between severe depressives' protestations of their worthlessness and their chronic belief that they have been unjustly slighted. He hypothesized that the depressives' self-accusations are really directed at significant others: ". . . everything derogatory that they say about themselves is at bottom said about someone else" (p. 248). He agreed with Abraham's contention that depressives have an impaired capacity for love even when they are not clinically depressed.

According to Freud, in normal mourning for a lost significant object (person, ideal, function, possession, etc.) reinvolvements with others tend to occur fairly soon. But if the lost or disappointing relationship was an intensely ambivalent one, as tends to be the case in persons predisposed to severe depressions, object loss (real or unconscious) results in partial identification with the lost object. Components of the previously *interpersonally* directed ambivalence are split and internalized. The conflict between the loving and hostile components of the ambivalent relationship is then reenacted intrapsychically (Freud, 1923, p. 54). The hostile component of the internalized ambivalence now in the service of the regressed, chastising super-ego treats the ego now identified with the lost object as the unconsciously hostile ego would like to have treated the object prior to the onset of the internalization and regression process. However, even in psychotic depressions, regression is only partial. Some of the original interpersonal hostility may still be outwardly directed and reinforced by the discomfort inflicted on significant others.

Freud further proposed that depression could result from overly high and critically enforced ego-ideals which the ego was unable to live up to. Like Abraham, Freud also contended that, ". . . the more a man checks his aggressiveness toward the exterior the more severe—that is aggressive—he becomes in his ego-ideal" (1923, p. 54).

Rado (1928), the third major contributor to classic analytic theory on depression, depicted the self-esteem of depressives as unduly dependent on external sources of interpersonal gratification such as love, approval, or recognition. The depression-prone are strongly motivated to control their love objects because even minor disappointments in relationships can severely deflate their self-regard. Prior to the onset of depressive episodes threats to their significant relations tend to elicit enraged rebellion. Depression ensues only if the rebellion fails to restore a gratifying relationship. Rado viewed depression as ". . . a great despairing cry for love". An intrapsychic cycle of guilt, atonement, and forgiveness develops which derives from learned, internalized, interpersonal sequences wherein the person transgresses, is punished, and then forgiven.

In neurotic depression, the depressive's unhappiness may have a manipulative component. But in psychotic depressions, unhappiness reflects intrapsychic events; the super-ego punishes the ego for its aggressive attitudes and behavior toward the love object. Thus, Rado shifted emphasis from the earlier stress on hostility and perfectionism, toward excessive interpersonal dependency.

Gero's (1936) account of several psychoanalytically treated cases of depression illustrates the application of these classic psychodynamic conceptions to case material in a reasonably comprehensible manner.

English Psychoanalytic School

In Klein's 1934 and 1940 papers (1948) the founder of the "English School of Psychoanalysis" contended that all infants respond to frustration with intense rage and sadistic fantasies. These hostile impulses induce severe anxiety and helplessness in the infant because of their destructive import and the resultant fears of retaliation. Rage toward significant others generates fears and fantasies of symbolically disguised and projected persecutors, which sometimes crystallize into animal phobias. Gradually, the infant internalizes representations of good experiences with the mother; this internalized "good object" becomes the source of infantile security. Even mild frustrations by the mothering one can trigger a sequence of rage, sadness, and guilt, leading the child to fear that its rage may have destroyed the good internalized object. Only with sufficient good experience and the development of object constancy does anxiety about destroying the internalized good object subside. Klein regarded the successful resolution of anxieties associated with this developmental phase, the so called "depressive position," as crucial to the development of a capacity for satisfying relations. Many depression-prone persons never receive enough good mothering to enable them to internalize stable good objects capable of neutralizing the hostility generated even by inevitable deprivations and frustrations. Such persons are a constant prey to thoughts and feelings of grief, sadness, and unworthiness. The defenses used by infants to alleviate anxiety related to the preservation of good internal and external objects are similar to those used by adult depressives. These defenses include reparation via suffering in hopes of atonement, denial of loss and/or of hostility, devaluation or overidealization of significant others, and obsessional efforts to control the self and others.

Ego Analysis

The two major ego-analytic contributors to theories of depression are Edith Jacobson and Bibring. According to Jacobson (1971), the psychic traumas that result in subsequent vulnerability to depression occur when the young child no longer believes itself to be omnipotent and thereby becomes increasingly aware of its helplessness and dependency. This realization disposes the child toward acceptance of a strong love-object which is perceived as providing security even if it deprives the child of pleasure. Development of self-esteem depends heavily on the extent to which the young child feels positively toward its parental figures. During early life, boundaries between internalized self and object representations are very permeable. Thus, if children are hostile and deprecating toward their parental figures, these negative feelings and attitudes tend to adversely affect their self-regard, which partly reflects their identifications with their parents. If the child overidealizes its parents and incorporates the parental ideals as part of its own ideals, unfortunate results may also occur. Self-esteem is largely regulated by one's perceived capacity to approximate these internalized standards. If these standards are excessively high in relation to relevant personality factors such as ability, motivation, ego strength and/or opportunities, then vulnerability to deflated self-esteem and depression is also likely to be high.

Bibring (1953) maintained that the *content* of standards relevant to self-esteem regulation is linked to epigenetic developmental stages. Fixation and regression to standards and concerns that are related to particular developmental stages account for why depressives vary in the extent to which the central issue in their depression relates to a sense of helplessness and hopelessness about achieving high, rigidly adhered to standards concerned with affectional deprivation, guilt, or inadequacy.

Interpersonal Variants

An "Intensive Study of Twelve Manic-Depressives" (Cohen, Baker, Cohen, Fromm-Reichman, & Weigart, 1954) was the first major psychodynamic paper to specifically address the interpersonal aspects of depression. Cohen et al.'s sample included patients with bipolar and nonbipolar mood disorders. Their paper attempted to explain the etiology, course, and treatment of mood disorders within a Sullivanian (1953) interpersonal framework. "Our purpose is to delineate as far as possible the experiences with significant people which made it necessary for the prospective manic-depressive to develop the particular patterns of interaction which comprise his character and his illness" (Cohen et al., 1954, p. 120). These interactions are assumed to have shaped the vulnerabilities, defenses, and adaptations of the patients, and to have resulted in their having unrealistic or conflicting goals, vulnerable self-esteem, and inappropriate or inadequate means of obtaining biological satisfactions and interpersonal gratifications essential to their having a secure sense of well-being. The Cohen et al. paper is presented in considerable detail despite its lack of methodological rigor because it has considerably influenced thought and research about interpersonal aspects of depression. Furthermore, it contains many potentially testable but unexamined hypotheses. Cohen et al. had two primary data sources: their interpretations of the transference phenomena which occurred during intensive interpersonal psychotherapy and their patients' accounts of their lives as related during treatment.

According to Cohen et al., families with depression prone persons typically view themselves as socially marginal and thus are very concerned with elevating family prestige. "Good" behavior, academic and economic success are seen as the main avenues for enhancing family prestige. Parents indoctrinate their children with strictly conventional concepts of good behavior which derive from the impersonal authority of the parents' perceptions of the values of their reference groups. The parents' own values are weakly held and poorly conceptualized, but their impersonal standards are strictly enforced. To compound difficulties, multiple adult authority figures with disparate values often reside in the household. Children within these families are valued not for who they are but for what they can do to enhance family status. Children selected to be the primary "standard bearers" of family prestige are especially prone to subsequent depression.

Parental blaming attitudes are common and negatively affect the predepressive's self-evaluation, which is largely dependent on the reflected appraisals of significant others. Frequently, the mother is "intensely ambitious" and prone to devalue the father as the cause of the family's marginal status. Fathers of patients are described as cold and unloving toward their wives, but as fearful of them and desirous of their approval. Fathers blame their wives for being cold and contemptuous. Fathers are often perceived by the children as weak but lovable, while the mothers are seen as the moral authority in the family. The fathers tend to accept their wives' blame and are dependent on them. The fathers seem to convey the message of "Do not be like me." The mothers' contemptuous attitude toward the fathers warns of what might befall the children if they fail to abide by her impersonal standards.

Cohen et al. speculated that the major unresolved anxiety-provoking experiences in depression prone persons occur toward the end of the first year of life when the young child is less intimately bound to the mothering person. At this stage, the child makes less use of identification with the mother than before, but still has a very limited capacity for relating to others as whole distinct persons. Cohen et al. assume that the child feels peculiarly alone and vulnerable to threats of abandonment during this developmental phase. The mothers of predepressives reputedly enjoy the intense dependency of their infants. Difficulties between mother and predepressive develop when the young child begins to exhibit increased independence and rebelliousness for which these mothers have little tolerance.

This transition in maternal behavior complicates the child's attempts to integrate the good and bad aspects of the mother as components of a whole person, which eventuates in the depressive's characteristic ambivalence and difficulties with authority figures. If pleased, important authorities are regarded as the source of all good things, but if displeased, they are perceived as tyrannical and punishing.

Predepressives often have a special role in the family that entails burdensome responsibilities and subjects them to intense envy by other family members. Along with the predepressive's heavy responsibilities often go a sense of loneliness and of being unduly accountable for the family's fate. Envy and competitiveness are typically kept from awareness in order to defend the family ethos, which requires that family members be mutually supportive against a hostile world. To counteract envy and competition, predepressives often undersell themselves and become exceptionally helpful to others, but in return they unconsciously expect complete acceptance and preference. Depressives' tendencies to undersell themselves not only serve to counter unconscious anxieties about envy and competitiveness but also to convey their intense needfulness. However, uncritical acceptance by others of their underselling can evoke the depressive's hatred both toward the other and toward themselves as fraudulent. Constant enactment of the excessively helpless dependent role can eventually convince the depression-prone that they lack capabilities well within their range.

As adults, predepressives tend to have a few intensely dependent, demanding relationships. Fears of abandonment that might result from giving or receiving offense are a major source of anxiety. This anxiety is largely handled by insensitivity to the emotional subtleties of interpersonal exchanges.

Most depressive episodes are precipitated by loss of a significant dependency relationship or by a change in the depressive's perception of such a relationship. Depressives need to keep the extent of their dependency from awareness lest they be overwhelmed with guilt and/or anxiety. This need makes it difficult for them to anticipate and cope effectively with situations that threaten impending loss. Depressive behaviors such as complaining and whining when feeling deprived often alienate needed others. When hopelessness about the restoration of dependency gratifications emerges, depression tends to ensue. Guilt and self-punitive behaviors are seen as attempts to placate and regain the approval of authority figures. Because depressives often do not try to change their unadaptive, dependent behavior, Cohen et al. assume that their guilty expressions do not express genuine regret.

Cohen et al. (1954) believe that the hostility of depressives is secondary to frustrations of their manipulative and exploitive attempts to sustain excessive dependency gratifications. Because of the annoying impact of depressives' dependency related demands Cohen et al. believe that the amount and primacy of hostility associated with depression have been exaggerated.

Another pioneering paper on the interpersonal and particularly the marital aspects of depression was the ego analyst, E. Jacobson's 1956 paper on interactions between depressive partners which she has since revised (1971). Unfortunately, like Cohen et al. she does not consistently distinguish between clinical material based on bipolar and nonbipolar depressives. Jacobson contends that married depressed persons tend to cling too closely to their partners, but often share few interests with them so that they have little to say to each other. The depressed patients are described as often self-sacrificing but domineering. They tend to describe their spouses as more passive, selfish, and demanding than themselves. When the depressives' partners were seen in treatment or for consultation, many of the complaints which depressed patients had voiced about their spouses appeared to be well-founded. Often the partners' praises of the patients were not congruent with their behavior toward the patient. Excessive demands by the partner seemed to frequently precipitate depression in the patient.

Jacobson noted that while the patient's symptoms tend to play on their partner's pity, sympathy, and guilt, the symptoms may also convey sadistic reproaches. Family members sometimes retaliate against the impact of these symptoms by cruel aggressiveness or avoidance which increase the patient's sense of worthlessness.

Certain features of the interpersonal relations of many depressives and borderline personalities may have common origins and similar adult manifestations. As DSM-III-R notes (p. 232) dysthymic and personality disorders frequently coexist. E. Jacobson (1971) among others has cited the tendency of depressives to oscillate between excessive idealization and devaluation of their significant others; pervasive ambivalence and fears of abandonment are reputedly common to both disorders. Psychodynamic and attachment theorists tend to attribute a significant amount of the relationship difficulties in these disorders to vicissitudes of the separation-individuation developmental phase. Melges and Swartz (1989) elaborate this theorizing for Borderline Disorder in a way that may well overlap with fluctuations in depressives' relationships. According to their conjectures, in persons prone to Borderline Disorder, moves toward engagement arouse dysphoria about being overcontrolled but attempted adaptations by withdrawal arouse dysphoric fears of abandonment. In this cybernetic feedback loop which is largely controlled by negative feedback, a sense of continuous loss of control may develop. Furthermore, "deviant amplification," wherein deviations amplify other deviations, can aggravate relationships. They cite the example of a person blaming another, leading to retaliation by the other, leading to further blame and a spiraling cycle of dysphoria and oscillation.

Melges and Swartz (1989) attribute adult manifestations of this pattern to a socialization wherein the person felt threatened by abandonment if they displayed too much autonomy. The offspring are prone to feeling victimized, dominated, abandoned, and helpless hence entitled to support.

Borderlines tend to split others into perceiving themselves as rescuers who see the borderline as helpless and victimized, or as rejectors who feel manipulated.

Because persons prone to becoming enmeshed in negative feedback cybernetic processes tend to be excessively concerned with others' reactions to them, they are very present focused and therefore unlikely to access memories of prior pleasurable experiences. As will be seen in the next chapter, social learning interaction theorists of depression such as Lewinsohn, Coyne, and Wortman share some quite similar concepts to those of Melges and Swartz.

Adlerian Analysis

While Adlerians (Adler, 1961; Bonime, 1966) reject orthodox psychoanalytic instinctual energy concepts and the overriding importance of early experience, they nonetheless accept the idea that much of the predisposition to depression stems from childhood interaction patterns with parents. They stress the tendency of parents of predepressives to be manipulative and to deprive the child of spontaneity and of self-regard despite their facade of oversolicitude. The reaction of the predepressive child is to feel chronically discouraged, worthless, and often vengeful. As adults they tend to be socially insecure due in part to their deficient social skills. Often they alienate the very sources of gratification they covet by their demandingness and inability to trust others' affection and concern as genuine rather than exploitive.

Adlerians view the resultant depressive suffering as an inevitable consequence of their *lifestyle* rather than as unconsciously sought atonement for hostile impulses. Furthermore, they see depression as a *practice* (Wachtel, 1982) rather than as a syndrome. The depressives' protestations of inadequacy are seen as exaggerated attempts to coerce support and to evade social responsibility. Depressives are reputed to experience attempts at social influence as aversive; they are described as unwilling to give gratification or to accept it, as being ruthless and disdainful toward others, and as unwilling to exert themselves in pursuit of their excessively high aspirations, but then of blaming others for their failure to attain these aspirations. Chronic anxiety sometimes accompanies depression; this anxiety is ascribed to depressives' apprehensions lest their manipulativeness prove to be unsuccessful.

Social Role Disruption

Contributions to this perspective have a strong sociological component. In marked contrast to the Adlerian formulations, E. Becker (1964) characterized depressives as excessively conforming, especially so with the desires of the significant others whose approval they seek. Their restricted social repertoire and sources of social reinforcement make them highly vulnerable to devastating losses. Their few relationships provide their principle sources of meaningful activity. Hence the loss of *meaningful role activity* may be fully as important an etiologic factor in depression as the loss of a significant other.

Oatley and Bolton (1985) though not psychodynamically oriented, have also developed a role centered social-cognitive theory of depression that synthesizes and elaborates aspects of Brown and Harris's (1978), Sullivan's (1953), Bibring's (1953) and E. Becker's (1964) theorizing. Basically, their notion is that depression tends to occur when loss jeopardizes or threatens to jeopardize the major role of persons who do not have substantial secondary roles available to them. One's sense of self or of identity is integrally bound-up with one's major role(s). Roles entail goals, plans, and expectancies. Their fulfillment defines a sense of worth and meaningfulness in life. Major role enactments typically involve reciprocal patterns of interaction with significant others.

If the significant other is unable or unwilling to engage in reciprocal behavior due, for example, to death, divorce, demoralization or unemployment, expectable role enactment is disrupted. Expectancies of the behavior of the "role-other" are incorporated into an internalized model with personal and societal rules governing interactional expectancies and outcomes. Major discrepancies from expectancies in major role enactments are depressogenic because they undermine one's sense of worth, meaningfulness, and self-esteem. Since goals are the sources of action, the loss of someone who is integrally associated with the role enactments essential to goal attainment can vitiate motivation. Thus, precipitants to depressive onsets often involve violated role mutuality.

Oatley and Bolton provide a rather ingenious account of the major symptoms of acute and chronic depressions within the framework of their theory. They view chronic depression as a major role wherein the regressive strategies (e.g, excessive dependency, complaining, sulkiness, etc.) for seeking worth and meaning preempt the development or expression of more realistically adaptive role behaviors.

Oatley and Bolton agree with attachment theorists and others (Costello, 1982) that the *basic vulnerability in depression probably resides in difficulties in forming and maintaining close relationships*. However, depressive vulnerability may also result from strategies and circumstances that are not conducive to forming new relationships as, for example, culture shock resulting from immigration to a markedly different culture or an inadequate repertoire of satisfying activities that involve the participation by others. Oatley and Bolton do not view cognitive bias as an important factor in depression.

Integrative Psychoanalysis

Arieti and Bemporad (1978) have sought to bridge the predominantly intrapsychic orientation of the Freudian and ego-analysts with the predominantly sociocultural orientation of the neo-Freudian psychodynamic schools. According to Arieti and Bemporad, the core problem in depression is the depressive's inability to seek or enjoy "autonomous gratification" and their overreliance on external support for gratifications, self-esteem, and a meaningful existence. They view the depressive as coerced into conformity with values that the dominant parent (typically mother for severe depressives and father for the less severely depressed) espouses but does not exemplify. Deviation from these values evokes severe anxiety. The depression-prone repeat this manner of relating with subsequent significant others.

Three types of depressives are identified, but all share an inability to experience direct spontaneous gratification. Rather gratification must be mediated by the approval of a dominant other, or by a specific role in an organization, or by the attainment of a dominant goal. These pursuits govern lifestyle including interpersonal modes of relating. In the "Dominant Other" type of depression, an implicit bargaining relationship exists wherein, if the depression-prone person (typically female due to cultural influences) conforms, she can at least fantasize approval by the dominant other. These depressives are described as attempting to extract support by engaging in passive, clinging, manipulative behaviors and by avoiding rebelliousness. A common variant in males is a similar compliant subservience to the perceived expectancies of an institution. In the Dominant Goal-Oriented depressive, self-esteem is centered on the fanatical pursuit of an achievement which is fantasized as totally fulfilling. Such persons are reputed to be seclusive, arrogant, and obsessive.

Episodic depressives can at least fantasize gratification which enables them to function reasonably well between episodes. But characterological depressives are chronically fearful of rejection or exploitation. They lead severely constricted lives characterized by pettiness, a chronic sense of futility, criticalness of self and others, and hypochondriasis. Chronic mild to moderately severe depressives are vulnerable to more severe episodes if they experience a full awareness of their sterile existence.

As Arieti and Bemporad construe depression, it largely results from the perpetuation of an inaccurate mode of cognitive processing that evolves largely during childhood but is thereafter repeated.

Nonbipolar Depressive Subtypes and Interaction Patterns

A principal shortcoming of most of these previously cited psychodynamic papers is their generality. Typically, there are very limited attempts to delineate distinguishing categorical or dimensional characteristics among diagnostic categories or among depressive subtypes, a shortcoming that is regrettably not limited to psychodynamic formulations.

Dependent Vs. Achievement Subtypes. As many writers, including Beck (1983) Arieti and Bemporad (1978), Blatt and Shichman (1983), Coyne and Gotlib (1983), and Chodoff (1973) have suggested, subtypes of nonbipolar depressives may have relatively specific vulnerabilities, provoking agents, resources, and coping capacities. These ideas are beginning to be empirically examined (e.g., Blatt, Quinlan, Chevron, McDonald, & Zuroff, 1982; Hammen, Ellicott, Gitlin, & Jameson, 1989; Klein, Harding, Taylor, & Dickstein, 1988). To a considerable extent, these subtypes derive from or were anticipated by the psychodynamic literature.

Because the interpersonal characteristics of these subtypes or dimensions overlap considerably, only the interpersonal aspects of Beck's (1983) subtypes are explicated. Beck indicates that "During 1980 we focussed a good deal of attention on the thesis proposed by Bowlby . . . that the disruption of social bonding was a critical factor in the production of depression" (p. 266). While this conceptualization fitted most of the cases of depression treated by him and his associates, a minority of cases shared enough attributes to warrant a second category. Depressions fitting the former category have been termed "sociotropic" (socially dependent) and those fitting the latter as "autonomous." He contends that these two constructs that are variously termed "types of cases," "personality dimensions," "problems," "modes of functioning" are characterized by typical premorbid personalities, systems of beliefs, assumptions and expectations, vulnerabilities to specific life stresses, symptom patterns and problems in treatment. These personality dimensions are not unique to depression, but in terms of more *traditional* depressive designations, the socially dependent (sociotropic) type conforms more to reactive depressions and the autonomous type to endogenous depressions. While Beck (1983) *very explicitly* (pp. 267–268) endorses multiple biopsychosocial causes of depressive disorders, his theory, research, and treatment center on "here and now factors," with an "overemphasis" (his statement) on intrapsychic aspects of depression, that is on the patient's construction of reality. Nonetheless he recognizes the important role of the social environment in depressive reactions (p. 269). He acknowledges that contexts can mobilize either sociotropic or autonomous tendencies, as for example, situations loaded with competitive versus loving implications; and likewise that conflicts between such tendencies may occur. From Beck's perspective, affect and behavior are primarily determined by how one construes events. Depressogenic constructs derive mostly from aversive experiences and consist largely of negatively stereotyped automatic cognitive patterns, "thoughtless thinking."

Persons with socially dependent personalities are strongly concerned with positive interactions with others. Their prime motif is receiving. They have powerful passive-receptive and narcissistic wishes (i.e., to be accepted, supported, admired), and their sense of well-being and quality of function are largely dependent on positive feedback from others.

In contrast, persons operating in an autonomous mode are chiefly concerned with "doing." They are invested in issues like independence, boundaries, integrity, and goal attainment.

Sociotropic persons (predominantly female) tend to seek close, stable, predictable, nurturant relationships. Rejection and abandonment are their chief fears. They are reluctant to risk alienating others because of their need for constant reassurance. Their symptoms chiefly express a need for succorance; when provided, they tend to perk-up and become more optimistic about the possibility of their lives' improving. Their self-criticalness centers on the theme of being socially undesirable. Often they appear to be sad and lonely.

Autonomous depressives (predominantly male) tend to be very self-judgmental, less influenced by social feedback, less sensitive to others, averse to permanent commitments, and more tolerant of variability and ambiguity. They dislike external pressures or seeking assistance. Pleasure is mainly derived from goal attainment. With regard to interpersonal symptoms, autonomous personalities tend to be less interested in and withdrawn from others. They can be quite hostile, rejecting of help, and pessimistic about its potential efficacy.

Socially dependent types feel and think of themselves as severely *deprived*, ". . . . they try to renew social bonding by calling on others' sympathy, understanding, and reassurance" (Beck, p. 276). In a sense they show consistent dependency pre and intramorbidly. In contrast, autonomous types believe themselves to be failures and switch from perceiving themselves as self-reliant premorbidly to perceiving themselves as passive, helpless, and guilt ridden intramorbidly.

In depressives, the evidence so far more strongly supports Beck et al.'s predictions about the specificity of certain types of vulnerability events and symptom manifestations to the social dependent dimension of the Sociotropy-Autonomy Scale than to the autonomy dimension (Robins & Block, 1988; Robins, Block, & Peselow, 1989).

Depressive Interaction Patterns. In a somewhat abstruse but stimulating paper, Wiener (1989) contends that the most useful way to understand and correct dysfunctional behaviors is to identify the patterns of transactions within which they occur. Based primarily on clinical observation and literature review, Wiener illustrates a number of interactional patterns that are frequently (but not uniquely) associated with distinctive aspects of depressive speech. A rationale for presenting Wiener's undocumented depressive interactive patterns is nicely reflected by Coyne, Burchill, and Stiles' (in press) able summary of the interaction perspective on depression. They point out that much of the evidence for its importance ". . is circumstantial and suggestive, rather than indicative of the complex processes by which depressed persons and those around them are influencing each other" (p. 3).

Wiener contends that dysfunctional behavioral patterns are usually quite normal within appropriate contexts but dysfunctional when displayed in inappropriate contexts. He takes a series of statements often associated with depression such as "I feel helpless" and analyzes their import within five prototypical patterns of interactions and attitudes, which he infers from the interpersonal behavior of depressives. The interactional matrices are labeled as follows:

1. Passive, Non-Initiating; Claim to Low Competence and Helplessness;
2. Emotionally labile, Egocentric; Claim to Powerlessness;
3. Withdrawn, Obsessive; Claim of Worthlessness or Guilt;
4. Intrusive, Agitated, Worried; Claim to Special Knowledge;
5. Physically Incapacitated.

According to Wiener, the words–action pattern conveying "I feel helpless" within his first context (also labeled Passive-Dependent-Incompetent) describes a self-presentation expressive of immaturity, incompetence, passivity, and helplessness. It implies that others are capable of more mature actions, and it tends to evoke a response of trying to succor the helpless person. If declarations of helplessness persist, others are likely to escape or avoid contact. Such reactions tend to escalate declarations of helplessness. Persons displaying this pattern are often viewed as shy and they complain about loneliness. "I can't" is a common statement within this pattern which tends to elicit pep talks about only needing to exert more effort.

The context for the "Narcissistic-Reactive-Powerless" behaviors in the second category are expressions of hurt stemming from powerlessness to cope with the excessive demands or expectancies of a significant other. Need for the good will of what the other is believed to be able to provide constrains expressions that might alienate the other. Incompetence is not displayed within this matrix. Furthermore, this matrix typically involves complaints to a third person about the excessive demands of someone. This behavior usually evokes support and validation from the third person. In short, one complains to someone about someone else's excessive demands and receives support.

The context for the third category, also labeled Self-Evaluative Withdrawal, is one of withdrawal, uncommunicativness, and claims of guilt and/or worthlessness. Perfectionistic and self-evaluative preoccupations are common. Persons who behave thusly tend to be perceived as uncomfortable and disinterested in social behavior. Negative self-statements from such persons elicit responses stressing the worth and achievements of the self-deprecator. Self-evaluations are more salient than others' evaluations except for a low tolerance of others' criticism. This pattern is believed to derive from contexts in which confession, contriteness, and retribution were associated with a return to acceptance. This stereotypic interaction pattern has normal antecedents in childhood, but unless an adult is physically incapacitated such declarations are not *age* appropriate.

The action matrix for category four, also labeled as agitated, worried, complaining involves a compulsion to complain indiscriminately about unspecified external threats. This pattern is traditionally referred to as paranoid or delusional. Wiener observes that it is as if only by communicating something of great importance could contact with others be justified. It tends to be quite effective at eliciting a response even if only of disbelief.

Wiener's fifth and last social interaction matrix involves physical disability. Everyone responds as though the person were no longer capable of conducting their premorbid social behavior. Persons respond with empathy, reassurance, reaffirmation of relationships, and validation of incapacity rather than pep talks about past attainments as indicators of worth. Disclaimers of the basis for worries may also figure in this matrix.

These interpersonal interaction patterns undoubtedly overlap each other, and as Wiener indicates, they are not exhaustive of characteristic depressive patterns. However, there are probably a finite number of validly discriminable interaction patterns, and it seems reasonable to expect that some of these patterns will be more strongly associated with certain diagnostic classifications and phases of maladaptive behavior than with others. Wiener has elaborated his interactional matrices to a degree of complexity beyond the efforts of most investigators. Their validity and utility seem well worth exploring.

ATTACHMENT AND DEPRESSION

As noted, most psychodynamic and social learning/cognitive theorists agree that a major factor in vulnerability to the onset, maintenance, and recurrence of depressive disorders relates to difficulties in developing and retaining close, secure interpersonal relationships. These concerns are the central focus of attachment theory. Attachment theory figures increasingly in studies of both early social development and of subsequent psychopathology (Paterson & Moran, 1988). The roots of attachment concepts lie in psychodynamic theory and in the biological and social sciences.

Attachment Defined

Bowlby (1988a) defines attachment as a bond with another discriminated and preferred individual who is typically perceived as being stronger and wiser. Attachment behaviors are designed to achieve or maintain closeness to the attachment object. These behaviors are directed toward particular individuals over considerable periods of time. Initially, they largely subserve survival needs.

When formed, maintained, or renewed, attachment bonds tend to be associated with strong positive affects and conversely when bonds are threatened or lost they tend to be associated with strong negative affects. The initiation and termination of attachment behaviors are activated by relatively specific conditions.

Evolutionary Adaptive Function of Attachment

From an evolutionary perspective, affective-cognitive-behavioral patterns develop and endure because they confer an added survival-reproductive advantage. Among mammalian young, especially some species of primates, depressive-like reactions to separation from, or to loss of, a very closely associated other are common. This observation has generated speculation about the possible adaptive value of such depressive-like reactions. Many students of depression (e.g., Klerman et al., 1984) surmise that among species in which the young have a prolonged extrauterine dependence on their mothers, the nurturance and support she provides fosters the development of attachment bonds. When these bonds are threatened by loss or separation such infants typically respond with anguish and despair which tends to elicit nurturance and protective reactions from the mothering one. The inherent dependency of human young typically leads to many repetitions of this pattern. The basic determinant then of early attachment is the mother's protective and nurturant response to the youngster's security needs (Bowlby, 1988a). This mother–infant interactive pattern appears to be largely genetically programmed. But since humans are less instinctually governed than other primate species, the potential for this supportive process going awry is substantial.

Early Attachment Patterns

Ainsworth (1989), a seminal attachment theorist and researcher, developed a research paradigm, the Strange Situation (Ainsworth, Blehar, Waters, & Wall, 1978), in order to systematically evaluate and elaborate her assumption that the parents' manner of interacting with the infant has significant implications for the infant's subsequent social relations. Strong advocates of this position (Bowlby, 1988b; Sroufe, 1985) argue that the mother's manner of relating to the child has markedly greater impact on many crucial aspects of the child's social and personality development than innate temperamental factors. However, they do not contend that early patterns of relationships are fixed or confined to a single pattern at a time; (e.g., the pattern can differ considerably between the child and each parent). Furthermore, attachment investigators have observed that changes in the parents' adaptive-emotional state predictably influence their manner of relating to their children, as well as the child's reactions to them and to others. These matters and their implications for depression become clearer as basic relationship patterns are explicated.

The Strange Situation research paradigm was developed primarily to investigate individual differences in the mother–infant dyad. Attachment within this framework is conceived of as a behavioral control system. The primary objective of the paradigm is to reveal the dynamic interplay between the child's autonomy-exploratory behaviors and its dependent needs for a secure base (typically mother). It is believed that aspects of the infant's models of itself, its parent, and their relationship are demonstrated within this context. The Strange Situation paradigm elicits attachment behaviors by progressively augmenting situational stressors. The behavioral patterns displayed in the Strange Situation have been shown to be representative of corresponding dyadic interactions at home (Gaensbauer, Harmon, Cytryn, & McKnew, 1984).

When secure or healthy attachment has occurred ("Type B"), the mother is perceived by the child as a reliable source of comfort and assistance. This fosters a sense of competence which enables the youngster to actively explore the environment. Mothers of Type B children foster autonomy but readily provide assistance if needed. Youngsters with such attachments are usually a pleasure to interact with. They tend to be adaptable, optimistic, and to be relatively undemanding and to have relatively high frustration tolerance.

Children with "anxious resistant attachments" ("Type C") tend to have mothers who provide inconsistent support initially and who use threats of abandonment as a means of control. As a result, these children may develop intense and enduring separation anxiety. Type C children are described as tense, impulsive, easily frustrated, passive, prone to helplessness and pessimism, clinging, whiny, and demanding of attention. Their exploratory behavior is curtailed by an excessive focus on mother. When these youngsters seek support, their mothers' responses are less predictable than mothers in the other interaction patterns. Maternal rejection is sometimes mixed with overintrusiveness (a combination inherent in high Expressed Emotion which has such untoward effects on adult depressives as discussed in Chapter 6). Such mothers actively discourage exploration and seek to use their children as their own attachment base.

Youngsters with "anxious avoidant attachment" ("Type A"), have been subjected to chronic rejection, abuse, or prolonged separation due to factors such as the mothering one having been institutionalized. Because these children anticipate rebuff when they feel needful of support, they try to avoid being aware of or expressing such needs. These youngsters tend to become emotionally detached, hostile, or chronically antisocial. Like the anxious resistant children, they have low frustration tolerance and are pessimistic.

Psychiatric Implications of Attachment

Bowlby (1977, 1980, 1988b) has been the principal elaborator of the psychiatric implications of attachment theory. His work is primarily derived from developmental psychologists (e.g., Ainsworth et al., 1978), psychoanalysts (e.g., Mahler, Pine, & Bergman, 1975), ethologists (e.g., Hinde, 1982; Lorenz, 1957), with branchings into information processing and cognitive psychology.

Bowlby contends that infants become attached to their caregivers regardless of the quality of care provided by the caregiver. But the quality of care and the resultant relationship between the provider and the infant significantly influence subsequent relationships. Bowlby attributes this durable influence to the inner working models or schematas that evolve from these early interactions. These internalized models which reflect the accrued expectancies and evaluations of self, others, and their interactions and which influence cognition, affect, and behavior are modifiable, but skewed toward congruence with extant models (Wachtel, 1982). Throughout life there is an ongoing interaction between attachment dispositions and interactions with significant others. While unfavorable interactions incline the developmental pathway toward increased vulnerability to or manifestations of psychiatric disorder, favorable interactions have the opposite effect. Bowlby contends that epidemiological findings on psychopathology, especially those of Brown and his associates (e.g., Brown & Harris, 1978), buttress the evidence for his model of developmental psychopathology.

Wortman and Silver's (1989) review of reactions to coping with loss take issue with the important aspect of psychodynamic and attachment theory that relates to the capacity for mature attachments and response to bereavement. These latter theorists generally contend that normal bereavement for a significant other usually entails acute grief followed by a "working through" phase during which the loss comes to be accepted and the grief resolved. According to Wortman and Silver's data, a high portion of the bereaved never go through an acute grieving phase. Those who initially grieve acutely are more likely to remain disturbed for prolonged periods than those who do not. These findings are contrary to prevailing theory which assumes that those who initially grieve over their loss are expected to have the better prognosis. Failure to grieve may sometimes reflect a pathological process, but it may also be associated with positive factors such as superior coping skills and adequate social support. Persons who lose a significant other suddenly and unexpectedly seem more vulnerable to protracted grief as do widows whose marriages had been highly conflictual. Bowlby's contention that those who do not grieve may be incapable of forming attachments is not supported by Wortman and Silver's study of parents who have lost a child from Sudden Infant Death Syndrome.

Bowlby's Psychopathological Subtypes

Bowlby (1977) delineates two broad patterns of disorder that may eventuate from disturbed attachment relationships. Persons afflicted by "anxious attachment" (largely an outgrowth of Type C-Anxious-Resistant Attachment) have chronic concerns about losing attachment figures and cope with this anxiety by excessive clinging, jealousy, manipulative testing, and chronic, intense, displaceable anger. They appear to resemble aspects of Beck's sociotropic depressives as well as of borderlines who often display depressive reactions.

The other major pattern of disorder (which is largely an outgrowth of Type A, Avoidant Attachment) is "compulsive self-reliance." Persons so afflicted despair of establishing satisfying attachment bonds. Fearful of involvements, they attempt to rely on their own resources. Persons with such patterns appear to share much with Beck's autonomous depressives. Bowlby conceptualizes other disorder patterns as combinations of these two basic patterns.

Attachment Studies of Depressed Mothers

Spieker and Booth (1988) have reviewed the data on several studies of interactions between mothers with diagnosable psychiatric conditions and their toddlers. Children with a depressed parent are much more likely to become depressed as adults than children with nondepressed parents (Eisenbruch, 1983). Data from the two studies that were regarded as methodologically adequate are presented in Table 5.1.

TABLE 5.1
Caregiver Psychopathology and Attachment Classifications

	Sameroff et al. (1982)	$n = 232$ age = 12 mos			
	avoidant	10%			
	borderline avoidant	10%			
	secure	51%			
	borderline secure	15%			
	insecure	14%			

	n	Age	A	B	C	AC
Gaensbauer et al. (1984)						
manic depressive parent	7	12 mos	29%	71%	0%	
	7	15 mos	57%	43%	0%	
	7	18 mos	86%	14%	0%	
matched control	7	12 mos	29%	71%	0%	
	7	15 mos	0%	86%	14%	
	7	18 mos	29%	57%	14%	
Radke-Yarrow et al. (1985)						
bipolar depression	14	30-47 mos	43%	21%	7%	29%
major unipolar depression	41	16-44 mos	27%	53%	2%	17%
minor depression	12	25-34 mos	17%	75%	8%	0%
no depression	31	25-39 mos	29%	71%	0%	0%

From Spieker and Booth (1988).

In the Gaensbauer et al. (1984) study, a male child from each of seven families with a bipolar parent (four mothers, three fathers) was seen with his mother in a modified Strange Situation at three points in time. No effects of a disturbed parent were evident at 12 months, but at each successive point in time the percentage of Anxious-Avoidant children of the disturbed parent group increased. Because *n*s in this study are so small, these data by themselves would be unimpressive. However, these data accord well with Anthony's (1975) moving clinical account of child development in homes with bipolar parents. Moreover, coupled with the much larger sample of 99 toddlers and their mothers in the Radke-Yarrow, Cummings, Kuczynski, and Chapman (1985) study, the results are more impressive and suggestive of more specific relationships. It appears that minor depression in the parent does not impair relationships with the child at least in the age range examined, whereas major affective disorder does have harmful effects. Radke-Yarrow et al. used a combined A and C (A/C) category in which infants display moderate-to-high maternal avoidance and moderate-to-high resistance during reunion. The A/C's also tend to look sad or to show a lack of affect. The mothers of children with the A/C pattern were the most severely depressed in the Radke-Yarrow et al. study.

Follow-up Studies of Children with Early Disturbed Attachment

Unfortunately, there are no long-term follow-ups of the social interactions of children of depressed mothers specifically but there are some follow-up studies into the early grade levels of children who had shown anxious attachments when quite young (Belsky & Nezworski 1988). These studies indicate that early relationship patterns are highly predictive of subsequent ones barring significant alterations in the stressfulness of living conditions for the child and/or his current significant others.

Older children whose early relationships were consistently secure tend to have more and better friendships, to be flexible, good stress copers, and to be neither victims nor victimizers. Anxious-avoidant children tend to become victims or victimizers and the anxious-resistant to become victimized. Again, developmental relationship patterns are not invariant, category shifts occur but these shifts do not appear to be spontaneous or endogenous but rather can usually be associated with identifiable environmental factors (Sroufe, 1988).

Nonetheless, the extent to which early internalized working models of relationships influence later relationships remains unclear, as does the extent to which immediate contexts influence the expression of these models. It seems likely that the earlier, more pervasive, and durable the skew from normal attachment experience, the more likely the resultant associated behavioral models and maladaptive patterns are strengthened and perpetuated.

Children in Sroufe's (1988) longitudinal sample who had definite psychiatric disturbances had all had anxious attachments as infants. Sroufe regards early anxious attachments as a *risk* or a *vulnerability* factor rather than as a *cause* of psychopathology. Even in vulnerable persons, significant recent stress and inadequate support appear to be requisites to the onset of most functional psychiatric disorders. Less vulnerable persons tend to have histories of secure attachments and to have developed good coping skills, resilience, and supportive resources (Sroufe, 1988). Apropos of the relatively durable importance which many attachment theorists attribute to mother-infant interactions, it should be noted that Rutter (1985) doubts that infants have sufficient cognitive equipment during the first several years of life for events occurring then to have much durable impact *independent of later life circumstances*. He notes that even psychopathologists who believe that psychosocial factors contribute significantly to psychopathology decreasingly attribute adult psychopathology primarily to such general factors as poor early affectional relationships or severe life events. The quest is for much greater specificity: that is, what differential kinds of life experiences, personality attributes, and life circumstances account for vulnerability to, the precipitation of, or resilient defenses against, particular kinds of psychopathology.

Rutter's misgivings about the lasting impact of early experience may have been colored by the heretofore common notion that the cognitive capacity for empathy does not develop until mid childhood. However, recent studies on empathy in infants (Goleman, 1989) indicate that infants experience the unhappiness of others as though it were happening to themselves. At about age one they begin to show signs of recognizing that another person is experiencing distress. Even then they engage in what has been termed "motor mimicry" that is, they emulate the suffering other.

According to Greenberg and Speltz (1988) Phase III of Bowlby's Developmental Attachment Theory, which begins at about 18 months, contributes substantially to the patterning of subsequent relationships. During this phase the child oscillates among wishes, needs, and fears of exploring the environment versus remaining close to the typically more secure caregiving attachment figure. If Phases I and II were characterized by effective caregiving, the child tends to be secure enough to engage in more extended exploration. In Phase IV, around year three, the dyadic relationship evolves toward a "goal-corrected partnership" wherein the relationship is more reciprocally determined by symbolic as well as behavioral interactions.

The parent's ability to negotiate joint planning which takes account of the child's needs and desires is likely to substantially mediate the child's security in social relationships. "Goal-corrected" partnership between parent and child in regard to separations for example are likely to make these potentially anxiety fraught situations less threatening. The child's acquisition of *negotiating skills* is highly dependent on the parents' modeling and reinforcement of such skills. Initially, of course, the parent controls the process and outcome of these "negotiations" but ideally the parent explicitly takes note of the child's wishes and, when practical, incorporates them in their plans.

Greenberg and Speltz use their so called "deficiency in planning" hypothesis to explain conduct disorder symptoms, but in a way that seems quite applicable to depressive behaviors. Negative attention seeking may be the only effective means the conduct-disordered child has for establishing contact with the parent. Children of depressed mothers often exhibit conduct disorders (Eisenbruch, 1983). Negative-attention seeking behaviors may be modeled as well as negatively reinforced by the parent. Parental coerciveness and lack of limit-setting tend to foster maladaptive behaviors in the child. Children reared within such regimens fail to learn the importance of considering others' needs and desires in pursuing their objectives. As the child moves into newer and broader social contexts, the short-term payoffs from negatively reinforced behaviors acquired during a socialization marked by serious deficiencies in the process of joint planning are likely to be short lived.

As repeatedly noted, the onset or aggravation of depressions are often associated with loss or threatened loss of a significant other. A critical aspect of socializing a secure child appears to be the caregiver's manner of dealing with separation. Ideally feelings are recognized and labeled, explanations are given for caregiver departures, attempts are made to structure such situations so that the child's concerns are acknowledged and, to the extent feasible, moderated by involvement with engaging activities. Given such practices, severely disruptive cognitive-affective states, such as acute separation anxiety is much less likely to ensue in the child and subsequent adult. If children and adults have the linguistic skills to identify the antecedents of their dysphoria and to logically analyze their response to it, they are less likely to feel helpless and hopeless about their plight. Quite likely, depressive-like behaviors by children with their caregivers reflect varying degrees of a need for establishing greater closeness, and their despair about the prospects of achieving closeness.

Selected Attachment Related Research on Adult Depressives

As noted, longitudinal work on attachment behavior in general is still at an early stage and on attachment in populations at high risk for depression at an even earlier stage. We agree with Bowlby's (1988a, 1988b) belief that the work of George Brown and his associates on adult depressives may be especially relevant to elucidating relationships between attachment and depression.

In Brown and Harris' (1978) formulation of the social aspects of depression, self-esteem plays a crucial role in vulnerability and resilience. Severe early disruption of affectional bonds seems to durably impair the persons' capacity for trust in others as well as in their own capabilities. Adversity if overcome often can foster diverse and flexible coping skills and self-confidence so that even when things are not going well the possibility of eventual satisfactions occurring can at least be envisaged.

George Brown (1979) and his associates have been developing a model and theory to explain social etiological factors in depression. Their most comprehensive study was conducted in the Camberwell district of South London (Brown & Harris, 1978). One sample in this study consisted of female depressed patients who were being seen for in- or outpatient psychiatric treatment; the other of a randomly selected sample of women not in treatment. Of the latter group, 240 were working class and 218 were middle class. Though some aspects of the methodology and analyses of this study have been criticized (summarized in Oatley & Bolton, 1985), it is probably the outstanding contribution to this literature to date. Brown et al. initially evolved a tripartite model that integrates aspects of vulnerability, provoking events, and symptom formation. They identified four factors that predispose women to depressive reactions: lack of a confidante, death of a mother before age 11, four or more children in the household younger than age 14, and lack of personal employment outside of the home. Provoking agents are primarily loss of a significant other but more generally, severe life events that anyone familiar with the context within which it occurred (i.e., the background and current circumstances of the person) would regard as a major loss or threat. Severe chronic difficulties like poverty or inadequate housing can also act as provoking agents though to a lesser extent. The final category in the model is symptom formation. The greater the number of premorbid losses, especially by death (including father, siblings, children, spouse, and mother) the greater the likelihood of a severe psychotic reaction.

Without at least one vulnerability factor, even catastrophic losses were unlikely to provoke clinical depression. Availability of an intimate confidante (spouse or boyfriend) conferred a high degree of protection even in the face of an adequate provoking agent plus several vulnerability factors.

In terms of theoretical speculation, Brown et al. conjecture that cognitions related to self-esteem regulation are critical to understanding the operation of their model. As Becker (1979) has shown, the socialization processes attributed to the development of low self-esteem and the independently described socialization processes of predepressives are strikingly similar. Brown et al. argue that loss per se is not inevitably devastating; many bereaved persons do not become clinically depressed. Rather it is the cognitions and experiences consequent to loss that largely account for its impact.

To digress briefly, recent refinements of the attributional theory of depression within a diathesis-stress model (Metalsky, Halberstadt, & Abramson, 1987) and related research reinforce the likelihood that proneness toward a particular *attributional style* associated with the negative outcomes of events in domains that are highly relevant to self-esteem, can act as a vulnerability factor in some depressions. For example, if a person regards the negative outcome of intimate interpersonal relationships as extremely important, and is inclined to make global and stable attributions for such negative outcomes, that person is more likely to become depressed than persons who make unstable, specific attributions or who attach considerably more importance to the outcome of achievement related events than to interpersonal events.

Brown et al. do not discount the contribution of biological factors to depression, but they contend that the role of social factors in etiology, course, and relapse have not been adequately recognized. While they attach somewhat more importance to contemporary factors in the etiology of depression than psychodynamic theorists, their thinking meshes well with its derivatives in attachment theory. For example, they cite a correlation of .60 (gamma) between early loss of mother and lack of an intimate relation with spouse or boyfriend. They do not contend that a direct, powerful, and irreversible relationship exists between disrupted early attachments and impaired subsequent ones, but rather that the consequences of early disruptions are conducive to subsequent life experiences that impair the capacity for adult intimacy.

They cite two major components in the implications of loss: it often entails the disruption of a primary attachment such as the loss of a spouse or of a mother by a young daughter, and it may additionally entail severe role disruption (E. Becker, 1964). As a result, belief in the worthwhileness of existence may be seriously impaired, and a low threshold for experiencing states of helplessness may ensue.

Brown et al. have mainly focused their depression research on women with children in working class districts because they have found this population to be at especially high risk for depression. A high proportion of these women lack adequate social support. Their studies are postdictive and predictive in that they typically deal with the occurrence of depression during the year prior to their initial interview as well as with new cases which occur during the intervals between the initial evaluation and annual follow-ups. Bifulco, Brown, and Harris (1987) conducted a study on the relations among childhood loss of parent, quality of parental care, and adult depression in Islington, an inner city area of London. In part, this Islington study sought to clarify why such mixed results had been obtained in earlier studies on the relationship between early parental (mainly maternal) loss and subsequent depression. Most of these earlier studies had a sampling bias because the probands were diagnosed depressives' undergoing treatment rather than depressives identified in community studies. Only a small proportion of diagnosable depressives seek treatment from mental health specialists. A prior study by Harris, Brown, and Bifulco (1986) as well as work by others which they review (Bifulco et al., 1987) have increasingly implicated the *quality* of care received by a bereaved child as a factor more predictive of vulnerability to depression than the loss of parent (or parents) per se.

The principal question investigated in the Islington study was the extent to which lack of nurturant care by parental figures operates as an independent vulnerability factor or as a mediator between the loss of a mother prior to age 17, the occurrence of an adequate precipitant, and the onset of depression. In a previous study, the Walthamstow survey (Harris et al., 1986), they had found that low self-esteem, premarital pregnancy, and marital separation might be additional intervening variables between lack of care and depression. Therefore, they also sought to replicate these findings.

Subjects in the Islington study were working class mothers with at least one child at home plus single mothers in the locale regardless of their social class. Of the 3000 women surveyed, 438 met subject criteria for a clinically significant depression; 93% of these participated in the first stage interviews and 69% of the latter completed the two annual follow-ups. Both the occurrence of a clinically significant depression (comparable to at least the severity of typical outpatients) and of provoking agents (contextually threatening life events and major chronic difficulties) were assessed for the year preceding the first interview and for each of the years intervening between follow-ups.

Two scales were developed to assess parental neglect of the subject for each period of at least one year during which the same parental figures were present during the first 17 years of the subject's life. One scale assessed *parental indifference* as gauged by lack of parental concern with school work, care and interest in friends, regular eating, and clean clothes. High ratings of neglect by raters required concrete examples from respondents. The other neglect scale assessed *parental control* in terms of discipline and supervision. A high rating reflects stringent restrictions often combined with severe punishment whereas low ratings reflect minimal attempts to enforce rules. An index, "*Lack of Care,*" combines the two scales of parental neglect. Interrater kappa for the index was .71 on 20 families.

Data from the Islington survey were analyzed in several stages; the first stage analyzed data obtained during the initial phase of the project. Even though 83% of the subjects had lost their mothers before age 17, only 5% had lost only their mother. Nevertheless, a logistical regression analysis indicated that loss of mother only, before age 17 predicted the prevalence of depression better than the loss of both parents or of father alone. Subjects' marital status and quality of marriage were linked to *early* childhood loss of mother and to current presence of a psychiatric disorder. As predicted from attachment theory, persons whose early attachment bonds had been disrupted had a greater likelihood of a poor marriage or of being never-marrieds and also of having a psychiatric disorder.

With regard to being depressed at the time of the initial interview, 34% of the women who reported having had a lack of parental care were clinically depressed versus 15% of those who did not ($p < .001$). One-third of those with clinical depressions reported a lack of care. Low parental control rarely occurred without parental indifference, and the latter occurred much more commonly. All subjects who had experienced loss or separation of at least a year from their mother or separation from their father reported more lack of care than subjects without loss or separation from either parent. Lack of care was a more powerful predictor of depression ($p < .001$) than loss of mother ($p < .01$).

A second set of analyses examined the role of maternal loss and lack of care as vulnerability factors in depression provided that an adequate provoking (or precipitating) agent had occurred. As the investigators noted, occurrence of these vulnerability factors is likely to increase the probability of life circumstances in which provoking agents occur. Alternatively, these life circumstances may cause people to be more susceptible to provoking agents (Baumeister & Scher, 1988), and of course both may be true. This second stage of analyses dealt with the 1-year follow-up data on subjects who had not had diagnosable (i.e., "case") depression when they were initially interviewed. Twenty percent of the women who had experienced a provoking agent during the prior year had onsets of case depression versus only 1% of those who had not had such an experience. Loss of mother did not predict the onset of depression among those who had had a provoking agent though there was a trend in the direction of earlier loss being more predictive of vulnerability than later loss or no such loss.

Earlier lack of care increased vulnerability to depression both directly and by doubling the likelihood of the occurrence of a provoking agent. Within the Lack of Control Index, parental indifference was again more strongly related to depressive onset than low control, though both usually occurred together.

The intervening environmental and psychological variables between lack of care and onset of depression that had been predictive of depressive onset in the Walthamstow survey were reconfirmed in the Islington follow-up data. More women who became depressed had experienced premarital pregnancy, been divorced or separated, or had a negative evaluation of themselves.

In sum, Bifulco et al. concluded that the impact of loss of mother on vulnerability to depression is chiefly mediated by lack of adequate care as exemplified mainly by parental indifference. Even in the absence of loss of mother, lack of care is still a powerful vulnerability predictor because of the disturbed relationships that tend to follow in its wake.

Oatley and Bolton (1985, p. 374) summarize nine studies that fully or partly replicate the Brown and Harris (1978) finding that having a confidante substantially reduces the likelihood of a depressive onset despite the occurrence of a recent provoking agent. The findings of the few longitudinal studies were consistent with the retrospective studies. As previously indicated, Oatley and Bolton's paper also contains a brief review of the numerous critiques of Brown and Harris' statistical analyses, the main thrust of which seems to survive reasonably intact.

Prior findings by Parker (1979, 1983), which differ somewhat from those of Brown et al. in regard to parental control, influenced the content of the Islington study. Parker, Tupling, and Brown (1979) developed the Parental Bonding Instrument (PBI) as a means of investigating hypotheses related to attachment theory and depression. This self-report measure assesses the adult respondents' perceptions of the caring and overprotectiveness or control provided by parental figures who most significantly influenced their upbringing. Studies (Parker,

1981, 1982, 1983) have indicated that the PBI scores probably reflect actual socialization transactions rather than patient perceptions only, and are not unduly influenced by state, neurotic trait or genetic factors. Parker (1979) reported several studies with the PBI comparing the response patterns of 52 outpatient neurotic depressives and 70 bipolars most of whom were in remission with nonpsychiatric controls. Subjects' responses to the PBI reflected their perceptions of their most, and next most influential childhood parent-figures. Findings indicated that mothers of neurotic depressives were perceived as less caring and somewhat more overprotective than controls, while fathers were perceived as less caring and either higher or lower in overprotectiveness than controls. Bipolars did not differ from controls regardless of whether their parents had been bipolar or not, which is surprising in light of findings such as Anthony's (1975).

From a methodological standpoint, Parker's (1982) findings on 232 postgraduate students were particularly interesting. Ninety-five percent reported episodes of depressed affect during the prior year with 14% reporting a depressive duration of weeks or months. The students took the PBI, Eysenck Personality Inventory, and a measure of self-esteem. Again as might be expected in part at least from attachment theory, those students who reported a socialization pattern of low care and high overprotection were the highest of the 5 comparison groups on trait depression and anxiety and lowest on self-esteem, had longer and more severe depressions, were more alienated and neurotic. Students with high care and low overprotection had virtually the reverse pattern of relationships.

Parker noted that his findings do not refute the possibility that children with depressive temperaments may elicit a pattern of low parental care and overprotectiveness. As he also indicated, a self-perpetuating pattern could ensue in which the child's temperament results in treatment that lowers the child's self-regard rendering it more susceptible to depression inducing events and reactions. These interactions could also result from the reduced social competence inherent in poor parental modeling and constricted opportunities for alternative models and reinforcement contingencies. Such interactions as Parker notes would be conducive to the learned helplessness response set suggested by Bibring (1953) and by Seligman and his associates (Peterson & Seligman, 1985) among others.

Parker (1983) replicated his findings on the relationship of low care–high overprotection in a further study of 125 outpatient neurotic depressives and nonpsychiatric controls. Data from this study indicated that inadequate care from the same-sexed parent is especially strongly associated with depression. He contends (Parker, 1982) that the so called "affectionless control" socialization pattern provides a promising risk indicator for neurotic disorders generally as distinct from psychotic disorders as well as from nonpsychiatric controls.

Retrospective studies of childhood socialization experiences in patients are always subject to the criticism of state related distortion. However, several lines of evidence and theory summarized by Perris et al. (1986) support the utility of considering such data. For example, Parker (1981) found that scores obtained on his Parental Bonding Instrument from parents and independent observers were highly correlated. Convergent findings from investigators using different instruments, depressive populations, and methodologies further strengthen the likelihood that a broad spectrum of depression prone persons tend to have experienced childhoods that were relatively deprived of emotional warmth. While it is true that most of these data are based on retrospective self-report, it has been argued that perceptions of past experience may be of greater import than the events that occurred.

SOCIAL SUPPORT AND DEPRESSION

In general the social support literature (Cohen & Wills, 1985) indicates that social support is positively associated with physical and psychological health. Social support tends to diminish feelings of helplessness and of lowered self-regard, while lack of social support tends to engender anxiety and depression which in turn may have negative effects on physical and mental health. These consequences may occur even in the absence of severe precipitating events.

An ongoing controversy concerns whether social support has a *direct effect* on well-being regardless of the level of stress experienced versus acting as a buffer under high stress conditions.

Following Cohen and Wills' conceptualization, in the former model the assumption is that integration into a sizable supportive network provides positive affect, predictability, stability, and validation of self worth. Such integration tends to *lessen the likelihood that negative experiences will occur.*

In the buffering model which applies only to conditions that are stressful or potentially so, social support may be helpful in mitigating distress at two points in the chain of events following the onset of the stressor(s). First, adequate social support may result in an appraisal of the events as nonthreatening (for a situation to be perceived as threatening it requires a response beyond the perceived coping ability of the event's appraiser). Second, even if the situation is perceived as threatening, adequate social support may result in a reappraisal which can attenuate the impact of the stressful event if the reappraisal facilitates adaptive responses and inhibits maladaptive responses.

Most relevant to the implications of psychodynamic and attachment theory for depression are studies on the role of confidantes as social supports. The availability of a confiding relation is classified as a functional or buffering measure by Cohen and Wills. Such a relationship usually provides esteem and informational support. Overall findings have indicated that the availability of a close confiding relationship provides a greater buffering effect for women than for men and that husbands and boyfriends are more effective in this capacity than other confidantes. With particular relevance to attachment, most studies find that while

". . . a single confidante is sufficient for stress buffering, a large range of social contacts is not" (Cohen & Wills, 1985, p. 348).

Many of the inconsistent findings on the role of social support in relation to various aspects of depression, especially onset, may have resulted from a failure to discriminate between attachment and affiliation in social relationships (Sheldon & West, 1989). Sheldon and West contend that most investigators implicitly assume that the same criteria can be used to identify these two constructs and that both serve the same functions although attachment involves a somewhat greater degree of intensity and intimacy.

Sheldon and West tested the hypothesis that adults organize distinctive relationship expectancies for attachment and affiliation. Their research shows considerable support for their assumption though both constructs are related to affectional bonds as Ainsworth (1989) had contended. The primary constituents of attachment are concerns with present and especially future security, that is with protection against threat. Affiliative relations which may closely resemble attachment behaviors tend to serve expanded interests that usually derive from having a secure attachment base.

Sheldon and West note important distinctions between infant–child and adult attachments (Weiss, 1982). Adult attachments are usually between peers and with care-givers; they do not preempt other important behavioral systems; and a sexual relationship is often involved. In the absence of attachments, adults tend to feel lonely despite participation in a friendship network.

Adult attachments are more difficult to assess than infant or child attachments because adult behaviors typically subserve multiple behavior systems. Thus the spouse in our society is usually not only a source of security but also gratifies affiliative needs as a confidante or best friend.

Major stressors arouse attachment needs which center on seeking and obtaining security. Sheldon and West buttress their argument for the primary prophylactic value of attachment rather than affiliative relations against depressogenic vulnerability to provoking agents by citing Brown and Harris' (1978) finding that only type *a* relationships which had to be "close, intimate and confiding" with a husband, boyfriend, or live-in woman friend conferred almost total protection. Type *b* relationships with a "mother, sister or friend" seen at least weekly provided essentially no protection. Presumably type *a* relations have a much heavier loading of attachment gratification; while type *b* relations are more loaded with affiliative gratification.

However, the results of Brown, Bifulco, Harris, and Bridge's (1986) longitudinal Islington study suggest the likelihood of a more complex relation among attachment, prophylaxis against stress and psychopathology than their earlier Camberwell, London study. In the Islington study, a confiding relationship for wives was unrelated to risk of depression, while just positive social support reduced risk in single mothers.

Sheldon and West suggest that in future research on relations among social support, stress and psychopathology, attempts should be made to independently assess the quality of attachment, affiliation, and of general social support.

Brugha et al. (1982) largely replicated findings in Dublin on attachment relations and social interaction in depressives originally done by Henderson, Duncan-Jones, McAuley, and Ritchie (1978) in Canberra. However, the replication held up better for depressed neurotic than for depressed outpatients with psychomotor retardation. Depressives reported as much pleasurable interaction with their social network as nonpsychiatric controls, but reported four times as much unpleasant interaction. Patients did less interacting overall, and had fewer attachment figures, relatives, or close friends.

Determinants of Satisfaction

Pagel, Erdly, and Becker (1987) in a study of Alzheimer's spouses as a group at high risk for depression (with an antecedent stressor clearly independent of the depression per se) investigated relations between social support and depression in a longitudinal predictive study. Most studies of relations between social network interactions and depression have used unidimensional measures of social support which do not differentiate between positive and negative components of such interactions. Caregivers' ratings of the helpful and upsetting aspects of their daily interactions with significant network members were investigated for their relations with overall network satisfaction and with depression initially and 10 months later. Regression analyses controlling for demographic factors and for Alzheimer patients' functional status indicated that caregivers' upset with their network bore a strong positive relationship with lower network satisfaction and greater depression at both time points. Caregivers' ratings of the helpfulness of their network interactions had minimal direct relation to network satisfaction or depression. Helpful aspects of network interaction did interact with network upset in predicting network satisfaction and depression.

The most severe depressions in the Pagel et al. study were related to networks rated high on both helpfulness and upset; upset in less helpful networks had much less depressogenic impact. A similar pattern was obtained for ratings of global network satisfaction. Pagel et al. speculate that network helpfulness is generally more expectable than upset when one is stressed. Dissatisfaction may have much greater salience and impact because of its unexpected quality. The lower expectancies of helpfulness by persons in relatively unhelpful networks may lessen the impact of such events.

Most importantly, as predicted after controlling for age, sex, patients' functional status, initial upset, and initial depression, follow-up depression increased as a function of increased upset with the interaction network and was unaffected by changes in helpfulness ratings. This longitudinal finding supports the argument that upset with the interaction network has an etiological and maintenance role and is not simply synonymous with depression. Additional regression analyses indicated that network helpfulness and upset influence depression indirectly via overall network satisfaction.

These findings do not, of course, refute the oft cited finding that satisfaction with the interaction network is inversely related to depression. Rather, they help to clarify the determinants of satisfaction with network interaction. Dissatisfaction seems to strongly outweigh helpfulness in determining overall satisfaction. Diener (1984) too has argued that positive and negative affect are largely independent constituents of subjective well-being.

Weissman's (1987) epidemiologic study on the relationship of marital status and satisfaction to depression underscores the high risk of a negative relationship with an intimate other. Wives dissatisfied with their marriages and unable to confide in their husbands constituted the highest risk group for depression. The negative effect of an unsatisfactory marriage considerably outweighed the benefits of a positive marital relationship. However, several studies indicate that satisfying marriages can lessen the impact of earlier unfortunate relationships. Unfortunately, depression prone individuals are prone to marry partners whose disturbed personalities are not conducive to positive marital relations (Brown, Bifulco, Harris, & Bridge, 1986). Coyne et al. (in press) review this literature extensively.

Clinical tradition had it that depression is a self-limited illness but recent studies have shown that nonrecovery rates from major depressive disorder are variable and substantial (George, Blazer, Hughes, & Fowler, 1989). George et al. examined the effects of social support on recovery in middle aged and elderly major depressives. Prior studies had failed to yield consistent predictors of recovery. On the basis of Henderson's (1978) prior work with neurotics, the investigators predicted that a subjective indicator, perceived adequacy of social support, would be more predictive of recovery than objective indicators such as network size. This prediction was supported. Some relationships of objective indicators to recovery were contrary to expectancy. Thus size of social network at baseline (in hospital) was negatively related to recovery 6 to 32 months later. Likewise marriage was negatively related to recovery. Much remains ambiguous about the relationship between network interaction and depression. In part, this reflects the inevitable hazards of attempting to relate two rather vaguely defined concepts. As yet there are no clear theoretical guidelines for what constitutes the social network.

SOME METHODOLOGICAL CAUTIONS

The advisability of relying on depressives or remitted depressives for accurate accounts of their premorbid patterns of interpersonal behavior such as dependency and sociability has been seriously questioned by Hirschfeld et al. (1989). They cite data suggesting that depression has residual effects on personality even after symptomatic remission. Furthermore, they raise the very troubling issue of when is premorbid really premorbid? Differences in personality self reports between high risk subjects tested before the onset of a first major depressive episode and their relatives may simply be due to prolonged subsyndromal affective disorders in those who subsequently decompensated. They also cite the need for careful attention to age and cohort effects as well as disorder specificity factors when interpreting vulnerability data. For example, while they found interpersonal dependency and first onset of a major depressive disorder were unrelated in their younger age group (17–30), premorbid interpersonal dependency was related to first onset in their older (31–41) age group. As Hirschfeld et al. note, the personality features predictive of onset in their *overall* sample lacked established theoretical relevance. The interpersonally and theoretically relevant variables of interpersonal dependency and introversion which had been expected to account for significant variance in onset were unrelated.

With regard to specificity, they cite findings by Reich et al. (1987) who reported very similar personality profiles in remitted depressives and panic disorder patients: both groups showed more interpersonal dependency and less emotional strength (adaptability to stress, emotional stability) than controls.

AN INTEGRATIVE SPECULATION

As indicated at the beginning of this chapter, there is no intent to minimize the probable role of biological factors in many depressive reactions. Therefore, we conclude with an interesting and promising approach to an integrated bio-psycho-social etiological theory of depression by Ehlers, Frank, and Kupfer (1988). According to Ehlers et al. biological theories of depression which heretofore had stressed the biogenic amine deficit hypothesis are increasingly shifting toward an emphasis on circadian rhythm dysregulation. "Social Zeitgebers" are a key concept in Ehlers et al. formulation. Social Zeitgebers are environmental events such as personality relationships, social demands, or tasks that tend to entrain biological rhythms. For example, marital partners tend to synchronize their rhythms: meal times, sleep, rest, and activity tend to be coordinated with a resultant modification of the natural rhythmic synchronies of each partner toward a compromise synchrony. Major life events such as bereavement, loss of job, or divorce are likely to have major disruptive affects socially, and biologically. Ehlers et al. for example cite data indicating that more than half of a sample of divorcing women experienced shortened REM latency and depressive symptoms, and widows and widowers who reported greater disruption in their social routines as a consequence of bereavement tend to be more depressed. Disruption of these social zeitgebers which in turn disrupt the synchronization of certain biological rhythms may precipitate the onset of major depressive disorder (MDD) episodes in vulnerable persons.

Patently, most people who experience major aversive life events do not become clinically depressed. Presumably, people differ considerably in their vulnerability to pathology inducing rhythmic disruptions. Less vulnerable persons are believed to have relatively high thresholds for disruptions and when disruptions occur they tend to be time-limited. At present, the best indicators of vulnerability to disruption appear to be personal and family histories of psychopathology. Ehlers et al. also endorse the importance of modulators of social zeitgebers citing G. Brown's work in particular. Thus, factors like social support, coping skills, and personal resources may act to lessen the disruptive impact of life events.

Most persons with MDD have relatively specific disturbances in biological rhythms related to their sleep/wake cycle and neuroendocrine systems. A phase advance in certain rhythms tends to occur. Changes such as short REM latency and increased REM activity occur during the first half of the night. Melatonin and thyroid stimulating hormone output decrease. Ninety percent of persons with MDD are reported to show at least one of the circadian rhythm anomalies associated with the disorder. Affected rhythms become desynchronized and more unstable. The disrupted biological rhythms in MDD seem to have a built in *time constant* for resynchronization; without treatment most episodes of MDD spontaneously remit within 6 months.

Ehlers et al. speculate that their theory may be able to account for subtypes of depression. Thus spontaneous (classic endogenous) MDD may result when the threshold for biological disruption is so low that environmental events seem virtually inconsequential; prolonged depression may stem from having an unusually long time constant for reentrainment of desynchronized rhythms to environmental conditions; atypical depressions with increased sleep, weight, and appetite may be caused by a tendency for disruption to cause *phase delay* rather than *phase advance* which is more typical.

An important implication of the threshold concept is that selective biases may occur in studies investigating relationships between stress and depression. Thus while Brown et al.'s approach may help to ensure that there is a clear separation between the occurrence of a stressor and the onset of depression in the samples which meet their criteria, they may be eliminating many cases precipitated by stress which do not meet their criteria (Coyne et al., in press).

Ehlers et al. attempt to account for the ameliorative impact of such diverse treatment interventions as tricylic antidepressants (TCAs), cognitive/behavioral and interpersonal psychotherapy. The assumption is that TCA's not only directly affect sleep but probably other biological rhythms as well. The psychotherapies presumably foster more and better routinized activity which should help to stabilize biological rhythms. They urge joint use of somatic and psychotherapeutic interventions and predict an additive effect. Evidence for the latter is less than compelling but neither of the psychotherapies most studied were specifically designed to entrain patients into more active, stress avoidant routines.

Ehlers et al. are quite aware that they have only adumbrated a theory but certainly a comprehensive explanation of nonbipolar depressions must eventually encompass and integrate biological and psychosocial factors. At a minimum, their theoretical excursion seems likely to stimulate fruitful attempts at validation or disconfirmation.

SUMMARY

As will be apparent in the following chapter and in other reviews of the empirical literature such as that by Coyne et al. (in press), and by Hokanson and Rubert (in press) well replicated, theoretically integrated knowledge about the pre-, intra-, and post-morbid interpersonal behavior of persons prone to depressive disorders is still relatively limited. Studies on interpersonal behaviors unique to depressives or depressive subtypes are even scantier. This is hardly surprising given that really active systematic empirical investigation has only been underway for about a decade, and that increased federal funding for longitudinal studies is even more recent.

Probably the best established facts about a sizable proportion of the depression prone is that they tend to come from troubled backgrounds and to have particular difficulties with intimate relations with others. Especially when depressed, their behavior tends to alienate others, though precisely how remains unclear. For many depressives, effective long-term treatment results appear to depend heavily on ameliorating their relationships with their most significant others. Symptomatic improvement from biological treatments does not seem to appreciably modify the relational difficulties of many depressives.

The psychodynamic and attachment literatures have clearly anticipated many contemporary findings. From Abraham on, mention is made of the annoying quality of depressive behavior, of their overly dependent and/or perfectionist tendencies, of their early social traumas, limited repertoire of social skills, difficulties with assertiveness and hostility, their tendency to integrate ungratifying, mutually frustrating interpersonal relationships, and the importance of social context in shaping socialization patterns. Patently, this literature often lacks internal consistency and many of its constructs do not readily lend themselves to systematic investigation. Nonetheless, as previously stated, we believe that many potentially fruitful observations in this literature may yet be recast as testable hypotheses.

REFERENCES

Abraham, K. (1945). *Selected papers*. London: Hogarth Press.
Adler, K. (1961). Depression in the light of individual psychology. *Journal of Individual Psychology, 17*, 56–76.

5. INTERPERSONAL ASPECTS OF DEPRESSION 165

Adler, T. (1989). Shy monkeys are born, not made. *Monitor*, August, p. 5.
Ainsworth, M. D. S. (1989). Attachments beyond infancy. *American Psychologist, 44*, 709–716.
Ainsworth, M. D. S., Blehar, M. D., Waters, W., & Wall, S. (1978). *Patterns of attachment*. Hillsdale, NJ: Lawrence Erlbaum Associates.
Akiskal, H. S., Rosenthal, T., Haykal, R. F., Lemmi, H., Rosenthal, R. H., & Scott-Strauss, A. (1980). Characterological depression: Clinical and sleep EEG findings separating subaffective dysthymias, from 'character spectrum disorders'. *Archives of General Psychiatry, 37*, 777–783.
American Psychiatric Association. (1987). *Diagnostic and statistical manual of mental disorders* (Third Edition-Revised). American Psychiatric Association: Washington, D.C.
Anthony, E. J. (1975). The influence of a manic-depressive environment on the developing child. In E. J. Anthony & T. Benedek (Eds.), *Depression and human existence* (pp. 279–317). Boston: Little, Brown.
Arieti, S., & Bemporad, J. (1978). *Severe and mild depression: A psychotherapeutic approach*. New York: Basic Books.
Barnett, P. A., & Gotlib, I. H. (1988). Psychosocial functioning and depression: Distinguishing among antecedents, concomitants, and consequences. *Psychological Bulletin, 104*, 97–126.
Baumeister, R. F., & Scher, S. J. (1988). Self-defeating behavior patterns among normal individuals: Review and analysis of common self-destructive tendencies. *Psychological Bulletin, 104*, 3–22.
Beck, A. T. (1983). Cognitive therapy of depression: New perspectives. In P. J. Clayton & J. E. Barrett (Eds.), *Treatment of depression: Old controversies and new approaches* (pp. 265–290). New York: Raven Press.
Becker, E. (1964). Depression, a comprehensive theory. From *The revolution in psychiatry, The new understanding of Man*, New York: The Free Press of Glencoe.
Becker, J. (1974). *Depression: Theory and research*. Washington, DC: Winston-Wiley.
Becker, J. (1979). Stress and self-esteem related factors in depression. In R. A. Depue (Ed.), *The psychobiology of the depressive disorders: Implications for the effects of stress* (pp. 317–334). New York: Academic Press.
Belsky, J., & Nezworski, T. (Eds.). (1988). *Clinical implications of attachment*. Hillsdale, NJ: Lawrence Erlbaum Associates.
Bibring, E. (1953). The mechanism of depression. In P. Greenacre (Ed.), *Affective disorders* (pp. 13–49). New York: International Universities Press.
Bifulco, A. T., Brown, G. W., & Harris, T. O. (1987). Childhood loss of parent, lack of adequate parental care and adult depression: A replication. *Journal of Affective Disorders, 12*, 115–128.
Blatt, S. J., Quinlan, D. M., Chevron, E. S., McDonald, C., & Zuroff, D. (1982). Dependency and self-criticism: Psychological dimensions of depression. *Journal of Consulting and Clinical Psychology, 50*, 113–124.
Blatt, S. J., & Shichman, S. (1983). Two primary configurations of psychopathology. *Psychoanalysis and Contemporary Thought, 6*, 187–254.
Bonime, W. (1966). The psychodynamics of neurotic depression. *Journal of the American Academy of Psychoanalysis, 4*, 301–326.
Bowlby, J. (1977). The making & breaking of affectional bonds II. *British Journal of Psychiatry, 130*, 421–431.
Bowlby, J. (1980). *Attachment and loss. Volume III: Loss, sadness and depression*. New York: Basic Books.
Bowlby, J. (1988a). *A secure base: Parent-child attachment and healthy human development*. New York: Basic Books.
Bowlby, J. (1988b). Developmental psychiatry comes of age. *American Journal of Psychiatry, 145*, 1–10.
Brown, G. W. (1979). The social etiology of depression—London studies. In R. A. Depue (Ed.),

The psychobiology of the depressive disorders: Implications for the effects of stress (pp. 263–291). New York: Academic Press.

Brown, G. W., Bifulco, A., Harris, T., & Bridge, L. (1986). Life stress, chronic subclinical symptoms and vulnerability to clinical depression. *Journal of Affective Disorders, 11,* 1–19.

Brown, G. W., & Harris, T. (1978). *Social origins of depression: A study of psychiatric disorder in women.* New York: The Free Press.

Brugha, T., Conroy, R., Walsh, N., DeLaney, W., O'Hanlin, J., Doner, E., Hickey, N., & Bourke, G. (1982). Social networks, attachments, and support in minor affective disorders: A replication. *British Journal of Psychiatry, 114,* 249–255.

Chodoff, P. (1973). The depressive personality. A critical review. *International Journal of Psychiatry, 11,* 196–217.

Cohen, M. B., Baker, G., Cohen, R. A., Fromm-Reichman, F., & Weigert, E. G. (1954). An intensive study of twelve cases of manic-depressive psychosis. *Psychiatry, 17,* 103–137.

Cohen, S., & Wills, T. A. (1985). Stress, social support, and the buffering hypothesis. *Psychological Bulletin, 98,* 310–357.

Costello, C. G. (1982). Social factors associated with depression: A retrospective clinical study. *Psychological Medicine, 12,* 329–339.

Coyne, J. C., Burchill, S. A. L., & Stiles, W. B. (in press). An interactional perspective on depression. In C. R. Snyder & D. O. Forsyth (Eds.), *Handbook of social and clinical psychology: The health perspective.* New York: Pergamon Press.

Coyne, J. C., & Gotlib, I. H. (1983). The role of cognition in depression: A critical appraisal. *Psychological Bulletin, 94,* 472–505.

Diener, E. (1984). Subjective well-being. *Psychological Bulletin, 95,* 542–575.

Ehlers, C. L., Frank, E., & Kupfer, D. J. (1988). Social Zeitgebers and biological rhythms. *Archives of General Psychiatry, 45,* 948–952.

Eisenbruch, M. (1983). Affective disorders in parents: Impact upon children. In D. P. Cantwell & G. A. Carlson (Eds.), *Affective disorders in childhood and adolescence* (pp. 279–335). New York: SP Medical and Scientific Books.

Erickson, E. H. (1963). *Childhood and society.* 2nd Edit. New York: W. W. Norton.

Feather, B. W., & Rhoades, J. M. (1972). Psychodynamic behavior therapy. I Theory and rationale; II Clinical Aspects. *Archives of General Psychiatry, 26,* 496–502 & 503–511.

Frank, E., Kupfer, D. J., & Perel, J. M. (1989). Early recurrence in unipolar depression. *Archives of General Psychiatry, 46,* 397–405.

Freud, S. (1917/1957). Mourning and melancholia. In J. Strachey (Ed.) *Collected works of Sigmund Freud: The standard edition.* Vol. 14. London: Hogarth Press.

Freud, S. (1923/1957). The ego and the id. In J. Strachey (Ed.), *The standard edition.* Vol. 19. London: Hogarth Press.

Gaensbauer, T. J., Harmon, R. J., Cytryn, L., & McKnew, D. H. (1984). Social and affective development in children with a manic-depressive parent. *American Journal of Psychiatry, 141,* 223–229.

George, L. K., Blazer, D. G., Hughes, D. C., & Fowler, N. (1989). Social support and the outcome of major depression. *British Journal of Psychiatry, 154,* 478–485.

Gero, G. (1936). The construction of depression. *International Journal of Psychoanalysis, 17,* 423–461.

Goleman, D. (1989, March 28). The roots of empathy are traced to infancy. *New York Times,* pp. 13, 21.

Greenberg, M. T., & Speltz, M. D. (1988). Attachment and the ontogeny of conduct problems. In J. Belsky & T. Nezworski (Eds.), *Clinical implications of attachment* (pp. 177–218). Hillsdale, NJ: Lawrence Erlbaum Associates.

Hammen, C., Ellicott, A., Gitlin, M., & Jamison, K. R. (1989). Sociotropy/Autonomy and vul-

nerability to specific life events in patients with unipolar depression and bipolar disorders. *Journal of Abnormal Psychology, 98,* 154–160.
Harris, T., Brown, G. W., & Bifulco, A. (1986). Loss of parent in childhood and adult psychiatric disorder: The role of parental care. *Psychological Medicine, 16,* 641–659.
Henderson, S., Duncan-Jones, P., McAuley, H., & Ritchie, K. (1978). The patient's primary group. *British Journal of Psychiatry, 132,* 74–86.
Hinde, R. (1982). *Attachment: Some conceptual and biological issues.* In C. M. Parkes & J. Stevenson-Hinde (Eds.), New York: Basic Books.
Hirschfeld, R. M. A., Klerman, G. L., Lavori, P., Keller, M. B., Griffith, P., & Coryell, W. (1989). Premorbid personality assessments of first onset major depression. *Archives of General Psychiatry, 46,* 345–353.
Hokanson, J. E., & Rupert, M. P. (in press). Interpersonal factors in depression. In D. G. Gilbert (Ed.) *Personality, social skills and psychopathology: An individual difference approach.* New York: Plenum.
Horowitz, M. J. (1988). *Psychodynamics and cognition.* Chicago: University of Chicago Press.
Jacobson, E. (1971). Transference problems in the psychoanalytic treatment of severely depressive patients. *Depression* (pp. 284–302). New York: International Universities Press.
Klein, M. (1948). A contribution to the psychogenesis of manic-depressive states (1934) *Contributions to Psycho-analysis 1921–1945* (pp. 282–311). London: Hogarth Press.
Klein, M. (1948). Mourning and the relation to manic depressive states (1940). *Contributions to psychoanalysis 1921–1945* (pp. 311–339). London: Hogarth Press.
Klein, D. N., Clark, D. C., Dansky, L., & Margolis, E. G. (1988). Dysthymia in the offspring of parents with primary unipolar affective disorder. *Journal of Abnormal Psychology, 97,* 265–274.
Klein, D. N., Harding, K., Taylor, E. B., & Dickstein, S. (1988). Dependency and self-criticism in depression: Evaluation in a clinical population. *Journal of Abnormal Psychology, 97,* 399–404.
Klerman, G. L., Weissman, M. M., Rounsaville, B. J., & Chevron, E. S. (1984). *Interpersonal psychotherapy for depression.* New York: Basic Books.
Lorenz, K. (1957). Der Kumpan in der Unvelt des Vogels. C. Schiller (Ed.) *Instinctive behavior.* New York: International Universities Press.
Mahler, M. S., Pine, F., & Bergman, A. (1975). *The psychological birth of the human infant: Symbiosis and individuation.* New York: Basic Books.
Melges, F. T., & Swartz, M. S. (1989). Oscillations of attachment in borderline personality disorder. *American Journal of Psychiatry, 146,* 1115–1120.
Mendelson, M. (1974). *Psychoanalytic concepts of depression* (2nd ed.). New York: Spectrum.
Metalsky, G. I., Halberstadt, L. J., & Abramson, L. Y. (1987). Vulnerability to depressive mood reactions: Toward a more powerful test of the diathesis-stress and causal mediation components of the reformulated theory of depression. *Journal of Personality and Social Psychology, 52* 386–393.
Miklowitz, D. J., Goldstein, M. J., Nuechterlein, K. H., Snyder, K. S., & Mintz, J. (1988). Family factors and the course of bipolar affective disorder. *Archives of General Psychiatry, 45,* 225–231.
Oatley, K., & Bolton, W. (1985). A social-cognitive theory of depression in reaction to life events. *Psychological Review, 92,* 372–388.
Pagel, M. D., Erdly, W., & Becker, J. (1987). Social networks: We get by with (and in spite of) a little help from our friends. *Journal of Personality and Social Psychology, 53,* 793–805.
Parker, G. (1979). Parental characteristics in relation to depressive disorders. *British Journal of Psychiatry, 134,* 138–147.
Parker, G. (1981). Parental reports of depressives. *Journal of Affective Disorders, 3,* 131–140.
Parker, G. (1982). Parental representations and affective symptoms: Examination for an hereditary link. *British Journal of Psychiatry, 55,* 57–61.
Parker, G. (1983). Parental "affectionless control" as an antecedent to adult depression: A risk factor delineated. *Archives of General Psychiatry, 40,* 956–960.

Parker, G., Tupling, A., & Brown, L. B. (1979). A parental bonding instrument. *British Journal of Medical Psychology, 52,* 1–10.
Paterson, R. J., & Moran, G. (1988). Attachment theory, personality development, and psychotherapy. *Clinical Psychology Review, 8,* 611–636.
Perris, C., Arrindell, W. A., Perris, H., Eisemann, J., Ende, V. D., & Von Knorring. (1986). Perceived deprived parental rearing and depression. *British Journal of Psychiatry, 148,* 170–175.
Peterson, C., & Seligman, M. E. P. (1985). The learned helplessness model of depression: Current status of theory and research. In E. E. Beckham & W. R. Leber (Eds.), Handbook of depression: Treatment, assessment, and research (pp. 914–940). Homewood, IL: Dorsey Press.
Radke-Yarrow, M., Cummings, E. M., Kuczynski, L., & Chapman, M. (1985). Patterns of attachment in two- and three-year olds in normal families and families with parental depression. *Child Development, 56,* 884–893.
Rado, S. (1928). The problem of melancholia. *International Journal of Psychoanalysis. 9,* 420–438.
Reich, J., Noyes, R., Hirschfeld, R., Coryell, W., & O'Gorman, T. (1987). State and personality in depressed and panic patients. *American Journal of Psychiatry, 144,* 181–187.
Robins, C. J., & Block, P. (1988). Personal vulnerability, life events, and depressive symptoms: A test of a specific interactional model. *Journal of Personality and Social Psychology, 54,* 847–852.
Robins, C. J., Block, P., & Peselow, E. D. (1989). Relations of sociotropic and autonomous personality characteristics to specific symptoms in depressed patients. *Journal of Abnormal Psychology, 98,* 86–88.
Rutter, M. (1985). Resilience in the face of adversity: Protective factors and resistance to psychiatric disorder. *British Journal of Psychiatry, 147,* 598–611.
Sheldon, A. E. R., & West, M. (1989). The functional discrimination of attachment and affiliation: Theory and empirical demonstration. *British Journal of Psychiatry, 155,* 18–23.
Spieker, S. J., & Booth, C. L. (1988). Maternal antecedents of attachment quality. In J. Belsky & T. Nezworksi (Eds.), *Clinical implications of attachment* (pp. 95–135). Hillsdale, NJ: Lawrence Erlbaum Associates.
Sroufe, L. A. (1985). Attachment classification from the perspective of infant-caregiver relationships and infant temperament. *Child Development, 56,* 1–14.
Sroufe, A. (1988). The role of infant-caregiver attachment in development. In J. Belsky & T. Nezworski (Eds.), *Clinical implications of attachment* (pp. 18–41). Hillsdale, NJ: Lawrence Erlbaum Associates.
Sullivan, H. S. (1953). *The interpersonal theory of psychiatry.* New York: Norton.
Wachtel, P. L. (1982). Interpersonal therapy and active intervention. In J. C. Anchin & D. J. Kiesler (Eds.), *Handbook of interpersonal psychotherapy.* New York: Pergamon Press.
Weiss, R. S. (1982). Attachment in adult life. In C. M. Parkes & J. Stevenson-Hinde (Eds.), *The place of attachment in human behavior.* New York: Basic Books.
Weissman, M. M. (1987). Advances in psychiatric epidemiology: Rates and risks for depression. *American Journal of Public Health, 77,* 445–451.
Wender, P. H., Kety, S. S., Rosenthal, D., Schulsinger, F., Ortmann, J., & Lunde, I. (1986). Psychiatric disorders in the biological and adoptive families of adopted individuals with affective disorders. *Archives of General Psychiatry, 43,* 923–930.
Wiener, M. (1989). Psychopathology reconsidered: Depressions interpreted as psychosocial transactions. *Clinical Psychology Review, 9,* 295–323.
Wortman, C. B., & Silver, R. C. (1989). The myths of coping with loss. *Journal of Consulting and Clinical Psychology, 57,* 349–357.

6 Empirical Studies of the Interpersonal Relations of Adult Depressives

Karen Schmaling
National Jewish Center for Immunology and Respiratory Medicine, and University of Colorado

Joseph Becker
University of Washington

Psychodynamic and attachment theories largely focus on how early social experiences predispose persons to subsequent maladaptive patterns of social perception, interaction, and reaction. In contrast, theories largely derived from general psychological theory especially learning, cognition, and social psychology, focus mainly on contemporary interactions with limited regard to their antecedents. Lewinsohn and Coyne have been the principle theoretical contributors to this domain.

Most of the research reviewed in the next section stems from earlier versions of Lewinsohn's and Coyne's models of depression. Lewinsohn's model of depression has evolved from an operant-interpersonal version toward a broader cognitive and social-learning model (Lewinsohn, Hoberman, Teri, & Hautzinger, 1985). However, a reduction in response contingent positive reinforcement continues to play a central role in what is sometimes referred to as Lewinsohn's social skills model. Low rates of environmental positive reinforcement and/or high rates of aversive experience are posited as causes of the depressive's dysphoria and low rates of behavioral activity. High rates of dysphoric inducing experience are variously attributed to the unavailability of positive reinforcements or low skill in acquiring them, or to inadequate coping with aversive events. Less stressed possibilities are that positive events may have lost some of their reinforcing properties or that aversive events may have acquired enhanced potency.

Lewinsohn's early models seemed to best account for the maintenance of depression but his revised model is designed to account for etiology as well as maintenance. They view disruptive stressors, particularly those involved with marital distress, social losses, or loss of work as particularly conducive to depression because they interfere with frequent automatic interactions with the environment. These disruptions shift the balance of reinforcement experienced toward greater negativity. Heightened self-awareness then ensues with associated self-devaluation and dysphoric mood. These result in an increased inability to meet standards, an enhanced sense of responsibility for perceived failures, and an increased pessimism about future prospects of successfully achieving important outcomes. This pessimism leads to a sense of futility and to social withdrawal which further diminishes the efficacy of self-enhancing defenses and adaptations. These processes lead to the typical behavioral, cognitive, and physiological changes associated with depression. A vicious cycle between symptoms and dysphoria develops.

Lewinsohn has made greater efforts than most investigators to obtain longitudinal data, use clinically depressed subjects, and nondepressed psychiatric controls.

In Coyne's (1976) original interactional model of depression, he contended that depressive symptoms had powerful aversive effects on others. These symptom arouse guilt in others and inhibit their counter expressions of annoyance and hostility. Others may initially respond with sincere support but persistent depressive behavior tends to induce depressed, anxious, hostile, and frustrated reactions leading the other to only partially sincere expressions of reassurance and support. The latter are accompanied by covert rejection and withdrawal from the depressed person. The depressive, perceiving the other's rejection, tends to increase depressive behavior in an effort to reinstate genuine trustworthy concern; this increase further escalates the spiraling cycle.

Although Coyne's model addresses an ongoing interpersonal process, his initial research and studies by others have mainly focused on brief interactions between mildly, often transiently state depressed college students and nondepressed students who are unacquainted with each other. These brief interactional studies have been extensively reviewed by Coyne, Kahn, and Gotlib (1987), and by Hokanson and Rubert (in press). Because of their largely inconsistent findings, and their questionable relevancy to more current theoretical formulations, these brief interactional studies are only briefly reviewed.

INTERACTION BETWEEN DEPRESSED PERSONS AND STRANGERS

Some authors have argued that acquaintanceship studies of depressed persons and strangers are virtually irrelevant to testing the validity of interpersonal models of depression (Doerfler & Chaplin, 1985). But Coyne (1985) has argued that such studies may at least shed light on the incipient disruption frequently observed when depressed persons interact with intimate others. As Coyne noted, studies of interactions between depressives and strangers have the advantage of not being confounded by either a prior history of their having been in conflict, or by the selective bias of examining intact relationships only. He contended that studies of interactions with strangers may provide broader generalizations and additional hypotheses about depressives' maladaptive interpersonal styles.

Research focused on the effects of strangers interacting with depressives have yielded inconsistent results. Some studies have reported that interaction with a depressed person induces dysphoric mood in the nondepressed participant as well as social rejection, and/or negative evaluation by the latter (Coyne, 1976; Gotlib & Beatty, 1985; Howes & Hokanson, 1979; Strack & Coyne, 1983; Winer, Bonner, Blaney, & Murray, 1981). However, Boswell and Murray (1981) found this pattern of results only for subjects interacting with male depressives, and other studies have failed to replicate Coyne's (1976) findings (King & Heller, 1984; McNeil, Arkowitz, & Pritchard, 1982). As King and Heller (1984) have suggested, these inconsistent findings may be due to differences in the interaction task (e.g., telephone conversations versus face-to-face unstructured versus problem-solving tasks), or the type of depressed person (e.g., mildly depressed college students versus confederate actors versus severely depressed psychiatric inpatients).

Dobson (1989) contends that prior findings more strongly support the contention that depressives are rejected by others than that depressives induce negative moods in others. However, Dobson's (1989) study failed even to support Coyne's contention that casual strangers tend to reject depressives after limited social interactions. Dobson's (1989) and Gotlib's (1983) work suggest that depressives may exaggerate the degree to which they have a negative impact on others. However, in Dobson's study, an exaggerated perception of having been rejected was not specific to depressed-anxious students, but applied equally to anxious nondepressed students.

In another study that also examined the specificity of reputed interpersonal antecedents and correlates of depressive disorders Hokanson et al. (1989) found appreciable differences between new cases of depression and normal controls but negligible differences between the depressives and persons with nondepressed psychopathology (mainly anxiety). Subjects were university student roommates. Depressives and the "other-psychopathology" group shared a constellation of personality—interpersonal characteristics that may be predictive of general psychopathology at least within a similar population. The constellation consisted of low self-esteem, sensitivity to stressful events and social behaviors typified by dependency, self-effacement, and aggrieved-mistrustful attitudes. Others react negatively to these behaviors; they seek and enjoy contact less, and are prone to display aggressive and competitive reactions. While this study uncovered little that was unique to depression it decidedly supplements its predecessors in that it dealt with longer term, closer relationships than most prior interactional studies of depressed persons. Its methodology has much greater potential for yielding results relevant to important aspects of social interaction theory than studies of casual acquaintances.

Whereas depressives may exaggerate their negative impact on others, other data suggest that depressives evaluate their level of social competence more accurately than nondepressives; that is, they rate themselves and are rated by others as having deficient social skills ("sadder but wiser": Alloy & Abramson, 1979) (Lewinsohn, Mischel, Chaplin, & Barton, 1980: Youngren & Lewinsohn, 1980).

Observational studies have found few *behavioral* differences between depressives and others in the acquaintanceship process (Gotlib, 1982; Jacobson & Anderson, 1982; Youngren & Lewinsohn, 1980). But as Coyne et al. (1987) have noted, investigators have largely confined themselves to frequently occurring, reliably measurable variables which may have little impact on the negative responses frequently elicited by depressives. Depressives exhibit situational specificity in their use of depressive behaviors depending upon whom they are interacting with (Meyer & Hokanson, 1985) and the context of the interaction (e.g., power relationships). A review of this pertinent literature by Coyne and Gotlib (1983) supports the contention that depressed persons do not consistently present themselves negatively or show consistently negative cognitions. Depressives may act and expect to be less depressed, for example, with a stranger, because they have not developed interpersonal expectations with that person. Hinchliffe, Hooper, and Roberts (1978) who observed differences in stranger-patient and spouse-patient interactions reported that interactions between a depressed inpatient and a stranger were less tense and self-absorbed as compared to patient-spouse interactions which were markedly more disturbed.

A recent review by Barnett and Gotlib (1988) suggests that dependency and introversion are stable traits characteristic of depressives. The consequences of such an interpersonal style may be narrowly derived self-esteem or overinvestment in a primary relationship. When disappointments such as losses and perceived failures occur within such a style, depression may be more likely to result. The following section reviews studies of the marital interactions of depressed persons.

SIGNIFICANCE OF MARITAL FACTORS AND CHARACTERISTICS OF MARITAL INTERACTION

Although studies of interactions between strangers and depressed patients have yielded relatively inconclusive results, interactions between depressives and their significant others are clearly dysfunctional and appear to be importantly related to the onset, course, and outcome of depression. The concurrence of depression and marital distress is much greater than would be expected by chance: Approximately 50% of depressed, married individuals are maritally distressed (Rounsaville, Weissman, Prusoff, & Herceg-Barton, 1979) compared to an estimate of only 20% of all married couples (Beach, Arias, & O'Leary, 1983).

The degree of marital distress has had a strong positive relationship to the level of depression in cross-sectional studies (cf. Briscoe & Smith, 1973; Coleman & Miller, 1975; Crowther, 1985; Ensel, 1982; Weiss & Aved, 1978), and, as noted, the lack of a confiding relationship is a significant vulnerability factor for depression (Brown & Harris, 1978). Marital friction is the most frequently reported stressful life event in the 6 months preceding the onset of a depressive episode (Paykel, Myers, Dienelt, Klerman, Lindenthal, & Pepper, 1969). Rounsaville et al. (1979) found that depressed women in distressed marriages were less likely to respond to psychotherapy unless concurrent changes in the quality of their marital relation also occurred.

Weissman and Paykel's (1974) interview-based study of the marital relationships of depressed women has probably been the single strongest stimulus to systematic observational studies of marital interaction. They characterized depressed women as hostile, lacking in affection, dependent, inhibited, and characterized by poor communication. The following section of our review focuses on those studies of the interaction of couples with a depressed spouse which used systematic observational measures.

Arkowitz, Holliday, and Hutter (1982) reported that the spouses of depressed wives rated themselves as more anxious after a problem-solving oriented interaction than the spouses of nondepressed patients or normal control couples. Husbands of both patient groups rated themselves as more hostile following these interactions. Depressed women and their husbands had significantly lower rates of positive nonverbal behavior than did partners in the other groups. Husbands of both patient groups had higher rates of negative nonverbal behavior than husbands in the normal control group. The authors suggest that while husbands of depressed wives may largely succeed in verbally disguising their negative feelings, their nonverbal behavior "leaks" (Ekman & Friesen, 1974) their discomfort.

Biglan et al. (1985) compared the problem-solving interactions of three groups of married couples: a normal control group, a group with depressed wives in distressed marriages, and a group with depressed wives in nondistressed marriages (which will be referred to as depressed-distressed and depressed-only couples, respectively). Control couples self-disclosed more than both depressed groups; depressed-distressed couples had lower rates of facilitative behavior (such as humor, approval, empathy) than depressed-only and normal control couples; and husbands in the depressed-distressed group proposed more solutions to the problem they were discussing than their wives. This last result is consistent with the notion that much of the interactive burden rests on the nondepressed partner (Coyne, 1976). Interestingly, depressed-distressed husbands were less likely to respond aggressively to their wives' depressive behavior than depressed-only and normal control husbands, and depressed-distressed wives were less likely to respond with depressive behavior to their husbands' aggressive behavior as compared to depressed-only and normal control couples. These functional relationships suggest that couples with a depressed spouse use aversive control techniques: Wives' depressive behavior is decreased by aggressive husband behavior and aggressive husband behavior is decreased by depressive wife behavior. Another study by the Oregon group found similar results using spouses' ratings of their feelings and reactions to their partners in hypothetical situations presented in a paper-and-pencil format (Biglan, Rothlind, Hops, & Sherman, 1989). Finally, the results presented by Hops et al. (1987) are largely an extension of Bigaln et al. (1985). Hops et al. (1987) examined the interaction of depressed mothers with their children. Half of the depressed patients and their spouses were maritally distressed. Marital discord exacerbated problematic interaction in these families. Depressed mothers' depressed affect made subsequent aggressive affect by other family members less likely. Family members' aggressive affect in turn made subsequent depressed affect by the mothers less likely.

Hautzinger and his colleagues (Hautzinger, Linden, & Hoffman, 1982; Linden, Hautzinger, & Hoffman, 1983) compared the interactions of distressed-only and depressed-distressed couples. Spouses with a depressed partner evaluated themselves more positively and their depressed partners more negatively than distressed-only couples.

Hinchcliffe and her colleagues did the earliest observational studies of the interaction of depressed patients and their spouses. Their results are summarized in *The Melancholy Marriage* (Hinchliffe, Hooper, & Roberts, 1978). Depressed inpatients' interactions with their spouses and with strangers were compared to inpatient surgery patient controls. The interactions of depressed couples were found to be more emotionally tense, disrupted and filled with pauses and interruptions, and to be self-absorbed and preoccupied. As in Weissman and Paykel's (1974) study, the female depressives negative expressiveness was independent of their clinical state which was not true for male depressives. Depressives engaged in much less negative expressiveness with strangers than with their spouses.

Hooley (1986) compared the discussions of depressed patients with spouses who were classified as exhibiting high or low levels of expressed emotion (EE) based on the number of critical comments they made about the patient during a separate interview. High EE spouses disagreed more, were less accepting, and made more critical comments about their depressed partners as compared with low EE spouses. Patients with high EE spouses did not differ from patients with low EE spouses in terms of negative verbal or nonverbal behavior, but they self-disclosed less and were more nonverbally neutral. The high EE patients may have been attempting to avoid confrontations by their self-protective and neutral stance, but they may have thereby given their spouses more openings for confrontations.

Kowalik and Gotlib (1987) used a highly structured experimental situation in which depressed outpatients, nondepressed outpatients, normal controls and their respective spouses rated the intent of their communications to their partner and the impact of their partner's communications on them. They were later asked to recall their original coding. Depressed patients coded fewer positive and more negative intents and impacts during their interactions with their spouses than subjects in the other groups and were more accurate in recalling their coding. Spouses of depressed outpatients recalled fewer positive and more negative intents than they had originally coded. These results suggest that negative reactions are elicited in the spouse when she or he interacts with the depressed person and that the depressed person has a negative perception of their environment. These results are consistent with a so called "self-focusing" style in which there is a bias toward focusing on negative outcomes to the neglect of focusing on positive outcomes (Pyszczynski & Greenberg, 1987). This phenomenon is similar to one noted among maritally distressed couples: Such couples tend to make negative (distress-maintaining) attributions for their spouse's behavior (Holtzworth-Munroe & Jacobson, 1985), to be focused on the negative aspects of the relationship to the virtual exclusion of the positive aspects, and to be more reactive to recent events, both positive and negative (Jacobson, Follette, & McDonald, 1982).

Although a number of studies have recorded less marital satisfaction and more marital conflict in couples with a depressed spouse as compared to couples without psychiatric disturbance, there has been little investigation of the specificity of the observed differences to depressed marital partners. Also, these studies have focused on dyads in which the wife was the diagnosed depressive. Gotlib and Whiffen (1989) compared three groups of marital partners: depressed, medical problems, or no history of psychiatric or serious medical problems. Some of the identified patients in the two patient groups were male. Variables examined were marital satisfaction, verbal and nonverbal interactions and reactions during and subsequent to dyadic discussions of typical marital problems rated by participants as serious. There were virtually no differences between depressed male and female patients except that females rated their affect more negatively after the interaction than their male counterparts and both male and female depressives rated the impact of interacting with spouses more negatively than spouses in the other two groups. As in a number of prior studies, depressed couples expressed less satisfaction and displayed more dysfunctional behavior by virtually every index than the normal controls. But most importantly the depressed couples differed little from the couples containing a partner with medical problems. Thus evidence for the specificity of dysfunctions previously identified with the marital interactions of depressed couples is called into question.

Merikangas, Ranelli, and Kupfer (1979) examined within-subjects changes in marital interaction as a function of response to antidepressant medication. The resolution of differences was preponderantly in favor of the patients' spouses initially but became more egalitarian as treatment progressed. Over time, the *frequency* of joint speech (i.e., both spouses talking at the same time which is often construed as a conflict indicator) decreased for medication responders, nonresponders, and their spouses. The *duration* of joint speech decreased for nonresponder patients and their spouses, and the *frequency* of responder couples' speech increased over time. The authors suggest that the changes in medication responders' interactions with their spouses reflected smoother, less choppy speech patterns indicative of improved social functioning.

Schmaling and Jacobson (in press) examined the interactions of 126 couples in a $2 \times 2 \times 2$ (depression $\times$ marital distress $\times$ sex of spouse) design. The couples discussed both neutral topics and topics involving marital disagreement and conflict. When the use of depressive behavior during neutral versus conflictual conversations was compared, couples with and without depressed wives were indistinguishable when they discussed neutral topics. When they discussed an area of conflict, however, couples with depressed wives showed significantly more depressive behavior than did nondepressed couples. A three-way interaction was found for aggressive behavior: Depressed women in nondistressed relationships exhibited high rates of aggressive behavior; in contrast, their husbands exhibited low rates of aggressive behavior. Spouses in distressed relationships, regardless of the level of the wives' depression, exhibited high rates of aggressive behavior. The study did not replicate the Biglan et al. (1985) findings that depressive behavior appeared to serve a coercive function. These results suggest that marital distress, not depression per se, may be the source of the dysfunctional interaction patterns frequently observed in depressed couples.

Using a subset of this sample, Schmaling, Whisman, Jacobson, Fruzzetti, & Truax (in preparation) examined couples' conversations as they defined areas of marital conflict. They found that husbands' increased use of behaviors that controlled and directed the content of the conversation were predictive of wives' greater self-reported depressive symptoms. These husband behaviors accounted for a significant proportion of the variance in wives' level of depression in addition to that attributable to marital distress. This suggests that, independent from the level of marital satisfaction, wives in couples with traditional husband-dominant power structures may be more depressed.

CHARACTERISTICS OF THE SPOUSES OF DEPRESSED PATIENTS

Several studies have examined the characteristics of the spouses of depressed patients. Coyne, Kessler, Tal, Turnbull, Wortman, and Greden (1987) found that living with a chronically or recurrently depressed patient during an episode imposes greater burdens than living with such a patient in remission. Forty percent of spouses of patients in active episodes evidenced sufficient psychological distress to justify referral for intervention. This study used a mixed bipolar and unipolar depressive sample. The results are comparable with Waring and Patton's (1984) who found that 36% of spouses of unipolar depressives reported significant symptoms of nonpsychotic emotional illness. Coyne et al. cite these findings as added evidence for the negative impact of depression on others. The design of the study reduced the likelihood that results were simply attributable to assortative mating. They urge that studies of the interpersonal context of depression are likely to prove more fruitful than the current emphasis on cognitive factors.

Krantz and Moos (1987) found that spouses of both remitted and nonremitted depressed patients reported poorer relationships, more conflict, and less cohesiveness with their patient-spouses than control couples. Spouse adaptation was unrelated to changes in the depression of the patient.

Hooley, Richters, Weintaub, and Neale (1987) suggest that aversive patient behaviors that are perceived as illness-related and uncontrollable by the spouse (i.e., positive symptoms, e.g., hallucinations) are less disturbing to the marital relationship, than behaviors perceived as controllable (i.e., negative symptoms, e.g., depression, lethargy), even though independent observers rated patients with positive symptoms as more impaired in terms of overall functioning. In this study, the investigators classified the controllability of the symptoms on an a priori basis. A goal for future research in this area would be to collect direct spousal attributions for the controllability of the symptom.

MARITAL INTERACTION FACTORS RELATED TO RELAPSE

Recovered formerly depressed patients with unimproved marriages are more likely to relapse than recovered patients whose marriages have also improved over the course of therapy (Rounsaville, Prusoff, & Weissman, 1980). While this and prior studies indicate that martial disharmony is predictive of relapse among depressed patients (cf. Kerr, Roth, & Shapira, 1974), few studies have used observational methods to examine the specific sorts of marital exchanges that are related to relapse in couples with a depressed spouse. Hooley, Orley, and Teasdale (1986) found that 59% of the formerly depressed patients with critical spouses had relapsed at 9 month follow-up whereas none of the formerly depressed patients with noncritical spouses had relapsed by then. An extension of this work (Hooley & Teasdale, 1989) found that an even better predictor of depressives' relapse was the patients' perceptions of how critical their spouses were of them. These studies echo the results of Vaughn and Leff (1976) who suggested that critical comments about the depressed patient by their family members were associated with increased relapse rates over a 9 month follow-up period. Critical comments are probably related to the degree of marital satisfaction in the couple. Thus, these results appear to replicate the linkage between marital distress and depression.

INTERACTIONS BETWEEN DEPRESSED MOTHERS AND THEIR CHILDREN

A number of studies have examined the impact of maternal depression on children. Again, results have not been very consistent, and sample n's have often been too small to have much statistical power. Lee and Gotlib (1989) briefly review this literature and report on one of the more adequately designed of these studies which compared internalizing and externalizing problems and social competence in the offspring of four groups: outpatient depressed mothers, outpatient nondepressed psychiatrically disturbed mothers, outpatient medically impaired mothers without diagnosable psychiatric problems, and nonimpaired controls. Analyses were based on mothers' ratings of their children and on interviewers' ratings of these children based on their self-reports. Ratings from these two independent sources were generally consistent. Results indicated no differences in externalizing problems or in social competence (except as influenced by socioeconomic differences) among children of the four groups. Children of the two psychiatric groups of mothers reported more internalizing problems than the two nonpsychiatric groups. Ratings were made during the initial stages of treatment of the psychiatric groups and then 8 weeks later. Despite considerable symptomatic improvement in the depressed mothers there was no corresponding improvement in their children's behavior.

The investigators concluded that disturbance in the offspring of psychiatric patients may be nonspecific though they conjecture that severity of maternal impairment may be positively related to social-behavioral dysfunction in their children. They endorse the importance of identifying the mechanisms and processes whereby maternal impairment effects offspring. Lee and Gotlib suggest maternal self-preoccupation and the tendency of psychiatric symptom displays to suppress aversive behavior by others as promising candidates for further investigation.

Dumas, Gibson, and Albin (1989) investigated relations between depressed mothers and their conduct disordered children from two perspectives: their interactions and the relationship of maternal distress to child adjustment. In a limited sense, these perspectives yielded conflicting results. On global ratings the conduct disordered children of depressed mothers were more maladjusted than the children of nondepressed controls, but the former were better adjusted on measures of specific interactions. When depressed mothers are more distressed their children become more maladjusted though selectively so. The investigators contend that increased interactional difficulties are probably attributable to disruption of the attentional and monitoring skills that are requisites of effective cognitive responding. The findings of Dumas et al. (1989) are generally supportive of Hops et al. (1987): maternal depressive behavior tends to result in conduct disordered children showing less aversive behavior and greater compliance toward their mothers.

METHODOLOGICAL CRITIQUE OF THE STUDIES

Definition of the Independent Variable and Heterogeneity of the Diagnostic Label. Drawing conclusive statements from the data reviewed is difficult because of several sources of heterogeneity in the literature. First, some of the studies have used depressed outpatients, and some have used depressed inpatients. Patient status may reflect differing levels of the severity of the depression. The methods used to classify a given subject as depressed or not have also varied significantly. The inconsistent application of the Beck Depression Inventory (Beck et al., 1961) is perhaps the best example of this phenomenon. A BDI score of 15 would classify a subject as depressed in one study (cf. Arkowitz et al., 1982) or as nondepressed in another (cf. Hautzinger et al., 1982). All but one study (Arkowitz et al., 1982) used structured diagnostic criteria or agreement between two diagnosticians to classify subjects as depressed or not. The use of "real" patients is laudable in studies of the interaction of couples with a depressed spouse as contrasted with numerous studies based on subclinically depressed college students (for a review see Doerfler, 1981). Depression is not a unitary phenomenon: two patients may both be diagnosed as being depressed yet have nonoverlapping symptoms. This underscores the need for increased specificity and homogeneity of the samples that are studied in order to be able to compare the results of several studies without having to attribute differences in the results to the possible effects of sample heterogeneity.

Definition of the Dependent Variable. The studies that used behavioral coding systems to examine the marital interactions of the depressed patients and their spouses all used independent observers with one exception (Kowalik & Gotlib, 1987) in which the spouses rated their own and their partner's behavior. All studies used different coding systems. Dependent variables which reflect the topography of couples' interactions (e.g., a measure of speech duration, Merikangas et al., 1979) versus those which reflect interactional content (cf. Hautzinger et al., 1982) may be measuring very different aspects of interaction. Results from studies that use diverse coding systems may not be comparable.

Investigators have been lax in their standards for the interrater reliability of their coding system (Biglan et al., 1985). Interrater reliability needs to be reported and the type of reliability coefficient needs to be clearly stated. With greater interrater variability, more error is introduced into the data, and the probability of Type II error (not rejecting the null hypothesis when it should be rejected) increases due to the use of insensitive dependent variables.

Sex Differences. Second, sex of the identified patient has been variously all-female or mixed in the studies reviewed earlier. Studies that have examined sex as a variable of interest have found differential reactions to depressed males as compared with depressed females (cf. Hammen & Peters, 1977). Hooley et al. (1986) found that fewer depressed men with critical wives relapsed as compared to depressed women with critical husbands. She speculated that spousal criticism may be associated with increased likelihood of divorce and that this may be differentially stressful (e.g., economically) for the sexes. It might be desirable to stratify samples according to the prevalence of depression by sex within the population, or to assume that different mechanisms are at work among depressed women as compared with men and to control for this potential source of variance. The latter seems probable given the relatively consistent finding that women have a much higher incidence and prevalence of depression than men (Weissman & Klerman, 1977). This latter tact may also be preferable given recent evidence that men and women respond to negative moods differently (Nolen-Hoeksema, 1987). Coyne et al. (1987) have suggested that power and satisfaction within the marriage might be particularly fruitful variables to investigate.

Generalizability and Type III Error. The studies have also varied according to the type of interactional task which the couples performed, particularly the degree of their involvement in the choice of topic(s) to discuss and the reactivity of the discussions. Most studies used a structured questionnaire about problems not specific to their marriage or a questionnaire about common areas of marital tension to arrive at areas of disagreement for discussion. How the couple approaches a contrived problem-solving task in a sterile laboratory setting may be quite different from their problem-solving in the natural environment. Some topics may be more evocative than others and the process through which a couple defines an area that is problematic for them is itself an area for further research (Schmaling et al., in preparation). Further work is needed to move away from examination of a contrived problem in a laboratory setting, to more valid problems discussed in laboratory settings, and to more ecologically valid problems discussed, e.g., in the home environment, though clearly these will present methodological challenges to researchers in the area. Type III error occurs when one interprets the results of an irrelevant study as support for one's hypothesis (Doerfler & Chaplin, 1985). A cautious approach should be taken to the generalization of results from laboratory studies as reflections of naturally occurring phenomena.

DESIGN AND ANALYSIS/STATISTICAL ISSUES

The sample sizes of the studies to date have been quite small. The N's of the studies have ranged from 4 and 5 per comparison group (Merikangas et al., 1979) to a maximum of 36 per cell (Schmaling & Jacobson, in press). Such small samples limit the generalizability of the results. If a study with a small sample does not find results that confirm their hypotheses, this may be due to a lack of statistical power rather than an inability to reject the null hypothesis. Most of the studies have involved between-subjects designs controlling for factors such as hospitalized patient status (Hinchliffe et al., 1978), psychiatric patient status (Arkowitz et al., 1982; Kowalik & Gotlib, 1987), or marital adjustment (Schmaling & Jacobson, in press). But none of the studies have controlled for the effects of depression, psychiatric patient status, and marital distress in a way that allows for identification of specific sources of interactional variability due to each of these effects. Sources of interactional variability uniquely attributable to marital distress and depression are in particular need of experimental control given the evidence for a strong relationship between them.

Other studies have used within-subjects designs. For example, Merikangas et al. (1979) examined interactional changes over the course of therapy comparing antidepressant medication responders and nonresponders. These designs are not without their own limitations, i.e., the effects of maturation, and the inability to rule out factors which change simultaneously with the treatment (Campbell & Stanley, 1963).

Additionally, past studies have used inadequate controls for Type I error (i.e., rejecting the null hypothesis when it should not be rejected), and/or have reported and interpreted statistically marginal results. Several studies have made many tests of their data without correcting for the probability of obtaining statistically significant results by chance. As the number of tests increases, so should the critical alpha level decrease to correct for Type I error (e.g., Bonferonni correction).

Much of the existing literature has asked questions that address the functional/temporal links between depressive behavior and other (antecedent and consequent) behaviors. Few studies, however, have used the appropriate design, dependent variables or statistical techniques to address these sorts of questions. One method of addressing functional/behavioral relationships is to observe the behaviors of interest, collect data in such a way as to preserve the temporal relationship of the behaviors, and examine the sequential structure of the interactions at a microanalytic level (e.g., Biglan et al., 1985; Schmaling & Jacobson, in press). The reader is referred to Sackett (1979) for an overview of observational methodology and sequential scoring and analytic methods. It should be noted, however, that the method proposed by Gottman (1980) should be used to examine sequential structure and calculate sequential reliability between observers. Longitudinal designs and regression-based analytic procedures would be a second direction for future research. With few exceptions, studies have used cross-sectional experimental designs and regression-based analysis procedures. Notable exceptions include the prospective studies of initially asymptomatic samples by Paykel et al. (1969) and Monroe, Bromet, Connell, and Steiner (1986). Barnett and Gotlib (1988) have understandably advocated the use of longitudinal designs to better assess the interaction between a psychosocial predictor variable, initial depressive symptoms, and to assess the predictor's relationship to changes in depressive symptoms over time.

TREATMENT IMPLICATIONS AND THEORETICAL IMPLICATIONS

Beach and O'Leary (1986) found that marital therapy and individual cognitive therapy were equally effective in reducing depressive symptoms among married, depressed women. Marital discord, however, was reduced only for the group receiving marital therapy. Preliminary results from another study (Jacobson, Dobson, Schmaling, Salusky, Follette, & Miller, in press) also suggest that among maritally distressed couples, marital therapy is as effective as cognitive therapy in reducing depressive symptoms. Rounsaville et al. (1980) found that remitted depressed women in unimproved distressed marriages were much more likely to relapse than were those patients with improved relationships. The work of Hooley et al. (1986) also suggests that a distressed marriage (i.e., having a critical spouse) is predictive of relapse. Thus, one would expect that successful marital therapy would also protect the patient from relapse. Unfortunately, no data addressing these questions are available. Marital therapy may be the primary treatment of choice for depressed patients who are in a distressed marriage.

REFERENCES

Alloy, L. B., & Abramson, L. Y. (1979). Judgment of contingency in depressed and nondepressed students: Sadder but wiser? *Journal of Experimental Psychology: General, 108,* 441–485.

Arkowitz, H., Holliday, S., & Hutter, M. (1982, November). *Depressed women and their husbands: A study of marital interactions and adjustment.* Paper presented at the meeting of the Association for Advancement of Behavior Therapy.

Barnett, P. A., & Gotlib, I. H. (1988). Psychosocial functioning and depression: Distinguishing among antecedents, concomitants, and consequences. *Psychological Bulletin, 104,* 97–126.

Beach, S. R. H., Arias, I., O'Leary, K. D. (1983). *Risk for depression as a function of social support.* Paper presented at the meeting of the Eastern Psychological Association in Philadelphia, PA. As cited in S. R. H. Beach and K. D. O'Leary (1986). The treatment of depression occurring in the context of marital discord. *Behavior Therapy, 17,* 43–49.

Beach, S. R. H., & O'Leary, K. D. (1986). The treatment of depression occurring in the context of marital discord. *Behavior Therapy, 17,* 43–49.

Beck, A. T., Ward, C. H., Mendelsohn, M., Mock, J., & Erbaugh, J. (1961). An inventory for measuring depression. *Archives of General Psychiatry, 4,* 561–571.

Biglan, A., Hops, H., Sherman, L., Friedman, L., Arthur, J., & Osteen, V. (1985). Problem solving interactions of depressed women and their spouses. *Behavior Therapy, 16,* 431–451.

Biglan, A., Rothlind, J., Hops, H., & Sherman, L. (1989). Impact of distressed and aggressive behavior. *Journal of Abnormal Psychology, 98,* 218–228.

Boswell, P. D., & Murray, E. J. (1981). Depression, schizophrenia, and social attraction. *Journal of Consulting and Clinical Psychology, 91,* 231–240.

Briscoe, C. W., & Smith, J. B. (1973). Depression and marital turmoil. *Archives of General Psychiatry, 29,* 811–817.

Brown, G. W., & Harris, T. O. (1978). *Social origins of depression: A study of psychiatric disorder in women.* New York: The Free Press.

Campbell, D. T., & Stanley, J. C. (1963). *Experimental and quasi-experimental designs for research.* Chicago: Rand McNally.

Coleman, R. E., & Miller, A. G. (1975). The relationship between depression and marital maladjustment in a clinic population: A multitrait-multimethod study. *Journal of Consulting and Clinical Psychology, 43,* 647–651.

Coyne, J. C. (1976). Toward an interactional description of depression. *Psychiatry, 39,* 28–40.

Coyne, J. C. (1985). Studying depressed persons' interactions with strangers and spouses. *Journal of Abnormal Psychology, 94,* 231–232.

Coyne, J. C., & Gotlib, I. H. (1983). The role of cognition in depression: A critical appraisal. *Psychological Bulletin, 94,* 472–505.

Coyne, J. C., Kahn, J., & Gotlib, I. H. (1987). Depression. In T. Jacob (Ed.), *Family interaction and psychopathology: Theory methods and findings* (pp. 509–533). New York: Plenum.

Crowther, J. H. (1985). The relationship between depression and marital maladjustment. *Journal of Nervous and Mental Disease, 173,* 227–231.

Dobson, K. S. (1989). Real and perceived interpersonal responses to subclinically anxious and depressed targets. *Cognitive Therapy and Research, 13,* 37–47.

Doerfler, L. A. (1981). Psychological research on depression: A methodological review. *Clinical Psychology Review, 1,* 119–137.

Doerfler, L. A., & Chaplin, W. F. (1985). Type III error in research on interactional models of depression. *Journal of Abnormal Psychology, 94,* 227–230.

Dumas, J. E., Gibson, J. A., & Albin, J. B. (1989). Behavioral correlates of maternal depressive symptomatology in conduct-disordered children. *Journal of Consulting and Clinical Psychology, 57,* 516–522.

Ensel, W. M. (1982). The role of age in the relationship of gender and marital status to depression. *Journal of Nervous and Mental Disease, 170,* 536–543.

Ekman, P., & Friesen, W. V. (1974). Nonverbal behavior and psychopathology. In R. Friedman & M. Katz (eds.), *The psychology of depression: Contemporary theory and research.* New York: Wiley.

Gotlib, I. H. (1983). Perception and recall of interpersonal feedback: Negative bias in depression. *Cognitive Therapy and Research, 7,* 399–412.

Gotlib, I. H. (1982). Self-reinforcement and depression in interpersonal interaction: The role of performance level. *Journal of Abnormal Psychology, 91,* 3–13.

Gotlib, I. H., & Beatty, E. (1985). Negative responses to depression: The role of attributional style. *Cognitive Therapy and Research, 9,* 91–103.

Gotlib, I. H., & Whiffen, V. E. (1989). Depression and marital functioning: An examination of specificity and gender differences. *Journal of Abnormal Psychology, 98,* 23–30.

Gottman, J. M. (1980). Analyzing for sequential connection and assessing interobserver reliability for the sequential analysis for observational data. *Behavioral Assessment, 2,* 361–368.

Hammen, C. L., & Peters, S. D. (1977). Differential responses to male and female depressive reactions. *Journal of Consulting and Clinical Psychology, 45,* 994–1991.
Hautzinger, M., Linden, M., & Hoffman, N. (1982). Distressed couples with and without a depressed partner: An analysis of their verbal interaction. *Journal of Behavior Therapy and Experimental Psychiatry, 13,* 307–314.
Hinchliffe, M. K., Hooper, D., & Roberts, F. J. (1978). *The melancholy marriage: Depression in marriage and psychosocial approaches to therapy.* Chichester: Wiley.
Hokanson, J. E., & Rubert, M. P. (in press). Interpersonal factors in depression. In D. G. Gilbert (Ed.), *Personality, social skills, and psychopathology: An individual difference approach.* New York: Plenum Press.
Hokanson, J. E., Rubert, M. P., Welker, R. A., Hollander, G. R., & Hedeen, C. (1989). Interpersonal concomitants and antecedents of depression among college students. *Journal of Abnormal Psychology, 98,* 209–217.
Holtzworth-Monroe, A., & Jacobson, N. S. (1985). Causal attributions of married couples: When do they search for causes? What do they conclude when they do? *Journal of Personality and Social Psychology, 48,* 1398–1412.
Hooley, J. M. (1986). Expressed emotion and depression: Interactions between patients and high- versus low-expressed-emotion spouses. *Journal of Abnormal Psychology, 95,* 237–246.
Hooley, J. M., Orley, J., & Teasdale, J. D. (1986). Levels of expressed emotion and relapse in depressed patients. *British Journal of Psychiatry, 148,* 642–647.
Hooley, J. M., Richters, J. E., Weintaub, S., & Neale, J. M. (1987). Psychopathology and marital distress: The positive side of positive symptoms. *Journal of Abnormal Psychology, 96,* 27–33.
Hooley, J. M., & Teasdale, J. D. (1989). Predictors of relapse in unipolar depressives: Expressed emotion, marital distress, and perceived criticism. *Journal of Abnormal Psychology, 98,* 229–235.
Hops, H., Biglan, A., Sherman, L., Arthur, J., Friedman, L., & Osteen, V. (1987). Home observations of family interactions of depressed women. *Journal of Consulting and Clinical Psychology, 55,* 341–346.
Howes, M. J., & Hokanson, J. E. (1979). Conversational and social responses to depressive interpersonal behavior. *Journal of Abnormal Psychology, 88,* 625–634.
Jacobson, N. S., & Anderson, E. A. (1982). Interpersonal skill and depression in college students: An analysis of the timing of self-disclosures. *Behavior Therapy, 13,* 271–282.
Jacobson, N. S., Dobson, K., Schmaling, K. B., Salusky, S., Follette, V., & Miller, D. (in press). Marital therapy and the treatment of depression. In B. Lerer & S. Gershon (Eds.), *New directions in affective disorder.* New York: Springer.
Jacobson, N. S., Follette, W. C., & McDonald, D. W. (1982). Reactivity to positive and negative behavior in distressed and nondistressed married couples. *Journal of Consulting and Clinical Psychology, 50,* 706–714.
Kerr, T. A., Roth, M., & Shapira, K. (1974). Prediction of outcome in anxiety states and depressive illness. *British Journal of Psychiatry, 124,* 125–133.
King, D. A., & Heller, K. (1984). Depression and the response of others: A re-evaluation. *Journal of Abnormal Psychology, 93,* 477–480.
Kowalik, D. L., & Gotlib, I. H. (1987). Depression and marital interaction: Concordance between intent and perception of communication. *Journal of Abnormal Psychology, 96,* 127–134.
Krantz, S. E., & Moos, R. H. (1987). Functioning and life context among spouses of remitted and nonremitted depressed patients. *Journal of Consulting and Clinical Psychology, 55,* 353–360.
Lee, C. M., & Gotlib, I. H. (1989). Maternal depression and child adjustment: A longitudinal analysis. *Journal of Abnormal Psychology, 98,* 78–85.
Lewinsohn, P. M., Hoberman, H. M., Teri, L., & Hautzinger, M. (1985). An integrative theory of depression. In S. Reiss & N. R. Bootzin (Eds.), *Theoretical issues in behavior therapy* (pp. 331–359). New York: Academic Press.

Lewinsohn, P. M., Mischel, W., Chaplin, W., & Barton, R. (1980). Social competence and depression: The role of illusory self-perceptions. *Journal of Abnormal Psychology, 89,* 203–212.
Linden, M., Hautzinger, M., & Hoffman, N. (1983). Discriminant analysis of depressive interactions. *Behavior Modification, 7,* 403–422.
McNeil, D. E., Arkowitz, H. S., & Pritchard, B. E. (1987). The response of others in face-to-face interaction with depressed patients. *Journal of Abnormal Psychology, 96,* 341–344.
Merikangas, K. R., Ranelli, C. J., & Kupfer, D. J. (1979). Marital interaction in hospitalized depressed patients. *Journal of Nervous and Mental Disease, 167,* 689–695.
Meyer, B. E. B., & Hokanson, J. E. (1985). Situational influences on social behaviors of depression-prone individuals. *Journal of Clinical Psychology, 41,* 29–35.
Monroe, S. M., Bromet, E. J., Connell, M. M., & Steiner, S. C. (1986). Social support, Life events, and depressive symptoms: A 1-year prospective study. *Journal of Consulting and Clinical Psychology, 54,* 424–431.
Nolen-Hoeksema, S. (1987). Sex differences in unipolar depression: Evidence and theory. *Psychological Bulletin, 101,* 259–282.
Paykel, E. S., Myers, J. K., Dienelt, M. N., Klerman, G. L., Lindenthal, J. J., & Pepper, M. P. (1969). Life events and depression. *Archives of General Psychiatry, 21,* 753–760.
Pyszczynski, T., & Greenberg, J. (1987). Self-regulatory preservation and the depressive self-focusing style: A self-awareness theory of reactive depression. *Psychological Bulletin, 102,* 122–138.
Rounsaville, B. J., Prusoff, B. A., & Weissman, M. M. (1980). The course of marital disputes in depressed women: A 48-month follow-up study. *Comprehensive Psychiatry, 21,* 111–118.
Rounsaville, B. J., Weissman, M. M., Prusoff, B. A., & Herceg-Barton, R. L. (1979). Marital disputes and treatment outcome in depressed women. *Comprehensive Psychiatry, 20,* 483–490.
Sackett, G. P. (1979). *Observing behavior: Data collection and analysis methods (Vol. 2).* Baltimore: University Park Press.
Schmaling, K. B., & Jacobson, N. S. (in press). Marital interaction and depression. *Journal of Abnormal Psychology.*
Schmaling, K. B., Whisman, M. A., Jacobson, N. S., Fruzzetti, A. E., & Truax, P. (in preparation). *Identifying areas of marital conflict: Interactional differences associated with depression.*
Strack, S., & Coyne, J. C. (1983). Social confirmation of dysphoria: Shared and private reactions to depression. *Journal of Personality and Social Psychology, 44,* 798–806.
Vaughn, C. E., & Leff, J. P. (1976). The influence of family and social factors on the course of psychiatric illness: A comparison of schizophrenic and depressed neurotic patients. *British Journal of Psychiatry, 129,* 125–137.
Waring, E. M., & Patton, D. (1984). Marital intimacy and depression. *British Journal of Psychiatry, 145,* 641–644.
Weiss, R. L., & Aved, B. M. (1978). Marital satisfaction and depression as predictors of physical health status. *Journal of Consulting and Clinical Psychology, 46,* 1379–1384.
Weissman, M. M., & Klerman, G. L. (1977). Sex differences in the epidemiology of depression. *Archives of General Psychiatry, 34,* 98–111.
Weissman, M. M., & Paykel, E. S. (1974). *The depressed woman: A study of social relationships.* Chicago: University of Chicago Press.
Winer, D., Bonner, T. O., Blaney, P., & Murray, E. (1981). Depression and social attraction. *Motivation and Emotion, 5,* 153–166.
Youngren, M. A., & Lewinsohn, P. M. (1980). The functional relation between depression and problematic interpersonal behavior. *Journal of Abnormal Psychology, 89,* 333–341.

7
Life Stressors, Social Resources, and the Treatment of Depression

Rudolf H. Moos
Stanford University and Veterans Administration Medical Centers, Palo Alto, California

Stressful life circumstances and lack of social resources play an important role in the onset and course of depression. However, researchers have not typically considered the way in which these life context factors influence the process of remission and relapse after treatment. In this chapter, I describe a conceptual framework for program evaluation that focuses on this issue. I use the framework to guide a review of existing literature and to present an overview of an ongoing program of research on depression. The research program applies the expanded evaluation paradigm and stress and coping theory to examine how depressed patients' life contexts affect the treatment they obtain and the outcome of treatment.

The expanded evaluation paradigm and stress and coping theory have broad applicability. I use them to examine the process of treatment selection and the determinants of treatment outcome, to compare remitted patients with nonremitted patients and demographically matched nondepressed case controls, and to show how spouses adapt to the stressors involved in living with a depressed partner. After considering these issues, I set forth some important directions for future research, such as applying the framework to other psychiatric disorders, focusing on variations in depressed mood in community groups, and clarifying the dynamics of the stress and coping process.

INTEGRATING THEORY AND PROGRAM EVALUATION

An expanded paradigm of evaluation research is needed to help program evaluations probe and refine a biopsychosocial perspective of depression. The biopsychosocial perspective is leading to revolutionary new approaches in medicine and psychology. Building on an ecological view of psychosomatic medicine, these approaches utilize a systems model of the causes of medical and psychiatric disorders and emphasize the influence of biological, psychological, and social factors in health and illness. The psychosocial aspects of the model are beginning to receive more emphasis in diagnostic assessment and treatment. For example, the American Psychiatric Association (APA, 1987) has developed a multiaxial diagnostic system, DSM-III-R, which considers the role of psychosocial stressors in depression as well as in other psychiatric and behavioral disorders. An evaluation paradigm should include information about such contextual factors and enable treatment providers to consider a patient's life situation when planning and evaluating treatment.

The Traditional Evaluation Paradigm

Many studies have used a "black-box" paradigm to evaluate treatment programs for depression (Howard, Kopta, Krause, & Orlinsky, 1986; Steinbrueck, Maxwell, & Howard, 1983). Following this summative paradigm, evaluators assess patients at intake and at one or more follow-ups, but pay little attention to the process of treatment (the "black box") or to other factors that might affect the patient. Such evaluations can gauge the overall outcome of a treatment program, but they reveal little about the process of treatment or about how to improve it.

Some recent evaluations have described the process of treatment for depression and the associations between specific aspects of treatment and outcome. For example, Rounsaville and his colleagues (1987) found that high therapist activity and warmth were associated with better outcome of interpersonal psychotherapy. Simons, Garfield, and Murphy (1984) noted that patients treated with antidepressant medication showed as much change in cognitive attributions as did patients in cognitive treatment. These process-oriented studies are leading to new causal mediational models of the role of cognition in depression (Hollon, DeRubeis, & Evans, 1987). By identifying how specific aspects of treatment are related to outcome and the presumed mediators of outcome, such studies can suggest new ways to make treatment more effective.

However, only a few studies have focused on how extratreatment factors influence the initiation and length of treatment for depression or the process of remission and relapse after treatment. Stressful circumstances and a lack of social resources can obscure the benefits of treatment, especially when treatment is brief and there is a long interval between the end of treatment and follow-up. In fact, such life context factors may be largely responsible for the high rate of relapse after treatment. A conceptual framework for program evaluation should consider how the interplay between treatment and life context factors can affect the process of remission and relapse in depression.

An Expanded Evaluation Paradigm

The expanded paradigm shown in Fig. 7.1 suggests that the outcome of treatment (personal resources and functioning at follow-up; Panel V) is influenced by personal resources at intake, including demographic factors, the severity and chronicity of depression, and other aspects of functioning (Panel II). Treatment outcome is also influenced by life context factors prior to intake (Panel I) and those that occur during the treatment and posttreatment interval (Panel IV), as well as by the patient's treatment experiences (Panel III). In addition, the model considers both personal and life context factors (that is, variables in Panels I and II) as determinants of entrance to treatment and of the amount and type of treatment (Panel III).

The model depicts some potential unidirectional "causal" influences (Panels I and II to Panels III, IV, and V). It also reflects the mutual interrelationships between life contexts, personal resources, and depression (the double-headed paths between Panels I and II and Panels IV and V), as well as those between treatment and life context (Panels I, III, and IV) and personal (Panels II, III, and V) factors. I focus primarily on unidirectional predictive associations here. Bill-

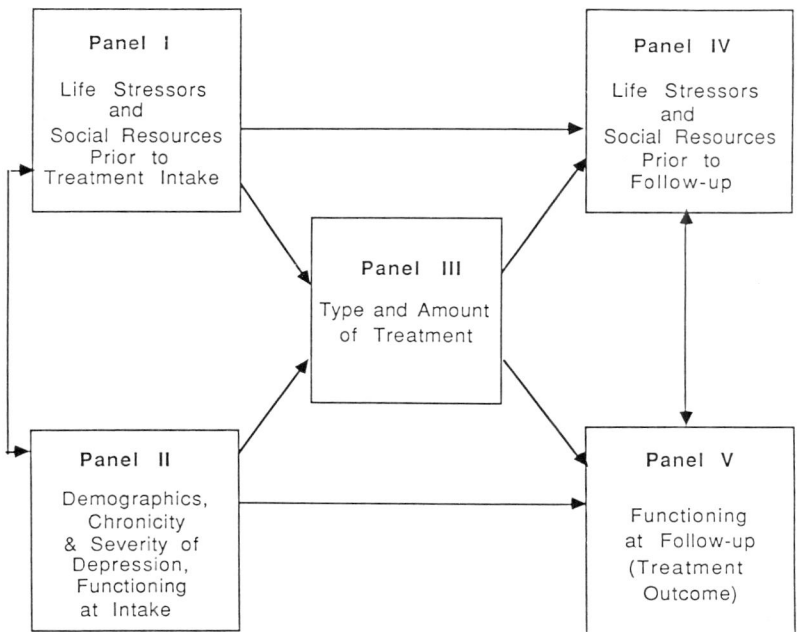

FIG. 7.1. The relationship between life context factors, treatment, and treatment outcome.

ings and Moos (1985c) discuss some of the reciprocal connections between life stressors, social resources, and depression, as well as how life stressors and coping patterns may change when depression develops into a syndrome that requires further coping efforts.

This expanded paradigm reflects two current trends in program evaluation. First, it encourages the careful study of treatment, including an assessment of how well treatment is implemented and an examination of the associations between specific treatment components and outcome. Second, it explicitly considers factors outside of treatment and how they influence treatment entry, treatment experiences, and treatment outcome. The paradigm reflects the complexity of the treatment and rehabilitation process and conceptualizes an intervention program as one of several sets of factors that influence outcome. The expanded paradigm can guide evaluations of pharmacological as well as psychosocial interventions and help to identify the processes involved in recovery without treatment.

Stress and Coping Theory

In order to make a generalizable impact, an evaluation should be guided by theory. The biopsychosocial perspective provides a broad framework for thinking about factors that foster and maintain depression, and for categorizing theories of etiology and the process of recovery and relapse. With the exception of a few general systems theory principles, however, it provides little in the way of explanatory principles that can account for depression. It is a perspective rather than a theory.

Our research is based on a systematic subset of psychosocial concepts within the biopsychosocial perspective; these concepts are derived from stress and coping theory. The theory posits that adaptation is influenced by the stressful life circumstances to which a person is exposed, by how such stressors are appraised, and by the personal and social resources available to manage them (Lazarus & Folkman, 1984). Although psychosocial stressors are risk factors for depression, they do not necessarily foreshadow depressed mood or a decline in functioning. Because no one can avoid all stressors, individuals necessarily face situations that can induce depression; their appraisal of the situation and their personal and social resources determine whether stressors lead to depression.

In general, stress and coping theory is consistent with theories that emphasize more specific sets of causal factors in depression, such as a lack of interpersonal and behavioral skills and maladaptive cognitive and self-regulatory processes. However, interpersonal and behavioral theories tend to highlight relatively enduring characteristics of individuals and cognitive and self-regulatory models typically focus on general and relatively stable patterns of attribution and self-focusing styles. In contrast, stress and coping theory places more emphasis on the environmental precursors of mood and behavior and conceptualizes appraisal and coping responses as somewhat situation-specific ways of managing stressful situations.

COMPARING DEPRESSED PATIENTS AND COMMUNITY CONTROLS

Patient and Community Groups

We are conducting a longitudinal study of patients who sought treatment for depression in a representative set of facilities. We drew a sample of 424 unipolar depressed patients as they entered psychiatric treatment in an inpatient or outpatient treatment facility. In order to be included, patients had to be 18 years of age or older and to have a diagnosis of major or minor depression according to the Research Diagnostic Criteria.

We also wanted to compare stress and coping processes in unipolar depressed patients and a normal group and to find out how well remitted patients and their family members function as compared to their nondepressed "neighbors." Accordingly, we randomly selected a community adult from within each patient's census tract and neighborhood. This sampling procedure enabled us to obtain a group of 424 men and women who were demographically comparable to the patients. The two groups were well-matched on gender (55% women; 45% men), marital status (45% married), age (average age of 40 years), and race (about 86% Caucasian). The community adults were somewhat better educated (14.1 vs. 13.4 years) and of somewhat higher occupational status (Billings, Cronkite, & Moos, 1983).

We obtained information on patients at the time they entered treatment and on spouses or partners who were living with the patients. We followed patients and their spouses or partners after 1 year and 4 years. The community group was assessed twice with a comparable interval between assessments. We completed 1-year and 4-year follow-ups on over 90% of the patients and controls who were still alive (18 patients had died by the 4-year follow-up).

The measures we obtained are based on the Health and Daily Living Form (HDL; Moos, Cronkite, Billings, & Finney, 1984), the Family Environment Scale (FES; Moos & Moos, 1986), and the Work Environment Scale (WES; Moos, 1986). The indices have been used in a number of studies and show moderate to high internal consistency and good construct and concurrent validity. Psychometric and normative information are in the manuals and other publications (Billings et al., 1983; Billings & Moos, 1985a, 1985b).

The indices of functioning include global depression (an 18-item index derived from the RDC definition of depression), physical symptoms (a 12-item index), self-esteem (an index composed of 6 adjectives rated on 5-point scales) and social activities with family members (an index of 12 such activities). Because we wanted to include a measure of clinically significant change, we also developed an index of remission (Billings & Moos, 1985b). As expected, at intake to treatment the patients were functioning more poorly in all areas than the matched nondepressed case controls. In addition to depression, the patients reported more physical symptoms and less self-esteem; they were less likely to participate in family social activities and to be employed either part-time or full-time (Billings et al., 1983).

Patients' Life Contexts at Intake to Treatment

Stressful life circumstances were measured by negative life events and by ongoing difficulties such as diagnosed medical conditions, spouse illness, child illness, family conflict, and stressful conditions at work (Table 7.1). In general, we focused on relatively serious life events that occurred in the 6 months prior to intake and that had long-term threatening implications. Much of the research in this area has considered only life events. However, life events and ongoing stressful circumstances are closely related; they both play an important role in the onset and course of depression (Brown & Harris, 1978, 1986). We have tried to maintain a distinction between new events and chronic difficulties by measuring them separately.

TABLE 7.1
Indices of Stressful Life Circumstances

1. Negative Life Events	number of serious undesirable events (0-15) experienced during the prior 6 months, such as separation, divorce, death of spouse or other immediate family member, and going deeply into debt
2. Medical Conditions	current diagnosed medical conditions (1 or more), such as arthritis, cancer, diabetes, and heart trouble
3. Spouse Illness	numbert of physical symptoms (0-12) experienced fairly often, such as headaches, indigestion, insomnia, and cold sweats
4. Children's Illnesses	number of health problems (0-13) experienced by children living in the household, such as allergies, asthma, headaches, and depression
5. Family Conflict	number of areas (0-14) of disagreement, such as money, relatives, sex, politics, and child discipline
6. Work Stressors	36-item index composed of 4 subscales from the Work Environment Scale that assess high work demands and supervisor control and lack of autonomy and clarity

As expected, depressed patients reported more negative events in the 6 months before intake than nondepressed controls did in a comparable 6-month interval. This was especially true for loss and exit events, which were reported by 30% of the patients and 16% of the controls. Compared to the case controls, depressed patients also reported more persistent stressors in each of the areas we assessed. They were more likely to have a diagnosed medical illness, to have an ill spouse or child, and to experience family conflict and problems at work. Such ongoing difficulties may eventually provoke a depressive episode or they may increase the likelihood of depression by exerting a cumulative influence together with a new stressful event. In this respect, 31% of the patients did not report a negative event in the 6 months before intake; however, the majority of these "event-free" patients (74%) experienced one or more chronic difficulties. Murphy (1982) also found that both severe stressful events and chronic difficulties were risk factors in the onset of depression. The risk was additive; a combination of a severe event and a major difficulty increased the likelihood of depression.

We measured social resources by positive events in the past 6 months and by indices of the number (number of network contacts, friends, close relationships) and quality (quality of a confidant, family support, work support) of personal relationships (Table 7.2). Compared to the case controls, the depressed patients at intake reported fewer positive events and fewer and less well-developed social resources. We found the largest group differences on two indices of the quality of social resources: the patient's relationship with a confidant and family support.

TABLE 7.2
Indices of Social Resources

1. Positive Life Events	number of desirable events (0-8) experienced during the prior 6 months, such as marriage, marital reconciliation, birth of a child, and substantial increase in income
2. Number of Network Contracts	sum of 5 items indexing visits with friends and relatives and attendance at clubs and organizations
3. Number of Friends	number of friends or people who are more than just casual acquaintances
4. Number of Close Relationships	number of close friends and persons who can be counted on for help when needed
5. Quality of Confidant	sum of 6 items rated on 5-point scales that describe the quality of a current significant relationship
6. Family Support	27-item index composed of 3 subscales from the Family Environment Scale that assess family cohesion, expressiveness,. and lack of aggression
7. Work Support	27-item index composed of 3 subscales from the Work Environment Scale that assess involvement, coworker cohesion, and supervisor support at work

Our findings replicate and extend prior case-control studies. In his review, Paykel (1985) identified 7 studies in which depressed patients were compared with general population groups. Patients experienced a higher level of threatening or undesirable events in all 7 comparisons. Individuals exposed to a causative or provoking factor were about six times as likely to become depressed in the subsequent 6 months as were individuals not so exposed. When we combined severe life events and major difficulties as risk factors, we obtained a relative risk of 4.4. The case-control studies have typically not considered patients' social resources. Our findings show that depressed patients experience a broad lack of social resources, as well as high levels of life events and chronic difficulties. Consistent with prior research (Brown & Harris, 1978), the lack of a confidant increased the relative risk (3.0) of developing depression among individuals who experienced a negative event or chronic difficulty.

Although the prevalence of depression is higher among women than among men, the psychosocial processes that underlie the onset of depression may be similar in both sexes. When we examined the case-control differences separately by gender, we found that virtually all of the overall group differences were significant for both men and women. Compared to men in the control group, men patients experienced more negative life events and ongoing difficulties and reported fewer and less extensive social resources. These findings imply that similar processes are involved in the development of depression among men and women.

The Accuracy of Depressed Patients' Reports

Depressed persons see themselves and their world in an excessively negative manner. Thus, some researchers have emphasized that depressed persons may overreport life stressors and underreport social resources. Our findings imply that the differences we observed between depressed and nondepressed persons are a reasonably accurate reflection of reality. For example, there were only low to moderate intercorrelations among the measures of stressors and social resources. Reports of the occurrence of several stressful events were not necessarily accompanied by reports of high levels of ongoing stressors. Likewise, reports of a lack of friends were essentially unrelated to reports of a poor relationship with a confidant. These results argue against any simple generalized response bias.

We also examined the correspondence between depressed patients' reports and those of their nondepressed partners. Where it was possible to evaluate an environmental factor shared by another person, such as the family milieu, we found significant agreement between the reports of the depressed patient and the nondepressed partner. The degree of agreement between respondents was comparable to that observed for the community group. Moreover, the depressed patients did not describe their environment as more stressful or less supportive than their nondepressed partners did (Billings et al., 1983; Billings & Moos, 1986).

Other studies support the validity of self-reports and imply that depressed persons can provide relatively accurate descriptions of their environment and behavior. Brown and Harris (1978) found that depressed persons and their relatives showed reasonably high agreement (about 80%) in the reported occurrence of negative events. Depressed patients' reports of the stressfulness of these events agreed with independent ratings made by the investigators. Zimmerman, Pfohl, and Stangl (1986) also found that depressed patients agreed with interviewers in rating the severity of psychosocial stressors in their lives. Moreover, Brown, Andrews, Harris, Adler, and Bridge (1986) noted that depressed and nondepressed women did not differ in their ratings of the helpfulness of crisis support. Depressed persons' negative cognitive biases affect their interpretations and causal attributions about their experiences more than the accuracy of their observations (Beck, 1987).

TREATMENT SELECTION AND ALLOCATION

We have seen that depressed men and women experience more negative events and chronic difficulties and report fewer social resources at intake to treatment than do matched nondepressed case controls. Next, we examined the extent to which the severity of patients' dysfunction and characteristics of their life contexts influenced treatment selection and assignment. Do patients who are more severely or chronically depressed obtain more intensive treatment? More important, do clinicians provide less treatment for patients who have recently experienced stressful events or for patients who have more social resources? These questions focus on the relationships between Panels I and II and Panel III in the model shown in Fig. 7.1.

To address these issues, we analyzed the association between patients' demographic characteristics, initial symptoms, and preintake life stressors and social resources, and the amount (number of treatment sessions) and type (individual therapy, group therapy, marital/family therapy, antidepressant medication) of treatment they received (Billings & Moos, 1984).

Patients' Functioning and Symptom Characteristics

As expected, we found some matching at the program level between the severity of patients' symptoms and treatment intensity. Inpatient programs treated more chronic patients who reported more severe depression and less self-esteem. Outpatients were less depressed, had fewer endogenous symptoms, received briefer treatment, and were less likely to receive medication.

After controlling for between-program differences, however, we found that more severely or chronically depressed patients obtained only slightly more treatment; this relationship occurred primarily among inpatients and was quite small. More severely depressed outpatients were more likely to receive psychoactive medication, but this relationship did not hold for inpatients. Similarly,

Keller and his colleagues (1982, 1986) found that the duration, severity, and endogeneity of depressive symptoms were only minimally related to the type and amount of treatment patients received. Overall, treatment programs seem to develop distinctive treatment orientations that are applied with little regard to variations in the symptoms of the patients they serve.

Patients' Life Stressors and Social Resources

A depressed patient's life context at intake may influence clinicians' beliefs about the appropriate type and length of treatment. We thought that clinicians might provide more intensive treatment for patients who did not have supportive relationships with family or friends. Such patients may take longer to develop a therapeutic alliance and may need more help before they improve. However, we found no associations between patients' social resources and the type or length of treatment they obtained.

Psychiatric disorders that arise in response to acute stressors are thought to have a better prognosis and to need less intensive treatment than those that do not. In fact, this idea provides the underlying rationale for Axis IV of DSM-III, which reflects clinicians' judgments of the presence and severity of psychosocial stressors. Clinicians' attributions about the locus of the patients' problems may influence the amount of treatment they provide (Fehrenbach & O'Leary, 1982). Clinicians may make situational attributions about the cause of depression for patients who report stressful environments and dispositional attributions about patients who are in seemingly benign circumstances.

Consistent with this rationale, we found that patients' life stressors at intake were related to the amount of treatment they received. Patients who reported more recent stressful events tended to obtain less treatment, as did patients who reported more family conflict and those whose spouses reported more physical illness. These findings were stronger among outpatients than among inpatients. As noted later, persons who experience depression in the context of an acute stressful event may recover somewhat more quickly than those whose depression occurs in the relative absence of acute stressors. In contrast, however, chronic stressors tend to predict poorer treatment outcome. Thus, clinicians need to discriminate between new life events and ongoing stressful circumstances when they make decisions about the type and amount of treatment to offer to depressed patients.

PRETREATMENT LIFE CONTEXTS, TREATMENT, AND TREATMENT OUTCOME

An extensive body of research has examined associations between the amount and type of treatment and treatment outcome among depressed patients (Howard et al., 1986; Steinbrueck et al., 1983). Cognitive, interpersonal, and behaviorally oriented individual psychotherapy, marital and family treatment, and antidepressant medication have been associated with positive outcomes in controlled treatment trials (Beckham & Leber, 1985).

In our model, we posit that patients' life stressors and social resources at intake (Panel I) also contribute to treatment outcome, in part by their influence on the amount of treatment required. Patients who experience less family conflict and have a close relationship with a confidant may need less intensive treatment, whereas patients who confront more psychosocial stressors and have fewer social resources may need more treatment. The joint examination of treatment and social context predictors of outcome may help clinicians identify high-risk patients and match patients more effectively with the appropriate amount and type of treatment.

Stressful Life Circumstances and Treatment Outcome

Stressful life circumstances contribute to the onset and course of depression; they may also play a role in remission and relapse after treatment. In fact, unipolar depression is often conceptualized as a direct reaction to environmental change. Many clinicians believe that reactive depressions have an especially good outcome and that the presence of precipitating stressors is a good prognostic sign.

Precipitating Life Stressors. A number of studies have focused on differences between reactive or situational depression and endogenous or nonsituational depression. Reactive depression is usually defined by a clinician's judgment of the presence of a precipitating event. However, endogenous depression is sometimes defined by a specific pattern of symptoms (such as psychomotor retardation or agitation, early morning wakening, diurnal variation with morning worsening) and sometimes by a presumed absence of precipitating stressors. This inconsistency has created some conceptual confusion. Moreover, there is little if any relationship between symptom patterns and the presence of precipitating stressors (Paykel, 1985).

Copeland (1984) used information on severe events and major difficulties preceding onset to divide depressed inpatients into those with reactive and endogenous illnesses. The two groups of patients did not show a distinctively different clinical picture. Moreover, there were no important group differences in treatment outcome at a 5-year follow-up. Situational or reactive patients may not even experience more psychosocial stressors than "nonsituational" patients do. Hirschfeld (1981) asked clinicians to make a diagnosis of situational depression only when they thought that the episode occurred in response to an external event or situation. However, additional data showed that "nonsituational" depressed patients experienced as many life stressors in the 6 months prior to onset as did "situational" patients.

A few researchers have taken a different approach; they have looked for an association between stressful events prior to intake and treatment outcome. Murphy (1983) found that antecedent negative events did not predict treatment outcome in a group of elderly depressed inpatients. In a study of depressed women in outpatient treatment, however, Monroe and his colleagues (1983) found that negative events in the year prior to treatment did predict better treatment outcome. The treatment protocol involved individual psychotherapy or social skills training. Patients who experience more stressful life circumstances may be able to use active psychosocial treatments to develop improved methods for coping and increased mastery of stressors, which lead to symptomatic relief.

Finally, some researchers have focused on the association between precipitating events and depressed patients' response to pharmacotherapy. Lloyd, Zisook, Click, and Jaffe (1981) found that preintake life events did not predict depressed patients' response to antidepressant medication. Zimmerman, Pfohl, Coryell, and Stangl (1987) found that more psychosocial stressors (higher Axis IV scores) were associated with *more* depressive symptoms on hospital discharge; they did not predict follow-up outcome. In general, there is only modest empirical support for the idea that precipitating stressors are associated with a more rapid recovery from depression.

New Life Events Versus Ongoing Difficulties. One reason for the variation in findings may be that researchers have not discriminated between life events and ongoing stressful circumstances. An onset of depression in response to an acute event may have a good prognosis, but this may not be true of a depressive episode that occurs in the context of chronic difficulties. In fact, chronic stressors at intake, such as physical health problems (Murphy, 1983) and high family conflict (Leff & Vaughn, 1985), are related to poorer treatment outcome and a higher likelihood of relapse among depressed patients. In contrast, depressed women who initially had no marital disputes (and those who were able to resolve such disputes during psychotherapy) showed more improvement at the end of treatment (Rounsaville, Weissman, Prusoff, & Herzeg-Barron, 1979).

The Interplay of Treatment and Stressful Life Circumstances. In our study, we examined the influence of stressful life circumstances and treatment on treatment outcome. More specifically, we used hierarchical multiple regression analyses to estimate the effect of preintake life context factors (Panel I) and the amount and type of treatment (Panel III) on treatment outcome (Panel V) after controlling for patients' demographic characteristics and functioning at intake (Panel II). The analyses were conducted on 118 inpatients and 265 outpatients who were studied at intake and at the follow-up 1 year later (for detailed findings on the outpatients, see Moos, 1990).

On average, both inpatients and outpatients improved after treatment. Both groups reported less depression; outpatients also reported fewer physical symptoms and more self-esteem. More intensive treatment was associated with better outcome among inpatients but not among outpatients. The associations between treatment and outcome may have been stronger among inpatients because they were treated quite intensively. On average, inpatients spent almost 7 weeks in hospital and participated in 40 treatment sessions. Longer inpatient treatment may have more impact because some life context influences are suspended when the patient is hospitalized; for example, stressful contacts with a critical spouse or family member may be curtailed or eliminated.

Preintake negative events were moderately associated with better outcome among inpatients; this finding provides some support for the idea that precipitating life events may be a good prognostic sign. However, the associations were not very strong and they did not show up among outpatients. Patients who experience negative events prior to intake are more likely to experience new negative events during the treatment/posttreatment interval. Preintake negative events may not be strongly related to better outcome because they foreshadow later negative events, which are related to poorer outcome. Moreover, negative events often reflect or produce chronic stressors, which also are related to poorer outcome. Thus, it is important to distinguish between new negative events and ongoing stressful circumstances.

In this respect, preintake medical conditions were associated with poorer outcome; they were also an independent risk factor for nonremission at both 1-year and 4-year follow-ups (Billings & Moos, 1985a; Krantz & Moos, 1988; Swindle, Cronkite & Moos, 1989). These findings are consistent with earlier research showing that both existing and new physical health problems are related to more depression and poorer treatment outcome. As noted by Murphy (1983), physical illness probably influences the course of depression through its meaning for the individual (as a potential sign of continuing physical impairment) rather than through a direct organic effect.

Antecedent family conflict was related to poorer treatment outcome among outpatients. In addition, we identified an interaction between treatment and family conflict (Moos, 1990). Among outpatients who had little family conflict at intake, brief treatment episodes were associated with less depression and more self-esteem. Among outpatients who experienced more family conflict at intake, however, more treatment was associated with better outcome in these two areas. More intensive treatment may reduce the risk associated with high family conflict for some depressed patients (Leff & Vaughn, 1985).

Social Resources and Treatment Outcome

Very little is known about the predictive role of social resources at intake to treatment. Monroe and his colleagues (1983) showed that positive events in the year prior to treatment predicted better outcome, whereas positive events in the treatment/posttreatment period did not. Steinmetz, Lewinsohn, and Antonuccio (1983) found that depressed clients who experienced their families as more supportive at treatment intake tended to improve more than clients who did not. Marziali (1987) noted that better pretreatment support was related to better treatment outcome among depressed psychiatric outpatients (see also Murphy, 1983).

In our own study, we found that a confidant and high family support at intake modestly predicted better outcome among outpatients. Family support may help to maintain remission after treatment as well as to protect an individual from the onset of a depressive episode. Contrary to Monroe et al. (1983), antecedent positive events did not predict outcome. Such events may not be related to outcome when they are followed by related negative events (such as a separation after an initial reconciliation) during treatment. In addition, some patients who experience positive events may be "let down" during life crises subsequent to intake (Brown, Andrews, et al., 1986).

Aside from these main effects, we identified some interactions between treatment and social resources among outpatients (Moos, 1990). Outpatients who had a good relationship with a confidant showed less depression (Fig. 7.2) and more self-esteem with brief treatment. Among outpatients with poorer relationships, however, brief treatment episodes were associated with more depression and less self-esteem. As the number of treatment sessions increased, treatment outcome improved.

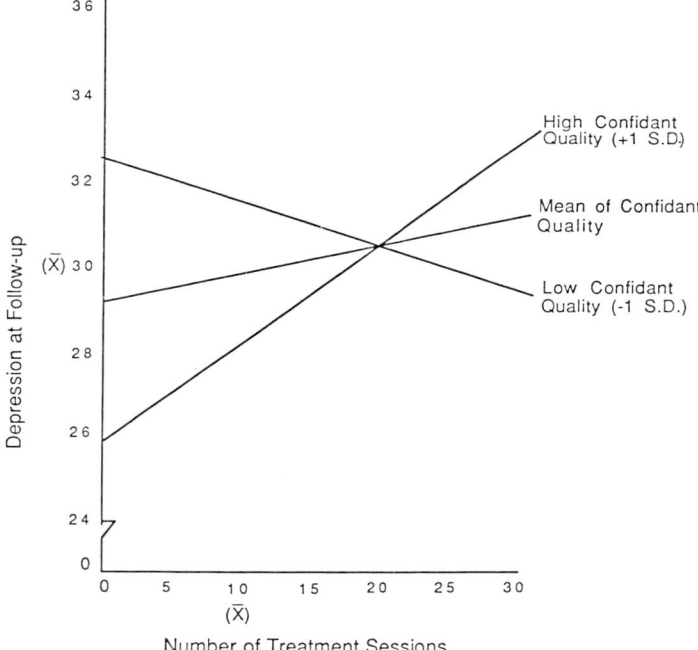

FIG. 7.2. Interaction of number of treatment sessions and quality of confident at intake on depression at follow-up (outpatients).

Treatment as a Social Resource

In many outpatient clinics, a large number of depressed patients receive brief treatment episodes of 6 sessions or fewer. Such brief treatment may be sufficient for outpatients who have a confidant and do not experience a high level of family conflict; longer treatment may pose a risk for such patients because it may upset an existing interpersonal balance. In contrast, more intensive treatment may be needed for outpatients who experience more family conflict and who do not have a confidant, in part because it takes them longer to form a therapeutic alliance (Koss, Butcher, & Strupp, 1986). Overall, these findings imply that treatment can provide patients with temporary support to compensate for a lack of current social resources.

Prolonged individual-centered treatment may not be especially beneficial for patients who experience depression in the context of severe chronic stressors and lack of ongoing interpersonal support. In such cases, treatment efforts need to focus on attempts to improve the patient's life situation. Similarly, Azrin, Sisson, Meyers, and Godley (1982) emphasized the importance of community treatment for alcohol abusers with few social resources and Ford, Bashford, and De Witt (1984) found that a minimal intervention was sufficient to improve communication skills among moderately cohesive couples, but that a more intensive intervention was needed for couples who initially reported low levels of cohesion.

As noted earlier, clinicians may provide somewhat less intensive treatment for patients who have experienced recent negative life events. However, the interaction between the length of treatment and pretreatment negative events did not predict treatment outcome. Thus, we found no support for the practice of providing shorter treatment for patients who experience recent stressful events prior to intake. In contrast, clinicians should provide more treatment for patients who experience chronic difficulties (especially physical ill health and family conflict) and who lack such social resources as support from a confidant (Krantz & Moos, 1988).

POSTTREATMENT LIFE CONTEXTS AND TREATMENT OUTCOME

Most studies of the psychosocial aspects of depression have focused on the onset and treatment phases of depressive episodes. There is considerable information about the deficits and risk factors associated with the onset of depression, but relatively little is known about the processes and correlates of remission or of failure to recover after treatment. We have described some associations between life stressors and social resources at intake and treatment outcome. It is important to recognize, however, that environmental factors such as family conflict and confidant support can change over time. Therefore, life context factors that characterize the treatment/posttreatment interval may be better predictors of long-term treatment outcome than those that characterize the interval prior to treatment.

Stressful Life Circumstances

Negative events that occur during the treatment/posttreatment interval tend to be related to poorer treatment outcome. Murphy (1983) noted that negative events in the year between intake and follow-up were associated with poorer outcome among elderly depressed patients (but see Monroe et al., 1983). This finding was especially striking when personal illness events were included. Severe events and long-term difficulties have also been related to the recurrence of depression after inpatient treatment (Surtees & Ingham, 1980). Similarly, Lloyd and her colleagues (1981) found that patients who experienced negative events subsequent to the initiation of antidepressant medication showed a poorer treatment response.

In our own study, we found that patients who experienced more negative events and chronic difficulties in the treatment/posttreatment interval improved less than expected at 1 year and 4-years after controlling for the severity of their dysfunction at intake. For example, negative events in the 12 months prior to follow-up, medical conditions, and family conflict were related to more depression and physical symptoms (Billings & Moos, 1985a; Swindle, Cronkite, & Moos, 1989).

The associations between ongoing stressors and treatment outcome were as strong and consistent as those for negative events. Overall, the evidence that posttreatment stressors affect the outcome of treatment is strengthened by considering chronic stressful circumstances as well as new life events. Brown, Bifulco, Harris, and Bridge (1986) noted that the majority of women whose chronic depressive symptoms improved reported a reduction in a severe difficulty shortly prior to remission.

Social Resources

Social resources available during the treatment/posttreatment interval are related to the outcome of treatment for depression. Surtees (1980) found that inpatients who had more close (presence of a confidant, contact with close relatives) and diffuse (contacts at work, with neighbors, at clubs or church) social resources were less severely depressed at follow-up. Compared to those who had adequate support, patients who had little or no support were more than twice as likely to be nonremitted. In addition, patients who had more residual adversity (life events and long-term difficulties) were more likely to be remitted if they had adequate social support.

We found that patients who had more supportive posttreatment social resources showed better treatment outcome than expected after controlling for demographic factors and the initial severity of dysfunction. Family support and the quality of a relationship with a confidant were associated with less depression and physical symptoms and more self-esteem at the 1-year follow-up. The quality of a confidant relationship were associated with these three criteria at the 4-year follow-up. Indices of the quality of support were somewhat more strongly related to outcome than were indices of the number of network members or social interactions (Billings & Moos, 1985a; Swindle, Cronkite, & Moos, 1989).

Positive events between the end of treatment and the 1-year follow-up were also associated with better outcome (Billings & Moos, 1985a). Most of these events were indicative of entrances to the social field (marriage, marital reconciliation, birth of a child) and some reflected newly available social resources (job promotion, increase in income). As noted by Monroe and his coworkers (1983), such newly acquired resources may reflect the beneficial influence of personal or social processes (such as the ability to form relationships and the presence of a support network) that help to provide a context in which remission can be maintained (see also Tennant, Bebbington, & Hurry, 1981).

The Robustness of Life Context Factors

The studies reviewed here point to a probable causal role for negative events, ongoing difficulties, and lack of social resources in the development and course of unipolar depression. In fact, our hierarchical regression analyses showed that postintake life stressors and social resources still predicted treatment outcome after the severity of depression at intake and the preintake levels of these life context factors were considered. Changes in life stressors and social resources during the treatment/posttreatment interval seem to have an independent influence on remission and relapse. More generally, personal and contextual factors can amplify each other. Chronic depression tends to impair an individual's functioning as spouse and parent, which can promote family conflict and erode family cohesion and thereby contribute to continued depression.

Life context factors play a relatively robust role in this mutual influence process. Among the outpatients we studied, for example, social background, the severity of depression at intake, and treatment together accounted for 25% of the variance in depression at follow-up. Life stressors and social resources at intake added 4% and postintake stressors and resources added another 17%. For the criterion of remission, 14% of the variance in outcome among outpatients was accounted for by demographic factors, the severity of depression at intake, and treatment; preintake and posttreatment stressors and social resources added 5% and 10%, respectively (Moos, 1990).

Overall, life context factors shape the course of depression almost as much as do demographic factors and symptom severity at intake to treatment. These findings support the value of a multiaxial diagnostic system such as DSM-III that considers psychosocial stressors. They also highlight the need to focus on psychosocial resources as well as stressors and to develop more systematic and conceptually integrated measures of these life context factors. More important, the finding that the conditions of life play an essential role in the process of remission from relatively severe depressive disorders is a hopeful sign. It implies that depression need not become a chronic disorder and that patients who are in relatively benign circumstances are likely to experience a remission.

REMITTED PATIENTS' FUNCTIONING AND LIFE CONTEXTS

How much do life stressors and social resources change among remitted patients after treatment? Do stressors that are elevated at intake decrease after treatment? Do remitted depressed patients enjoy more numerous and supportive social resources after treatment? More generally, do remitted patients establish life contexts that are comparable to those of nondepressed community controls?

Information about the adaptation and life contexts of matched nondepressed controls provides a realistic baseline or social comparison that helps to judge the extent to which remitted patients are functioning adequately. It also helps to estimate the personal and social deficits experienced by patients who remain depressed. Although a number of studies have contrasted depressed patients at intake to treatment with case controls (Paykel, 1985), few if any have compared these groups after treatment. Paykel (1974) found that the rate of new negative life events among remitted depressed patients decreased on follow-up, but it did not drop to the level of a normal control population.

We examined these issues by comparing remitted patients, partially remitted patients, and nonremitted patients with each other and with the matched nondepressed controls (for the remission criteria, see Billings & Moos, 1985b). As expected, patients whose depressive symptoms remitted tended to report improvement in other aspects of functioning, such as self-esteem and social activity. Remitted patients were no more depressed than the community group, but they did report more physical symptoms. In contrast, nonremitted and partially remitted patients reported poorer functioning than remitted patients and than nondepressed case controls.

Compared to the level they experienced at intake, the remitted patients reported fewer stressors during the treatment/posttreatment interval. Remitted patients experienced more new negative events during the follow-up interval than the normal comparison group did, but the difference was relatively small. They also reported more illness among their children. Thus, remitted patients reported a decline in psychosocial stressors from intake to follow-up, but they did not quite reach "normal" levels.

In contrast, the remitted patients' social resources improved markedly in all areas at follow-up; the largest increases were in family support and the quality of a relationship with a confidant. Remitted patients did not differ from case controls in the number of network contacts, quality of a confidant, or work support; however, they still had somewhat fewer close friends and less family support. Overall, the remitted patients moved toward but did not fully reach the level of social resources enjoyed by the community group.

As expected, nonremitted and partially remitted patients reported substantially more stressors and fewer social resources than the remitted patients and the normal group. Nonremitted patients experienced more than twice as many new negative events and much more illness among their spouses. The level of stressors experienced by the partially remitted and nonremitted patients did not decline from intake to follow-up, and the level of social resources showed only a modest increase (Billings & Moos, 1985b).

These findings show that the psychosocial stressors that contribute to the onset of depression do not necessarily decline after treatment. The high rate of nonremission and relapse among patients treated for unipolar depression may be due to new stressful events and ongoing difficulties that place this group at risk for recurrent depression. Although remitted patients attain near-normal levels of social resources, they still experience somewhat more stressful life circumstances than their nondepressed "neighbors."

THE SPOUSES OF DEPRESSED PATIENTS

The spouses of depressed patients tend to experience their own problems. They are often psychiatrically impaired (Merikangas, 1984), and they report more depression and physical symptoms, more illness, and less family support than comparable spouses of nondepressed persons. The functioning and life circumstances of spouses are important, both because they may be influenced by the depressed partner's symptoms and associated role impairments and because they can affect the depressed partner's recovery. The spouse plays a central role in determining the partner's quality of social resources. In turn, the depressed partner's remission and improved functioning can reduce the strain on the spouse. Coyne and his colleagues (1987) found that partners of former patients who were not currently in a depressive episode reported less distress than partners of depressed persons in treatment.

Life Stressors, Social Resources, and Spouse Functioning

We examined the functioning and life contexts of the spouses of our depressed patients at the patient's treatment intake and again after 1 year. We defined three groups of spouses according to their depressed partner's status at follow-up:

remitted, partially remitted, or nonremitted. We compared these spouse groups with each other and with the spouses of the community controls.

Spouses who experienced more negative events, more long-term difficulties, and a lack of family support prior to their depressed partner's intake to treatment reported more depressed mood. Spouses' levels of adaptation were not related to changes in the depressive symptoms of their partner. However, when the partner's depression improved, there was some improvement in the spouses's life context: more family cohesion and social activities, a less negative home environment, and fewer work stressors (Krantz & Moos, 1987). In turn, changes in these life context factors are associated with improvements in the spouses' adaptation.

At the time that patients whose depression later remitted sought treatment, their spouses reported more family conflict and less family cohesion than the control spouses did. The initial life contexts of the spouses of nonremitted partners were much worse than those of control spouses and somewhat worse than those of spouses whose partners remitted. The status of the groups of spouses remained largely the same at follow-up: Compared to control spouses, spouses of remitted patients continued to report more conflict and less cohesion. The spouses of remitted patients were already functioning quite well and they showed no improvement during the year, even though their partners were no longer seriously depressed. However, the spouses of nonremitted patients had somewhat more difficulties at follow-up than when the patient began treatment. Family conflict increased and family cohesion and the quality of their relationship with their partner declined. In addition, the spouses showed somewhat less self-esteem.

The Influence of a Partner's Impairment on the Spouse

As a next step, we need to develop a general model of spouse adaptation that considers role impairments and aspects of the partner's functioning other than depression, as well as other characteristics of the spouse's life context. Spouses of remitted patients face continuing problems. They may be affected by the absence of a dramatic change in their partner, disappointed if the remission does not meet their expectations, and concerned about relapse if the partner has psychological problems other than depression. Moreover, well-established maladaptive interchanges between spouses seem likely to continue, even after the depressive symptoms of one partner diminish.

In a study of alcoholic patients, we found that the spouses of remitted patients functioned as well as matched normal-drinking controls in almost all areas (Moos, Finney, & Cronkite, 1990). Unlike our findings on remitted depressed patients' spouses, the social and family contexts of the spouses of remitted alcoholic patients were comparable to those of spouses of matched case controls. A remitted alcoholic person may have fewer residual problems than a remitted depressed person. We also found that children of remitted alcoholic parents were functioning as well as normal controls (Moos et al., 1990), whereas children of remitted depressed parents showed deficits in functioning relative to case controls (Billings & Moos, 1986). A person's depression may have a long-term residual impact on child and family functioning (for a review, see Beardslee et al., 1983).

We formulated a conceptual framework to focus on the predictors of health and well-being among spouses of alcoholic partners (Finney, Moos, Cronkite, & Gamble, 1983). The impairment of the alcoholic partner in both drinking and nondrinking areas, other life stressors (such as negative events and children's health problems), and family social resources were each predictably related to spouse functioning. Such efforts may stimulate comparable research on spouses of other groups of impaired partners, and ultimately help to develop a general theory in this area.

FUTURE DIRECTIONS

I have described a psychosocial perspective that focuses on the onset and course of depression. The perspective integrates stress and coping theory with an expanded paradigm for program evaluation. It points to some of the risk and resistance factors involved in the process of remission and relapse; moreover, it applies to spouses and children of depressed patients as well as to patients themselves. The findings that emerge from research guided by this perspective imply that life stressors and social resources play an important role in the development of clinical depression, in the allocation and outcome of treatment, and in the posttreatment process of recovery for patients and their families. These findings and their potential applications suggest some important directions for future research, two of which involve applying the perspective to other psychiatric disorders and examining stress and coping among nonclinical groups.

Applications to Other Psychiatric Disorders

Life stressors and social resources play a significant role in a variety of psychiatric disorders. We have dealt with depression here, but other research has examined the influence of life context factors on remission and relapse in substance abuse and schizophrenia. For example, in 6-month, 2-year, and 10-year follow-ups of residentially treated alcoholic patients, we found that posttreatment stressors and lack of social resources were associated with higher levels of alcohol consumption and more depressed mood and physical symptoms. Relapsed alcoholics experienced more stressful life circumstances and fewer social resources than did their remitted counterparts and demographically matched normal-drinking controls (Finney, Moos, & Mewborn, 1980; Moos et al., 1990).

Schizophrenic patients who relapse experience more stressful events over the course of their disorder than do matched controls and schizophrenic patients who maintain their remission. Vaughn, Snyder, Jones, Freeman, and Falloon (1984) found that schizophrenic patients who returned to families characterized by parental conflict and excessive criticism were more likely to relapse; regular medication provided patients some protection against relapse, but only if they had limited contact with overly critical family members. However, when neuroleptic medication was combined with intensive family treatment, the incidence of relapse was markedly reduced (Falloon et al., 1982).

Even though there are some common risk factors in a variety of psychiatric disorders, there may be variation in the specific level of a factor that connotes risk. Leff and Vaughn (1985) showed that just two or more critical comments from relatives predicted relapse among depressed patients, whereas seven or more was the cutoff point for schizophrenic patients. This finding is consistent with the idea that depressed persons are especially sensitive to criticism. The identification of risk factors common to several disorders or unique to a particular form, and differences in the cutoff points to define risk, can yield important refinements in our models of psychopathology and its treatment. These ideas also apply to understanding psychosocial outcomes among children and adults with chronic medical conditions.

Stress, Coping, and the Continuum of Depression

A psychosocial stress and coping perspective can help to integrate the findings of epidemiological and community studies of depression with those of studies of treated depressed patients. The model seems to apply to the onset of severe depression in community groups and to clarifying the factors that underlie fluctuations in depressed mood among normal men and women. The salient variables and processes that influence normal variations in mood and behavior may be comparable (albeit attenuated) to those involved in the development of diagnosable psychiatric and behavioral disorders.

Brown and Harris (1986) have noted that there is considerable overlap in the severity of depression between psychiatric cases and "cases" identified in community surveys. In addition, there is remarkable consistency in the psychosocial risk factors for depressive symptoms and unipolar depressive disorders. Negative events and chronic difficulties are related to the onset of depression among women who do not have a good relationship with a confidant (Brown & Harris, 1978, 1986). More than 90% of women who had an onset of depression had experienced a severe event or a major difficulty in the prior 6 months; women who had low self-esteem and high marital conflict were especially likely to become depressed after a stresssful event (Brown, Andrews, et al., 1986).

We have examined these issues in two studies of community men and women. In one group of 267 married couples, negative events, chronic difficulties (such as the husband's alcohol consumption), and lack of family support were associated with the wife's depressed mood (Cronkite & Moos, 1984). In a separate group of over 400 adults, negative events and lack of family support were associated with both depressed mood and physical symptoms (Holahan & Moos, 1987). The presence of common processes related to normal fluctuations in depressed mood and to severe depression provides a conceptual bridge between epidemiological and clinical research on depression. It also raises an important question: Why is it that many individuals who experience depressed mood under adverse circumstances do not develop severe depression? To address this issue, we need to learn more about the dynamics of the stress and coping process and the positive consequences of adversity.

Dynamics of the Stress and Coping Process

Most prior research has focused on how stress and coping factors are related to health and well-being. However, to really understand the stress and coping process, we need to consider the associations among the mediating factors involved in this process. One question is whether life stressors and social resources change each other over time. Do stressful circumstances erode an individual's social resources? Conversely, can social resources reduce subsequent stressors? When we examined these questions in a subset of our depressed patients, we found that an increase in ongoing stressors was associated with a later decline in family support. Although high levels of family support did not lead to a decline in ongoing stressors, patients who had more close friends at intake experienced fewer stressors during the year (Mitchell & Moos, 1984).

Future research should examine the strength of the connection between life stressors and social resources in specific areas (such as family and work) and the ways in which social resources in one area (such as family support) may help an individual cope with problems in a different area (such as work stressors). In this respect, individuals occupy multiple environments that influence each other. To fully understand the potential outcome of specific life stressors and social resources, we need to consider their connections to other aspects of an individual's life context.

Another issue involves the close connection between life events and ongoing difficulties (Brown & Harris, 1986). People who are in chronically stressful contexts may be more likely to experience new negative events. Such events may lead to an increase in chronic stressors and a decline in social resources. When we examined this issue, we found that respondents who reported more ongoing stressors and fewer ongoing resources tended to experience more new stressful events. In turn, new stressful events foreshadowed increases in ongoing stressors and led to a decline in ongoing social resources (Moos, 1988). We may learn more about the influence of life events on adaptation by clarifying the processes by which events alter existing life situations.

Finally, we should consider the social context of coping. Do social resources influence an individual's reliance on particular types of coping responses? Do some coping responses change the existing level of social resources? Consistent with Thoits's (1986) conception of social support as a source of coping assistance, we found that depressed patients who had more social resources sought more information and support and engaged in more active problem solving. Increases in family support were related to increases in problem-solving coping among women and to a decline in emotional discharge among men. Increases in work support were associated with greater reliance on affective regulation among women and with more information/support seeking among men (Fondacaro & Moos, 1987).

More generally, we need to develop better concepts and measures of coping. Indices of appraisal-focused, problem-focused, and emotion-focused coping provide a useful first step, but more work is needed to construct measures of specific aspects of these three broad coping domains. There is growing evidence that certain cognitive (such as logical analysis) and behavioral (such as information seeking and problem solving) coping responses are related to good adaptation. The next step is to identify the personal and contextual determinants of reliance on these more effective types of coping responses.

Positive Consequences of Adversity

Some individuals develop depression when confronted by stressful life circumstances, but many people are remarkably resilient in the face of adversity. They may emerge from a crisis with new coping skills, more maturity and self-confidence, closer relationships with family and friends, and a richer appreciation of life. Such outcomes are remarkably common. When asked about the impact of a life crisis they have experienced, a substantial number of people, typically 50% or more, report some positive consequences (Schaefer & Moos, in press).

Positive outcomes of coping with stress are consistent with a dialectical perspective in which change is seen as necessary for human development as well as with the view that life crises may be "constructive confrontations" that challenge an individual and spur development. We need to broaden our conceptual approach to encompass the idea that stressful life circumstances can lead to greater personal maturity and effectiveness and to identify the nature and determinants of such outcomes. An understanding of the process of personal growth under adversity may help clinicians develop intervention programs to prevent and alleviate depression in vulnerable individuals.

IMPLICATIONS FOR CLINICIANS AND PROGRAM EVALUATORS

An expanded evaluation paradigm and a stress and coping perspective can sensitize clinicians and evaluation researchers to the personal and contextual factors involved in the development and remission of depression and other health problems and to the need to consider coping and social resources in planning and evaluating treatment. The framework may help to explain why conceptually different interventions seem to be equally effective in alleviating depression. Because there are direct connections between the domains shown in the framework, changes in a domain targeted by a specific treatment procedure may cause a change in one of the other domains. For example, cognitive treatment is oriented toward modifying maladaptive attributions, but it may also alter individuals' coping responses and help them develop better social resources. Similarly, an intervention designed to strengthen problem-solving skills may also help patients increase their social resources and resolve some stressful life circumstances.

An ecologically oriented psychosocial perspective points to the need for a fundamental shift in our thinking about intervention programs and their effects. An intervention program is but one of the many factors that influence health and well-being. Current life context factors also shape mood and behavior. Many of the hard-won gains of intervention programs fade away over time. This is precisely what we should expect on the basis of our knowledge about environmental impact and the diversity of influences to which people are exposed. Inherent in the belief that an intervention program can promote change is the assumption that other more recent environmental factors can modify such change. Conversely, if current life context factors can alter individuals, so can intervention programs. The use of an ecological systems framework may make it possible to identify convergent cross-setting effects and formulate more integrated and powerful intervention programs.

ACKNOWLEDGMENTS

The research reported here was supported in part by Veterans Administration Medical and Health Services Research and Development Service research funds and by NIAAA grants AA02863 and AA06699. John Finney and Ralph Swindle made helpful comments on an earlier draft of the manuscript.

REFERENCES

American Psychiatric Association. (1987). *Diagnostic and statistical manual of mental disorders* (3rd ed., rev.). Washington, DC: American Psychiatric Association.

Azrin, N. H., Sisson, R. W., Meyers, & Godley, M. (1982). Alcoholism treatment by disfulfiram and community reinforcement therapy. *Journal of Behavioral Therapy and Experimental Psychiatry, 13,* 105–112.

Beardslee, W. R., Bemporad, J., Keller, M. B., & Klerman, G. L. (1983). Children of parents with major affective disorder: A review. *American Journal of Psychiatry, 140,* 825–832.

Beck, A. T. (1987). Cognitive models of depression. *Journal of Cognitive Psychotherapy: An International Quarterly, 1,* 5–37.

Beckham, E. E., & Leber, W. R. (1985). The comparative efficacy of psychotherapy and pharmacotherapy for depression. In E. E. Beckham & W. R. Leber (Eds.), *Handbook of depression: Treatment assessment and research* (pp. 316–340). Homewood, IL: Dorsey Press.

Billings, A., Cronkite, R., & Moos, R. (1983). Social environmental factors in unipolar depression: Comparison of depressed patients and nondepressed controls. *Journal of Abnormal Psychology, 92,* 119–133.

Billings, A. G., & Moos, R. H. (1984). Treatment experiences of adults with unipolar depression: The influence of patient and life context factors. *Journal of Consulting and Clinical Psychology, 52,* 119–131.

Billings, A., & Moos, R. (1985a). Life stressors and social resources affect posttreatment outcomes among depressed patients. *Journal of Abnormal Psychology, 94,* 140–153.

Billings, A., & Moos, R. (1985b). Psychosocial processes of remission in unipolar depression: Comparing depressed patients with matched community controls. *Journal of Consulting and Clinical Psychology, 53,* 314–325.

Billings, A., & Moos, R. (1985c). Psychosocial stressors, coping, and depression. In E. Beckham & W. Leber (Eds.), *Handbook of depression: Treatment, assessment, and research* (pp. 940–974). Homewood, IL: Dorsey Press.

Billings, A., & Moos, R. (1986). Children of parents with unipolar depression: A controlled one-year follow-up. *Journal of Abnormal Child Psychology, 14,* 149–166.

Brown, G. W., Andrews, B., Harris, T., Adler, Z., & Bridge, L. (1986). Social support, self-esteem and depression. *Psychological Medicine, 16,* 813–831.

Brown, G. W., Bifulco, A., Harris, T. O., & Bridge, L. (1986). Life stress, chronic subclinical symptoms, and vulnerability to clinical depression. *Journal of Affective Disorders, 11,* 1–19.

Brown, G., & Harris, T. (1978). *Social origins of depression: A study of psychiatric disorder in women.* New York: The Free Press.

Brown, G. W., & Harris, T. (1986). Establishing causal links: The Bedford College Studies of Depression. In H. Katschnig (Ed.), *Life events and psychiatric disorders: Controversial issues* (pp. 107–200). Cambridge, England: Cambridge University Press.

Copeland, J. R. M. (1984). Reactive and endogenous depressive illness and five-year outcome. *Journal of Affective Disorders, 6,* 153–162.

Coyne, J. C., Kessler, R. C., Tal, M., Turnbull, J., Wortman, C. B., & Greden, J. F. (1987). Living with a depressed person. *Journal of Consulting and Clinical Psychology, 55,* 347–352.

Cronkite, R., & Moos, R. (1984). The role of predisposing and moderating factors in the stress-illness relationship. *Journal of Health and Social Behavior, 25,* 372–393.

Falloon, I. R. H., Boyd, J. L., McGill, C. W., Razani, J., Moss, H. B., & Gilderman, A. M. (1982). Family management in the prevention of exacerbations of schizophrenia. *New England Journal of Medicine, 306,* 1437–1440.

Fehrenbach, P. A., & O'Leary, M. R. (1982). Interpersonal attraction and treatment decisions in inpatient and outpatient psychiatric settings. In T. A. Wills (Ed.), *Basic processes in helping relationships* (pp. 13–36). New York: Academic Press

Finney, J., Moos, R., Cronkite, R., & Gamble, W. (1983). A conceptual model of the functioning of married persons with impaired partners: Spouses of alcoholic patients. *Journal of Marriage and the Family, 45,* 23–34.

Finney, J., Moos, R., & Mewborn, R. (1980). Posttreatment experiences and treatment outcome of alcoholic patients six months and two years after hospitalization. *Journal of Consulting and Clinical Psychology, 48,* 17–29.

Fondacaro, M., & Moos, R. (1987). Social support and coping: A longitudinal analysis. *American Journal of Community Psychology, 15,* 653–673.

Ford, J. D., Bashford, M. B., & De Witt, K. N. (1984). Three approaches to marital enrichment: Toward optimal matching of participants and interventions. *Journal of Sex and Marital Therapy, 10,* 41–48.

Hirschfeld, R. M. A. (1981). Situational depression: Validity of the concept. *British Journal of Psychiatry, 139,* 297–305.

Holahan, C. J., & Moos, R. (1987). Risk, resistance, and psychological distress: A longitudinal analysis with adults and children. *Journal of Abnormal Psychology, 96,* 3–13.

Hollon, S. D., DeRubeis, R. J., & Evans, M. D. (1987). Causal mediation of change in treatment for depression: Discriminating between nonspecificity and noncausality. *Psychological Bulletin, 102,* 139–149.

Howard, K. I., Kopta, S. M., Krause, M. S., & Orlinsky, D. E. (1986). The dose-effect relationship in psychotherapy. *American Psychologist, 41,* 159–164.

Keller, M. B., Klerman, G. L., Lavori, B. W., Fawcett, J. A., Coryell, W., & Endicott, J. (1982). Treatment received by depressed patients. *Journal of the American Medical Association, 248,* 1848–1855.

Keller, M. B., Lavori, P. W., Klerman, G. L., Andreasen, N. C., Endicott, J., Coryell, W., Fawcett, J., Rice, J. P., & Hirschfeld, R. M. A. (1986). Low levels and lack of predictors of somatotherapy and psychotherapy received by depressed patients. *Archives of General Psychiatry, 43,* 458–466.

Koss, M. P., Butcher, J. N., & Strupp, H. H. (1986). Brief psychotherapy methods in clinical research. *Journal of Consulting and Clinical Psychology, 54,* 60–67.

Krantz, S., & Moos, R. (1987). Functioning and life context among spouses of remitted and nonremitted depressed patients. *Journal of Consulting and Clinical Psychology, 55,* 353–360.

Krantz, S., & Moos, R. (1988). Risk factors at intake predict nonremission among depressed patients. *Journal of Consulting and Clinical Psychology, 56,* 863–869.

Lazarus, R. S., & Folkman, S. (1984). *Stress, appraisal, and coping.* New York: Springer Publishing.

Leff, J., & Vaughn, C. (1985). *Expressed emotion in families: Its significance for mental illness.* New York: Guilford.

Lloyd, C., Zisook, S., Click, M. Jr., & Jaffe, K. E. (1981). Life events and response to antidepressants. *Journal of Human Stress, 7,* 2–15.

Marziali, E. A. (1987). People in your life: Development of a social support measure for predicting psychotherapy outcome. *Journal of Nervous and Mental Disease, 175,* 327–338.

Merikangas, K. R. (1984). Divorce and assortative mating among depressed patients. *American Journal of Psychiatry, 141,* 74–76.

Mitchell, R., & Moos, R. (1984). Deficiencies in social support among depressed patients: Antecedents or consequences of stress? *Journal of Health and Social Behavior, 25,* 438–452.

Monroe, S. M., Bellack, A. S., Hersen, M., & Himmelhoch, J. M. (1983). Life events, symptom course, and treatment outcome in unipolar depressed women. *Journal of Consulting and Clinical Psychology, 51,* 604–615.

Moos, R. (1986). *Work Environment Scale manual: Second edition.* Palo Alto, CA: Consulting Psychologists Press.

Moos, R. (1990). Depressed outpatients' life contexts, amount of treatment, and treatment outcome. *Journal of Nervous and Mental Disease, 178,* 105–112.

Moos, R. (1988). Life stressors and social resources influence health and well-being. *Psychological Assessment, 4,* 133–158.

Moos, R., Cronkite, R., Billings, A., & Finney, J. (1984). *Health and Daily Living Form manual.* Palo Alto, CA: Social Ecology Laboratory, Stanford University and Veterans Administration Medical Center.

Moos, R., Finney, J., & Cronkite, R. (1990). *Alcoholism treatment: Context, process, and outcome.* New York: Oxford University Press.

Moos, R., & Moos, B. (1986). *Family Environment Scale manual: Second edition.* Palo Alto, CA: Consulting Psychologists Press.

Murphy, E. (1982). Social origins of depression in old age. *British Journal of Psychiatry, 141,* 135–142.

Murphy, E. (1983). The prognosis of depression in old age. *British Journal of Psychiatry, 142,* 111–119.

Paykel, E. S. (1974). Recent life events and clinical depression. In E. K. Gunderson & R. H. Rahe (Eds.), *Life stress and illness* (pp. 134–163). Springfield, IL: C. C. Thomas.

Paykel, E. S. (1985). Life events, social support, and clinical psychiatric disorder. In I. Sarason (Ed.), *Social support: Theory, research, and applications* (pp. 321–347). Dordrecht, The Netherlands: Martinus Nijhoff.

Rounsaville, B. J., Chevron, E. S., Prusoff, B. A., Elkin, I., Imber, S., Sotsky, S., & Watkins, J. (1987). The relation between specific and general dimensions of the psychotherapy process in interpersonal psychotherapy of depression. *Journal of Consulting and Clinical Psychology, 55,* 379–384.

Rounsaville, B., Weissman, M., Prusoff, B., & Herzeg-Barron, R. (1979). Process of psychotherapy among depressed women with marital disputes. *American Journal of Orthopsychiatry, 49,* 505–510.

Schaefer, J., & Moos, R. (in press). Life crises and personal growth. In B. N. Carpenter (Ed.), *Personal coping: Theory, research, and applications.* New York: Praeger.

Simons, A. D., Garfield, S. L., & Murphy, G. E. (1984). The process of change in cognitive therapy and pharmacotherapy for depression: Changes in mood and cognition. *Archives of General Psychiatry, 41,* 45–51.

Steinbrueck, S. M., Maxwell, S. E., & Howard, G. S. (1983). A meta-analysis of psychotherapy and drug therapy in the treatment of unipolar depression with adults. *Journal of Consulting and Clinical Psychology, 51,* 856–863.

Steinmetz, J. L., Lewinsohn, P. M., & Antonuccio, D. O. (1983). Prediction of individual outcome in a group intervention for depression. *Journal of Consulting and Clinical Psychology, 51,* 331–337.

Surtees, P. G. (1980). Social support, residual adversity, and depressive outcome. *Social Psychiatry, 15,* 71–80.

Surtees, P. G., & Ingham, J. G. (1980). Life stress and depressive outcome: Application of a dissipation model to life events. *Social Psychiatry, 15,* 21–31.

Swindle, R., Cronkite, R., & Moos, R. (1989). Life stressors, social resources, coping, and the 4-year course of unipolar depression. *Journal of Abnormal Psychology, 98,* 468–477.

Tennant, C., Bebbington, P., & Hurry, J. (1981). The short-term outcome of neurotic disorders in the community: The relation of remission to clinical factors and to "neutralizing" life events. *British Journal of Psychiatry, 139,* 213–220.

Thoits, P. A. (1986). Social support as coping assistance. *Journal of Consulting and Clinical Psychology, 54,* 416–423.

Vaughn, C. E., Snyder, K. S., Jones, S., Freeman, W., & Falloon, I. (1984). Family factors in schizophrenic relapse: Replication in California of British research on expressed emotion. *Archives of General Psychiatry, 41,* 1169–1177.

Zimmerman, M., Pfohl, B., & Stangl, D. (1986). Life events assessment of depressed patients: A comparison of self-report and interview formats. *Journal of Human Stress, 12,* 13–19.

Zimmerman, M., Pfohl, B., Coryell, W., & Stangl, D. (1987). The prognostic validity of DSM-III Axis IV in depressed inpatients. *American Journal of Psychiatry, 144,* 102–106.

8
An Integrative Perspective on Recurrent Mood Disorders: The Mediating Role of Personality

Hagop S. Akiskal, M.D.
University of Tennessee, Memphis

Research generated during the past 2 decades (Becker, 1974; Whybrow, Akiskal, & McKinney, 1984; Willner, 1985) has been generally consistent with a multifactorial conceptualization of depression deriving from primate (Akiskal & McKinney, 1973) and human data (Akiskal & McKinney, 1975). The emerging data further suggest that the predisposition to mood disorders is to be sought in childhood, and that life events and somatic stressors in adulthood serve as triggering factors that determine the timing of episodes (Akiskal, 1986). This position is strengthened by the increasing realization that mood disorders are recurrent in nature (Zis & Goodwin, 1979), and if one were to consider temperamental antecedants (Akiskal, Downs, Jordan, Watson, Daugherty, & Pruitt, 1985) and briefer untreated episodes (Angst, Merikangas, & Scheidegger, in press), they often begin much earlier in life than previously thought (Akiskal & Weller, 1989).

The present focus on the more recurrent forms of mood disorders is justified by the fact that much of the research conducted on these disorders is based on recurrent samples. Moreover, personality maladjustment is prevalent in such patients (Cassano, Maggini, & Akiskal, 1983) who, as is well-known, pose the greatest challenge to the clinician. Although much of the reported maladjustment represents postaffective personality complications (Akiskal, Hirschfeld, & Yerevanian, 1983b), in this chapter I develop the thesis that certain personality traits might play a mediating role between remote predisposing and proximate precipitating factors. As my main objective is to illustrate the heuristic value of such a conceptualization for both clinical and theoretical endeavors, I selectively focus on those studies of personality in affective illness that can serve to integrate the increasingly complex data deriving from diverse perspectives.

CONCEPTUAL AND METHODOLOGIC CONSIDERATIONS

Personality attributes observed in the affectively ill can be conceptualized as (1) predisposing factors, (2) as interpersonal complications which result from clinical episodes, or (3) as merely coexisting conditions which pathoplastically modify the clinical presentation or outcome of the illness. As discussed elsewhere (Akiskal, 1984), these three positions are not entirely incompatible; although much of the research evidence has been in favor of the second and third positions, a long tradition in both psychiatry and clinical psychology is predicated on the belief that affective episode arise from predisposing personality attributes. This belief, for instance, is embodied in Kretschmer's statement (1936) that "the endogenous psychoses are nothing but accentuation of normal types of temperament." While Kretschmer, as a follower of Kraepelinian tenets (1921), emphasized gentically determined (temperamental) contributions, much of the psychoanalytic and the more recent behavioral-cognitive literature has focused on learned (characterologic) attributes believed to be a legacy from life's vicissitudes. Despite differences in the relative importance accorded to specific experiences or constitutionally based vulnerability to such experiences, it is nonetheless impressive that all three of the major theoretical approaches to psychopathology tend to derive clinical depression and other major mood disorders from preexisting personality traits.

Ideally, the study of personality in a given patient should begin prior to the first onset of affective episodes. Assessing personality during an episode of illness is unsatisfactory because affective states may bias or exaggerate the patient's personality profile (Hirschfeld, Klerman, Clayton, Keller, McDonald-Scott, & Larkin, 1983). Even when the affectively ill are examined during euthymic periods, illness episodes—or the treatments provided for them—could have significantly altered personality structure. For these reasons, very few studies have succeeded in prospectively assessing the contribution of personality to mood disorders. Despite such thorny methodologic barriers, many interesting findings on the relevance of enduring personality characteristics to mood disorders have been reported (Akiskal et al., 1983b).

For the sake of clarity, I find it useful to define the various components that enter into the concept of personality and personality disorder (Akiskal, 1989; Rutter, 1987). Thus, affective temperaments (constitutionally determined subaffective expressions of mood disorders) are distinguished from characterologic disturbances (acquired attributes which are believed to develop early in life and are activated or accentuated by key life experiences). Affective illness, especially that with high rates of recurrence, often leads to much interpersonal disturbances, which in many cases eventually become incorporated into the habitual self of the patient (Akiskal, 1988); clinicians typically evaluate patients at this stage and what is diagnosed "personality disorder" more often than not represents a postmorbid phenomenon. In this chapter the term *personality* is used in the broadest possible sense to refer to long-term traits, whether they be temperamental, characterologic, or postmorbid. These distinctions are important—as I hope to demonstrate—because they refer to different phases in the pathogenetic chain of recurrent affective episodes.

The specific position I develop in this chapter builds on earlier explorations (Akiskal, 1986, 1987, 1988) suggesting that an interaction between heredofamilial and developmental factors translates into subaffective—i.e., temperamental—instability, with the implication that the disorder is probably always active at a subepisodic level. I further submit that it is such instability which creates the very circumstances—both psychologic and somatic—involved in the precipitation of major episodes. In the model to be expounded here, temperamental attributes play an intermediary role in the hypothesized pathogenetic chain of mood disorder. By contrast, characterologic disturbances are considered *orthogonal* factors, i.e., coexisting or postaffective factors which are largely noncausal, but which could nevertheless modify the clinical picture of depression or its prognosis.

HEREDOFAMILIAL FACTORS AND AFFECTIVE TEMPERAMENTS

Individuals who have a first-degree biological relative with a mood disorder are at increased risk of developing clinical depression. This risk is highest in the relatives of "schizoaffective" bipolars, followed by those of bipolar I and bipolar II (Gershon et al., 1982). It has been estimated that heredity may contribute as much as 50% of the variance in the pathogenesis of recurrent mood disorders (Gershon, Dunner, & Goodwin, 1971). Although the risk for depression is relatively modest in the relatives of unipolar depressives, many unipolars—especially those with high episode frequency—come from families with bipolar illness. This is best interpreted to mean that some apparently "unipolar" depressions are in fact less penetrant forms of bipolar illness (Akiskal, Walker, Puzantian, King & Drannon, 1983a). These depressions typically have early onset, are hypersomnic-retarded in symptom pattern, may exhibit brief switches to hypomania when treated with heterocyclic antidepressants, monoamine oxidase inhibitors, electroconvulsive therapy, or sleep deprivation, and may show preferential responses to lithium carbonate (Akiskal & Akiskal, 1988).

The importance of heredofamilial factors in the origin of depression is most dramatically illustrated by comparing the risk in the general population (which approximates the risk for the offspring of unaffected parents) with that of individuals who have one affected parent (*single matings*) or both parents affected (*dual matings*). The risk is tripled from the population baseline for single matings and increased at least tenfold for dual matings (Gershon et al., 1982). Increased familial risk of course is not synonymous with increased genetic risk. Definite evidence for genetic contributions has come principally from adoption studies and monozygotic-dizygotic differences in concordance rates in recurrent or cyclical mood disorders. Thus, adoption studies (e.g., Mendelwicz & Rainer, 1977; Cadoret, 1978; Wender, Kety, Rosenthal, Schulsinger, Ortmann, & Lunde, 1986) have demonstrated increased risk for mood disorders in subjects born to parents with such disorders but raised by normal adoptive parents. However, genetic contributions appear negligible in pure depressive disorders with a less recurrent course, where the risk for depression seems to depend on being raised by a parent—whether biologic or adoptive—who has been treated for depression (Von Knorring, Cloninger, Bohman, & Sigvardson, 1983; Cadoret, O'Gorman, Heywood & Troughton, 1985).

The wide difference in monozygotic-dizygotic concordance also indicates a strong genetic component in cyclic mood disorders (Bertelsen, Harvald, & Hauge, 1977); concordance is the same for monozygotic pairs regardless of whether they are reared together or apart from birth (Price, 1968). As with the adoption studies, genetic contributions appear less impressive in low episode frequency depressions. Furthermore, the fact that concordance is less than 100% even in the most genetic (bipolar) forms of mood disorders suggests that nongenetic familial and other environmental factors are of importance in the predisposition to affective episodes. It is also of great theoretical interest that where monozygotic pairs are discordant for affective breakdowns, the unaffected twin often exhibit subsyndromal mood instability (Bertelsen et al., 1977). This suggests the hypothesis that affective illness is not inherited as such, but may be transmitted in the form of temperamental disturbances (Akiskal, 1989).

This hypothesis is further suggested in a recent study (Akiskal et al., 1985a) that found such temperamental disturbances in nearly 50% of the juvenile—especially prepubertal—offspring of adult bipolars; these disturbances preceded the occurrence of major episodes. Prospective observations in prepubertal children (Kovacs & Gastsonis, 1989) have also found evidence for dysthymic tendencies later complicated by major depressive and hypomanic episodes; furthermore, infants of bipolar, compared with those of control, parents have been found to display extreme emotionality with minimal external provocation (Pellegrini et al., 1986). These high risk studies support Kraepelin's (1921) position which conceptualized the affective temperaments as the foundation from which major episodes arose. In these temperaments, the genetic potential for affective episodes is considered to be subclinically active—and to be easily triggered into clinical illness by environmental challenge. Table 8.1 summarizes the two basic affective types, the depressive (dysthymic) and the hyperthymic; the cyclothymic type oscillates between these two extremes of behavior.

Other lines of evidence which link these temperaments to major mood disorders have come from clinical and epidemiologic studies of young adults with these temperaments. For example, family rates of classic bipolar disorder are

TABLE 8.1
University of Tennessee Operationalization of Depressive and Hyperthymic Temperaments Based on Schneider's Typology

A. The Depressive Type

1. Gloomy, pessimistic, humorless or incapable of fun
2. Passive and nonassertive
3. Introverted
4. Living a life out of action
5. Skeptical, hypercritical, or complaining
6. Self-critical, self-reproaching, and self-derogatory
7. Preoccupied with inadequacy, failure, and negative events, sometimes to the point of morbid enjoyment of one's failures
8. Habitual long sleeper (> 9 hours)

B The Hyperthymic Type

1. Cheerful, overoptimistic or exuberant - though irritability can also occur
2. Overconfident, self-assured, boastful, bombastic or grandiose
3. High energy level - vigorous, full of plans, improvident, or rushing off with restless impulse
4. Overtalkative
5. Warm, people-seeking, or extraverted
6. Overinvolved or meddlesome
7. Uninhibited or stimulus-seeking, sometimes to the point of being promiscuous
8. Habitual short sleeper (< 6 hours)

Modified from Akiskal and Mallya (1987).

comparable in hyperthymic, cyclothymic, and depressive temperaments and classic bipolar illness (Akiskal, 1984). Furthermore, during prospective examination, the clinical course of both cyclothymic and dysthymic individuals is more like patients with affective disorder than noneffective personality controls (Akiskal, Djenderedjian, Rosenthal, & Khani, 1977; Akiskal et al., 1980; Depue, Slater, & Worfstetter-Kausch, 1981); even hyperthymic individuals are subject to depressive states, albeit of brief duration (Akiskal, 1984, 1989; Eckblad & Chapman, 1986). Thus, all three temperaments are at risk to develop depression under "natural" conditions; by contrast, the risk for hypomania—and this is even true for dysthymics—is augmented by exposure to tricyclic antidepressants. Such findings should be placed in the context of recent Italian work (Kukopulos, Reginaldi, Laddomada, Floris, Serra, & Tondo, 1980)—supported by U.S. experience (Akiskal & Mallya, 1987; Wehr & Goodwin, 1987)—which has shown that tricyclic antidepressants may actually accelerate the inherent cyclicity of mood disorders in hyperthymic and cyclothymic individuals. It would therefore appear that certain affective personalities are at high risk of developing depressive states under conditions of environmental challenge; they are also prone to hypomanic and manic states under pharmacologic challenge, as well as under other reactive conditions discussed in a subsequent section of this chapter.

The foregoing considerations lead to the suggestion that one mechanism whereby genetic factors might predispose to affective episodes is via the instability of the affective temperaments. This viewpoint is strengthened by the recent demonstration of shortened REM latency and related sleep neurophysiologic disturbances in individuals with dysthymic and hyperthymic temperaments (Akiskal, 1984), very much like the findings in individuals experiencing full-blown major depressions. This sleep neurophysiologic abnormality might represent a trait marker of vulnerability (Rush et al., 1986), and is not merely due to the stress of depression (Akiskal et al., 1984). Although the specificity of REM sleep findings to depressive illness—like other putative biological markers of depression—leaves much to be desired, shared neurophysiologic abnormalities between affective temperaments and full-blown clinical episodes tend to support the hypothesis of at least some continuity between subaffective and major affective episodes.

EARLY DEVELOPMENT AND CHARACTER PATHOLOGY

Temperamental contributions appear to have greater relevance in the recurrent and cyclic forms of mood disorder (Akiskal, 1984). In the more purely depressive forms of these disorders, a mixture of dependency and obsessiveness has long been hypothesized as a predisposing factor (Chodoff, 1972; Pilkonis, 1988). In psychoanalytic jargon, one can speak of "anaclitic" and "introjective" mechanisms (Blatt, Quinlan, Chevron, McDonald, & Zuroff, 1982). In the specific language of DSM-III (Shea, Glass, Pilkonis, Walkins & Docherty, 1987), depressed patients would fall primarily in the "anxious cluster" (e.g., compulsive-dependent-avoidant), with some overlap with the "dramatic cluster" (e.g., histrionic-borderline). Other formulations based on behavioral and cognitive approaches (Lewinsohn, 1974; Kovacs & Beck, 1978) have emphasized, respectively, an inadequate repertoire of social skills for rewarding social interactions and idiosyncratic thinking patterns which view one's efforts, the world and the future in negative light. All of these psychologic formulations, which have been developed largely through retrospective reconstruction of the premorbid characteristics of already depressed subjects, have typically derived from a relatively small clinical base, have not always taken the heterogeneity of mood disorders into consideration, have not used personality measures that can be compared across studies and, most seriously, have generally tended to confuse state and trait. Although reformulation of the earlier cognitive-behavioral position (Abramson, Seligman, & Teasdale, 1978) and subsequent research (reviewed in Alloy, 1988), have focused on more clearly defined depressive subgroups and have shown greater methodologic and theoretical sophistication, they too have relied on the logic of retrospective reconstruction.

We begin this discussion of characterologic aspects of depression by considering the classic psychoanalytic approach—based on Abraham's (1911) and Freud's (1917) work—which has long traced adult depression to early deprivations that preclude adequate mastery of loss situations. A neo-Freudian version of this approach formulated by Bowlby (1961) stipulates that the failure to successfully mourn object losses during childhood provides the behavioral sensitization to adult depressions; these individuals develop what is termed "anxious attachments." In another modification of the psychoanalytic theory of depression, Brown and Harris (1978) have traced the high rates of depression in women who lack confidants to the helplessness that has been their legacy as a result of having been maternally bereaved in childhood or adolescence. Arguing against the proposed relationship between childhood loss and adult depression is the fact that such loss is absent in two-thirds of adult patients with major affective diagnoses (Lloyd, 1980a); furthermore, the cumulative retrospective evidence—also reviewed by Lloyd (1980a)—has been generally nonsupportive of the specificity of childhood loss to adult mood disorder. Accordingly, in his latest writings, Bowlby (1977) has broadened his formulation to include in the consequences of early loss a large spectrum of adult characterologic dysphorias with impulsive tendencies.

While failing to specifically relate adult depression to childhood object loss, the available research evidence does suggest several interesting links in line with Bowlby's formulations. For instance, we now know from the work of Perris (1966) that unipolar depressives who experience developmental object loss have an illness onset 10 years earlier than those depressives without such loss. Others (Levi, Fales, Stein, & Sharp, 1966; Hill, 1969) have reported that suicide attempts are more common in depressive subjects who have sustained early traumatic separations. Studies in the author's research program (Akiskal, Bitar, Puzantian, Rosenthal, & Walker, 1978; Rosenthal, Akiskal, Scott-Strauss, Rosenthal, & David, 1981), conducted on "neurotic" and chronic depressives, have further shown that developmental losses are associated with such characterologic attributes as immaturity, hostile dependency, manipulativeness, impulsiveness, and low threshold for alcohol and drug abuse. It is finally relevant to cite evidence (Beck, Sethi, & Tuthill, 1963) that depressives with early loss have the highest scores on Beck's Depression inventory known to be loaded on such cognitive factors as low self-esteem, helplessness, hopelessness, and futurelessness; this finding need not indicate a more severe depression, but merely a characterologic tendency—in those with early loss—to overendorse certain cognitive items of depression. Although cumulatively results of these studies illustrate how breaks in early attachments could hypothetically relate to certain clinical aspects of depression—i.e., a pattern of clinging or "anxious attachment"—the characterologic attributes under consideration rather than being the complications of early object loss, might alternatively reflect the adverse psychosocial sequelae of having an alcoholic parent or one with severe personality disorder (VanValkenburg, Lillienfeld, & Akiskal, 1987).

While not causing depressive illness, developmental object loss might pathoplastically modify the clinical expression of the adult disorder. The characterologic propensity toward hostile dependency could, hypothetically, prepare a fertile soil of interpersonal friction that facilitates a depressive onset earlier than that determined by innate genetic factors. Another possible mechanism whereby early losses could hypothetically influence the occurrence of adult depression is by creating conditions favorable to the development of character traits associated with what Seligman (1975) refers to as "learned helplessness," or with the self-denigrating and generally pessimistic mental schemata described by Beck (1967). It is reasonable to assume that situations wherein the individual has failed to master a series of tasks can lead to subsequent helplessness when faced with similar situations. Early separations from parent(s), without adequate substitutes, might prevent the emergence of a sense of mastery of the environment. Such children may become anxious-insecure adults who then feel unable to face the challenge of new situations. It should be noted, however, that the mere presence of parents would not necessarily immunize against the trait of helplessness; developing a sense of mastery requires a suitable role model and the opportunity to cope with a series of life events of increasing complexity.

Such formulations, while plausible, have not been subjected to prospective testing in clinical populations. Despite their clinical popularity (Arieti & Bemporad, 1978), there is no convincing evidence that the proposed characterologic disturbances actually precede major affective episodes in an unselected population. The characterologic attributes of affectively ill individuals given prominence in the psychoanalytic and cognitive-behavioral literature constitute, in almost all circumstances, post-affective or interepisodic observations. These postmorbid personality features, commonly observed in recurrent mood disorders (Kraines, 1957; Akiskal et al., 1978; Cassano et al., 1983; Winokur, 1985) are summarized in Table 8.2. The three published prospective studies (Nystrom & Lindegard, 1975; Lewinsohn, Hoberman, & Rosenbaum, 1988; Hirschfeld et al., 1989) that searched for such characterologic abnormalities *prior* to the onset of major episodes failed to identify significant deviations in the personalities of those who eventually broke down with major depressive episodes. Whatever minor trends occurred, tended to support a subaffective hypothesis, i.e., the existence of low-grade subclinical affective symptomatology prior to major epi-

TABLE 8.2
Postmorbid Affective Personality Patterns

Social withdrawal	Sensitivity
Helpless dependency	Suspiciousness
Pessimism	Demandingness
Low self-esteem	Manipulativeness
Rigidity	Labile-hostility

sodes. While specific premorbid characterologic factors did not appear to be predictive of affective episodes, premorbid traits of high aggressiveness, impulsivity and related attributes were found predictive of suicide in a fourth prospective study—known as the Zurich study—that has been published only in part (Angst & Clayton, 1986).

It would therefore appear that early deprivations such as parental bereavement do not, on the average, lead to measurable characterologic disturbances prior to the onset of major affective episodes. Early traumatic experiences of this genre might then represent markers of some yet unknown variable that predispose to much interpersonal disruption once an affective episode occurs. These interpersonal sequelae are usually transient, but in a third of patients they tend to crystallize into chronic postdepressive personality maladjustments. These considerations lead to the hypothesis that given specific predisposition to mood disorder, the experience of being raised in a broken home would predict the occurrence of much interpersonal disruption following major affective episodes. In the extreme, these characterological disturbances can even take the form of what North American psychiatrists refer to as "borderline" features (Akiskal, Chen, Davis, Puzantian & Kashgarian, 1985b) which, in the author's view, are best regarded as epiphenomenal (postaffective). The observations of Freidman, Clarkin, Corn, Aronoff, Hurt, & Murphy (1982) on an adolescent inpatient unit are quite convincing in this regard: in almost all instances, borderline diagnoses postdated the diagnosis of affective illness by months to years.

The evidence thus far reviewed further suggests that having an affectively ill parent might represent a double jeopardy—i.e., the possibility of inheriting the biologic predisposition to affective dysregulation, and developmental disruptions arising from the fact of having an affectively ill parent. Such destabilizing influences could be conceivably enhanced by the presence of mood disorder, alcoholism, sociopathic or related characterologic tendencies in the other parent (Rosenthal et al., 1981). Research conducted at the Karolinska Institute (Asberg, Schalling, Traskman-Bendz, & Wagner, 1987) has shown that affectively labile individuals—who often have low cerebrospinal indices of Serotonin function—are more likely to die from violent suicides; this eventuality is not necessarily linked with a clinically diagnosable mood disorder. Actually, such serotonergic deficits have been hypothesized by Van Praag et al. (1987) as being generic to a large class of psychopathologic entities—including bulimia, alcoholism, suicide and violence against others—and clinically mediated by high impulsivity and related characterologic attributes. This factor appears relevant to both sexes and, in the presence of mood disorder, might color the affective clinical picture with concurrent character pathology.

The failure of prospective observations to uphold the existence of measurable characterologic pathology in the premorbid history of adults with mood disorders runs so contrary to clinical opinion that for long have linked them together, that this conclusion deserves further commentary. One possibility is that pencil-and-paper tests are inadequate for the task of measuring characterologic propensities, because the latter are best elicited by specific interpersonal cues. A related possibility—alluded to earlier—is that what is termed "character disorder" represents essentially a postaffective pathology resulting from an interaction between early losses or the developmental instability surrounding them, premorbid functioning based on temperamental attributes, and the disruptive effect of affective episodes. A final possibility is that while correlated with early object disruptions, characterologic disturbances play a relatively minor role in the origin of affective episodes; the prominence of characterologic disturbances in clinical samples of mood disorders could then be explained by the increased likelihood that such joint pathology would come to clinical attention.

GENDER, TEMPERAMENT, AND AFFECTIVE EPISODES

Women are more likely to receive unstable characterologic labels such as "borderline"; they are also more prone to depressive recurrences (Weissman & Klerman, 1977). Although it is customary to invoke psychosocial variables to account for this increased vulnerability, several biological parameters—known to be exclusively limited or more prevalent in women—appear at least equally relevant (reviewed in Akiskal, 1987, 1988). As discussed elsewhere (Akiskal, 1987), neither premenstrual nor postpartal emotional changes appear specific to mood disorders, but they could color, accentuate, or determine the recurrence of affective experiences in those women suffering from such disorders. Biological factors which might have greater relevance to women's increased vulnerability to depression include marginal hypothyroid indices (Gold, Potash, Mueller, & Extein, 1981)—especially relevant to rapid-cycling (Cowdry, Wehr, Zis, & Goodwin, 1983)—and an elevated level of the enzyme monoamine oxidase (Robinson et al., 1971). Increased activity of the latter enzyme, now known to be controlled by the X-chromosome (Kochersperger et al., 1986), might hypothetically account in part for the anxious-depressive clinical picture, the "atypical" (hypersomnic-lethargic-bulimic) depressive coloring (Akiskal & Lemmi, 1987), and the relative selectivity of the class of monoamine oxidase inhibitor antidepressants for women as contrasted to the greater utility of tricyclic antidepressants for men (Davidson & Pelton, 1986).

It is also of interest that recent collaborative research between the University of Pisa and the University of Tennessee, Memphis (Perugi, Musetti, Simonini, Piagentini, Cassano, and Akiskal, in press) has shown that women are more likely to exhibit depressive temperaments and men hyperthymic temperaments. These findings could, in part, explain Nolen-Hoeksema's (1987) formulation according to which the higher prevalence of depression in women might be due to the greater difficulty they have on the average, compared with men, of coming out of a depression. These considerations, in their turn, could account for the observed greater prevalence of recurrent depressions in women, and the equal sex ratio in classical bipolar illness. The Pisa-Memphis data complement earlier findings by Angst, Felder, and Frey (1979) of higher frequency of depressive episodes in women and mania in men.

AN INTERACTIONAL MODEL

As conceptualized in classical continental European psychiatry (Kraepelin, 1921; Kretschmer, 1936; Von Zerssen, 1977), episodic forms of mood disorder arise from a background of cyclothymic, hyperthymic and depressive temperaments. Danish work on monozygotic twins, cited earlier (Bertelsen et al., 1977), suggests that the lowest unit of inheritance observed at the level of a behavioral phenotype is represented by moodiness that does not reach a diagnosable threshold of mood disorder (Akiskal, 1988, 1989). This, in turn, suggests the hypothesis that the genetic potential to develop affective episodes might be transmitted as affective temperamental dysregulation. To what extent and in what specific ways developmental experiences impact on such dysregulation is uncertain at this point. These temperaments seem to emerge as subaffective expressions and, typically, precede frank affective episodes. Such temperamental propensities might subsequently interact with other risk factors—some independent, but more often resulting from their social or physiologic repurcussions—to bring about major affective breakdowns (Fig. 8.1). In this model, characterologic disturbances largely evolve as postepisodic interpersonal sequelae or complications.

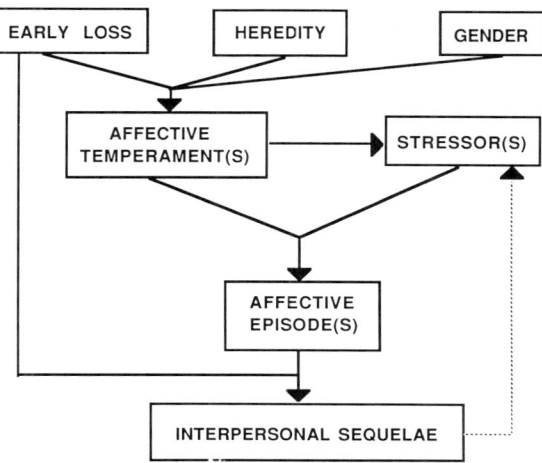

FIG. 8.1. The role of affective temperaments and characterologic (interpersonal) factors in the hypothesized pathogenetic interactional model of mood disorders.

PRECIPITATING CIRCUMSTANCES

Affective episodes are often temporally related to external and internal circumstances. The preceding discussion suggests that in vulnerable individuals affective disturbance is present subclinically—and that it is activated into overt clinical episodes by environmental challenge. Environmental circumstances may determine the precipitation of the initial episodes and, perhaps, the timing of subsequent recurrences (Akiskal, 1986, 1987). These circumstances are extremely varied and include psychosocial, biologic, and seasonal factors.

Although the majority of individuals exposed to losses and other aversive life circumstances do not sink into morbid despair, those predisposed to mood disorders may do so at such times. The lifetime risk for clinical depression is about 12% (Helgason, 1979), yet no more than 5% of those exposed to "exit" type life events decompensate into clinical depression (Paykel, 1976; Clayton, 1979; Lloyd, 1980b). Furthermore, history of previous depressive episodes is a stronger predictor of depression in the face of life stressors than the characteristics of the stressors and their social context (Warheit, 1979). Even individuals predisposed to mood disorders—measured as a function of previous episodes or positive family history—do not seem, on the average, to develop affective episodes in the face of a major loss; rather, other concurrent or antecedent events appear to influence the effect of such events (Akiskal, 1986, 1987). These include unresolved childhood loss, concurrent life events, impact of life events on life style, symbolic meaning of the life event, inadequate social support, deficient social skills and, as already discussed, temperament.

The fact that clinically significant depression occurs, on the average, in about 15% of the medically ill (Cavanaugh, 1983)—which approximates the lifetime risk for clinical depression—is an indication that medical contributions to depression are also in the nature of precipitant rather than cause. Reserpine-induced depressions (Goodwin & Bunney, 1971) illustrate this point in that two-thirds of these cases represent "pseudodepressions" secondary to the sedative side effects of the drug, which reverse as medication is discontinued; melancholia persisting in an autonomous fashion despite withdrawal of the offending chemical occurs in the remaining third, and is largely limited to those with past personal history or predisposition for depression.

It would appear that neither life events nor chemical events represent sufficient cause for the occurrence of clinical depressions: They seem to exert a depressant influence in the presence of predisposing factors. The same generally appears to be the case with the precipitation of hypomania or mania. The relevance of life events—especially losses—is suggested by Ambelas' study (1979). Obviously such losses can easily result from premorbid cyclothymic or hyperthymic instability in mood (Akiskal, 1984). The best known precipitants of hypomania—and to a lesser extent of mania—are catecholaminergic drugs or certain circadian disruptions (Vogel, 1975; Bunney, 1978; Wehr, Sack, & Rosenthal, 1987; Ehlers, Frank, & Kupfer, 1988). These include the noradrenergic tricyclics, the monoamine-oxidase inhibitors, ephedrine, L-dopa, cocaine, amphetamine-like drugs, REM-deprivation, total sleep deprivation, and transmeridian travel. These factors, which often represent medically or self-administered treatments in vulnerable temperaments—and, in the case of circadian disruptions, a manifestation of the hyperthymic or cyclothymic individuals' decreased need for sleep or increased involvement in activity—are more consistent in their association with a switch from depression to hypomania than from euthymia to hypomania. Thus, the pharmacological switch is largely limited to individuals with a bipolar diathesis—measured as a function of personal or family history of mania (Akiskal et al., 1983a). The same applies generally to postpartum affective episodes, whether manic, mixed, or retarded depressive. Another class of precipitating circumstances that has received recent attention is seasonality (Rosenthal et al., 1984), largely relevant to relatively milder cases of bipolar II disorder.

To summarize, this discussion on precipitating circumstances suggests that the onset of affective episodes is most commonly associated with an interaction between predisposing and triggering factors. Many, though not all, of these triggering factors themselves develop as a result of complex interactions between the environment and the temperament of the patient predisposed to mood disorders.

FUTURE PERSPECTIVES

The substantial findings on personality and affective illness reviewed in this chapter are compatible with the position which regards patients with cyclic and recurrent (i.e., bipolar) mood disorders to be "less neurotic" (MacVane, Lange, & Brown, 1978) and more temperamental (dysthymic, cyclothymic, or hyperthymic) than their strictly unipolar counterparts who are, on the average, deemed to be quite neurotic (i.e., anxious-compulsive or hostile-dependent). Although this conclusion is compatible with Kraepelinian, psychoanalytic, *and* cognitive-behavioral descriptions, it is open to different interpretations, from a causal perspective.

With respect to cyclic and recurrent mood disorders, this chapter has emphasized the specific theoretical proposal that personality as subaffective expression represents an intermediary step between remote predisposing and proximate precipitating factors. This means that the putative temperamental attributes and affective episodes are, in part, contiguous constructs that cannot be easily discriminated on a categorical basis (Akiskal, 1984; Widiger, 1989). It is of course quite uncertain why only selected individuals with affective temperaments make the clinical *jump* to major affective episodes. Stating that the origin of these episodes is multifactorial does not resolve this dilemma because most, if not all, affective temperaments are likely to be exposed to the factors considered in the multifactorial concept. Because in many patients it is not simply a matter of understandable transition from premorbid self to an affective episode, future research must more precisely define the parameters or circumstances—both internal and external—that render individuals acutely vulnerable to "episodegenic" influences.

This model, which links temperaments to genetic factors on the one hand—an area that has greatly benefited from Cloninger's (1987) fascinating explorations—and to the biopsychosocial sphere involved in episode precipitation on the other, provides opportunities for prevention (Akiskal, 1987). Thus, sleep deprivation, transmeridian travel, use of catecholaminergic drugs could all be subjected to prevention efforts. Likewise, the effects of adult object loss could, in principle, be attenuated by psychotherapy and, possibly, by psychopharmacotherapy. Most importantly, if temperamental disturbances—with underlying serotonergic mechanisms—are involved in young suicides, then preventive strategies can be designed and prospectively tested. Thus, the recent alarming rise of suicide in adolescent and young adult age cohorts (reviewed in Pfeffer, 1989)—often associated with substance abuse—might potentially be reversed by specific pharmacologic interventions. Furthermore, our finding of greater prevalence of polysubstance abuse in the offspring of adult manic depressives (Akiskal et al., 1985a), especially among adolescents manifesting depressive or cyclothymic temperaments, lends some support to the self-medication hypothesis of substance abuse. This consideration, coupled with the recent finding (Brent et al., 1988) of high rates of bipolar disorder in the first-degree relatives of substance-abusing adolescents, further suggests the potential benefit of prophylactic lithium trial as an approach to suicide prevention in vulnerable juvenile subjects.

That the promise of pharmacotherapy could extend to the underlying biology of the temperamental disturbances in mood disorders is best illustrated by the attentuation of the sombre personalities in dysthymia (Akiskal et al., 1980; Kocsis et al., 1988), the interpersonal—especially rejection—sensitivity in the atypical depressions of the "hysteroid dysphoric" type (Liebowitz & Klein, 1979; Liebowitz et al., 1988), and the tempestuous interpersonal storms in cyclothymic (Akiskal, Khani, & Scott-Strauss, 1979; Peselow, Dunner, Fieve, & Lautin 1982) or borderline conditions (Cowdry & Gardner, 1988). Although psychotherapeutically trained clinicians tend to dismiss such findings—and, admittedly, much more definitive data is needed in this difficult realm of psychopharmacologic application—the cited literature is provocative and testifies to the progress already achieved.

Given that the roots of affective illness, especially as regards to temperamental disturbances, are to be found in early development, supports the wisdom of investing in high risk studies that begin prospective observations in the early years of life. Observations on the anlagé of mood disorders in temperamental peculiarities would not only provide information as to which individuals—under what circumstances—would make the transition to a clinical affective episode, but it could also provide some understanding as to which conglomeration of factors leads to artistic creativity and eminence in a substantial minority of mild bipolars (bipolar II's and cyclothymics) as opposed to the more prevalent and disruptive manifestations of mood disorders (Akiskal & Akiskal, 1988). These temperamental characteristics then might provide links between the basic biology of mood and social attributes. A related social parameter, productivity in work, appears paradoxically enhanced in the interepisodic phase of certain types of depressions where leisure functions are deficient (Delisio et al., 1966; Perugi, Maremmani, McNair, Cassano, & Akiskal, 1988). Such "work-addicted" depression-prone individuals (Telenbach, 1980) have been commented as well by Schneider in his empirical description of the "depressive psychopath" (1958) and Simons in his discussion of a "masochistic type" in relation to depression (1987). These considerations present yet another major future challenge—to incorporate the realm of sociocultural forces in any coherent theory of depressive illness (see Kleinman & Good, 1985).

The reader will note that omitted from this review is the relationship between anxiety and depressive disorders which, among other areas of overlap, appear to share certain personality attributes involving neuroticism, sensitive-avoidant and phobic tendencies (Akiskal, 1988). The hypothesis that these attributes represent subclinical expressions of neurotic suffering is not easily discriminable from that which assigns them to an epiphenomenal status in the course of long-standing neurotic and dysphoric arousal. Since the present review focused on recurrent and cyclic mood disorders, this more or less chronic area of neurotic suffering was deemed somewhat peripheral to our main theme. It provides, nonetheless, an excellent illustration of the difficulty of distinguishing traits from states and the subaffective, from the complication, hypotheses. In chronic and recurrent conditions like neurotic and affective disorders, there may well be little to choose between these competing hypotheses.

Such thorny methodologic issues notwithstanding, this chapter has defended the thesis that the pathogenetic chain proceeds from affective temperament to affective episodes and, finally, to personality disorder. That is, temperamental disturbances are conceptualized to appear early in the life history of affectively ill individuals; whereas character disorders—especially as represented by the DSM-III personality disorder constructs—tend to appear much later in the course of the illness, which is typically after major episodes have declared themselves.

The unresolved etiologic status of characterologic factors—as well as other developmental experiences traditionally linked with them—will benefit from rigorous studies in developmental epidemiology (Rutter, 1988). Such studies will ultimately decide whether such factors represent etiologic factors in a multifactorial chain, or represent correlates of clinical referral indicating comorbidity, greater severity, and prognostic weighting of multiple factors. Comorbid mental conditions are prevalent in settings that treat severe mental disorders. Characterologic disturbances—and associated social disruptions, substance abuse and suicidal tendencies—with mental, especially affective, disorders represent not only one of the most challenging questions for theory, but provide the practitioner with a major source of therapeutic resistance and countertransference. This area has emerged as one of the priority areas of research in mental illness.

REFERENCES

Abraham, K. (1911/1960). Notes on the psychoanalytic investigation and treatment of manic-depressive insanity and allied conditions. In *Selected Papers on Psychoanalysis* (pp. 137–156). New York: Basic Books.

Abramson, L. Y., Seligman, M. E. P., & Teasdale, J. (1978). Learned helplessness in humans: Critique and reformulation. *Journal of Abnormal Psychology, 87,* 49–74.

Akiskal, H. S. (1984). Characterologic manifestations of affective disorders: Toward a new conceptualization. *Integrative Psychiatry, 2,* 83–88.

Akiskal, H. S. (1986). A developmental perspective on recurrent mood disorders: A review of studies in man. *Psychopharmacology Bulletin, 2,* 579–586.

Akiskal, H. S. (1987). Overview of biobehavioral factors in the prevention of mood disorders. In R. Munoz (Ed.), *Depression prevention: Research directions* (pp. 263–280). New York: Hemisphere.

Akiskal, H. S. (1988). Personality as a mediating variable in the pathogenesis of mood disorders: Implications for theory, research, and prevention. In T. Helgason & R. Daly (Eds.), *Depressive illness: Prediction of course and outcome* (pp. 131–164). Heidelberg: Springer-Verlag.

Akiskal, H. S. (1989). Validating affective personality types. In L. Robins & J. Barrett (Eds.), *The validity of psychiatric diagnosis* (pp. 217–227). New York: Raven Press.

Akiskal, H. S., & Akiskal, K. (1988). Re-assessing the prevalence of bipolar disorders: Clinical significance and artistic creativity. *Psychiatrie et Psychobiologie, 3,* 29s–36s.

Akiskal, H. S., Bitar, A. H., Puzantian, V. R., Rosenthal, T. L., & Walker, P. W. (1978). The nosological status of neurotic depression: A prospective three-to-four year examination in light of the primary-secondary and unipolar-bipolar dichotomies. *Archives of General Psychiatry, 35,* 756–766.

Akiskal, H. S., Chen, S. E., Davis, G. C., Puzantian, V. R., Kashgarian, M., & Bolinger, J. M. (1985b). Borderline: An adjective in search of a noun. *Journal of Clinical Psychiatry, 46,* 41–481.

Akiskal, H. S., Djenderedjian, A. H., Rosenthal, R. H., & Khani, M. K. (1977). Cyclothymic disorder: Validating criteria for inclusion in the bipolar affective group. *American Journal of Psychiatry, 134,* 1227–1233.

Akiskal, H. S., Downs, J., Jordan, P., Watson, S., Daugherty, D., & Pruitt, D. B. (1985a). Affective disorders in the referred children and younger siblings of manic-depressives: Mode of onset and prospective course. *Archives of General Psychiatry, 42,* 996–1003.

Akiskal, H. S., Hirschfeld, R. M. A., & Yerevanian, B. I. (1983b). The relationship of personality to affective disorders: A critical review. *Archives of General Psychiatry, 40,* 801–810.

Akiskal, H. S., Khani, M. K., & Scott-Strauss, A. (1979). Cyclothymic temperamental disorders. *Psychiatric Clinics of North America, 2,* 527–554.

Akiskal, H. S., & Lemmi, H. (1987). Sleep EEG findings bearing on the relationship of anxiety and depressive disorders. In G. Racagni & E. Smeraldi (Eds.), *Anxious depressions: Assessment and treatment* (pp. 153–159). New York: Raven Press.

Akiskal, H. S., Lemmi, H., Dickson, H., King, D., Yerevanian, B. I., & VanValkenburg,

C. (1984). Chronic depressions: Part 2. Sleep EEG differentiation of primary dysthymic disorders from anxious depressions. *Journal of Affective Disorders, 6,* 287–295.
Akiskal, H. S., & McKinney, W. T. (1973). Depressive disorders: Toward a unified hypothesis. *Science, 182,* 20–28.
Akiskal, H. S., & McKinney, W. T. (1975). Overview of recent research in depression: Integration of ten conceptual models into a comprehensive clinical frame. *Archives of General Psychiatry, 32,* 285–305.
Akiskal, H. S., & Mallya, G. (1987). Criteria for the "soft" bipolar spectrum: Treatment implications. *Psychopharmacology Bulletin, 23,* 68–73.
Akiskal, H. S., Rosenthal, T. L., Haykal, R. F., Lemmi, H., Rosenthal, R. H., & Scott-Strauss, A. (1980). Characterological depressions: Clinical and sleep EEG findings separating "subaffective dysthymias" from "character-spectrum" disorders. *Archives of General Psychiatry, 37,* 777–783.
Akiskal, H. S., Walker, P. W., Puzantian, V. R., King, D., Rosenthal, T. L., & Drannon, M. (1983a). Bipolar outcome in the course of depressive illness: Phenomenlogic, familial and pharmacologic predictors. *Journal of Affective Disorders, 5,* 115–128.
Akiskal, H. S., & Weller, E. (1989). Mood disorders and suicide in children and adolescents. In H. I. Kaplan & B. J. Sadock (Eds.), *Comprehensive textbook of psychiatry* (pp. 1981–1994). Baltimore, MD: Williams & Wilkins.
Alloy, L. B. (Ed.). (1988). *Cognitive processes in depression.* New York: The Guilford Press.
Ambelas, A. (1979). Psychologically stressful events in the precipitation of manic episodes. *British Journal of Psychiatry, 135,* 15–21.
Angst, J., & Clayton, P. J. (1986). Premorbid personality of depressive, bipolar and schizophrenic patients with special reference to suicidal issues. *Comprehensive Psychiatry, 27,* 511–532.
Angst, J., Felder, W., & Frey, R. (1979). The course of unipolar and bipolar affective disorders. In M. Schou & E. Stromgren (Eds.), *Origin prevention and treatment of affective disorders* (pp. 215–226). New York: Academic Press.
Angst, J., Merikangas, K., & Scheidegger, P. (in press). Recurrent brief depression: A new subtype of affective disorder. *Journal of Affective Disorders, 19,* 87–98.
Arieti, S., & Bemporad, J. (1978). *Severe and mild depression.* New York: Basic Books.
Asberg, M., Schalling, D., Traskman-Bendz, L., & Wagner, A. (1987). Psychobiology of suicide, impulsivity, and related phenomena. In H. Y. Meltzer (Ed.), *Psychopharmacology: The third generation of progress.* New York: Raven Press.
Beck, A. T. (1967). *Depression—Causes and treatment.* Philadelphia: University of Pennsylvania Press.
Beck, A., Sethi, B., & Tuthill, R. (1963). Child bereavement and adult depression. *Archives of General Psychiatry, 9,* 295–302.
Becker, J. (1974). *Depression: Theory and research.* Washington, D.C.: V. H. Winston & Sons.
Bertelsen, A., Harvald, B., & Hauge, M. A. (1977). A Danish study of manic-depressive disorders. *British Journal of Psychiatry, 130,* 338–351.
Blatt, S. J., Quinlan, D. M., Chevron, E. S., McDonald, C., & Zuroff, D. (1982). Dependency and self-criticism: Psychological dimensions of depression. *Journal of Consulting and Clinical Psychology, 50,* 113–124.
Bowlby, J. (1961). Childhood mourning and its implications for child psychiatry. *American Journal of Psychiatry, 118,* 481–498.
Bowlby, J. (1977). The making and breaking of affectional bonds. I: Aetiology and psychopathology in the light of attachment theory. *British Journal of Psychiatry, 130,* 201–210.
Brown, G.W., & Harris, T. (1978). *Social origins of depression.* London: Tavistock.
Brent, D. A., Perper, J. A., Goldstein, C. E., Kolko, D. J., Allan, M. J., Allman, C. J., & Zelenak, J. P. (1988). Risk factors for adolescent suicide. *Archives of General Psychiatry 45,* 581–588.
Bunney, W. E. (1978). Psychopharmacology of the switch process in affective illness. In M. A.

Lipton, A. Dimascio, & K. F. Killam (Eds.), *Psychopharmacology: A generation of progress* (pp. 1249–1259). New York: Raven Press.

Cadoret, R. J. (1978). Psychopathology in adopted-away offspring of biologic parents with antisocial behavior. *archives of General Psychiatry, 25,* 1–15.

Cadoret, R. J., O'Gorman, T. W., Heywood, E., & Troughton, F. (1985). Genetic and environmental factors in major depression. *Journal of Affective Disorders, 9,* 155–164.

Cassano, G. B., Maggini, C., & Akiskal, H. S. (1983). Short-term, subchronic and chronic sequelae of affective disorders. *Psychiatric Clinics of North America, 6,* 55–67.

Cavanaugh, S. (1983). The prevalence of emotional and cognitive dysfunction in a medical population. *General Hospital Psychiatry, 5,* 15–24.

Chodoff, P. (1972). The depressive personality: A critical review. *Archives of General Psychiatry, 27,* 666–673.

Clayton, P. J. (1979). The sequelae and nonsequelae of conjugal bereavement. *American Journal of Psychiatry, 136,* 1530–1534.

Cloninger, C. R. (1987). A systematic method for clinical description and classification of personality variants. *Archives of General Psychiatry, 44,* 573–588.

Cowdry, R. W., & Gardner, D. L. (1988). Pharmacotherapy of borderline personality disorder. *Archives of General Psychiatry, 45,* 111–119.

Cowdry, R. W., Wehr, T. A., Zis, A. P., & Goodwin, F. K. (1983). Thyroid abnormalities associated with rapid-cycling bipolar illness. *Archives of General Psychiatry, 40,* 414–420.

Davidson, J., & Pelton, S. (1986). Forms of atypical depression and their response to antidepressant drugs. *Psychiatry Research, 17,* 87–95.

Delisio, G., Maremmani, I., Perugi, G., Cassano, G. B., Deltito, J., & Akiskal, H. S. (1986). Impairment of work and leisure in depressed outpatients: A preliminary communication. *Journal of Affective Disorders, 10,* 79–84.

Depue, R. A., Slater, J. F., & Wolfstetter-Kausch, H. (1981). A behavioral paradigm for identifying persons at risk for bipolar depressive disorder: A conceptual framework and five validation studies. *Journal of Abnormal Psychology, 90,* 381–437.

Eckblad, M., & Chapman, L. J. (1986). Development and validation of a scale for hypomanic personality. *Journal of Abnormal Psychology, 95,* 214–222.

Ehlers, C. L., Frank, E., & Kupfer, D. J. (1988). Social zeitgebers and biological rhythms. *Archives of General Psychiatry, 45,* 948–952.

Freidman, R. C., Clarkin, J. F., Corn, R., Aronoff, M. S., Hurt, S. W., & Murphy, M. C. (1982). DSM-III and affective pathology in hospitalized adolescents. *Journal of Nervous and Mental Disease, 170,* 511–521.

Freud, S. (1917/1962). *Mourning and melancholia,* Vol. 14, standard ed. London: Hogarth Press.

Gershon, E. S., Dunner, D. L., & Goodwin, F. K. (1971). Toward a biology of affective illness: Genetic contributions. *Archives of General Psychiatry, 25,* 1–15.

Gershon, E. S., Hamovit, J., Guroff, J. J., Dibble, E., Leckman, J. E., Sceery, W., Targum, S. D., Nurnberger, J. I., Goldin, L. R., & Bunney, W. E. (1982). A family study of schizoaffective, bipolar I, bipolar II, unipolar and normal control probands. *Archives of General Psychiatry, 39,* 1157–1167.

Gold, M. S., Pottash, A. C., Muller, E. A., & Extein, I. (1981). Grades of thyroid failure in 100 depressed and anergic psychiatric inpatients. *American Journal of Psychiatry, 138,* 253–255.

Goodwin, F., & Bunney, W. F. (1971). Depression following reserpine: A reevaluation. *Seminars in Psychiatry, 3,* 19–53.

Helgason, T. (1979). Epidemiological investigations concerning affective disorders. In M. Schou & E. Stromgren (Eds.), *Origin, prevention and treatment of affective disorders* (pp. 241–255). London: Academic Press.

Hill, O. (1969). The association of childhood bereavement with suicide attempt in depressive illness. *British Journal of Psychiatry, 115,* 301–304.

Hirschfeld, R. M. A., Klerman, G. L., Clayton, P. J., Keller, M. B., McDonald-Scott, P., & Larkin,

B. H. (1983). Assessing personality: Effects of the depressive state on trait measurement. *American Journal of Psychiatry, 140,* 695–699.
Hirschfeld, R. M. A., Klerman, G. L., Lavori, P., Keller, M. B., Griffith, P., & Coryell, W. (1989). Premorbid personality assessments of first onset of major depression. *Archives of General Psychiatry, 46,* 345–350.
Kleinman, A., & Good, B. (1985). *Culture and depression.* Berkley: University of California Press.
Kochersperger, L. M., Parker, E. L., Siciliano, M., Darlington, G. J., & Denny, R. M. (1986). Assignment of genes for human monoamine oxidases A and B to the X chromosome. *Journal of Neuroscience Research, 16,* 601–616.
Kocsis, J. H., Frances, A. J., Voss, C., Mann, J. J., Mason, B. J., & Sweeny, J. (1988). Imipramine treatment for chronic depression. *Archives of General Psychiatry, 45,* 253–257.
Kovacs, M., Beck, A. T. (1978). Maladaptive cognitive structures in depression. *American Journal of Psychiatry, 135,* 525–533.
Kovacs, M., & Gastsonis, C. D. (1989). Stability and change in childhood-onset of depressive disorder: Longitudinal course as a diagnostic validator. In L. N. Robins & J. E. Barrett (Eds.), *The validity of psychiatric diagnosis* (pp. 57–73). New York: Raven Press.
Kraepelin, D. (1921). *Manic-depressive insanity and paranoia.* Edinburgh: Livingstone.
Kraines, S. H. (1957). *Mental depressions and their treatment.* New York: The MacMillan Company.
Kretschmer, E. (1936). *Physique and character* [E. Miller, Trans]. London: Kegan Paule, Trench, Trubner and Co.
Kukopulos, A., Reginaldi, D., Laddomada, P., Floris, G., Serra, G., & Tondo, L. (1980). Course of the manic-depressive cycle and changes caused by treatments. *Pharmacopsychiatria, 13,* 156–167.
Levi, D. L., Fales, C. L., Stein, M., Sharp, V. H. (1966). Separation and attempted suicide. *Archives of General Psychiatry, 15,* 158–164.
Lewinsohn, P. M. (1974). A behavioral approach to depression. In R. J. Fredieman & M. M. Katz (Eds.), *The psychology of depression: Contemporary theory and research.* New York: Wiley.
Lewinsohn, P. M., Hoberman, H. M., & Rosensbaum, M. (1988). A prospective study of risk factors for unipolar depression. *Journal of Abnormal Psychology, 97,* 251–264.
Liebowitz, M. R., & Klein, D. F. (1979). Hysteroid dysphoria. *Psychiatric Clinics of North America, 2,* 555–575.
Liebowitz, M. R., Quitkin, F. M., Stewart, J. W., McGrath, P. J., Harrison, W. M., Markowitz, J. S., Rabkin, J. G., Tricamo, E., Goetz, D. M., & Kleinm, D. F. (1988). Antidepressant specificity in atypical depression. *Archives of General Psychiatry, 45,* 129–137.
Lloyd, C. (1980a). Life events and depressive disorder reviewed. I: Events as predisosing factors. *Archives of General Psychiatry, 32,* 285–305.
Lloyd, C. (1980b). Life events and depressive disorder reviewed. II: Events are precipitating factors. *Archives of General psychiatry, 37,* 541–548.
McVane, J. R., Lange, J. D., & Brown, W. A. (1978). Psychological functioning of bipolar manic depressives in remission. *Archives of General Psychiatry, 35,* 1351–1354.
Mendlewicz, J., & Rainer, J. D. (1977). Adoption study supporting genetic transmission in manic depressive illness. *Lancet, 268,* 327–329.
Nolen-Hoeksema, S. (1987). Sex differences in unipolar depression: Evidence and theory. *Psychological Bulletin, 101,* 259–282.
Nystrom, S., & Lindegard, B. (1975). Predisposition for mental syndromes: A study comparing predisposition for depression, neurasthenia and anxiety state. *Acta Psychiatria Scandinavica, 51,* 69–76.
Paykel, E. S. (1976). Life stress, depression and attempted suicide. *Journal of Human Stress, 2,* 3–12.
Pellegrini, D., Kosisky, S., Nackman, D., Cytryn, L., McKnew, D. H., Gershon, E., Hamovit, J., &

Cammuso, K. (1986). Personal and social resources in children of patients with bipolar affective disorder and children of normal control subjects. *American Journal of Psychiatry, 143,* 856–861.
Perris, C. A. (1966). A study of bipolar (manic-depressive) and unipolar recurrent depressive psychoses. *Acta Psychiatria Scandinavica, 42* (Suppl.), 118–152.
Perugi, G., Maremmani, I., McNair, D. M., Cassano, G. B., & Akiskal, H. S. (1988). Differential changes in areas of social adjustment from depressive episodes through recovery. *Journal of Affective Disorders, 15,* 39–43.
Perugi, G., Musetti, L., Simonini, E., Piagentini, F., Cassano, G. B., & Akiskal, H. S. (in press). Gender mediated clinical features of depressive illness: The importance of temperamental differences. *British Journal of Psychiatry.*
Peselow, E. D., Dunner, D. L., Fieve, R. R., & Lautin, A. (1982). Lithium prophylaxis of depression in unipolar, bipolar II and cyclothymic patients. *American Journal of Psychiatry, 139,* 747–752.
Pfeffer, C. R. (Ed.). (1989). *Suicide among youth: Perspectives on risk and prevention.* Washington, DC, American psychiatric Press.
Pilkonis, P. (1988). Personality prototypes among depressives: Themes of dependency and autonomy. *Journal of Personality Disorders, 2,* 144–152.
Price, J. (1968). The genetics of depressive behavior. In A. Coppen & A. Walk (Eds.), *Recent developments in affective disorders. British Journal of Psychiatry* (spec. publ.), *2,* 37–54.
Robinson, D. S., Davis, J. M., Nies, A., Ravarais, C. L., & Sylvester, D. (1971). Relation of sex and aging to monoamine oxidase activity of human brain, plasma, and platelets. *Archives of General Psychiatry, 24,* 536–539.
Rosenthal, N. E., Sack, D. A., Gillin, J. C., Lewy, A. J., Goodwin, F. K., Davenport, Y., Mueller, P. S., Newsome, D. A., & Wehr, T. A. (1984). Seasonal affective disorder. *Archives of General Psychiatry, 41,* 72–80.
Rosenthal, T. L., Akiskal, H. S., Scott-Strauss, A., Rosenthal, R. H., & David, M. (1981). Familial and developmental factors in characterological depression. *Journal of Affective Disorders, 3,* 183–192.
Rush, A. J., Erman, M. K., Giles, D. E., Schlesser, M. A., Carpenter, G., Vasavada, N., & Roffwarg, H. P. (1986). Polysomnographic findings in recently drug-free and clinically remitted depressed patients. *Archives of General Psychiatry, 43,* 878–884.
Rutter, M. (1987). Temperament, personality and personality disorder. *British Journal of Psychiatry, 150,* 443–58.
Rutter, M. (1988). Epidemiological approaches to developmental psychopathology. *Archives of General Psychiatry, 45,* 486–495.
Schneider, K. (1958). *Psychopathic Personalities* (M. W. Hamilton, Trans.). London: J. Cassell.
Seligman, M. D. (1975). *Helplessness: On depression, development, and death.* San Francisco: Freeman.
Shea, M. T., Glass, D. R., Pilkonis, P. A., Watkins, J., & Docherty, J. P. (1987). Frequency and implications of personality disorders in a sample of depressed outpatients. *Journal of Personality Disorders, 1,* 27–42.
Simons, R. C. (1987). Psychoanalytic contributions to psychiatric nosology: Forms of masochistic behavior. *Journal of American Psychoanalytic Association, 35,* 583–608.
Telenbach, H. (1980). *Melancholia* (E. Eng, Trans.). Pittsburgh, PA: Duquesne University Press.
van Praag, H. M., Kahn, R. S., Asnis, G. M., Wetzler, S., Brown, S. L., Bleich, A., & Korn, M. L. (1987). Denosologization of biological psychiatry or the specificity of 5-HT disturbances in psychiatric disorders. *Journal of Affective Disorders, 13,* 1–8.
VanValkenburg, C., Lillienfeld, S., & Akiskal, H. S. (1987). The impact of familial personality disorder and alcoholism on the clinical features of depression. *Psychiatrie et Psychobiologie, 2,* 195–201.
Vogel, G. W. (1975). A review of REM sleep deprivation. *Archives of General Psychiatry, 32,* 749–761.

Von Knorring, A. L., Cloninger, C. R., Bohman, M., & Sigvardson, S. (1983). An adoption study of depressive disorders and substance abuse. *Archives of General Psychiatry, 40,* 943–950.

Von Zerssen, D. (1977). Premorbid personality and affective psychoses. In G. D. Burrows (Ed), *Handbook of studies on depression.* Amsterdam: Excerpta Medica.

Warheit, G. J. (1979). Life events, coping, stress and depressive symptomatology. *American Journal of Psychiatry, 136,* 502–507.

Wehr, T. A., & Goodwin, F. K. (1987). Can antidepressants cause mania and worsen the course of affective illness? *American Journal of Psychiatry, 144,* 1403–1418.

Wehr, T. A., Sack, D. A., & Rosenthal, N. E. (1987). Sleep reduction as a final common pathway in the genesis of mania. *American Journal of Psychiatry, 144,* 201–204.

Weissman, M. M., & Klerman, G. L. (1977). Sex differences and the epidemiology of depression. *Archives of General Psychiatry, 34,* 98–111.

Wender, P. H., Kety, S. S., Rosenthal, D., Schulsinger, F., Ortmann, J., & Lunde, I. (1986). Psychiatric disorders in the biological and adoptive families of adopted individuals with affective disorders. *Archives of General Psychiatry, 43,* 923–929.

Whybrow, P. C., Akiskal, H. S., & McKinney, W. T. (1984). *Mood disorders: Toward a new psychobiology.* New York: Plenum Press.

Widiger, T. A. (1989). The categorical distinction between personality and affective disorders. *Journal of Affective Disorders, 3,* 77–91.

Willner, P. (1985). *Depression: A psychobiological synthesis.* New York: Wiley.

Winokur, G. (1985). The validity of neurotic-reactive depression. *Archives of General Psychiatry, 42,* 1116–1122.

Zis, A. P., & Goodwin, F. K. (1979). Major affective disorder as a recurrent illness. *Archives of General Psychiatry, 36,* 835–839.

Author Index

A

Abbott, S., 76, 77, 78, 81, 92, 96
Abou-Saleh, M. T., 24, 31, 33
Abraham, K., 132, 133, 164, 221, 230
Abramson, L. Y., 153, 167, 220, 230
Adler, K., 139, 164, 165
Adler, Z., 12, 32, 117, 126, 195, 200, 208, 212
Ainsworth, M. D. S., 146, 147, 159, 165
Akiskal, H. S., 27, 31, 40, 61, 103, 123, 125, 130, 131, 165, 215, 216, 217, 218, 219, 220, 221, 222, 223, 224, 225, 226, 227, 228, 229, 230, 231, 232, 234, 235
Albala, A. A., 24, 33
Allan, M. J., 228, 231
Allman, C. J., 228, 231
Alloy, L. B., 220, 231
Ambelas, A., 226, 231
Andreasen, N. C., 22, 25, 31, 34, 35, 115, 117, 127, 196, 213
Andrews, B., 12, 32, 195, 200, 208, 212
Aneshensel, C. S., 21, 31
Angst, J., 27, 30, 31, 32, 122, 125, 215, 223, 225, 231
Anthony, E. J., 150, 157, 165
Anthony, J. C., 16, 21, 30, 31, 32
Antonuccio, D. O., 199, 214, 231
Aronoff, M. S., 223, 232
Arrindell, W. A., 84, 92, 157, 168
Asberg, M., 223, 231
Asnis, G. M., 25, 37
Ayuso-Mateos, J. L., 26, 36
Azrin, N. H., 201, 211

B

Babor, T. F., 28, 36
Badger, L., 81, 94
Bailey, J., 24, 33
Barlow, D. H., 16, 32
Barnett, P. A., 132, 165
Barrett, J., 22, 32
Bashford, M. B., 201, 212
Baumeister, R. F., 156, 165
Beardslee, W. R., 207, 211
Bebbington, P., 29, 33, 80, 98, 101, 104, 111, 114, 115, 125, 120, 125, 128, 130, 203, 214
Beck, A. T., 1, 36, 43, 44, 50, 55, 58, 59, 61, 62, 132, 140, 142, 143, 153, 154, 160, 165, 167, 195, 211, 220, 221, 222, 231, 233
Becker, J., 215, 231
Beckham, E. E., 197, 212
Beiser, M., 81, 82, 92
Bellack, A. S., 116, 118, 120, 129, 198, 199, 200, 202, 203, 213
Belsky, J., 150, 165
Bemporad, J., 141, 142, 165, 195, 211, 215, 231

Berchick, R. J., 1, 36
Bergman, A., 147, 148, 167
Berner, P., 26, 34
Bertelsen, A., 218, 225
Bibring, E., 135, 140, 157, 165
Bifulco, A. T., 12, 21, 27, 32, 34, 80, 93, 113, 117, 125, 126, 154, 155, 159, 161, 165, 166, 167
Billings, A. G., 190, 191, 192, 194, 195, 199, 202, 203, 204, 205, 207, 212, 213
Binder, J., 27, 30, 31, 36
Bird, H., 78, 90, 93
Birley, J. L. T., 18, 37, 85, 93
Bitar, A. H., 27, 31, 221, 222, 230
Blackburn, I. M., 25, 33
Blackwood, D. H. R., 25, 33
Blanchard, E. B., 16, 32
Blatt, S. J., 142, 165, 220, 231
Blazer, D. G., 75, 92, 161, 166
Blehar, M. D., 146, 147, 165
Bleich, A., 25, 37
Blignault, I., 116, 117, 120, 129
Block, P., 143, 168
Bloom, J., 73, 88, 89, 90, 96
Blumenthal, M. D., 17, 32
Bohman, M., 218, 235
Bolinger, J. 223, 230
Bolton, W., 140, 153, 156, 167
Bonime, W., 139, 165
Booth, C. L., 149, 168
Boulton, D. M., 60, 64
Bourke, G., 160, 166
Bourne, E., 69, 98
Bowlby, J., 107, 126, 142, 145, 146, 147, 148, 152, 165, 221, 231
Boyd, J. H., 2, 14, 32, 79, 98
Boyd, J. L., 208, 212
Bravo, M., 78, 90, 93
Breier, A., 39, 40, 46, 47, 62, 115, 123, 126, 130,
Brenner, R., 79, 87, 92
Brent, D. A., 228, 231
Bridge, L., 12, 32, 113, 125, 126, 159, 161, 166, 195, 200, 208, 212

Briggs, J., 70, 92
Brockington, I, F., 29, 34, 35
Bromet, E. J., 12, 20, 32
Broverman, D. M., 75, 92
Broverman, I., 75, 92
Brown, C. H., 16, 21, 32
Brown, G. W., 1, 4, 10, 11, 12, 13, 15, 16, 17, 19, 20, 21, 23, 26, 27, 32, 33, 34, 35, 36, 65, 75, 77, 78, 80, 81, 84, 93, 97, 108, 109, 110, 111, 112, 113, 117, 123, 125, 126, 127, 129, 140, 148, 152, 153, 154, 156, 159, 161, 166, 167, 192, 194, 195, 200, 202, 208, 209, 212, 221, 231
Brown, L. B., 156, 168
Brown, S. L., 25, 37
Brown, W. A., 227, 233
Brugha, T. S., 114, 115, 125, 126, 160, 166
Buhl-Auth, J., 78, 81, 85, 98
Bunney, W. E., 115, 128, 217, 226, 232
Burchill, S. A. L., 143, 161, 163, 164, 166
Burke, J., 28, 36, 73, 75, 97
Burr, B. D., 86, 94
Butcher, J. N., 201, 213
Byrne, D. G., 4, 33

C

Caballero, L., 26, 36
Cadoret, R. J., 218, 232
Calloway, S. P., 115, 118, 122, 126, 127
Cammuso, K., 218, 233, 234
Campbell, T., 83, 84, 85, 93
Canas, F.,, 26, 36
Cane, D. B., 41, 49, 63
Canino, G., 78, 84, 90, 93
Carey, G., 46, 47, 52, 58, 60, 62, 64
Carney, M. W. P., 18, 24, 33
Carpenter, G., 220, 234
Carpenter, W. T., 21, 35
Carroll, B. J., 24, 33, 43, 62
Carstairs, G. M., 79, 93

Carver, C. S., 44, 62
Cassano, G. B., 215, 222, 224, 226, 229, 232, 234
Cavanaugh, S., 226, 232
Celentano, D., 82, 97
Chagnon, N., 70, 71, 93
Chahal, R., 16, 21, 32
Chapman, L. J., 219, 232
Chapman, M., 149, 150, 168
Charney, D. S., 25, 26, 35, 39, 40, 46, 47, 62, 123, 126
Charon, F., 121, 128
Chen, S. E., 223, 230
Cheung, F. M., 89, 93
Chevron, E. S., 131, 142, 146, 165, 167, 188, 214, 220, 231
Chodoff, P., 142, 166, 220, 232
Clark, D. C., 131, 167
Clark, L. A., 40, 42, 43, 44, 45, 46, 47, 49, 50, 51, 52, 55, 57, 58, 60, 62, 64, 65
Clark, V. A., 21, 31
Clarkin, J. F., 223, 232
Clarkson, F. E., 75, 92
Clayton, P. J., 25, 34, 101, 115, 117, 126, 127, 223, 226, 231, 232
Cleary, P. A., 52, 54, 62
Click, M., Jr., 120, 128, 198, 213
Cloninger, C. R., 218, 228, 232, 235
Cochrane, C., 39, 56, 63
Cohen, J., 43, 62
Cohen, M. B., 135, 136, 138, 166
Cohen, S., 124, 126, 158, 159, 166
Collier, J., 79, 93
Collis, R., 88, 93
Comrey, A. L., 42, 50, 62
Conroy, R., 114, 126, 160, 166
Cooke, D. J., 17, 33, 101, 108, 112, 115, 126
Cooper, B., 105, 126
Cooper, J. E., 3, 4, 5, 18, 33, 37, 52, 63
Copeland, J. R. M., 4, 20, 33, 197, 212
Copolov, D. L., 25, 33
Coppen, A., 24, 31, 33, 36
Cordero-Villafafila, A., 26, 36

Corenthal, C., 43, 65
Corn, R., 223, 232
Coryell, W. H., 19, 24, 25, 34, 37, 43, 65, 125, 127, 161, 162, 167, 168, 196, 198, 213, 214, 216, 222, 233
Costa, P. T., 57, 62
Costello, C. G., 42, 50, 52, 62, 140, 166
Costes, H., 90, 93
Covi, L., 52, 54, 63, 65
Cowdry, R. W., 224, 228, 232
Coyne, J. C., 86, 91, 93, 107, 127, 142, 143, 161, 163, 164, 166, 205, 212
Craig, T. K. J., 4, 11, 12, 20, 21, 27, 32, 33, 75, 79, 93, 113, 114, 126
Cronkite, R. M., 191, 192, 194, 199, 202, 203, 206, 207, 209, 212, 213, 214
Cross, C., 77. 79. 80, 94
Croughan, J., 2, 3, 17, 20, 29, 36, 52, 64
Cummings, E. M., 149, 150, 168
Cytryn, L., 147, 149, 150, 166, 218, 233, 234

D

Dansky, L., 131, 167
Darlington, G. J., 224, 233
Daugherty, D., 215, 218, 228, 230
Davenport, Y., 60, 64, 227, 234
David, M., 221, 223, 234
Davidson, J., 224, 232
Davidson, S., 13, 32
Davis, G. C., 223, 230
Davis, J. M., 224, 234
Day, R., 81, 93
De Souza, F. V. A., 115, 118, 126, 127
De Witt, K. N., 201, 212
de la Selva, 73, 85, 86, 91, 95
de Vigne, J. P., 24, 33
Dean, C., 9, 33
DeLaney, W., 160, 166
DeLay, P., 81, 93
Delisio, G., 229, 232
Deltito, J., 229, 232

Deluty, B. M., 44, 62
Deluty, R. H., 44, 62
Denny, R. M., 224, 233
Depue, R. A., 104, 107, 110, 118, 126, 127, 219, 232
Derogatis, L. R., 17, 33, 40, 52, 54, 62, 63
DeRubeis, R. J., 188, 213
DeVos, G., 67, 68, 69, 95
Dew, M. A., 12, 20, 32
Dibble, E., 217, 232
Dickinson, J. K., 5, 34
Dickson, H., 220, 230, 231
Dickstein, S., 142, 167
Dienelt, M., 84, 97
Diener, E., 57, 62, 161, 166
DiNardo, P. A., 6, 32
Djenderedjian, A. H., 219, 230
Dobler-Mikola, A., 27, 30, 31, 32
Dobson, K. S., 41, 49, 62
Docherty, J. P., 220, 234
Dohrendwend, B. P., 2, 33, 36, 87, 93, 109, 110, 127
Dohrenwend, B. S., 87, 93
Dolan, R. J., 115, 118, 122, 126, 127
Doner, E., 160, 166
Doran, A. R., 115, 118, 130
Dowie, C., 39, 63
Dowland, J., 16, 35
Downs, J., 215, 218, 228, 230
Drannon, M., 217, 227, 231
Dressler, W., 81, 94
Dryman, A., 30, 32
Dube, K., 81, 93
Duncan-Jones, P., 4, 10, 11, 33, 34, 160, 161, 167
Dunn, L. O., 12, 20, 32
Dunner, D. L., 217, 228, 232, 234

E

Eaton, J., 83, 94
Eaves, L. J., 46, 63, 123, 127, 128
Ebigbo, P., 70, 88, 90, 94
Eckblad, M., 219, 232

Eckman, K. M., 39, 44, 65
Edgerton, R., 73, 94
Egger-Zeidner, E., 17, 18, 23, 34, 115, 116, 127
Egri, G., 2, 33
Ehlers, C. L., 162, 166, 227, 232
Eisdorfer, C., 107, 127
Eisemann, J., 157, 168
Eisemann, M., 84, 92
Eisenbruch, M., 149, 152, 166
Ekman, P., 68, 94
Elkin, I., 188, 214
Ellicott, A., 142, 166, 167
Elliot, G. R., 107, 127
Emmons, R. A., 57, 62
Ende, V. D., 157, 168
Endicott, J., 3, 9, 22, 24, 25, 31, 33, 34, 35, 36, 37, 125, 127, 196, 213
Engelsmann, F., 83, 94
Enriquez, E., 78, 96
Erbaugh, J. K., 43, 50, 62
Erdly, W., 160, 167
Erickson, E. H., 132, 166
Erman, M. K., 220, 234
Ernberg, G., 81, 93
Estrada, A. L., 21, 31
Evans, M. D., 188, 213
Extein, I., 224, 232
Eysenck, H., 42, 62
Eysenck, S. B. G., 42, 62
Ezquiaga, E., 122, 127

F

Fairchild, C. J., 26, 36
Fales, C. L., 221, 233
Falloon, I. R. H., 85, 91, 98, 208, 212, 214
Farias, P., 83, 94
Farmer, A. E., 28, 29, 33, 34, 36
Farmer, P., 71, 94
Farnham, C., 79, 94
Faust, S., 81, 93
Fava, G., 90, 94
Fawcett, J. A., 22, 37, 196, 213

Feather, B. W., 133, 166
Fehrenbach, P. A., 196, 212
Feinberg, M., 24, 33, 43, 62
Felder, W., 225, 231
Fenton, F., 92, 96
Field, M. J., 76, 78, 94
Fieve, R. R., 228, 234
Finder, E., 117, 118, 128
Finlay-Jones, R., 10, 11, 12, 16, 34, 101, 112, 123, 127
Finney, J., 191, 206, 207, 212, 213
Firth, C. D., 39, 63
Fleiss, J. L., 1, 36, 52, 63
Floris, G., 219, 233
Foa, E. B., 39, 63
Foa, U. G., 39, 63
Folkman, S., 190, 213
Folstein, M., 16, 21, 32
Fonagy, P., 115, 118, 122, 126, 127
Fondacaro, M., 210, 212
Ford, J. D., 201, 212
Forster, B., 117, 118, 128
Fournier, L., 20, 35
Fowler, N., 161, 166
Fowles, D. C., 56, 63, 114, 127
Frances, A. J., 228, 233
Frank, E., 131, 162, 166, 227, 232
Frank, J. D., 2, 34, 54, 63
Freeman, C. P., 25, 33
Freeman, W. B., 85, 91, 98, 208, 214
Freud, S., 133, 134, 166, 221, 232
Frey, R., 225, 231
Friedman, B., 22, 34, 35
Friedman, R. C., 223, 232
Fromm-Reichman, F., 135, 136, 138, 166
Fulton, C. L. 26, 36

G

Gaensbauer, T. J., 147, 149, 150, 166
Gaines, A., 71, 94
Gamble, W., 207, 212
Gammon, G. D., 83, 98
Gardner, D. L., 228, 232

Garfield, S. L., 188, 214
Garmany, G., 105, 110, 127
Garside, R. F., 23, 24, 33, 34, 52, 64
Gastsonis, C. D., 218, 233
Gauron, E. F., 5, 34
Gebhart, J., 81, 93
Geertz, H., 68, 69, 71, 72, 94
Gentry, K. A., 13, 36
George, L. K., 75, 92, 161, 166
Gero, G., 134, 166
Gersh, F. S., 56, 63, 114, 127
Gershon, E., 217, 218, 232, 233, 234
Ghiselin, M. T., 8, 34
Gilderman, A. M., 208, 212
Giles, D. E., 26, 36, 220, 234
Gillin, J. C., 60, 64, 227, 234
Gitlin, M., 142, 166, 167
Glass, D. R., 220, 234
Godley, M., 201, 211
Goetz, D. M., 228, 233
Gold, A., 39, 63
Gold, M. S., 224, 232
Goldberg, D. P., 2, 5, 26, 34, 35
Goldin, L. R., 217, 232
Goldstein, C. E., 228, 231
Goldstein, M. J., 131, 167
Goleman, D., 151, 166
Gomez, E., 43, 62
Gonzales, L. G., 78, 94
Good, B., 69, 71, 72, 74, 80, 82, 83, 86, 87, 88, 89, 91, 94, 95, 229, 233
Good, M.-J., 69, 72, 80, 82, 83, 86, 87, 88, 89, 94
Goodwin, D. W., 59, 63
Goodwin, F. K., 60, 64, 215, 217, 219, 224, 226, 227, 232, 234, 235
Gorman, D. M., 13, 34
Gorsuch, R. L., 43, 50, 64
Gotlib, I. H., 41, 42, 49, 63, 132, 142, 165, 166
Gottesman, I. I., 46, 62
Gourlay, A. J., 4, 33
Graham, P., 18, 37,
Greden, J. F., 24, 33, 43, 62, 86, 91, 93, 205, 212

Green, L. M., 5, 36
Greenberg, M. T., 151, 166
Griffith, P., 161, 167, 216, 222, 233
Grove, W. M., 25, 34
Gruenberg, E. M., 16, 21, 32, 73, 75, 97
Guarnaccia, P., 83, 91, 94, 95
Guevara, L., 78, 90, 93
Gurland, B. J., 52, 63
Gurney, C., 52, 64
Guroff, J. J., 217, 232
Gutierrez, J. L. A., 122, 127
Guze, S. B., 59, 63
Guzman, A., 90, 93

H

Haberman, P. W., 87, 94
Halberstadt, L. J., 153, 167
Hamilton, M., 14, 15, 34, 43, 45, 63
Hammen, C., 142, 166, 167
Hamovit, J., 217, 218, 232, 233, 234
Hansell, M. J., 21, 31
Harding, J. S., 86, 95
Harding, K., 142, 167
Harmon, R. J., 147, 149, 150, 166
Harris, T. O., 4, 10, 11, 12, 15, 16, 17, 19, 20, 21, 23, 26, 27, 32, 33, 34, 35, 75, 77, 78, 80, 81, 84, 93, 97, 108, 109, 110, 111, 112, 113, 114, 123, 125, 126, 129, 140, 148, 152, 153, 154, 155, 156, 159, 161, 165, 166, 167, 192, 194, 195, 200, 202, 208, 209, 212, 221, 231
Harrison, W. M., 228, 232
Harvald, B., 218, 225, 231
Harwood, J., 24, 33
Haskett, R. F., 24, 33
Hauge, M. A., 218, 225
Haykal, R. F., 131, 165, 219, 228, 231
Heath, A. C., 46, 63
Heath, H. C., 123, 127, 128
Helgason, T., 226, 232
Helzer, J. E., 2, 3, 17, 20, 28, 29, 34, 36, 52, 64, 73, 75, 97

Henderson, A. S., 46, 63
Henderson, S., 4, 33, 160, 161, 167
Hendrie, H. C., 115, 130
Heninger, G. R., 39, 40, 46, 47, 62, 123, 126
Hersen, M., 116, 118, 120, 129, 198, 199, 200, 202, 203, 213
Herzeg-Barron, R., 198, 214
Heywood, E., 218, 232
Hickey, N., 160, 166
Hill, O., 221, 232
Himmelhoch, J. M., 116, 118, 120, 129, 198, 200, 202, 203, 213
Hinde, R., 148, 167
Hinkle, L. E., Jr., 105, 127
Hirschfeld, R. M. A., 22, 25, 31, 37, 77, 79, 80, 94, 115, 117, 127, 161, 162, 167, 168, 197, 213, 215, 216, 222, 230, 233
Hoberman, H. M., 222, 233
Hoell, N. L., 43, 62
Hokanson, J. E., 164, 167
Hoke, D. J., 101, 108, 112, 126
Holahan, C. J., 209, 213
Holden, N. L., 24, 34
Hollingshead, A. B., 84, 97
Hollon, S. D., 188, 213
Holmes, T. H., 107, 127
Hooley, J., 85, 95
Hopkins, T. R., 39, 44, 65
Hordern, A., 5, 36
Horowitz, M. J., 132, 167
Hough, R., 82, 98
Howard, G. S., 188, 196, 214
Howard, K. I., 188, 196, 213
Howell, E., 75, 76, 95
Hsu, F., 67, 68, 69, 96
Hughes, D. C., 161, 166
Hurry, J., 101, 114, 115, 120, 125, 130, 203, 214
Hurt, S. W., 223, 232
Hyman, H. H., 6, 34

I

Imber, S., 188, 214
Ingham, J. G., 21, 34, 117, 120, 128, 202, 214
Isaacs, A. D., 18, 37
Izard, C., 68, 95

J

Jablenski, A., 28, 36, 81, 92, 93, 96
Jackson, S. W., 102, 103, 127
Jacobson, E., 135, 138, 167
Jaffe, K. E., 120, 128, 198, 212
James, N. M., 24, 33
Jamison, K. R., 142, 166, 167
Jardine, R., 46, 63
Jegede, R. O., 88, 95
Jenkins, J. H., 70, 73, 83, 85, 86, 88, 89, 91, 95
Jenner, F. A., 24, 37
Johnstone, E. C., 39, 63
Jones, S., 85, 91, 98, 208, 214
Jordan, K., 75, 92
Jordan, P., 215, 218, 228, 230

K

Kahn, R. S., 25, 37
Kameoka, V. A., 49, 64
Kanner, A. D., 107, 127
Kaplan, A., 8, 34
Kapur, R. L., 79, 93
Karno, M., 73, 77, 78, 85, 86, 90, 91, 95,
Kashgarian, M., 223, 230
Katon, W., 74, 75, 95
Katschnig, H., 17, 18, 23, 26, 34, 101, 111, 112, 127
Katz, R., 29, 33, 104, 114, 115, 125, 128
Keller, M. B., 22, 25, 31, 34, 35, 37, 115, 117, 125, 127, 161, 167, 196, 207, 211, 213, 216, 222, 233
Kelman, H. C., 54, 63
Kendall, P. C., 57, 65
Kendell, R. E., 5, 9, 23, 35, 56, 63

Kendler, K. S., 46, 63, 123, 127, 128
Kern, R., 109, 110, 127
Kerr, T. A., 52, 64
Kessler, R. C., 86, 91, 93, 205, 212
Kety, S. S., 131, 168, 218, 235
Khani, M. K., 219, 228, 230
Kidd, K. K., 83, 98
King, D., 217, 227, 231
King, D., 220, 231
Kirkpatrick, J., 69, 99
Kirmayer, L., 74, 95
Klein, D. F., 4, 24, 28, 35, 36, 47, 63, 228, 233
Klein, D. N., 131, 142, 167
Klein, M., 134, 167
Klein, R., 76, 77, 78, 81, 92
Kleinman, A., 69, 71, 74, 75, 81, 86, 87, 89, 91, 95, 229, 233
Klerman, G. L., 17, 33, 40, 42, 44, 60, 62, 65, 75, 76, 98, 107, 115, 117, 121, 125, 127, 128, 131, 146, 161, 167, 196, 207, 211, 213, 216, 222, 224, 233, 235,
Klibansky, R., 102, 103, 104, 128
Kochersperger, L. M., 224, 233
Kocsis, J. H., 228, 233
Kolko, D. J., 228, 231
Kolody, B., 82, 98
Kopta, S. M., 188, 196, 213
Korn, M. L., 25, 37
Korten, A., 81, 93
Kosisky, S., 218, 233, 234
Koss, M. P., 201, 213
Kotin, J., 43, 62
Kovacs, M., 218, 220, 233
Kovess, V., 20, 35
Kraepelin, D., 216, 218, 225, 233
Kraepelin, E., 102, 128
Kraines, S. H., 222, 233
Kramer, M., 16, 21, 32
Krantz, S., 199, 201, 206, 213
Krause, M. S., 188, 196, 213
Kreitman, N. B., 21, 34, 117, 120, 128
Kretschmer, E., 216, 225
Kronfol, Z., 24, 33

Kuczynski, L., 149, 150, 168
Kukopulos, A., 219, 233
Kupfer, D. J., 104, 118, 128, 131, 162, 166, 227, 232

L

Laddomada, P., 219, 233
Lamphere, L., 79, 97
Landerman, R., 75, 92
Lange, J. D., 227, 233
Langer, T., 87, 98
Lautin, A., 228, 234
Lavalle, J., 82, 89, 96
Lavori, P. W., 22, 34, 35, 37, 125, 127, 161, 167, 196, 213, 216, 222, 233
Lazarus, R. S., 105, 107, 127, 128, 190, 213
Leber, W. R., 197, 212
Lechman, J., 83, 98
Leckman, J. F., 39, 46, 63, 123, 128, 217, 232
Leeka, J., 57, 62
Leff, J. P., 4, 9, 37, 85, 91, 98, 198, 199, 208, 213
Leff, M. J., 115, 128
Leighton, A., 86, 95
Leighton, D. C., 86, 95
Lemmi, H., 131, 165, 219, 220, 224, 228, 230, 231,
Lemyre, L., 15, 33
Leon, C. A., 81, 93
Leon, D., 104, 128
Lesser, I. M., 117, 118, 128
Levav, T., 2, 36
Levi, D. L., 221, 233
LeVine, R., 69, 98
Levine, S., 60, 64
Levy, R., 68, 70, 96
Lewinsohn, P. M., 59, 63, 199, 214, 220, 222, 233
Lewis, A. J., 39, 63
Lewy, A. J., 60, 64, 227, 234
Libet, J., 59, 63
Liebowitz, M. R., 228, 233

Lillienfeld, S., 221, 234
Lin, T. -Y., 86, 96
Lindegard, B., 222, 233
Link, B. G., 109, 110, 127
Linkowski, P., 121, 128
Linnoila, M., 115, 118, 130
Lipman, R. S., 17, 33, 40, 52, 54, 62, 63, 65,
Lloyd, C., 101, 112, 120, 128, 198, 213, 221, 226, 233
Locke, B. Z., 2, 37, 43, 65, 75, 92
Lohr, N., 24, 33
Lopez, A. G., 122, 127
Lopez, S., 73, 95
Lorenz, K., 148, 167
Luks, O., 27, 35
Lumsden, D. P., 105, 128
Lunde, I., 131, 168, 218, 235
Lushene, R. E., 43, 50, 64
Lutz, C., 69, 70, 96

M

MacCarthy, B., 114, 115, 125
Macklin, D. B., 86, 95
MacMillan, A., 86, 95
Maggini, C., 215, 222, 232
Mahler, M. S., 147, 148, 167
Mallya, G., 219, 231
Mander, A. J., 25, 33
Manicavasagar, V., 116, 117, 120, 129
Mann, J. J., 228, 233
Mann, S. A., 4, 9, 37
Manson, S., 73, 88, 89, 90, 96
Manton, K., 75, 92
Mapother, E., 39, 63, 101, 128
Maremmani, I., 229, 232, 234
Margolis, E. G., 131, 167
Markowitz, J. S., 109, 110, 127, 228, 233
Marmot, M., 21, 35
Marsalla, A., 67, 68, 69, 73, 81, 91, 92, 93, 96
Marten, S., 13, 36
Martin, C. J., 26, 35

Martin, N. G., 46, 63, 123, 127, 128
Martinez, R., 78, 90, 93
Marziali, E. A., 199, 213
Maser, J. D., 47, 64
Mason, B. J., 228, 233
Mason, J. W., 105, 128
Mattsson, N. B., 54, 65
Matussek, P., 27, 35, 115, 128
Maxwell, S. E., 188, 196, 214
McAuley, H., 160, 161, 167
McCrae, R. R., 57, 62
McDonald, C., 142, 165, 220, 231
McDonald-Scott, P., 22, 34, 35
McEvoy, L. T., 29, 34
McGill, C. W., 208, 212
McGrath, P. J., 228, 233
McGuffin, P., 29, 33, 104, 114, 115, 125, 128
McKinney, W. T., 215, 231, 235
McKnew, D. H., 147, 149, 150, 166, 218, 233, 234
McNair, D. M., 229, 234
McPherson, K., 39, 63
McVane, J. R., 227, 233
Meehl, P. E., 31, 35
Meinhardt, K., 78, 81, 85, 98
Melges, F. T., 139, 167
Melville, M., 75, 92
Mendels, J., 39, 56
Mendelsohn, F. S., 2, 33
Mendelson, M., 43, 50, 62, 132, 167
Mendez de Leon, C-F., 78, 96
Mendlewicz, J., 121, 128, 218, 233
Merchant, A., 16, 21, 32
Merikangas, K.R. ,39, 46, 63 83, 98, 123, 128, 205, 213, 215, 231
Metalsky, G. I., 153, 167
Metcalfe, M., 24, 33
Mewborn, R., 207, 212
Michael, S., 87, 98
Miklowitz, D. J., 131, 167
Miller, P. McC., 21, 34, 117, 120, 128
Miln, P., 24, 33
Mintz, J., 73, 95, 131, 167
Mirande, A., 78, 96

Mitchell, R., 209, 213
Mitchell, S., 76, 96
Mock, J. E., 43, 50, 62
Mollica, R., 82, 89, 96
Monroe, S. M., 17, 19, 35, 101, 104, 106, 110, 111, 116, 118, 120, 124, 126, 127, 129, 198, 199, 200, 202, 203, 213
Montego, M. L., 26, 36
Moos, B., 191, 213
Moos, R. H., 195, 198, 199,200, 201, 202, 203, 204, 205, 206, 207, 209, 210, 212, 213, 214
Moradi, R., 72, 82, 83, 88, 94
Moran, G., 145, 168
Moss, H. B., 208, 212
Mountjoy, C. Q., 40, 64
Mueller, P. S., 60, 64, 227, 234
Muller, E. A., 224, 232
Munoz, R. A., 13, 36, 82, 97
Murillo, N., 69, 96
Murphy, E., 10, 11, 34, 193, 197, 198, 199, 200, 202, 214
Murphy, G. E., 188, 214
Murphy, H. B. M., 88, 96
Murphy, M. C., 223, 232
Musetti, L., 224, 234
Myers, F., 69, 96
Myers, J. K., 2, 14, 32
Myers, J.R., 75, 79, 84, 97, 98

N

Nackman, D., 218, 233, 234
Nagel, D., 27, 35
Ndetei, D., 77, 81, 96
Nedetei, D. M., 80, 98
Neilson, E. M., 21, 35
Nelson, J. C., 25, 26, 35
Nestadt, G. R., 16, 21, 32
Newsome, D. A., 60, 64, 227, 234
Nezworski, T., 150, 165
Ni Bhrolchain, M., 17, 23, 35
Nielsen, E., 22, 34, 35
Nielsen, J., 81, 93

Nies, A., 224, 234
Nixon, J. M., 4, 9, 37
Nolen-Hoeksema, S., 224, 233
Noyes, R., 162, 168
Nuechterlein, K. H., 131, 167
Nurnburger, J. I., 217, 232
Nystrom, S. 222, 233

O

O'Connell, M. M., 12, 20, 32
O'Gorman, T., 162, 168, 218, 232
O'Hanlin, J., 160, 166
O'Leary, M. R., 196, 212
Oatley, K., 140, 153, 156, 167
Obeyesekere, G., 72, 73, 88, 96
Ochs, E., 71, 96
Oei, T. I., 111, 129
Ohlenhuth, E. H., 54, 65
Olatawura, M., 81, 93
Oreland, L., 118, 124, 129
Orley, J., 73, 77, 85, 95, 96
Orlinsky, D. E., 188, 196
Orsulak, P. J., 26, 36
Ortmann, J., 131, 168, 218, 235
Orvaschel, H., 73, 75, 97
Ots, T., 74, 97
Owens, D. G. C., 39, 63

P

Pagel, M. D., 160, 167
Pakesch, G., 17, 18, 23, 34, 115, 116, 127
Panofsky, E., 102, 103, 104, 128
Parker, E. L., 224, 233
Parker, G., 29, 35, 84, 97, 116, 117, 120, 129, 156, 157, 167, 168
Parloff, M. B., 54, 63
Paterson, R. J., 145, 168
Paul, S. M., 115, 118, 130
Pauls, D. L., 39, 46, 63, 123, 128
Paykel, E. S., 80, 84, 85, 97, 98, 111, 115, 121, 129, 194, 197, 204, 214, 226, 233

Pellegrini, D., 218, 233, 234
Pelton, S., 224, 232
Pennybacker, M., 75, 92
Perel, J. M., 131, 166
Perper, J. A., 228, 231
Perris, C., 84, 92, 157, 168
Perris, H., 114, 118, 122, 124, 129, 157, 168
Persky, H., 39, 44, 65
Perugi, G., 224, 229, 232, 234
Peselow, E. D., 143, 168, 228, 234
Peterman, A. M., 101, 119, 129
Peterson, C., 157, 168
Peto, J., 23, 32
Pfohl, B., 19, 24, 25, 37, 111, 130, 195, 198, 214
Piagentini, F., 224, 234
Pickar, D., 115, 118, 130
Pickens, R., 28, 36
Pilkonis, P. A., 220, 234
Pilowsky, I, 60, 64
Pine, F., 147, 148, 167
Plutchik, R., 68, 97
Poland, R. E., 117, 118, 128
Pollitt, J., 39, 64
Ponce, C., 26, 36
Pottash, A. C., 224, 232
Pottenger, M., 2, 37, 43, 65
Potter, J., 114, 115, 125
Price, J., 218, 234
Prudo, R., 10, 11, 12, 16, 33, 34, 35, 77, 78, 97, 123, 129
Pruitt, D. B., 215, 218, 228, 230
Prusoff, B. A., 2, 37, 39, 42, 43, 44, 46, 63, 64, 65, 83, 98, 123, 128, 188, 198, 214
Pulver, A. E., 21, 35
Puzantian, V. R., 27, 31, 123, 130, 217, 221, 222, 223, 230, 227, 231
Quinlan, D. M., 142, 165, 220, 231
Quitkin, F. M., 228, 233

R

Rabkin, J. G., 4, 28, 35, 36, 228, 233

AUTHOR INDEX 247

Radloff, L. S., 2, 26, 75, 77, 97
Rado, S., 134, 168
Rahe, R. H., 107, 127
Rainer, J. D., 218, 233
Ramos-Brieva, J. A., 26, 36
Rao, A. V., 73, 97
Rao, B. M., 115, 129
Rao, V. A. R., 24, 36
Ratcliff, K. S., 2, 3, 17, 20, 29, 36, 52, 64
Ravaraos. C., 224. 234
Rawson, S. G., 43, 62
Razani, J., 208, 212
Rees, W. L., 105, 129
Regier, D., 28, 36, 73, 75, 97
Reginaldi, D., 219, 233
Reich, J., 162, 168
Reich, T., 25, 31
Rhoades, J. M., 133, 166
Richman, J., 78, 97
Rickels, K., 52. 54. 63, 65
Rickman, E. E., 43, 62
Riley, G., 39, 63
Ring, J., 82, 97
Rios, B., 26, 36
Riskind, J. H., 1, 36
Ritchie, K., 160, 161, 167
Rivera, A., 26, 36
Roatch, J. F., 115, 128
Robbins, P. R., 60, 64
Robertson, B. M., 83, 97
Robins, C. J., 143, 168
Robins, E., 9, 13, 24, 36
Robins, L. N., 2, 3, 17, 20, 28, 29, 30, 34, 36, 73, 75, 97
Robinson, D. S., 224, 234
Roessler, R. L., 43, 62
Roffwarg, H. P., 26, 36, 220, 234
Rogler, L. H., 84, 97
Romanoski, A. J., 16, 21, 32
Rosaldo, M., 68, 69, 79, 97
Rosen, G., 74, 75, 95, 105, 129
Rosenbaum, M., 222, 233
Rosenkrantz, P. S., 75, 92

Radke-Yarrow, M., 149, 150, 168
Rosenthal, D., 131, 168, 218, 235
Rosenthal, N. E., 60, 64, 131, 165, 226, 227, 234, 235
Rosenthal, R. H., 219, 221, 223, 228, 230, 231, 234
Rosenthal, S. H., 60, 64
Rosenthal, T. L., 27, 31, 123, 130, 131, 165, 217, 219, 221, 222, 223, 227, 228, 230, 223, 231, 234
Roth, M., 23, 24, 33, 34, 40, 52, 64
Rounsaville, B. J., 131, 146, 167, 188, 198, 214
Roy, A., 115, 118, 129, 130
Rubin, R. T., 25, 33, 117, 118, 128
Rubio, M., 78, 93
Rubio-Stapec, M., 90, 93
Ruch, A. J., 26, 36
Rupert, M. P., 164, 167
Rush, A. J., 220, 234
Rutter, M., 151, 168, 216, 229, 234

S

Sack, D. A., 60, 64, 226, 227, 234, 235
Sanday, P., 79, 97
Sandifer, M. G., 5, 36
Santana, F., 73, 86, 95
Sartorious, N., 3, 4, 5, 18, 28, 36, 37, 81, 86, 92, 93, 96, 97
Sashidharan, S. P., 9, 21, 25, 33, 34, 117, 120, 128
Saxl, F., 102, 103, 104, 128
Sceery, W., 217, 232
Schaefer, C., 107, 127
Schaefer, J., 210, 214
Schalling, D., 223, 231
Scharfetter, C., 27, 36
Scheftner, W. A., 22, 25, 31, 37
Scheidegger, P., 215, 231
Scheper-Hughes, N., 84, 97
Scher, S. J., 156, 165
Schieffelin, B., 71, 96
Schieffelin, E., 69, 70, 97
Schlesser, M. A., 26, 36, 220, 234

Schmale, A. H., 107, 130
Schmid, I., 27, 36
Schneider, K., 229, 234
Schukit, M. A., 13, 36
Schulberg, M. C., 12, 20, 32
Schulsinger, F., 131, 168, 218, 235
Schweder, R., 69, 97, 98
Scott-Strauss, A., 131, 165, 219, 221, 223, 228, 230, 231, 234
Seligman, M. D., 222, 234
Seligman, M. E. P., 157, 168, 220, 230
Selye, H., 105, 107, 130
Serra, G., 219, 233
Sesman, M., 78, 90, 93
Sethi, B., 221, 231
Seyfried, W., 29, 36
Shaffer, M., 59, 63
Shapiro, S., 16, 21, 32
Sharp, V. H., 221, 233
Shea, M. T., 220, 234
Sheffield, B. F., 18, 24, 33
Sheldon, A. E. R., 159, 168
Shepherd, M., 11, 36
Shichman, S., 142, 165
Shisana, O., 82, 97
Sholomskas, D., 2, 37, 43, 65
Shore, J., 73, 88, 89, 90, 96
Shrout, P. E., 2, 33, 36, 78, 90, 93, 109, 110, 127
Siciliano, M., 224, 233
Sigvardson, S., 218, 235
Silver, R. C., 148, 168
Simonini, E., 224, 234
Simons, A. D., 188, 214
Sisson, R. W., 201, 211
Slater, E., 122, 130
Slater, J. F., 219, 232
Slater, P., 122, 130
Smith, T. W., 60, 64
Smouse, P. E., 43, 62
Snyder, K. S., 85, 91, 98, 131, 167, 208, 214
Soldner, M. L., 27, 35
Sotsky, S., 188, 214
Speiker, S. J., 149, 168

Speltz, M. D., 151, 166
Spielberger, C. D., 43, 50, 64
Spitzer, R. L., 1, 3, 9, 24, 33, 36, 37
Spiznagel, E. L., 29, 34
Srole, L., 87, 98
Sroufe, L. A., 146, 150, 151, 168
Staddon, J. E. R., 7, 8, 36
Stangl, D., 19, 24, 25, 37, 111, 130, 195, 198, 214
Steer, R. A., 1, 36
Stein, M., 21, 233
Steinbrueck, S. M., 188, 196, 214
Steiner, M., 24, 33
Steiner, S. C., 106, 124, 129
Steinmetz, J. L., 199, 214
Stewart, J. W., 228, 233
Stiles, W. B., 143, 161, 163, 164, 166
Stoltzman, R. K., 29, 34
Stromgren, E., 81, 93
Strupp, H. H., 201, 213
Sturt, E., 9, 37, 114, 115, 125
Sullivan, H. S., 136, 140, 168
Surtees, P. G., 9, 21, 33, 34, 117, 120, 128, 202, 214
Swartz, M. S., 139, 167
Sweeny, J., 228, 233
Swindle, R., 199, 2302, 203, 214
Sylvester. D., 224. 234

T

Takahashi, R., 81, 93
Tal, M., 86, 91, 93, 205, 212
Tanaka-Matsumi, J., 49, 64
Tanck, R. H., 60, 64
Tanner, J., 121, 129
Targum, S. D., 217, 232
Tarika, J., 24, 33
Taylor, C. N., 115, 129
Taylor, E. B., 142, 167
Teasdale, J., 85, 95, 220, 230
Tellegen, A., 48, 57, 58, 64, 65
Telles, C., 73, 95
Tennant, C., 80, 98, 101, 114, 115, 116, 120, 125, 129, 130, 203, 214

Thayer, R., 57, 60, 64
Thoits, P. A., 124, 130, 210, 214
Thompson, W., 2, 14, 32
Thomson, K. C., 115, 130
Tondo, L., 219, 233
Torres-Matrullo, C., 78, 98
Toussignant, M., 70, 72, 88, 98
Towle, L. H., 28, 36
Traskman-Bendz, L, 223, 231
Tricamo, E., 228, 233
Troughton, F., 218, 232
Tuma, A. H., 47, 64
Tupling, A., 156, 168
Turnbull, J., 86, 91, 93, 205, 212
Tuthill, R., 221, 231
Tyrer, P., 123, 130

U

Uhlenhuth, E. H., 52, 54, 63
Ullrich, H., 77, 98

V

Vadher, A., 77, 80, 81, 96, 98
Valle, R., 82, 98
Van der Ende, J., 84, 92
Van Natta, P., 75, 79, 93
Van Praag, H. M., 25, 37
Van Valkenburg, C., 123, 130, 220, 221, 230, 231, 234
Vasvada, N., 220, 234
Vaughn, C., 85, 91, 98, 198, 199, 208, 213, 214
Vega, W., 78, 81, 82, 85, 98
Vermilyea, J., 16, 32
Vlissides, D. N., 24, 37
Vogel, G. W., 226, 234
Vogel, S. R., 75, 92
von Knorring, A. L., 84, 92, 118, 124, 129, 157, 168, 218, 235
von Korff, M. R., 16, 21, 32
Von Zerssen, D., 225, 235
Voss, C., 228, 233
Vye, C., 44, 64

W

Wachtel, P. L., 139, 148, 168
Wagner, A., 223, 231
Wakeling, A., 115, 118, 122, 126, 127
Walker, P. W., 27, 31, 217, 221, 222, 227, 230, 231
Wall, S., 146, 147, 165
Walsh, N., 160, 166
Ward, C. H., 43, 50, 62
Warheit, G. J., 15, 37, 78, 81, 85, 98, 226. 235
Warner, R., 79, 87, 98
Waters, W., 146, 147, 165
Watkins, J., 188, 214, 220, 234
Watson, D., 42, 44, 48, 49, 50, 51, 52, 57, 58, 60, 62, 64, 65
Watson, S., 215, 218, 228, 230
Wehr, T. A., 60, 64, 219, 224, 226, 227, 232, 234, 235
Weigert, E. G., 125, 136, 138, 166
Weil, R., 83, 94
Weinstein, N., 39, 56
Weiss, R. S., 159, 168
Weissenburger, J. E., 26, 36
Weissman, M. M., 2, 14, 32, 37, 39, 43, 46, 63, 65, 73, 75, 76, 79, 83, 85, 97, 98, 123, 128, 131, 146, 161, 167, 168, 198, 214, 224, 235
Weller, E., 215, 231
Wender, P. H., 131, 168, 218, 235
West, M., 159, 168
Wetzler, S., 25, 37
White, G., 69, 73, 98, 99
Whitehouse, A. M., 25, 33
Whybrow, P. C., 215, 235
Widiger, T. A., 227, 235
Wiegand, M., 115, 128
Wiener, M., 143, 168
Wierzbicka, A., 68, 99
Wig, N., 81, 93
Wilkinson, G., 11, 36
Williams, C., 83, 99
Williams, H. V., 54, 65

Williams, J. B. N., 1, 36, 24, 37
Willner, P., 104, 130, 215, 235
Wills, T. A., 124, 126, 158, 159, 166
Wilson, S., 43, 65
Wing, J. K., 3, 4, 5, 9, 18, 28, 36, 37, 73, 77, 85, 93, 96
Winokur, G., 25, 34, 222, 235
Wittchen, H. U., 28, 36
Wober, M., 88, 99
Wolfstetter-Kausch, H., 219, 232
Woodbury, M., 75, 92
Wortman, C., 86, 91, 93, 148, 168, 205, 212
Wykes, T., 114, 115, 125
Wynne, L. C., 81, 93
Wyshak, G., 82, 89, 96

Y

Yeh, E. K., 86 99
Yerevanian, B. I., 215, 216, 220, 230, 231
Young, E., 24, 33
Young, J., 39, 64
Young, M. A., 22, 37

Z

Zavalla, I., 78, 81, 84, 99
Zelenak, J. P., 228, 231
Zimmerman, M., 19, 24, 25, 37, 39, 43, 44, 65, 111, 130, 195, 198, 214 215, 224, 232, 235
Zisook, S., 120, 128, 198, 213
Zung, W. W., 50, 65
Zuroff, D., 142, 165, 220, 231
Zwart, F. M., 111, 129

Subject Index

A

Affective disorders,
  psychosocial factors in, 131-164
Affiliations/social support,
  confidantes as, 158, 201
  depression and, 158-161
Age-specific depression, 77-78
Alcohol, 221, 228
  depression and, 27, 28
  measurement and, 13, 14
Antidepressants, 163
Anxiety, 56-61, 114-124
  (see Depression)
Attachment,
  adult, 158-161
  defined, 145-146
  depressed mothers and, 149
  disturbed, 150-152
  early, 146-147
  evolutionary perspective, 146
  loss of mother and, 154-156
  psychopathological, 147-149
  self-esteem and, 152-154
  strange situation paradigm, 147
Autonomous depressives, 143

B

Beck Depression Inventory (BDI), 43-44, 50, 58-60, 90
Bedford College scheme, 9-11
Biological Factors, 102-103, 117-118, 154, 162, 16

circadian rhythms, 162-163 (see Genetics)
Borderline cases, 12
Brooding, as a symptom, 6

C

Caseness,
  borderline, 11-12
  depression and, 9-10
  social class differences, 12-13
  vulnerability, 12-13
CATEGO, 9
Children, depressed parents and, 83-84, 178-179
Circadian clock, 162-163, 226-227
  (see Biological factors; Genetics)
Classification, 23
  marginal cases, 11
Community response and depression, 86-92
Community treatment facilities, 191-196, 201-203, 211
Comorbidity, 122-124
Composite Intelligence Diagnostic Interview (CIDI), 28-30
Covi Anxiety Scale, 43
Cross-cultural depression, 67-92
  communication of symptoms, 87-89
  context variables, 68-70, 90-91
  depression symptoms, 86-91
  notions of self, 90-91
  problems of context, 88-90
  validity, 89-90

vulnerability, 69-79
Culture, Depression and, 69-74
Cyclic mood disorders, 59-60, 215-229

D

Darwinian measurement, 7-8
Depression, (*see also*, Emotion)
  attachment and, 145-160
  anxiety and, 39-61
  biological theories, 162-163
  body signs, 11
  borderline, 12
  caseness and, 9-10
  categorizing, 56
  children, 157, 178-179
  community response to, 86-92
  cross-cultural, 67-92
  cycles, 59-60 (*see* Biological)
  defining, 8, 16
  effects of, 161-162
  episodic, 27
  factor analytic studies, 51, 52
  family studies, 46, 47
  gender, 78-79, 180
  genetic determinants, 46, 56, 83-84, 154 (*see* Genetic factors)
  H-P-A axis, 117-118
  immigrants and, 81-83
  interpersonal relations, 136, 143-144, 168-182
  insomnia, 40
  loss, 122-124, 154-156
  measurement, 40-48
  medication, 163, 181
  models of, 103-105
  nonacculturation, 78-83
  onset, 18-21, 162
  overlap, 22, 46-48
  panic disorder, 39, 52-53, 162
  pharmacologic studies, 40-47
  population studies, 27-31
  postpartum, 227
  predisposition, 58-61, 132
  reliability accounts, 161-162

remission, 204-205
schizphrenia, 85-86, 207
seasonality, 60, 227
self-report, 42-47
social class and 78-79
spouses, 205-207
strangers, 170-172
stress, 102-103
subtypes, 22-28
temperament, 157
variables, 40
Depressive affect,
  cross-cultural, 73-79
  somatic symptoms, 73-74
  suffering and, 69-73
  vulnerability, 75-79
Diagnosis, 1-10,19-21, 28-29, 56
  aspects, 48-49
  implications, 55-56
  instruments, choice of, 28-30
  intuition, 22,-23
  overlap, 46-48 (*see* Instruments, Measurement)
Diagnostic category, 16,
  criteria, 9-11
  flexibility, 17
  hierarchical rules, 16
Diagnostic Interview Schedule (DIS), 22, 28-30
Dysfunctional family, 83-84

E

Eating disorders, 29
Emotion,
  biological similarity, 68-70
  cultural similarity, 68-71
  egocentric view, 69-70
  ethnopsychology of, 69
  family view, 69
  societal view, 69-70
Endogenous depression, 20-26
Epidemiologcal research, 1-31

F, G

Family structure, 83-87
  (*see* Depression, Emotion)
Gender, 180, 224,
Genetic factors, 46, 56, 84-84, 154, 217-223
  affective disorders and, 131-132
  predisposition, 132
  recurrence, 224-225

H

Hamilton Scale for Depression (HRSD), 43-45
Heredity (*see* Genetics)

I

Immigrants, 78-84 (*see also* Depression, Cross-cultural depression)
Index of Definition of Psychiatric Disorders, 9
Instruments, 2-6, 30-31 (*see also* Measurement, Depression)

M

Measures,
  Dexamethasone Suppression Test (DST), 18, 25
  heterogeneity and, 17-18
  Newcastle scale, 18, 24-25
Measurement, 2-4, 14-15
  alcohol and, 13, 14
  bias in, 5-6
  convergence of, 43-44
  Darwin and, 7-8
  defined, 6
  diagnostic impressions, 5-6
  discriminitive power in, 41-42
  negative affinity trait, 42, 50-56
  respondent-based measures, 2-4
  self-report vs. clinical, 41-46
  systems, 21-22
  validity, 41

Measurement scales
  Beck Depression Inventory, 43-44, 50, 58-60, 90
  Costello-Comrey Anxiety Scale, 50-51
  medication, 188, 217, 226-228
  MMPI, 50-51
  Raskin Depression Scale, 43
Mood disorders, 215-230
  gender, 224
  genetics, 217-218
  predisposition to, 215-227
  temperament, 216-220, 227-229

P

Panic disorder, 39, 52-54, 162
Parental Bonding Instrument (PBI), 156-158
Personality, effects of depression on, 161-162, 215-219
Predepressives, 137-139
Predisposition, 58-61, 132
Psychiatric Epidemiology Research Interview (PERI), 2
Psychodynamic models,
  Adlerian analytic, 139
  classical, 132-134
  Ego-analysis, 135
  English, 134-135
  Integrative psychoanalysis, 141
  Interpersonal variants, 135-139
  Social role disruption, 140

Q

Questionnaires, 3 (*see* Measurement)

R

Rating systems, 2 (*see* Measurement)
Reliability, scales for convergence, 43
Raskin Depression Scale, 43
Research Diagnostic Criteria (RDC), 9, 10

254 SUBJECT INDEX

S

Scaling models, 58-60
Screening scales, 2
 culture-specific scales, 90
Screening instruments, 5, 89-90
Self-esteem, 21-22, 221
 attachment and, 152-154
Self-report, 42-47, 56-57, 194-195
 cross-cultural notions, 90-91
 positive/negative affect, 56-60
Social support systems, 158-161
Sociotropic persons, 143
Stress, 101-125
 biological differences, 117-118 (see Biological factors)
 clinical differences, 116-120
 concept of, 105-107
 confidantes, 201
 intervention programs, 211
 life context factors, 203
 measurement of, 108-113
 onset, 18-21, 118-119, 162
 program evaluation, 187-200
 recurrence, 121-122
 relapse, 120-121
 remission, 120
 social resources, 194-196, 201-203
 standardization criteria, 119-120
 stress and coping theory, 190-196
 subtypes, 22-28, 113-116
 symptomatic distinctions, 114
Stress disorder interactions, 102-125
Strange situation paradigm (see Attachment)
Subtypes, 22-28, 105-107, 113-116
Symptoms, 2-4, 16, 19-21, 58-59
 categorizing, 1
 clusters of, 1
 core, 13-14
 diagnostic categories,
 documentation of, 20-21
 formation of, 27
 hostility, 261
 measurement of, 4-5

recording, 3 (see Measurement)
rules concerning, 5-7
syndromes, 27-28

T

Temperament, 216-220, 227-229
 children 157
 twins, 224
Testing, validity in, 28-29 (see Measurement)
Treatment evaluation, 188-202

V

Validity studies, 84-87
 across populations, 67
 diagnostic, 46-48